Using the *Teach Yourself* in 24 Hours Series

Welcome to the *Teach Yourself in 24 Hours* series! You're probably thinking, "What, they want me to stay up all night and learn this stuff?" Well, no, not exactly. This series introduces a new way to teach you about exciting new products: 24 one-hour lessons, designed to keep your interest and keep you learning. Because the learning process is broken into small units, you will not be overwhelmed by the complexity of some of the new technologies that are emerging in today's market. Each hourly lesson has a number of special items, some old, some new, to help you along.

Minutes

The first 10 minutes of each hour lists the topics and skills that you will learn about by the time you finish the hour. You will know exactly what the hour will bring with no surprises.

Minutes

Twenty minutes into the lesson, you will have been introduced to many of the newest features of the software application. In the constantly evolving computer arena, knowing everything a program can do will aid you enormously now and in the future.

Minutes

Before 30 minutes have passed, you will have learned at least one useful task. Many of these tasks take advantage of the newest features of the application. These tasks use a hands-on approach, telling you exactly which menus and commands you need to use to accomplish the goal. This approach is found in each lesson of the *24 Hours* series.

Minutes

You will see after 40 minutes that many of the tools you have come to expect from the *Teach Yourself* series are found in the *24 Hours* series as well. Notes and Tips offer special tricks of the trade to make your work faster and more productive. Warnings help you avoid those nasty time-consuming errors.

Minutes

By the time you're 50 minutes in, you'll probably run across terms you haven't seen before. Never before has technology thrown so many new words and acronyms into the language, and the New Terms elements found in this series will carefully explain each and every one of them.

Minutes

At the end of the hour, you may still have questions that need answered. You know the kind—questions on skills or tasks that come up every day for you, but that weren't directly addressed during the lesson. That's where the Q&A section can help. By answering the most frequently asked questions about the topics discussed in the hour, Q&A not only answers your specific question, it provides a succinct review of all that you have learned in the hour.

What's New with Windows 95

Different, better, and still the same best describes how Windows 95 compares to previous versions of Windows. Despite the similarities, there are major differences in Windows 95 that you should know about ahead of time so that you can use Windows 95 the way it is supposed to be used. Microsoft designed Windows 95 so that you can concentrate on using your software and hardware rather than concentrate on using Windows 95.

Although Windows 95 has been released for a while, many people have yet to make the switch. If you are new to Windows 95, consider yourself fortunate! You are about to be impressed. If you've already used Windows 95 for some time you will find lots of tips and tidbits that will lessen your Windows 95 load and make Windows 95 work better for you. Some of the Windows 95 key features are

- The taskbar that acts like a jukebox for programs from which you can select whatever program you want to activate next.

- Explorer, a new navigational feature, replaces the File Manager and Program Manager.

- You can use longer filenames. Filenames now can contain from 1 to 255 characters compared to the 8-character filenames Windows 3.x carried.

- The Find option on the Start menu searches your computer for a file that matches a certain filename pattern (using wildcards) or a specific modification and creation date. You even can search every file's contents for a word or phrase that you know is in the file and search across networks and the Internet.

- The MS-DOS window now contains a menu and a toolbar.

- The Plug-and Play-feature enables you to plug new devices into your computer without having to set hardware switches or determine appropriate interrupt settings.

- One of the benefits that Windows 3.1 users will appreciate is that Windows 95 does not require as many mouse clicks and double-clicks asprevious versions of Windows did.

- The My Computer window displays the contents of your computer system. This window enables you to manage files, set up hardware, organize network connections, manage printers, and execute programs.

☐ Synchronize your document files by using the Windows 95 Briefcase tool so your work remains current.

☐ The Microsoft Network is an online service that gives you access to the Internet and other specific Microsoft services. Windows 95 makes Microsoft Network access simple.

☐ If you use the Internet, Windows 95 includes one-click Internet access and provides a uniform Internet access method throughout most of Windows 95.

Teach Yourself
WINDOWS 95

in 24 Hours,
Second Edition

Greg Perry

SAMS
PUBLISHING

201 West 103rd Street
Indianapolis, Indiana 46290

This book is for a man who serves, does right, and risks the consequences: Mr. Steve Largent.

Copyright © 1997 by Sams Publishing

SECOND EDITION

International Standard Book Number: 0-672-31006-6

Library of Congress Catalog Card Number: 96-70716

2000   99   98   97   4

Interpretation of the printing code: the rightmost double-digit number is the year of the book's printing; the rightmost single-digit, the number of the book's printing. For example, a printing code of 97-1 shows that the first printing of the book occurred in 1997.

Composed in AGaramond and MCPdigital by Macmillan Computer Publishing

Printed in the United States of America

Trademarks

Publisher and President: Richard K. Swadley

Publishing Manager: Dean Miller

Director of Editorial Services: Cindy Morrow

Director of Marketing: Kelli S. Spencer

Assistant Marketing Managers: Kristina Perry, Rachel Wolfe

Acquisitions Editor
Grace M. Buechlein

Development Editor
Brian-Kent Proffitt

Indexer
Johnna L. VanHoose

Technical Reviewer
John Nelsen

Editorial Coordinator
Katie Wise

Technical Edit Coordinator
Lynette Quinn

Editorial Assistants
Carol Ackerman
Andi Richter
Rhonda Tinch-Mize

Cover Designer
Tim Amrhein

Book Designer
Gary Adair

Copy Writer
David Reichwein

Production Team Supervisors
Brad Chinn
Charlotte Clapp

Production
Mona Brown
Brad Lenser
Donna Martin
Gene Redding
Andrew Stone

Overview

Contents

Acknowledgments

My sincere thanks go to the editors and staff at Sams Publishing who strive to produce computer books that teach all levels of computer users from beginners to experts. The people at Sams Publishing take their jobs seriously because they want readers to have only the best books possible.

As I've said before, Sam's Dean Miller deserves praises and raises. Dean has his hand somewhere in most of my successful books and my books are better because of Dean.

Other editors and staff at Sams who produced this book, namely Grace Buechlein, Brian Proffitt, and Cindy Morrow, are also responsible for this book's excellence, and I alone am responsible for any problems if there are any.

Mr. Bob Enyart and his wonderful wife Cheryl continue to add spice to my life. Rarely can one have friends who challenge, teach, and love as much as the Enyarts do and I'm so very grateful for both them.

My lovely and gracious bride, Jayne, stands by my side day in and day out. Thank you, my Dear Jayne. Thanks also to my Dad and Mom, Glen and Bettye Perry, who are my biggest fans. I love you all.

Greg Perry

About the Author

Greg Perry is a speaker and writer on both the programming and the applications sides of computing. He is known for his skills at bringing advanced computer topics down to the novice's level. Perry has been a programmer and trainer since the early 1980s. He received his first degree in computer science and then a master's degree in corporate finance. Perry is the author of more than 40 computer books, including *Absolute Beginner's Guide to Programming*, *Absolute Beginner's Guide to C*, *Teach Yourself Office 97 in 24 Hours*, *C Programming in 12 Easy Lessons*, and *Visual Basic 4 Starter Kit*. He also writes about rental-property management, loves to travel, and helps produce a nationally syndicated television show.

Tell Us What You Think!

As a reader, you are the most important critic and commentator of our books. We value your opinion and want to know what we're doing right, what we could do better, what areas you'd like to see us publish in, and any other words of wisdom you're willing to pass our way. You can help us make strong books that meet your needs and give you the computer guidance you require.

Do you have access to CompuServe or the World Wide Web? Then check out our CompuServe forum by typing GO SAMS at any prompt. If you prefer the World Wide Web, check out our site at http://www.mcp.com.

JUST A MINUTE

If you have a technical question about this book, call the technical support line at 317-581-3833.

As the publishing manager of the group that created this book, I welcome your comments. You can fax, e-mail, or write me directly to let me know what you did or didn't like about this book—as well as what we can do to make our books stronger. Here's the information:

FAX: 317-581-4669

E-mail: opsys_mgr@sams.samspublishing.com

Mail: Dean Miller
           Sams Publishing
           201 W. 103rd Street
           Indianapolis, IN 46290

Introduction

You probably are anxious to get started with your 24-hour Windows 95 tutorial. Take just a few preliminary moments to acquaint yourself with the design of this book described in the next few sections.

Who Should Read This Book

This book is for *both* beginning and advanced users of Windows. Readers rarely believe that lofty claim for good reason, but the design of this book and the nature of Windows 95 make it possible for this book to address such a wide audience. Here is why: Windows 95 is a major improvement over the previous Windows 3.11 for Workgroups and Windows 3.1 operating environments. (This book refers to both versions collectively as *Windows 3.1*.)

Readers unfamiliar with windowed environments will find plenty of introductory help to bring them up to speed quickly. This book teaches you how to start Windows 95, how to exit Windows 95, and how to manage almost every aspect of Windows 95. This book talks to beginners but does not talk *down* to beginners.

For readers who presently use Windows 3.1, this book also addresses you. Here is how: There are several sidebars labeled *3.1 Step-Up* that explain how a specific Windows 95 feature improves upon or replaces a Windows 3.1 feature. With your fundamental base of Windows 3.1 understanding, you'll appreciate the new Windows 95 feature. In addition to the Step-Ups, keep in mind that Windows 95 operates using a completely new style from previous versions. Although Windows 95 is similar to Windows 3.1, almost every Windows 95 action differs slightly from the Windows 3.1 equivalents. There are more than enough new features to keep Windows 3.1 users interested and happy for a long time.

For special insight into Windows 95, current Windows 3.1 users might want to read Appendix B, "Quick Help for Windows 3.1 Users." It compares areas of Windows 3.1 to their equivalent and improved features in Windows 95.

What This Book Will Do for You

Although this is not a reference book, you'll learn almost every aspect of Windows 95 from the user's point of view. There are many advanced technical details that most users will never need, and this book does not waste your time with those. This book knows that you want to get up to speed with Windows 95 in 24 hours, and this book fulfills its goal.

This book presents both the background and the theory that a new Windows 95 user needs. In addition to the background discussions, this book is practical and provides more than 75 useful step-by-step tasks that you can work through to gain hands-on experience. The tasks guide you through all the common Windows 95 actions you'll need to make Windows 95 work for you, instead of you working to use Windows 95.

Can This Book Really Teach Windows 95 in 24 Hours?

Yes. You can master each chapter one hour or less (by the way, chapters are referred to as "hours" in the rest of the book). Although some chapters are longer than others, the material is balanced. The longer chapters contain several tasks, and the shorter chapters contain background material. The balance provided by the tasks, background, and insightful explanations and tips make learning Windows 95 using this book fresh at every page.

What You Need

This book assumes that you have a Windows 95-compatible computer with Windows 95 installed. Just in case you are brand new to computers, you are not out of luck; if you need introductory computer help, Appendix A, "Understanding Your Computer," reviews fundamental concepts of computer hardware and software.

Conventions Used in This Book

Each chapter contains a glossary to explain the important new terms in the chapter. There is a question-and-answer section at the end of each chapter to reinforce ideas. This book also uses several common conventions to help teach the Windows 95 topics. Here is a summary of the typographical conventions:

- ☐ The first time a new term appears, the term is *italicized.*
- ☐ Commands and computer output appear in a special monospaced computer font.
- ☐ Words you type appear in a boldfaced computer font.

☐ If a task requires you to select from a menu, the book separates menu commands with a vertical bar. Therefore, this book uses File | Save **As** to select the Save **As** command from the **File** menu.

☐ Windows 95 uses underlining to indicate hot keys on the screen. (Hot keys are keyboard alternatives to using the mouse to choose menu items and dialog box options.) This book indicates hot keys with a boldface character. For example, in the menu commands **F**ile|Save **A**s, the F and A are hot keys.

In addition to typographical conventions, the following special elements are included to set off different types of information to make them easily recognizable:

JUST A MINUTE

Special notes augment the material you are reading in each hour. They clarify concepts and procedures.

TIME SAVER

You'll find numerous tips that offer shortcuts and solutions to common problems.

CAUTION

The caution sections warn you about pitfalls. Reading them will save you time and trouble.

Current Windows 3.1 users will advance quickly by reading the Step-Ups provided for them.

Review the Basics

Windows Minutes are sections that provide background information for users who have never used a windowed operating environment before. Windows Minutes can be from a paragraph to a page or two long.

Each Windows Minute includes a heading so you can tell quickly whether it contains information you need.

Although these sections are intended for beginners, experienced users may find them useful as a refresher course on the topic or procedure at hand.

PART
I

Wake Up
Windows 95!

Hour

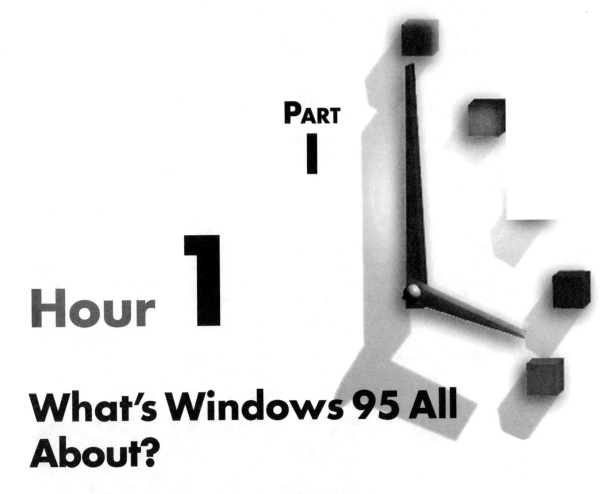

**PART
1**

Hour 1

What's Windows 95 All About?

Who says that a productive computer user cannot have fun being productive? Windows 95 from the Microsoft Corporation, is fun, friendly, and powerful. This hour introduces you to Windows 95. You will learn some of the goals that the Microsoft programmers had in mind when they designed Windows 95. Also, you will learn how Windows 95 improves upon previous versions of Windows and other operating environments.

The highlights of this hour include:

- [ ] How Microsoft designed Windows 95 to be as easy and intuitive as possible
- [ ] What makes Windows 95 more powerful than many other operating environments
- [ ] How to start Windows 95
- [ ] Why you may have to log on to Windows 95
- [ ] How to access and manipulate common Windows 95 controls such as command buttons and checkboxes
- [ ] When you need to perform a shut down of Windows 95

Getting a Feel for Windows 95

Most users like the look and feel of Windows 95, and they appreciate the fact that Windows 95 is also enjoyable to use. Although Windows 95 is both fun and easy to master, it is also a computer interface system that offers tremendous power for anyone who uses PCs. With Windows 95 you will be able to access your computer's hardware and data files easily even if you have not used a computer much before. As a matter of fact, Microsoft spent many hours and many dollars streamlining the way that Windows 95 helps people work.

Windows 95 contains a computer interface that attempts to please all groups of people including novice computer users, current Windows 3.1 and MS-DOS users, and advanced computer programmers. In order to achieve the lofty goal of pleasing a broad spectrum of users, Microsoft designed an interface that is intuitive without being intrusive.

Figure 1.1 shows the typical Windows 95 screen that Windows 95 users see much of the time. The Windows 95 screen is often called a *desktop* and you'll learn to manage items on the Windows 95 desktop just as you do with your own desktop where you sit. Other than some pictures and text here and there, the Windows 95 desktop screen is very clean and clear of the clutter that previous Windows users so often saw.

Figure 1.1.

The Windows 95 screen, like a clean desktop, is free of clutter.

The pictures that appear on the Windows 95 desktop's background are called *icons*. Figure 1.1 contains seven icons along the left side of the screen. Icons can also appear elsewhere, such as on the ribbon across the bottom of Figure 1.1's desktop.

1

JUST A MINUTE

Your Windows 95 screen may contain more or fewer icons than Figure 1.1's screen, depending on the way your version of Windows 95 is configured. For example, if your PC is not connected to a computer network, you will not see the icon labeled Network Neighborhood. In addition, you may see artwork in your Windows 95 desktop's background.

The artwork that forms the background for a Windows 95 screen is called *wallpaper*. The wallpaper comes from a graphics file called a *bitmap* file. In Hour 3, "Understanding the My Computer Window," you'll see how you can change or remove the wallpaper if you don't like the artwork used on your system. Figure 1.2 shows the same Windows 95 desktop as before, only the desktop contains a graphical wallpaper file to make things more interesting.

Figure 1.2.

Wallpaper can make your desktop less boring.

The Windows 95 screen acts like a desktop from which you'll work on your computer. If you want to write letters using a word processor, you'll start the word processor program from the Windows 95 environment. Windows 95 always remains in the computer's memory to help you interact with your programs and with the computer hardware.

In ancient times (less than ten years ago!), people controlled computers by typing all kinds of cryptic commands that the computer responded to. MS-DOS is one such environment that requires typed, and sometimes difficult, commands. These commands take a long time to learn and are often hard to remember.

Computers controlled by graphical user interfaces (*GUIs*), such as Windows 95, no longer require the tedium of typed commands. Windows 95 is extremely graphical in nature. Instead of typing a command that directs the computer to start a program, you'll use the mouse or keyboard to point to an icon on the screen to activate the icon's matching program.

Microsoft developers proudly promote the effort they put into the Windows 95 interface. In designing Windows 95, Microsoft took people who had never before used a computer and placed them in front of other operating environments, such as previous versions of Windows, and requested that the new users perform certain tasks such as starting game programs. As a result, Microsoft learned a lot about the way people approach a visual environment. Windows 95 is the result of countless hours of this kind of usability testing.

3.1 ▶
Step Up
When you used to start Windows 3.1, you saw all kinds of Program Manager icons. These icons represented different program groups. Program groups still exist in Windows 95, but they are much more integrated into the system and remain out of the way until you are ready for them.

If you are fairly new to computers, you may not understand why you would want to use Windows 95. Perhaps you've used a word processor or a spreadsheet but never taken the time to learn about MS-DOS or find out what this Windows stuff is all about. Other newcomers to Windows 95 may have migrated to the PC world from a Macintosh or from a mainframe computer. In a nutshell, Windows 95 is all of the following:

☐ An operating system that manages your hardware and software interactions. Windows 95 provides uniform access to your system so that programs can more accurately use your system's resources (such as disks and printers). Windows 95 eases many of the burdens that previous PC users had to go through when installing new software.

☐ A graphical user interface (GUI) that lets you start programs and control hardware graphically.

☐ A *32-bit environment,* which is a fancy computer technical term meaning that Windows 95 utilizes your computer's internal architecture to its fullest, unlike Windows 3.1 and MS-DOS, which are only 16-bit environments. A 32-bit environment does not necessarily guarantee double-speed performance, but programs often run much faster than in 16-bit environments.

☐ An improved replacement for MS-DOS—based computers. DOS stands for *disk operating system.*

☐ A networked interface that helps seamlessly integrate a network and the Internet into your work environment. If you do not currently use a network or the Internet, Windows 95 will help you transition to either of those new technologies when you are ready.

1

If one were to state the single greatest reason to use Windows 95, that reason would be this: Microsoft designed Windows 95 so that you can concentrate on using your software and hardware—*not* so you have to concentrate on using Windows 95. As you'll see throughout this book, use of the keyboard and mouse complement each other to give you easy control over every aspect of Windows 95.

How To Operate the Mouse

The odds are good that you've used a mouse if you've used a computer before. Using the mouse involves following the *mouse cursor* around the screen. The mouse cursor is the pointing arrow that moves as you move your mouse. In Hour 3 you'll learn how to change the mouse cursor shape from the arrow to something else.

Here's a quick review of the possible mouse actions you can perform:

☐ When you move the mouse, you physically move the mouse across your desk. (Some mice are actually trackballs; trackballs remain stationary and you spin the trackball's sphere to move the mouse.) The screen's mouse cursor follows your mouse movements. When you point to an object on the screen, you are moving the mouse to that object.

☐ When you click the mouse, you press and immediately release either the left or right mouse button. To select graphical screen objects, you'll often click the left button. You will use your right mouse button displaying special pop-up menus. Hour 3 explains how to swap the left and right mouse button actions if you are left-handed.

☐ When you double-click, you press and immediately release the left or right mouse button twice in succession.

☐ When you drag screen objects with the mouse, you'll move the mouse cursor over an object that you want to move to another screen location. With the mouse cursor over the object, press and hold the left mouse button and keep the button pressed. The item under the mouse cursor is now temporarily welded to the mouse cursor. As you move the mouse (while still holding the mouse button), the screen object moves with the cursor. When you eventually release the mouse button, Windows 95 anchors the object in the mouse cursor's new position.

You can almost always use the keyboard instead of the mouse to perform just about any Windows 95 operation. Remember, though, that using the mouse is a lot easier than using the keyboard for most Windows 95 operations. If you are uncomfortable with using a mouse, don't fret, because the mouse actions soon become second nature.

One of the benefits that Windows 3.1 users learn about Windows 95 is that Windows 95 does not require as many mouse clicks and double-clicks as previous versions of Windows did.

First Things First

Starting Windows 95 is easier than starting previous versions of Windows. The first requirement that users of earlier versions of Windows needed to master was how to enter the Windows environment. Engineers designed PCs to be controlled by an operating system such as MS-DOS. When Microsoft designed Windows originally, Windows ran *in addition to* MS-DOS. Therefore, after users would start their computers, which first loaded MS-DOS, they would also have to issue a separate command to start Windows.

Windows 95 contains a complete native operating system (called the *kernel* because the operating system is the heart of everything you do on the computer), in addition to a graphical user interface. Except in rare cases where someone configures his or her computer to run Windows 95 along with another version of Windows, Windows 95 starts automatically when you turn on your PC. Therefore, you don't have to learn how to start Windows 95; Windows 95 automatically loads itself when you turn on your computer or *reboot* it (which means to reset the computer using the strange Ctrl+Alt+Del keystroke sequence).

JUST A MINUTE

> The keystroke Ctrl+Alt+Del might be confusing to you. To issue that key combination, you press and hold down the keys sequentially: Press and hold down the Ctrl key, then press and hold down the Alt key, and then press the Del key (you'll actually hold down all three keys). Let up on all three keys at once to begin the reboot process.

Logging On

If you are not connected to a network, nothing in this section applies to you. Even if you access the Internet, you will not need to know this section's material if your computer is not part of a wired networking system. You may skip ahead to the next section entitled, "Welcome to Windows 95."

If your PC is connected to a network, you will have to *log on* to the network. When you log on, you type a user name and password that you or a *System Administrator* in your company has set up. Figure 1.3 shows the logon screen that you might see if you are running in a networked computer environment.

1

Figure 1.3.
Network users will have to log on to Windows 95.

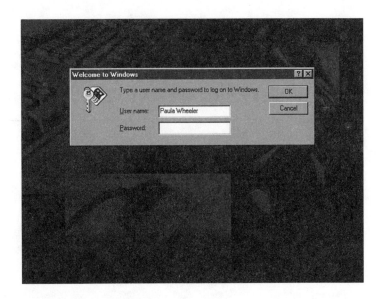

Task 1.1: Logging On to Windows 95

Step 1: Description

There is no way for this book to know your user name and password. You'll have to ask the person responsible for installing the networked Windows 95 on your PC for the logon information. Once you get the user name and initial password, you can log on to the computer and then be able to access Windows 95.

Step 2: Action

1. When you see the logon screen, type your user name exactly as the System Administrator set it up. Often, your user name is your full name or your first initial and last name.

2. Press the Tab key.

3. Type your password exactly as the System Administrator set it up. Asterisks appear in place of the actual password you type so that no one looking over your shoulder will be able to read your password.

4. Press Enter to start Windows 95.

Step 3: Review

If you get an error message, you will have to check with the System Administrator to make sure you are properly authorized to use the networked Windows 95. If this is the first time you or anyone else has logged on with your user name, the initial password that you enter will be the permanent password unless you change the password later. Windows 95 will request that first password twice to be sure that you type the initial password exactly as it should be.

JUST A MINUTE

By design, networks allow more than one user access to the same files. In other words, assuming that you have the proper electronic authorization, you can access files stored on any person's PC that is connected to your PC. The extra benefits that a network provides also require extra security precautions so that unauthorized users do not bother other people's files.

TIME SAVER

Your Network Administrator can set up different *user profiles* for each network user. A user profile defines your interface preferences and the file access you have. The Windows 95 interface is customizable, as you'll see throughout this book. When you log on, your custom interface, such as a particular desktop wallpaper you prefer, can appear. If another user uses your computer, that user's profile will determine that user's interface design.

You can change your password by double-clicking the Windows 95 Control Panel's Password icon and entering your current and new password. If you need further help with the Control Panel, you'll learn how to use the Control Panel for managing your system in Hour 3.

Welcome to Windows 95

Windows 95 is helpful. In fact, Windows 95 is *extremely* helpful! Each time when you first turn on your PC and start it, Windows 95 displays the *Welcome Screen* with a different tip (such as the one shown in Figure 1.4).

Figure 1.4.

Learn something new every time you start Windows 95.

The Welcome Screen is an example of a *window*. In Windows 95, windows appear all over the place, often overlapping and hiding other windows. Keep in mind that Windows 95 works as if it were a 3D set of images on your screen. If one window covers up a screen object (such as text, an icon, or another window), the objects the new window covers are still underneath the new window. When you move the window or make the window disappear (called *closing* the window), you'll see the hidden objects once again.

The Welcome Screen is a helpful screen that you might want to see the first few times you start Windows 95. In addition to a different tip, you can access any of the following services from the Welcome Screen:

- ☐ Browse a brief on-screen tour of Windows 95.
- ☐ Find out how Windows 95 differs from its predecessor Windows 3.1.
- ☐ Use your modem (if one is connected to your PC) to register your copy of Windows 95 so Microsoft can inform you of its latest products (and fill your mail box with *lots* of mail).
- ☐ Learn what other Microsoft products are available.
- ☐ Read additional tips.

Much of the time, you'll read the Welcome Screen tip and then close the Welcome Screen window with the button labeled Close, so you can begin working with Windows 95. After a while, the tips will begin to repeat themselves, and you won't need the services of the Welcome Screen any longer. Uncheck the caption next to the checkbox at the bottom of the screen when you want to stop seeing the Welcome Screen.

Command Controls

As you work with Windows 95, you'll see all kinds of windows appear and disappear. The Welcome Screen window shown in Figure 1.4 is sometimes called a *dialog box*. Dialog box windows contain all kinds of various *controls* with which you can manage Windows 95.

There are six *command button* controls down the right side of the Welcome Screen. Command buttons (often just called *buttons*) give you push-button access to various options. These on-screen graphical buttons look and act as if they are physical pushbuttons. There are three ways to select an on-screen command button:

1. Click the button with the mouse.
2. Press Tab to highlight the buttons in succession. Shift+Tab moves backwards. You'll know that a button is highlighted when a dotted outline appears around the button's caption. Moving the highlight between on-screen controls is called *changing the focus*. Once the focus (the dotted highlight) appears on the button you want to select, press Enter to activate that button.

▲

3. Press Alt plus the underlined letter on the button's caption. This combined keystroke is called a *hot key*. For example, you can select the Welcome Screen's Next **T**ip command button by pressing Alt+T. (Hot keys appear bold in this text.)

There is another kind of control at the bottom of the Welcome Screen called a *checkbox*. Certain windows need checkboxes to indicate a yes or no possibility. If the Welcome Screen's checkbox is checked (a check mark appears in the white box when checked), Windows 95 shows the Welcome Screen (with a different tip) the next time you start Windows 95. If you uncheck the checkbox, Windows 95 will not show the Welcome Screen again.

There are three ways to check (or uncheck) a checkbox:

1. Click either the checkbox or the message next to the checkbox with the mouse.
2. Move the focus to the checkbox text (by pressing Tab or Shift+Tab) and press Enter.
3. Press Alt plus the hot key of the checkbox's message.

Perhaps you just started Windows 95, but the Welcome Screen did not appear. The last person to use your PC may have unchecked the Welcome Screen's checkbox control so the screen does not appear for you. If you'd like to see a Welcome Screen tip when you start Windows 95, you'll learn how to add the Welcome Screen to the startup sequence in Hour 7, "A Call for Help!" Although activating the Welcome Screen is not difficult to do, you need some additional Windows 95 skills before you should try this task.

3.1 ▷
Step Up
You will quickly see that Windows 95 takes on an entirely different look from Windows 3.1. The command buttons have a more chiseled 3D appearance, and window buttons, such as the resizing and control buttons, look different and make more sense in Windows 95 than they did before.

Even programs written for Windows 3.1 will take on the rejuvenated look of Windows 95 programs when you run those programs under Windows 95. Figure 1.5 shows the Microsoft Word menu bar as it looks running under Windows 95. Notice that the same menu items and window-control icons appear in Windows 95 just as you are used to from Windows 3.1 but that the Windows 95 version is different and less bulky looking. (Many new Windows 95 programs, such as Word 97, show a button depression when you move your mouse over the menu item, as Figure 1.5 shows.)

Close the Welcome Screen window if it still appears on your monitor. When you close a window, the window goes completely away. You can close the window by clicking the command button labeled with an x (the *Close* button). In Hour 2, "What's Windows 95 All About?," you'll learn how to leave a window without completely closing the window; the window will be out of your way, but you will be able to return to that window whenever you want.

1

Figure 1.5.
Windows 95 makes a new fashion statement.

1

Keep Before You Quit

You are probably anxious to get started, but before you learn more about using Windows 95, you must learn how to quit Windows 95 properly. Due to the integration of Windows 95 and your computer's hardware and software, you must take a few extra steps when quitting your Windows 95 session and turning off your computer.

CAUTION

> If you do not properly shut down Windows 95, you could very easily lose work that you just completed. At the worst, you could damage a Windows 95 configuration file that will mess up Windows 95 the next time you start your PC.

Surely you've noticed the button in the lower-left corner of the Windows 95 screen labeled Start. This area of the screen is known as the *taskbar,* and this button is called the *Start button.* The taskbar is perhaps the most important element in Windows 95 because you'll use it, the taskbar, to launch and switch between several programs. Windows 95 lets you run more than one program at the same time. In other words, you could be downloading a file from another computer, printing a spreadsheet, listening to an opera on an audio CD, and typing with a word processor, all at the same time. The taskbar grows to list each program currently running. Figure 1.6 shows a taskbar that lists four programs running in memory at the same time.

Figure 1.6.
The taskbar lists every program running.

Taskbar buttons   Taskbar   Clock

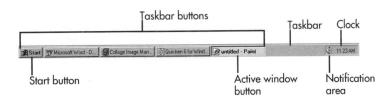

Start button   Active window   Notification
                      button   area

TIME SAVER

> Think of the taskbar as acting like a television channel changer. On a television, there are several channels with programs going at the same time; you can switch between the channels using the remote control. When you run more than one Windows 95 program, you can switch among the programs by clicking the program names in the taskbar at the bottom of the screen.

The taskbar does more than list and manage running programs. The taskbar is the starting point for just about everything you will do in Windows 95. If you want to rearrange files, start programs, change screen colors, modify the mouse, or view the contents of files, the taskbar contains the power to do all those things and more. The taskbar is the launch pad for just about everything you'll want to do in Windows 95.

The taskbar also contains the commands you'll need to shut down Windows 95 and your computer. In Hour 4, "Take Windows 95 to Task," you'll delve much more deeply into the operations of the taskbar. At this point though, you'll learn just enough to master the Windows 95 shutdown process, because without the proper shutdown you face risky consequences of data loss as I described at the start of this section.

TIME SAVER

Place the mouse cursor over the Start button but do not click the mouse button. After a brief pause, Windows 95 displays a small caption box next to the mouse cursor that reads, "Click here to begin." If you are unsure as to what a Windows 95 button does, move the mouse cursor over the button and wait for a moment. Most of the time, Windows 95 displays a message, such as the Start button's, that describes what the button would do if you were to click it.

When you click the Start button on the taskbar, you'll see the *Start menu* pop up above the Start button as shown in Figure 1.7. The Start menu gives you access to every part of your computer. Table 1.1 describes what each option of the Start menu does. From the Start menu, you can start programs, check disk space, manage files, and properly shut down the computer. The latter, shutting down the computer, is the concern of this section.

Table 1.1. The Start menu commands.

Command	Description
Programs	Displays lists of program groups and names that you can run.
Documents	Displays a list of documents, or data files, that you've recently opened and may want to return to again. As you'll learn in Hour 5, "Cruise with Documents and Windows," Windows 95 works from a data-driven viewpoint. Windows 95 lets you work on your data without worrying about tedious program-starting details.
Settings	Lets you change the configuration of Windows 95.
Find	Lets you search your computer's files for specific data.
Help	Gives you online help for the various tasks you can perform in Windows 95.

Command	Description
Run	Gives you the ability to execute programs or open program group folders if you know the proper MS-DOS commands to do so.
Sh**u**t Down	Lets you safely shut down your computer without losing data that you might otherwise lose if you did not shut down properly.

Figure 1.7.
The Start menu is the command center for the rest of Windows 95.

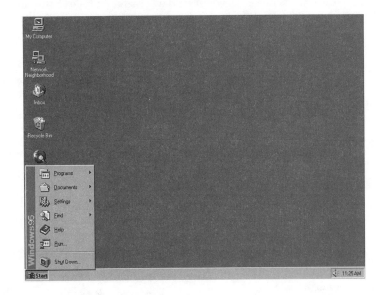

 The taskbar's Programs command takes the place of the bulky Program Manager that you know about from Windows 3.1.

Although you can select the various Start menu commands, please understand that the most important command on the start menu is the Shut Down command. Before you do too much, even before you really master the ins and outs of the Start menu, you should read the rest of this section to learn how to shut down your computer safely. You don't want to write the first chapter of a best-selling novel only to find that Windows 95 sent the chapter into oblivion because you did not shut down the computer properly before turning off the power.

JUST A MINUTE

Actually, the data on your computer is fairly safe in most cases. If you did not shut down the computer before turning off the power, you'd *probably* not lose any data 99 times out of 100. Why take the chance though? The Shut Down command is quick and easy to use and ensures that all data and Windows 95 settings are safely recorded so you can turn off the computer without the worry of data loss.

Activating Menu Commands

Windows 95 menus list various options and commands available to you at the time. When confronted with a menu, such as the Start menu, there are several ways you can select any item you want from the menu.

If you use your mouse, you can point to an item on the menu. As you move the mouse cursor over the menu items, you'll see that a highlight follows the mouse cursor through the menu, clearly showing you which menu item the mouse cursor is over. If your hands are on the keyboard when you display a menu, you can press the up and down arrow keys to move the highlight through the menu's commands.

Some menu commands, such as the Shut Down command, contain ellipses (...) to the right of the command name. The ellipses indicate that if you choose this command, a dialog box will appear requiring additional information.

Some menu commands, such as the Start menu's Programs and Documents commands, display arrows to the right of the command names. The arrows indicate that other command menus appear if you select from those commands. Sometimes, Windows 95 menu commands *cascade* (trigger additional menus) several levels deep, such as the one shown in Figure 1.8. You can decrease the cascade, removing one or more of the extra cascaded menu levels, simply by moving the mouse to the left one menu or by pressing the Esc key.

Figure 1.8.

Some menus trigger other menus producing a cascaded menu look.

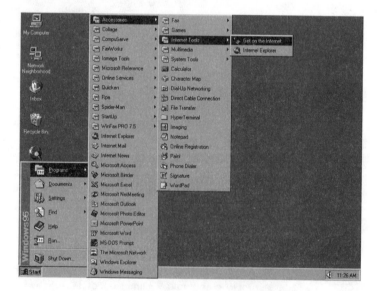

1

Some menu commands, such as **H**elp, do not contain anything to the right of the command name. These commands perform an immediate service, such as displaying a Help screen, displaying a menu, or starting a program from your disk drive.

If a menu command contains an underlined letter, such as **H**elp, you can select that menu command by pressing Alt plus the letter. Alt+H activates the **H**elp menu command.

To display a cascading menu, you don't have to click the mouse as you would in Windows 3.1. As a matter of fact, Windows 95 changes all your Windows applications, such as the pull-down menus in Microsoft Excel. When you display a menu, you only have to move the mouse cursor through the menu options to highlight those commands. In Windows 3.1, if you wanted to highlight a menu command, you would have to use the up and down arrow keys or click on the menu command with the mouse button.

Are you beginning to see how Windows 95 improves your use of Windows without taking away any functionality? Through the cascading menus, you can see all your program groups, but those program groups don't appear 100% of the time, getting in your way as they did in Windows 3.1. Also, the menus are sometimes called *sticky* menus because you don't have to press a mouse button to highlight a menu command. The commands highlight themselves as you move the mouse cursor through them (the commands *stick* to the mouse cursor).

If you just explored a bit and displayed a cascaded menu or selected another command from the Start menu, press Esc until the Start menu disappears and the Start button returns to normal. As mentioned earlier, this is an important time to learn about the Sh**u**t Down command.

Press the Start button once again and select the Sh**u**t Down command. The ellipses after the words Sh**u**t Down indicate that a dialog box window will appear. Figure 1.9 shows the resulting Shut Down window. There is more than one way to shut down your computer depending on what your current need is.

Figure 1.9.

You must make a decision as to how you want to shut down the computer.

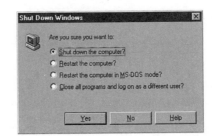

WINDOWS MINUTE

Shut Down Options

The Shut Down window demonstrates a new kind of control in Windows 95. The three lines inside the Shut Down window represent captioned *option buttons*. A dot inside one of the option buttons indicates that this option is the selected option. When you first display the Shut Down window, the first option, "**S**hut down the computer?" is the selected option. If you were to select another option, Windows 95 would *deselect* the first option, thereby ensuring that only one is active at any one time.

Here are three ways to select an option from a list of option button choices:

☐ Point to one of the options with the mouse and click the mouse button.

☐ Use the keyboard's up and down arrow keys to move the focus (the focus's dotted line surrounds the selected option button) among the selections.

☐ Press Alt plus the underlined letter of the option you want to select. Alt+R chooses the "**R**estart the computer?" option.

Simply selecting an option does not trigger any action. Once you select the desired option, you'll then have to activate the Yes command button (sometimes labeled OK) to execute that option's command. If you choose No, Windows 95 removes the Shut Down window and returns you to the Windows 95 environment. If you push the Help command button, Windows 95 displays online help that describes the options in more detail. (Hour 7 explains the Windows 95 online help system in detail.)

TIME SAVER

If you want to restart Windows 95 without rebooting your computer, hold down a Shift key when you select the **R**estart the computer? option. Continue holding Shift until you see the message, Restarting Windows 95. Windows 95 will restart, but your computer won't go through the time-consuming reboot and memory test.

Table 1.2 describes each of the three shut down options. Most of the time, you'll select the first one because you are turning off the computer. When you select the first option, Windows 95 pauses briefly, and then displays a message telling you that you can turn off the computer's power. Go ahead and select the first option now. Select the first option button and click the Yes button to initiate the shut down.

TIME SAVER

When you see command buttons, Windows 95 will highlight one of them by darkening the button's edges a bit as done on the Yes button in Figure 1.9. If you were to press Enter, Windows 95 would activate the Yes button for you. As a shortcut to using Windows 95 and command buttons, you can always press Enter to trigger the activation of the highlighted button instead of using the mouse or keyboard to find and press that same button.

Table 1.2. The Shut Down commands and their descriptions.

Command	Description
Shut down the computer?	Closes all open files and programs as well as writes any remaining unwritten data to the disk.
Restart the computer?	Performs a shut down, but then reboots the computer for you. Sometimes, you'll be instructed to restart Windows 95 after installing a new program or after changing a Windows 95 option.
Restart the computer in MS-DOS Mode?	Performs a shut down, but then restarts the computer in MS-DOS mode without putting you directly into Windows 95. Only those users who understand MS-DOS commands would want to use this command. From the MS-DOS mode, you can type the word exit to leave MS-DOS and enter Windows 95.

You may have to develop the habit of shutting down Windows 95 properly before turning off the computer. Perhaps you can stick a note to the computer's on/off switch until you get used to running the Shut Down command. Again, the Shut Down command is cheap insurance against data loss, and the Shut Down habit is a good one to develop.

TIME SAVER

If you shut down the computer but change your mind, you don't have to turn off the machine. Instead of turning off the computer and then turning it back on again, you can press Ctrl+Alt+Del to reboot the computer and Windows 95 will reload after a few moments.

Ten Good Reasons to Switch to Windows 95

Still not convinced that you want to change from the familiar Windows 3.1 to Windows 95? Here are ten good reasons to make the switch:

1. Windows 95 is faster than Windows 3.1. Windows 95 requires fewer keystrokes and mouse clicks to get work done. Most applications will run faster as well.

2. Windows 95 provides a technical feature known as *preemptive multitasking* that offers much smoother operation of several programs at the same time. Despite the promises, Windows 3.1 was not adept at downloading a file while you did something else on the computer, such as print a spreadsheet. Windows 95 offers better multitasking and lets you download files in the background without loss of data.

3. The Windows 95 screen, although much cleaner than the Windows 3.1 screen, makes all your PC's programs available to you when you need them, but does not needlessly clutter the screen.

4. Windows 95 contains integrated networking and Internet capabilities if you work in a networked environment. As a matter of fact, for those on a budget, Windows 95 offers a direct-connect pseudo-networking feature that lets you connect two PCs together with just a cable.

5. Windows 95 contains a much-improved MS-DOS with true cut-and-paste capabilities and the power to run MS-DOS-based programs (such as your favorite games!) as quickly as you can run those programs in a native MS-DOS environment.

6. You will not have to match switch settings or worry about those pesky things called DMAs and IRQs when installing new hardware. With the new *Plug-and-Play* feature, Windows 95 detects when you add or change hardware and adjusts all the computer's settings automatically. (Not all hardware is approved for Plug-and-Play compatibility yet.)

7. Windows 95 has the capability to detect when you insert a CD-ROM in the drive and start (or install) the software stored on the CD-ROM. This *AutoPlay* feature eliminates the need for users to issue start-up instructions when they want to run a program from a CD-ROM. In addition, other areas of multimedia are more integrated into Windows 95 than before. For example, you can place a volume control at the bottom of the screen to control the speaker volume for audio playback of CDs.

8. Windows 95 utilizes that right-hand button on your mouse. Clicking the right button pops up a context-sensitive menu that gives you instant access to common tasks you may want to perform (see Hour 2 for details).

9. Windows 95 supports filenames longer than 8 characters with a three-character extension! If you want to give a 250-character name that even includes spaces to a file, go ahead! (The limit is 256 characters.)

10. Perhaps the most important day-to-day improvement you'll find is Windows 95's replacement for Windows 3.1's Program and File manager called *Explorer* (covered in detail in Hour 6, "Explore the Windows 95 System"). Explorer makes managing hardware and files actually easy for a change.

Summary

You are off to a great start! It's time to push your own Start button, gear up your mind's memory chips, and begin exploring Windows 95 to see how to use Windows 95 and what it can do for you. Over the next 23 hours of study and tutorial, you'll be mastering the Windows 95 environment and learning all kinds of shortcuts along the way.

Keep in mind that Windows 95 is not an end in itself. The application programs that you want to run are the most important parts of your computer usage. It is Windows 95's job to help you work with your applications as painlessly as possible.

Workshop

Term Review

AutoPlay   The Windows 95 feature that starts the loading and execution of CD-ROMs as soon as you place the CD-ROM in your computer's CD-ROM drive.

bitmap   The technical name for a graphics file. Windows 95 often uses bitmaps for the Windows 95 wallpaper.

checkbox   A Windows 95 control that appears next to each item in a list which you use to select one or more items from the list.

click   The process of pressing and immediately releasing one of the mouse buttons.

command button   A Windows 95 control that appears and acts like a push button on the screen.

cursor   A pointing device, such as the arrow that represents the mouse pointer location and the insert bar that represents the Windows 95 text location. The cursor moves across the screen as you type or move the mouse.

desktop   The Windows 95 screen and background.

dialog box   A window containing text and one or more screen controls that you use to issue instructions to Windows 95.

disk operating system   The program inside memory that controls all the hardware and software interactions.

dragging   The process of moving an image or selected text from one screen location to another using the mouse. To drag the mouse, you move the mouse while holding the mouse button. When you've dragged the item to the final position, release the mouse to anchor the item in that position.

focus   The highlighted command button or control in a dialog box that Windows 95 automatically selects when you press enter.

GUI   A graphical user interface, such as Windows 95, that lets the user interact with the computer primarily through graphic images as opposed to a more traditional text-based interface that requires typed commands.

hot key   The combination of an Alt keypress combined with another key that selects command buttons. The key you press with Alt is displayed with an underlined letter in the command button you want to select.

icons   Small pictures that represent commands and programs in Windows 95.

kernel   The internal native operating system that controls the hardware and software interaction.

log on   The process that lets you gain access to a networked computer.

multitasking   The process of a computer that is running more than one program at the same time.

Option buttons   A Windows 95 control that appears next to each item in a list which you use to select one and only one item from the list.

Plug-and-Play   The feature inside Windows 95 that detects and automatically configures the operating system to match new hardware that you install in your computer system.

point   The action made by the screen's mouse cursor when you move the mouse.

reboot   The process of restarting your computer through the keyboard (by pressing Alt+Ctrl+Del) without shutting off the computer's power.

Start button   The button at the left of the taskbar that displays the Windows 95 cascading menu of choices. When you click the Start button, the Windows 95 Start menu appears.

Start menu   A Windows 95 system and program menu that appears when you click the taskbar's Start button.

System Administrator   The person in charge of assigning user names and setting up new users on networked environments.

1

Taskbar   The bar at the bottom of a Windows 95 screen where running program icons appear along with the system clock.

User profile   The customized interface and file-access rules setup for each networked user.

wallpaper   The background graphics that appear on the Windows 95 desktop.

Q&A

Q For whom did Microsoft write Windows 95?

A Microsoft wrote Windows 95 for everybody including beginners, intermediate users, advanced users, and programmers. The primary Windows 95 goal is to be easy enough for newcomers, and yet powerful enough for those who need that power.

Q When will I have to log on to Windows 95?

A If your computer is connected to a network, the chances are good that you will have to log on before you can use Windows 95. In a network environment, computers have connections to each other so users have physical access to other people's files. By delegating user names and passwords, the system administrator assigns protection and privileges to all users on the system.

Q Why do asterisks appear when I enter my network password?

A Asterisks appear in place of the actual characters that you type so that someone looking over your shoulder cannot steal your password.

Q I've read all the Welcome Screen tips, and I don't want to see them anymore. Can I stop having to see a Welcome Screen every time I start Windows 95?

A Yes. Click the checkbox at the bottom of the Welcome Screen when you next start Windows 95. Afterwards, Windows 95 will no longer display the Welcome Screen when you first start Windows 95.

Q What happens if I do not use the Shut Down procedures for my computer?

A If you do not Shut Down your computer before turning off the power, you could lose data files or even system configuration files. Most of the time, you'd probably be okay if you did not Shut Down the computer, but your data is worth too much not to get into the habit of properly shutting down the system and safely storing all data.

Hour 2

Tour Windows 95 Now

For the next hour, you are going to learn a lot about Windows 95's interface. You will become comfortable with managing windows and icons.

There are several examples to follow along in this hour. Some people who have used Windows for years may not know more than you'll learn this hour. Once you master the fundamental approach to managing Windows 95's screens and elements, you'll see that this hour's techniques will follow you and help you manage almost every other aspect of Windows 95 that you work with in the future. In other words, once you master the basics of the window and screen management tools, you'll use those abilities in all your Windows 95 applications work.

The highlights of this hour include:

- ☐ Why windows management is important
- ☐ What the parts of a window are called
- ☐ How to resize and move windows
- ☐ When the Control menu is useful

Windows appear all over the place when you work with Windows —
that's why it's called *Windows*! Therefore, taking a moment to learn
proper windows management now will reap big-time savings and reduce
confusion in the future.

I Do Do Windows!

The first window that you will work with is called the My Computer window. In this hour
you will look at that window to learn how to work with windows. Once you master window
management in this hour, the next hour will explain how to use the contents of the My
Computer window. Locate the My Computer icon on your Windows 95 desktop. Double-
click the icon to open the My Computer window. Most icons on the desktop open to
windows when you double-click them as you'll see throughout this book.

Figure 2.1 shows the My Computer window with all its control buttons and window
components labeled. You will find this same window structure in almost every window that
you open. You will even find windows like these in the Windows 95 applications that you
run, such as a database program. Although you saw a couple of simpler windows in this book's
previous hour, the window in Figure 2.1 is more typical of the windows you'll work with most
often.

Figure 2.1.

*Use a window's controls
and menus to manage the
window.*

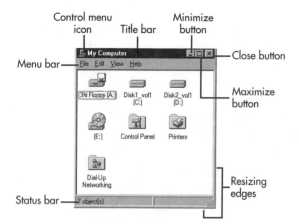

Familiarize yourself now with the buttons and window sections called out in Figure 2.1 because almost every window contains these windows controls or a subset of them. Here are some of the more general things you can do with such a window on the screen:

☐ You can shrink the window down to an icon on the taskbar, eliminating the window from the screen, but keeping the window active. This is called *minimizing a window.*

☐ You can enlarge a minimized window to partial- or full-screen size. When you size a window to take up the entire screen, the window is known to be *maximized.*

☐ You can move a window from one location to another on the screen.

☐ You can bring a window to the top of a stack of windows so you can work within that window. (Due to Windows 95's multitasking capability, hidden windows can still perform data processing, such as calculating and printing.)

☐ You can close a window completely, removing its icon from the taskbar and stopping the application that is running inside the window.

You can have one or more windows on your screen, some overlapping other windows, some completely covering others, and you will sometimes see windows side by side or above other windows. In a typical Windows 95 user's day, the user may have two or more applications running at the same time. Each of those applications might display one or more windows of its own.

You must learn how to manage all those windows if you want to be as productive as possible. Don't jump to the conclusion, though, that all those windows result in confusion. On a typical desk, even the desks of the most organized people (the author not being one of them!), you'll find all sorts of paper stacks, and those stacks don't imply disorganization. The desk's user simply has to know how to organize the stacks and bring the most important stacks to the forefront when he or she wants to work on them.

JUST A MINUTE

When you start a program, the taskbar gets a new taskbar button with the name of that application appearing on the taskbar button.

Some applications display single windows. Other applications might display multiple windows. For example, there are word processors that can display two documents side by side in two different windows.

Minimizing Windows

If you temporarily finish working with a window, you can minimize that window by pressing the window's Minimize button. Minimizing a window keeps the program in the window loaded and active but puts the program out of the way until you are ready to return to that program again. Even if you minimize a window, the window's icon and description remain on the taskbar at the bottom of the screen. The taskbar continues to hold the application's button until you completely close the application.

 Notice how the icons on Windows 95's control buttons illustrate the purpose of those buttons better than the equivalent control buttons in Windows 3.1.

Task 2.1: Minimizing a Window

Step 1: Description

The Minimize button clears the window from your desktop. The program that you have running inside the window is still loaded and active, but the program no longer takes up screen space. The taskbar continues to list the program because the program is still active.

Step 2: Action

1. Find the Minimize button on your My Computer window.
2. Click the button with your mouse pointer. Look closely at the screen as you minimize the window. You'll see that Windows 95 graphically and quickly shrinks the outer edges of the window down into the taskbar button labeled My Computer.

Step 3: Review

When you minimize a window, whatever window or icon is behind that window will then appear. Remember that the way you know a window is still active is that its icon and description still appear on the taskbar as shown in Figure 2.2.

Figure 2.2.

The window's taskbar button still appears after you minimize a window.

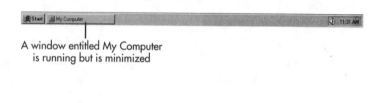

A window entitled My Computer
is running but is minimized

The taskbar button in Figure 2.2 contains the caption My Computer. The caption says My Computer because the minimized window's title bar contained the title My Computer. The taskbar button always contains the same title listed in the application's title bar.

JUST A MINUTE

> Depending on the length of the title and the number of items in the taskbar, the taskbar may only show the first few letters of a window's title.

2

Enlarging Windows

Windows 95 supplies several ways to enlarge a window. You can enlarge a minimized window from its taskbar status to the window's regular size. You can also maximize a window that's already showing, to take up the entire screen space. Here are the ways to enlarge a window:

- ☐ Click the window's taskbar button when the window is minimized
- ☐ Click the window's Maximize button to enlarge the window to full screen
- ☐ Drag one of the window's corners or edges outward to increase the size of the window or inward to shrink the size of the window manually

This section discusses the first two window enlarging methods that utilize buttons, and the next section explains how to enlarge a window manually.

Task 2.2: Enlarging a Minimized Window

Step 1: Description

Use the taskbar buttons to display minimized windows. In other words, if you have one or more minimized windows and want to work with one of those window's programs, click the matching taskbar button, and the window reappears at its original size before you minimized the window.

Step 2: Action

1. Click the My Computer taskbar button. The My Computer window reappears.
2. Notice how the window quickly and visually grows from the taskbar back to its original size? Perhaps you want to see that again. Minimize the now enlarged My Computer window once again to shrink the window down into the taskbar.
3. Click the My Computer taskbar button and watch the window return to its original and enlarged state.

Step 3: Review

The taskbar lists windows that represent all running programs. Some of those programs may have their windows showing on the screen; other programs are minimized so they take no screen space but are still loaded. Clicking a taskbar button causes a minimized window to return to its original size.

JUST A MINUTE

You'll see icons other than the open windows on your taskbar. At the right of most taskbars lie the time of day along with other icons such as the speaker icon.

Task 2.3: Maximizing a Window

Step 1: Description

As long as a window contains a Maximize button, you can maximize that window to the screen's full size. (Some windows are designed to be no larger than a preset size; these windows do not have Maximize buttons.) When you want to dedicate the entire screen to a window, you can usually maximize the window by clicking the window's Maximize button.

TIME SAVER

You also can maximize a window by double-clicking the window's title bar.

Step 2: Action

1. Click the My Computer window's Maximize button. The window grows to consume the entire screen. Figure 2.3 shows what you will see when you click the My Computer window's Maximize button. The My Computer window does not contain a lot of items, so maximizing the My Computer window does not produce much benefit other than the practice that you're getting here. The more a window contains, the larger you'll want to make that window so that you can see the contents. For example, if your computer contained several disk drives and was networked to other machines, you may need to maximize the window to see all the icons that represent your computer's peripherals.

   There is no need for Windows 95 to keep a Maximize button on a window that's already maximized. Therefore, Windows 95 changes the Maximize button to a Restore button as soon as you maximize any window. The Restore button, noted in Figure 2.3, always restores the window to the size it measured before you maximized it.

Figure 2.3.

A maximized window fills the entire screen.

A Restore button replaces the Maximize button

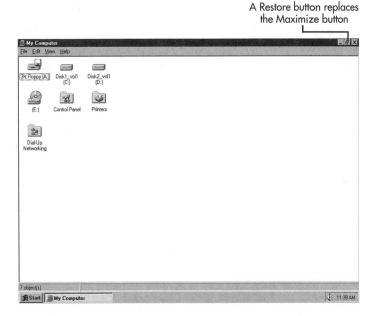

2. Click the My Computer window's Restore button. The window resizes (down) to its original size. As soon as you restore the window's size, you'll see that the Restore button switches back to a Maximize button once again.

3. Give it another maximizing whirl, but this time, double-click the My Computer window's title bar (point the mouse anywhere over the title in the window's title bar before double-clicking). Double-clicking the title bar maximizes a window just as pressing the Maximize button does.

4. Restore the My Computer window's original size again by clicking the Restore button.

Step 3: Review

You will often want to maximize a window if you are doing a lot of work within that window's program. For example, most word processor users maximize the word processing window while typing a document so that more screen real estate goes to that document and, therefore, more of the document appears on the screen at one time. You can maximize a window by clicking the window's Maximize button or by double-clicking the title bar.

TIME SAVER

> If you have loaded several programs and one program's window is covering up another program, you can click the hidden program's taskbar button to bring that covered window to the top of the window stack and into view.

Manually Changing Window Sizes

So far, you've seen how to minimize a window so it shrinks to a taskbar button. You've seen how to maximize a window to fill the screen. You've also seen how to restore that maximized window to its original size. This section shows you how, by dragging the mouse, you can resize a window to any size you want.

When you point to any window's edge or corner, the mouse cursor changes from its default shape (the pointing arrow) to a bidirectional arrow. The bidirectional arrow indicates that you are at one of the edges of the window and that you can drag that edge or corner inward or outward to change the size of the window.

When you drag one of the four straight edges, the window grows or shrinks left, right, up, or down. When you drag one of the four window corners the window grows or shrinks in both height and width in the direction of the cursor's bidirectional diagonal shape. (See the Windows Minute "How to Operate the Mouse," or the terms review in Hour 1, for common mouse actions including how to drag the mouse.)

Task 2.4: Manually Resizing a Window

Step 1: Description

Figure 2.4 shows the My Computer window after it is expanded down and to the right. In this task, you'll duplicate the figure's window size by manually enlarging your own My Computer window's size.

2

Figure 2.4.
You can manually enlarge a window with the mouse.

Step 2: Action

1. Point to the right edge of the My Computer window. Notice that the cursor changes to a horizontal bidirectional arrow. The horizontal arrow indicates that you could manually resize the window by dragging the right edge inward or outward.

2. Now point to the lower-right corner of your My Computer's window. Notice that the cursor changes to a diagonal, bidirectional arrow.

3. Drag the corner down (be sure that the cursor is a diagonal bidirectional arrow before pressing the mouse button) and to the right until your My Computer window is approximately the same size as Figure 2.4. Let up on the mouse button when the window obtains the desired size.

Step 3: Review

When you touch the corner of the window, the mouse cursor's shape changes to a bidirectional arrow that indicates manual resizing is now available. When the bidirectional arrow appears, you can drag the mouse left, right, up, down, or diagonally to move that edge or corner of the window and resize the window.

JUST A MINUTE

> You cannot resize some windows due to the way they are designed. Some windows will only enlarge or shrink to dimensions pre-set by the window's programmers. The Welcome screen that you see when you start up Windows 95 is one such screen. You cannot resize or minimize the Welcome screen.

Moving Windows

The windows that appear on your Windows 95 desktop don't always appear in the location you want. That's okay. Using the mouse, you can easily drag a window to another location on the screen. The title bar acts like a handle for the window—to move the window, you drag the window's title bar.

Task 2.5: Moving a Window

Step 1: Description

Sometimes, you'll need to rearrange the windows on your screen so they form a more logical appearance as you work. To move a window, drag its title bar. As you move the window by dragging the title bar, an outline of the window follows the mouse. When you release the mouse button, the window appears in the new location.

Step 2: Action

1. Move the My Computer window by dragging the title bar and moving the mouse. You'll see the outline of the window move with the mouse.

2. Let up on the mouse button to end the dragging session and anchor the window in its new location.

3. Move the window once again. Move the window off the edge of the screen. As you can see, when you move a window over the screen's edge, Windows 95 *truncates* (chops off) a portion of the window. When you move the window back into full view, the window reappears in its entirety.

Step 3: Review

 Any time the order of your screen's windows is inappropriate, you can move one or more windows to different locations.

2

Closing a Window

Windows 95 is obviously full of windows and those windows contain executing programs that work with data values of all kinds. This windowed concept gives you a flexible and manageable way to run and control several programs at one time. When you open a window in the real world, you are using that window to let air inside a building. *Opening* a window in Windows 95 means that you are using the program or data area located within that window. Whenever you start a windowed program or enlarge a window that's been minimized, you are opening the program's window.

When you're through with an open window, both in the real world and in Windows 95, you must *close* the window. Closing a window eliminates the window from view and if that window contained a running program (as most do), that program will cease executing. The window's taskbar button will no longer appear on the taskbar.

CAUTION

Remember that *closing* a window differs from *minimizing* the window. Closing a window stops a program; minimizing a window keeps it running in the background.

If you open a window from an icon, as you did when you first opened the My Computer window earlier in this hour, closing the window eliminates the window from your desktop area, but the window's icon will remain on the screen in its original place. Unless you take some advanced steps to erase the icon and its contents, the icon remains on your Windows 95 desktop area whether the corresponding window is open or closed.

TIME SAVER

You can rearrange icons on your screen by dragging them with the mouse just as you rearrange windows.

Keep in mind that some windows contain running programs (such as the window you see when typing in a word processor program) while other windows contain icons and even more windows (such as the My Computer window). You can close both kinds of windows by clicking the Close button. When running a program you can also close its primary window, and hence terminate the entire program, by double-clicking the program's icon in the upper-left corner of the window or by terminating the program (normally by selecting **F**ile | E**x**it from the program's menu).

Unlike Windows 3.1, Windows 95 contains *folder* icons. These icons, when you double-click them, open up still more folders or windows of icons. In Windows 3.1, a program group could not contain other program groups, but Windows 95's folders (the new representation for program groups) can contain other folders. Folders also represent directories on your disk when you see folder icons in file listings.

Task 2.6: Closing a Window Using the Mouse

Step 1: Description

When you're done with a window, you can close the window by clicking the Close button (the window control button with an X that appears in the upper-right corner of the window), double-clicking the window's icon, or (if the window represents a running program) using the program's termination commands to close the program and the window.

Step 2: Action

1. Click the Close button on the My Computer window. The window will instantly disappear from view.

2. Look at the taskbar for the My Computer icon. You will see no My Computer icon! Remember that a closed window is different from a minimized window in that a minimized window is still active and loaded.

3. Open the My Computer window once more by double-clicking the My Computer icon on your desktop.

Step 3: Review

Closing a window is like taking a paper file off your desktop and storing that file away in a file cabinet. The window is completely gone from your work area just as the paper file would be. If you want to work in the window again you'll have to reinitiate the commands that displayed the window to begin with (usually by double-clicking an icon that represents the window).

Using the Control Menu

All windows contain icons in their upper-left corners. The icon is the same icon that you'll see when the window is closed. For example, you clicked a large PC icon on the Windows 95 desktop to open the My Computer window. Once opened, the My Computer window contains a small icon that matches the start-up icon you double-clicked to start the program.

Earlier (in the section labeled, "Closing a window") you learned to double-click this icon to close a window. The icon also represents a *Control menu* with which you can control the window's size and placement. Figure 2.5 shows the Control menu for the My Computer window. Almost every Windows 95 program contains this same menu.

Figure 2.5.
You can control a window's size and placement through the Control menu.

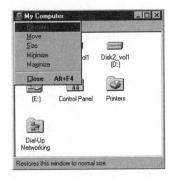

What's on the Menu?

Just as a menu in a restaurant is a list of food items you can choose, a Windows *menu* is a list of commands you can select. The Control menu is a typical Windows 95 menu. Many menus operate the same way that the Control menu operates—that is, the list of menu choices stays out of the way until you are ready to choose from it. You've seen another kind of menu in Hour 1: The Start menu. Once you display a menu, you can move through the menu selections using the keyboard's up and down arrow keys, as well as with the mouse.

The first thing you'll notice about Figure 2.5 is that the top choice, **R**estore, is *grayed out.* Often one or more menu items will be grayed out, meaning that the choice is unavailable at this time but, depending on circumstances, may be available from this menu at a later time.

Just like the Start menu, the Control menu offers a list of *shortcut keys* with which you can quickly select a menu item. For example, Alt+N selects the Control menu's Mi**n**imize command as long as the Control menu is shown at the time you press Alt+N.

There's another kind of shortcut key you'll see on the Control menu. Both Alt+C *and* Alt+F4 select the Control menu's **C**lose command. The Alt+F4 key, however, is an *accelerator* key meaning that the Control menu does not have to be showing when you press Alt+F4 to close the window. Accelerator keys generally involve function keys and appear to the right of their associated menu choices.

As with the Start menu, you can also select from the Control menu using the mouse. You now know everything there is to know about using and choosing from Windows 95 menus!

Just a Minute

If you accidentally open a window, such as the Start or Control menu, press Esc to close the menu.

Time Saver

Later in this hour, when you use the My Computer window's menu bar (shown previously in Figure 2.1), you'll select commands and shortcut keys from the menu bar just as you do from the Control menu. The only difference is that the commands on the menu bar always appear at the top of the window whereas the Control menu appears only when you click the Control menu icon.

Table 2.1 explains what each Control menu command does.

Table 2.1. The Control menu commands.

Command	Description
Restore	Restores a window that you've maximized. The Restore command is available (not grayed out) only when the window is maximized.
Move	Moves a window on the screen to a different location.
Size	Resizes a window by enlarging or shrinking the window.
Minimize	Shrinks the window to the taskbar icon and description.
Maximize	Enlarges the window to full-screen size.
Close	Closes the window. If the window is a running program, the program terminates.

Task 2.7: Closing a Window Using the Keyboard

TASK

Step 1: Description

Today, Windows users do not often use the Control menu for window sizing and placement because the mouse is so much easier to use. However, long ago in the computers of olden times (at least five years ago), many people owned computers without a mouse attached. The Control menu gives you a way to manage window sizes and move windows using the keyboard.

2

Step 2: Action

1. Display the My Computer window's Control menu.

2. Using only the keyboard, press the down arrow key. The Control menu's highlight bar will move down through the choices as you press the down arrow. Highlight the Size menu command and press Enter. (You also could have pressed Alt+S or clicked Size with the mouse.) The mouse cursor changes to four pointing arrows. The mouse cursor indicates that you can now resize the window using the keyboard.

3. Press the left arrow key and the new mouse cursor jumps to the left edge of the screen and changes to a resizing cursor.

4. Press the right arrow key three times and you'll shrink the My Computer window by about half an inch.

5. Press Enter. Pressing Enter tells Windows 95 that you're through with the resizing or moving and you're ready to return to work doing other things.

Step 3: Review

The Control menu lets you use the keyboard to mimic window commands available with the mouse and window buttons. The Control menu also contains the Alt+F4 accelerator key that closes the window at the press of a keystroke even when the Control menu is not displayed at the time.

Mastering fundamental windows management, as you've done so far this hour, is like learning to drive a car. You have to learn the basics before getting into traffic. Now you are ready to begin traveling the road toward the Indy 500, by seeing what Windows 95 can really do. The first step requires understanding how Windows 95 views your specific computer, and the contents of the My Computer window shows you just that.

Summary

This hour taught you the ins and outs of windows management. Learning how to manage windows is a fundamental skill that Windows 95 users must understand. Windows 95 lets you open, resize, move, and close windows. The windows on your desktop contain the running applications, and part of running Windows 95 programs requires being able to position those windows where you want them.

Workshop

Term Review

accelerator key   A key found on a menu, usually a function key used in conjunction with the Alt key (such as Alt+F4), that lets you initiate a menu command from the keyboard without first having to display the menu.

closing a window   The practice of eliminating a window from view and terminating any program that might be running within the window at the time.

Control menu   A menu available on all windows within Windows 95 that lets you move and resize windows from the keyboard; it is accessed by clicking the window's icon in the upper-left corner of the window.

folder   A special icon that contains other icons which are displayed when you double-click the folder icon; a grouping of related files stored under the same subdirectory.

maximized window   A window that you've expanded to the size of the entire screen.

minimized window   A window that you've shrunk down to a taskbar icon.

opening a window   The process of starting a program in a window or double-clicking an icon to display a window.

shortcut key   An underlined letter on a menu that you can combine with the Alt key to issue a menu command.

Q&A

Q What's the difference between a shortcut key and an accelerator key?

A Both shortcut (or hot) keys and accelerator keys involve selecting commands from Windows 95 menus. The shortcut keystrokes appear as underlined letters in menu commands. When you combine the Alt key with the underlined letter (such as Alt+R to select **R**estore), the matching menu item executes.

Accelerator keys have the added distinction of enabling the user to select menu commands by pressing keystrokes without first having to display a menu. Accelerator keys appear at the right of their corresponding menu commands.

2

Q Why would I use the Control menu instead of the mouse to resize a window?

A If you have a mouse, you'll find that using the mouse to move and resize the window is a lot easier than using the Control menu. The Control menu was originally designed to be used by people without a mouse attached to their computer.

Q Why would I want to minimize a window?

A Often, Windows 95 users will run several programs at once. Instead of all those program windows appearing all over the screen, you can minimize the windows you aren't using currently but may need again shortly so that the windows are out of the way.

To return to the minimized window, you need only to click the window's icon on the taskbar. Therefore, the window remains active and loaded, ready to be used, but out of the way until you need the window.

2

Hour 3

Understanding the My Computer Window

The My Computer icon opens to a window as you learned in the previous hour. The My Computer window contains information that relates to your computer's hardware and software. You will often open the My Computer window when you add or remove both hardware and software. The My Computer window provides access to many different areas of your computer, as you will see as you progress through this book.

Many computer beginners and advanced users ignore the My Computer window more than they should. The My Computer window, which always appears on your Windows 95 desktop, lets you access every hardware device on your system in a uniform fashion.

In this hour you will use the My Computer window to change the behavior of your mouse and also to modify the screen background that you see. You must look at the desktop often, so changing the graphics behind the desktop can break the monotony that you might otherwise face with a dull Windows 95 desktop screen. People often spend the first few sessions with any new operating environment getting to know the environment and modifying the appearance to suit their own preferences. This hour lets you learn about the My Computer window while you modify your work environment.

The highlights of this hour include:

☐ What the contents of the My Computer window are

☐ Where to go for mouse control changes

☐ How to change the screen's wallpaper

☐ How to test your modem

☐ Why a startup disk can help you locate system problems

Searching My Computer

Your computer system is a mixture of hardware (the system unit, monitor, keyboard, CD-ROM, and so on), *firmware* (the internal memory), and software (for example, Windows 95, MS-DOS, word processors, spreadsheets, and games). There are several ways to access your computer's hardware and software through different areas of Windows 95. The My Computer window contains one of the most helpful hardware and software management resources available in Windows 95.

3.1 ▶
Step Up
As you will see throughout this book, you can manage files, set up hardware, and execute programs from the My Computer window. There are several other places in Windows 95 where you can do those things as well. Windows 3.1 was more limited in its approach, often giving you only a single place from which to access specific computer components and files.

If your My Computer window is still not open from the previous hour, open the My Computer window now by double-clicking the icon. When you double-click the My Computer icon, Windows 95 displays the My Computer window shown in Figure 3.1.

JUST A MINUTE

> Your open My Computer window may differ somewhat from Figure 3.1 depending on the configuration of your system. If you do not see an open window, you may have clicked the My Computer icon too slowly. Double-click again until you open the icon's window. If you have trouble double-clicking the icon, you can open the icon by clicking once on it (thus highlighting the window's icon) and pressing Enter.

3

Figure 3.1.
The My Computer window displays the contents of your computer system.

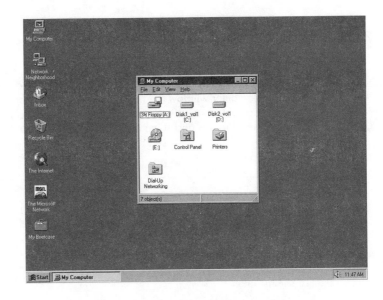

Introducing the My Computer Window

The My Computer icon is always on your Windows 95 desktop when you start Windows 95. Surely that icon must be important or Microsoft would have put it more out of the way. The My Computer icon *is* important, and its importance will show itself in many ways throughout this book and in your own work as you learn more about Windows 95.

People's needs for the My Computer window will differ greatly, depending on which systems they use to run Windows 95. For example, a network user would probably display the My Computer window more often than a single user working primarily on a spreadsheet program.

 The My Computer window works a lot like a mixture between the Windows 3.1 Program Manager and the Control Panel program group. The My Computer window contains a list of all hardware and software on your computer.

To keep things simple, this book uses a PC with a fairly simple system: a floppy disk drive labeled A, two hard disk drives labeled C and D, a CD-ROM labeled E, a modem, and a printer. Almost all of today's Windows 95 users will have these basic hardware devices. You may have more or fewer devices depending on your needs. Whatever configuration your computer uses, the My Computer window works in a uniform manner across all kinds of hardware and software setups.

TIME SAVER

If you have a computer that is Plug-and-Play compatible and you add Plug-and-Play hardware to the computer such as a new internal high-speed modem, Windows 95 should be able to detect that you've installed that new modem. A modem icon will automatically appear inside the My Computer window the next time you start the computer and open the My Computer window. Some devices, such as *PC card* devices that plug into most laptops and some desktop systems, automatically configure themselves when you insert the cards; they don't require that you first turn off your computer.

Before looking at a sample My Computer window work session, you should understand that there are two ways to view the My Computer window as well as most other Windows 95 windows:

- ☐ In the icon view
- ☐ In the list view

The icon view is the default view that is set when you install Windows 95. The My Computer window figures shown throughout this hour have all shown the icon view format. Newcomers prefer the familiarity that an icon view provides. In other words, later you will learn how to move files from one disk drive to another by dragging a file to the disk icon where you want to put that file instead of typing a disk drive name as computer users of older operating systems have to do.

As you progress, you may prefer to switch to a list view. A list view lists window contents down the screen in a list of items more like a table of contents. Although small icons still appear next to most of the items in a list view of the My Computer window, the icons are extremely small. The list view gives you the ability to see more items at once without the clutter of icons filling the screen.

When you first open the My Computer window, the difference between the views is not extremely important because the My Computer window shows a high-level overview of the system. Figure 3.2 shows an icon view of the My Computer window, and Figure 3.3 shows the list view of the same window. Notice that the list view is more difficult to see when only a few items are present in the window. If many more items appeared in the window, however, the list view would provide more information at one time because you would not have to click *scroll bars* (vertical and sometimes horizontal bars) as often to see all the items listed in the window.

3

Figure 3.2.

The My Computer window shown in icon view.

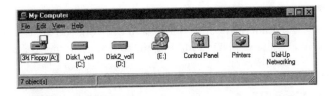

Figure 3.3.

The My Computer window shown in list view.

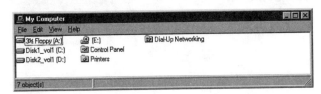

When you first explore the My Computer window, just look around for a bit. The next task walks you through a sample exploration session of the My Computer window so that you'll quickly get acquainted with some of the window's more useful investigative features.

Task 3.1: Navigating the My Computer Window

Step 1: Description

The best way to begin learning about the My Computer window is to work within the window. Follow the steps in this task to see some of the things that are possible with My Computer.

Step 2: Action

1. Open the My Computer window if you don't have it open already.

2. From the menu bar, select **View | List**. The view instantly changes to the list view.

3. Select **View | Details**. The list view expands to tell you more about each item such as free space and total space on the disk and CD-ROM drives.

4. Go back to the **View | Large** Icons display. (The **View | Small** Icons display provides extremely small icons on most systems that do not add any readability over the list view.)

5. Maximize the My Computer window by clicking the Maximize button or by double-clicking the title bar.

6. Double-click the C disk drive icon. When you do, you should see a window of folders and other icons appearing similar to the one shown in Figure 3.4. Each folder represents a *subdirectory* on your disk drive. A subdirectory is a list of files

stored together in one group. The subdirectory name appears under each file folder. Anytime you see a folder icon, you are looking at a subdirectory icon. If you also see a hand holding the folder, the folder is known as a *shared folder* available to others on the network you're working on.

Figure 3.4.

Looking at the directories on drive C.

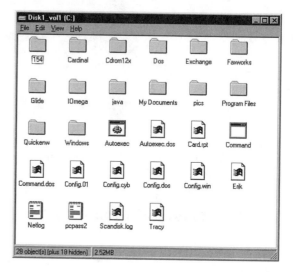

JUST A MINUTE

The folders let you group similar files together so that you can work with the entire group at once instead of having to work with the entire contents of the subdirectory when you want to work with the set of files.

The icons that look like pieces of paper are document icons that represent individual files, including programs and text files, on your system's C drive. You'll find other kinds of icons as well. If you see the list view when you display the C disk drive, use **View | Large Icons** to see the icons.

The window you're now looking at is a completely different window from the My Computer window. Minimize the window to see the My Computer window, which was originally hidden, come back into view.

7. Maximize the C window (click the taskbar button). To look at the contents of a file folder, double-click the file folder. When you do, yet another window will open up. You are leaving a trail of windows on your system that describe your hard drive.

8. Close the folder's window so that you return to the drive C window. If you have lots of files on drive C, and most people do, you may have to use the scroll bars to see all of the window's contents.

9. Close the C window to return to the My Computer window. Leave the My Computer window open for the next section.

Step 3: Review

The My Computer window displays information about your computer and its contents. All the computer's hardware and files are located on the disk. As you add more hardware, you'll see more icons appearing in the My Computer window. The view that you select determines how much information you can see at one time and how that information appears with a corresponding icon.

JUST A MINUTE

The Printers folder contains information about the printer or printers attached to your computer. You'll learn how to manage the Printers folder in Hour 15, "Increase Printing Power."

Scrolling Along

Your computer screen has a limited amount of display area. Within that area, you'll open one or more windows that each have even smaller display areas. Many times, there is simply too much information to display everything in a window at once. When Windows 95 senses that the available screen space will not hold all the contents of the window, Windows 95 attaches scroll bars to the window's borders. Windows 95 may attach a vertical scroll bar, horizontal scroll bar, or both, depending on the direction the window holds the data being displayed.

With scroll bars, the window works like a camera panning all around a large scene. You can scroll up and down with a vertical scroll bar, or left and right with a horizontal scroll bar. Figure 3.5 shows a resized My Computer drive C window with one scroll bar. The figure tells the names of the scroll bar parts.

Clicking on either scroll arrow moves ("pans") the window up, down, left, or right by a small amount. If you want to scroll the window farther than the scroll arrows allow, click within the scroll bar shaft for a larger scrolling jump.

The scroll box is sometimes called a "thumb" because you can drag the scroll bar to a specific position anywhere within the scroll shaft and Windows 95 will instantly scroll the window directly to that exact position without your having to scroll incrementally with the scroll arrows. The size of the thumb is large when the majority of the window's contents is within view, and the thumb shrinks if the window is showing only a small portion of the window's contents. Windows 3.1 users are accustomed to a uniform thumb size, but the resizing thumb offers a better gauge and lets you determine more accurately how far down a list you have scrolled.

Figure 3.5.
*Scroll bars let you
look at lots of data.*

Scroll box (thumb)
Minimum scroll position
Scroll arrow

Vertical
scroll bar

Scroll arrow
Maximum scroll position
Scroll bar shaft

Introducing the Control Panel

The Control Panel icon lets you adjust and manage the way hardware devices are attached
to and respond to your computer. From the My Computer window, double-click the
Control Panel icon, and you'll see a window like the one in Figure 3.6. From the Control
Panel, you can change or modify system and hardware settings.

Figure 3.6.
*Modify the system settings
from within the Control
Panel.*

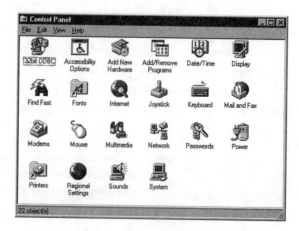

3

CAUTION

Be very sure that you know what to change before modifying values within the Control Panel. You could change a required setting that might be difficult to reverse later. The Control Panel does not offer any kind of undo command.

As with the previous section, this section is not going to explain the ins and outs of the Control Panel because much of the rest of this book covers the Control Panel and its functions. Nevertheless, the next task demonstrates one safe use of the Control Panel so that the Control Panel will not be foreign to you.

Task 3.2: System Modification with the Control Panel

TASK

Step 1: Description

One of the safest ways to explore the Control Panel is to modify the behavior of your mouse. This task changes the mouse cursor's default shape and lets you reverse the buttons on your mouse.

Step 2: Action

1. Open the Control Panel window within the My Computer window, if you have not yet done so.

2. Double-click the Mouse icon. The icon indicates that the mouse settings are found here. You'll see the Mouse Properties dialog box appear as shown in Figure 3.7.

Figure 3.7.

You can change the behavior of the mouse.

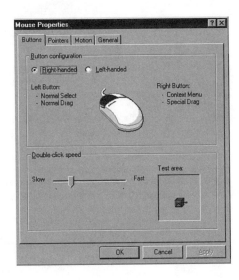

3. If you are left-handed but your mouse is set for a right-handed user, you can select the option button marked **Left-Handed** to change the mouse button functions. The buttons then change their functionality as described in the text beneath each button after the change. (The change will not take effect until you close the Mouse Properties dialog box or click the **A**pply button.) You can change the button back to its original state by clicking on the other hand.

4. Click the tab marked Pointers at the top of the Mouse Properties dialog box. From the Pointer portion of the dialog box, you can change the default appearance of the mouse. A scrolling list of mouse shapes indicates all the kinds of cursor shapes that appear when certain Windows 95 events take place.

5. To change the normal mouse cursor (called the *Normal Select* shape), double-click the row with the Normal Select text. Windows 95 displays yet another screen, shown in Figure 3.8. Different mouse cursors appear for different reasons. The Pointers dialog box lets you select shapes for the various mouse cursors that can appear.

Figure 3.8.

Select a mouse cursor shape file.

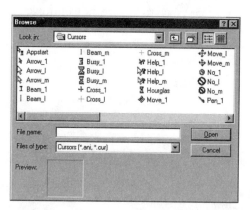

6. Windows 95 needs to know the name of the file that holds a cursor image you want to make the new mouse cursor. (This screen is not the easiest screen in Windows 95 to figure out, by the way.) Just for grins, double-click the Hourglass row in the choices listed under Look **in**, and Windows 95 changes the pointing cursor arrow to an hourglass.

CAUTION

It's best to stick with the default cursor shape and *not* keep this change permanent so that others who use your computer will know what the cursor indicates. Even you may forget which shape means what if you were to change the mouse cursors to other shapes.

3

7. Before leaving the Mouse Properties window, click the Use Default button to return the standard mouse cursor to its default pointer shape. If you've already returned to the Control Panel, you'll have to click the Mouse icon again to set the cursor back to its default shape.

8. Click OK and close the Control Panel. You can now close the My Computer window as well.

Step 3: Review

Through the Control Panel located in the My Computer window, you can change various hardware settings so that Windows 95 interacts with your computer's hardware differently. This task peeked into the Control Panel by showing you how to reverse the mouse buttons and change the default mouse shapes.

JUST A MINUTE

> Hour 4, "Take Windows 95 to Task," explains more about tabbed dialog boxes such as the Mouse Properties dialog box.

TIME SAVER

> Windows 95 supports *animated cursors* that move when they appear. If you use Microsoft's add-on Windows 95 product called *Plus!*, or if you've installed one or more of the numerous software products that add animated cursors to your system (such as Office 97), you can select cursors that change shape during their display. Instead of looking at the standard hourglass cursor while you wait on your computer, why not display a hand patiently tapping on the desktop? The animated cursors all reside in files that have the .ANI filename extension. If your cursor name display (see Figure 3.8) does not show filename extensions, click on the cursor names and look at the Preview area of the dialog box to see whether the cursor provides animation.

The Right Mouse Button

If you use a right-handed mouse, you probably have had little use for that right mouse button. The same is true for the left mouse button for left-handed users. Beginning with Windows 95, Microsoft added a shortcut feature to the often-unused mouse button: Depending on where you are pointing the mouse, clicking the right mouse button (or left if you are left-handed) brings up a menu of choices of things you can do at that time.

The menu is *context-sensitive* which means that Windows 95 looks at what you are doing when you click the right mouse button. Depending on the context, Windows 95 displays commands appropriate to that task.

Task 3.3: Using the Right Mouse Button

Step 1: Description

This task shows that you don't always need the My Computer window to make changes to your system. In Hour 1, "What's Windows 95 All About?," you learned that *wallpaper* is the name for the background you see on the screen when you start Windows 95 and work within its windows. You can change that wallpaper to a different picture or eliminate the wallpaper altogether with a right mouse click.

Step 2: Action

1. With all windows closed, move the mouse cursor over the wallpaper in the middle of the screen. If your screen has no picture behind the icons but displays only a solid color, you *do* have wallpaper, but it's boring!

2. Click the right mouse button if you are right-handed or the left mouse button if you are left-handed. Windows 95 looks to see that your mouse is pointing to the wallpaper and displays a menu of choices that are relevant to your position.

3. Select the Properties command from the menu. Windows 95 opens the Display Properties screen shown in Figure 3.9.

Figure 3.9.

A right click displays a wallpaper selection screen.

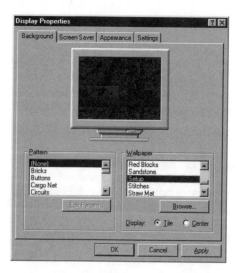

3

4. Find the lower-right section entitled **W**allpaper. Scroll through the list of choices looking for an interesting name, such as Red Bricks, and click on that selection. Windows 95 models the new wallpaper style in the small screen to give you a preview of that style. You can go with that selection or choose another.

5. When you are happy with your selection, click the OK button and *presto*, you've hung new wallpaper without messy cutting or gluing!

Step 3: Review

You'll learn other uses of the right mouse button as you progress through this book. You learned here how to change the wallpaper pattern so that you don't get too bored by the same old look.

Test Your Modem

Due to its technical nature, communications can be difficult to understand and troubleshoot. If you are having trouble communicating with another computer, the first place to look is the My Computer's Control Panel folder. Learn how to diagnose your modem problems now so that you will know what to do if you experience the problems that invariably come with modem usage.

Task 3.4: Using the Right Mouse Button

Step 1: Description

This task shows you how to let Windows 95 find a potential problem. Windows 95 includes a modem diagnostic tool that tests your modem connection and lets you know if everything is fine or if a problem exists.

Step 2: Action

1. Double-click the My Computer window.

2. Double-click the Control Panel folder to open the Control Panel window.

3. Double-click the Modems icon to open the Modems Properties tabbed dialog box.

4. Click the Diagnostics tab.

5. Click your modem's port name (such as COM1) to highlight your modem.

6. Click the **M**ore Info button. After a brief pause, Windows 95 will display a More Info… dialog box similar to the one in Figure 3.10. If the More Info… dialog box found an error, you will see the error.

Figure 3.10.
The modem is
responding properly.

7. Click the OK button to close the More Info… dialog box.

8. Close the Modem Properties dialog box and the My Computer window.

Step 3: Review

The Windows 95 modem test is another one of those nice features that even Windows 95 gurus often forget exists. Although the modem test will not describe detailed problems that might exist with your modem, you will learn whether Windows 95 recognizes your modem properly when you experience communications troubles.

Startup in Emergencies

Now that you've familiarized yourself with Windows 95, its environment, and the Control Panel, this would make a great time to ensure against a minor or major disaster. During the course of using Windows 95, you will add hardware and software. Windows 95 makes adding such components relatively easy, but in some cases, problems may occur. Perhaps you receive a bad installation disk, or a hardware conflict arises that freezes up Windows 95.

By making a *startup disk*, you can safely get your computer started and access your hard disk when you otherwise cannot start your machine. The startup disk is little more than an MS-DOS boot disk, although the disk does contain several MS-DOS and Windows 95 utility programs (such as the Scan Disk utility explained in Hour 17's chapter) that can help you locate disk and memory troubles that can cause boot problems.

3

If you use a laptop on the road, *always* carry a startup disk with you! The startup disk will help save you when you do not have Windows 95 installation disks, MS-DOS disks, or utility programs readily available.

Task 3.5: Making a Startup Disk

TASK

Step 1: Description

This task shows you how to create a startup disk. Before beginning this task, locate a high-density formatted disk. Make sure the disk contains no data that you need, because the startup process overwrites all data on your disk.

Step 2: Action

1. Click the Start button.
2. Select **S**ettings | **C**ontrol Panel to display the Control Panel window.
3. Double-click the Add/Remove Program icon.
4. Click the Startup Disk tab to display Figure 3.11's Startup Disk page.

Figure 3.11.

Create a startup disk for emergencies.

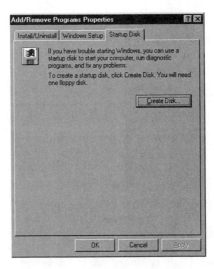

5. Click the **C**reate Disk button. The dialog box will let you know when you need to insert the disk you'll use for the startup disk.

6. Once the startup disk creation process ends, close the Control Panel and put away the startup disk in a safe place.

Step 3: Review

Once you create a startup disk, you'll have a disk in case of emergencies. If you find that you cannot access your hard disk or boot your computer because your system files are corrupt, you'll be able to regain hard disk access by inserting the startup disk and rebooting your computer. The startup disk will not be able to cure any problems, but you will have system access once again so that you may begin tracing the difficulties.

Summary

This hour taught you how to use the My Computer window. Don't be dismayed that this hour just skimmed the surface of what's available in the My Computer window because the My Computer icon provides a launching point for many powerful hardware and software interactions that sometimes take quite a while to master. The typical Windows 95 user does not have to know all the details of the My Computer window to use Windows 95 effectively.

Workshop

Term Review

animated cursors   Cursors that display movement during the cursor's display, such as a cursor showing a picture of a running horse or a playing piano.

context-sensitive   The process Windows 95 uses to respond to what you're doing.

Control Panel   A folder window within the My Computer window that lets you change your computer's system settings.

desktop   The Windows 95 screen and background.

firmware   The computer's internal memory, also known as *RAM*, which stands for Random Access Memory. Firmware memory is volatile, meaning that the contents remain in memory only as long as the PC is turned on. The disk drive is hardware, not firmware, because the disk drive retains its contents after the computer is turned off.

3

folder   A special icon that contains other icons which are displayed when you double-click the folder icon; a grouping of related files stored under the same subdirectory.

scroll bars   Windows 95 controlling tools that enable you to view a window's contents more fully.

shortcut key   An underlined letter on a menu that you can combine with the Alt key to issue a menu command.

startup disk   A disk you create from the Control Panel so that you can start your computer when your hard disk's system files get corrupted due to a hardware or software problem.

Q&A

Q Will I use the My Computer icon a lot?

A This question's answer differs with different people. Some people use their computers primarily for one or two application programs. These people don't modify their computers very often and do not perform a lot of file interaction or system management, so they would rarely, if ever, need to open the My Computer window.

On the other hand, if you modify the hardware on your computer often, you might have to access the My Computer window often. As described in the previous hour, Windows 95 is designed for use with Plug-and-Play hardware, which means that you don't have to configure Windows 95 every time you change hardware on your computer. Not all hardware devices are Plug-and-Play compatible, however, and you may have to modify some Windows 95 system settings using the My Computer window when you install new computer hardware, such as a second printer.

In Hour 5, "Cruise with Documents and Windows," you'll learn how to work with files and disk drives through Windows 95. When you begin to work with more files on your system, you'll sometimes use the My Computer window to access the contents of your disks.

Q I like the animated cursors, but will they slow down my computer?

A If you use a slow computer, you don't want to do anything that will drain more speed from the processor. Nevertheless, the animated cursors do not seem to cause much of a drain on the processor's resources. The animated cursor icons are small and efficient. Therefore, you should feel free to use whatever cursors you want to use.

3

Q What do I do if the modem test fails?

A Unfortunately, this book cannot answer that question because the answer could
come from myriad sources. The Windows 95 modem test is nice to remember
because it gives you a first-step approach to tracing communications problems. If
your modem test goes well but you experience communications problems, the
problems are either with your software or with the computer on the other end of
the telephone line. If the modem diagnostic fails, look into reinstalling the modem
drivers that came with your modem. You can also try a different modem, which
will solve the problem if the original modem you used is bad.

Hour 4

Take Windows 95 to Task

The taskbar and the Start button are closely related. Most Windows 95 users use the Start button to display the Start menu, then execute a program. As you've already seen, when the program begins running, the taskbar displays a button with an icon along with a description that represents that running program.

The taskbar, Start button, and the Start menu are the most important components Microsoft put in Windows 95. Previous versions of Windows offered less intuitive startup procedures for programs. The taskbar is the cornerstone of Windows 95; as a matter of fact, the taskbar is *so* important, we'll spend this hour discussing nothing but the taskbar. This hour describes the taskbar and its Start menu in detail and explains how to customize the taskbar to make it perform in a manner that best suits your computing style.

The highlights of this hour include:

- ☐ Where the Start menu comes from
- ☐ How to move and resize the taskbar
- ☐ When to change the appearance and performance of the taskbar
- ☐ What tabbed dialog boxes are all about
- ☐ Why the Start menu's **P**rograms command may not execute a program

A Quick Taskbar and Start Button Review

In Hour 1, you saw the Start menu and used it to shut down your computer properly. Clicking the taskbar's Start button produces the Start menu shown in Figure 4.1. The Start menu does all these things and more:

Figure 4.1.

The Start menu gives you access to all other areas of Windows 95.

☐ It makes itself available to you no matter what else you are doing in Windows 95. Even if you work inside a full-screen MS-DOS session you can display the Windows 95 Start menu.

☐ It displays a list of all programs on your system using the Start menu's cascading system.

☐ It provides you with an easy-access list of recently opened documents that you can look at or edit no matter which Windows 95-compatible word processor or editor you originally used to create those documents.

☐ It provides a search engine that navigates through all your files looking for the one you need.

☐ It activates the Windows 95 help engine that provides online help for working within Windows 95 (Hour 7, "A Call for Help!," describes how to use the help system).

The next few sections explain how you can customize the taskbar and its associated Start menu, so when you are ready to use the Start menu for these items, the Start menu will act and look the way you expect.

TIME SAVER

If you do not see the Start button, your taskbar may be hidden or you may be working within a full-screen MS-DOS session. Press Ctrl+Esc to display the Start menu if you need to use the Start menu and cannot see it. Many Windows 95 experts forget about the Ctrl+Esc shortcut keystroke. If you were working in a full-screen MS-DOS session when you pressed Ctrl+Esc,

4

Windows 95 switches back to the Windows 95 desktop to display the Start menu, but the MS-DOS session remains active. You can then switch back to the MS-DOS session by clicking the taskbar button or by pressing Alt+Tab when you finish with the Start menu.

Moving the Taskbar Around

The taskbar does not have to stay at the bottom of your screen. Depending on your application, you can move the taskbar to either side of your monitor, or even to the top of your screen. The taskbar placement is easy to change, as you will see in this hour.

JUST A MINUTE

Figure 4.2 shows that a side taskbar does not have the width necessary to display lengthy taskbar descriptions. When you place the taskbar at the bottom or top of the screen, the taskbar is wide and has more room for longer descriptions of programs and windows you currently have open.

4

Figure 4.2.

You can place the taskbar on any edge of your screen.

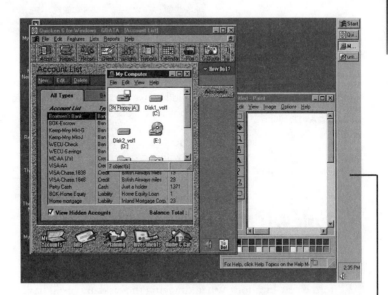

The newly placed taskbar

If you place the taskbar at the top of the screen, the Start menu falls down from the Start button, whereas the Start menu pops up from the Start button when you place the taskbar at the bottom of the screen. Figure 4.3 shows the Start menu coming down from a taskbar that is placed at the top of your screen.

Figure 4.3.

The Start menu drops down from a taskbar at the top of the screen.

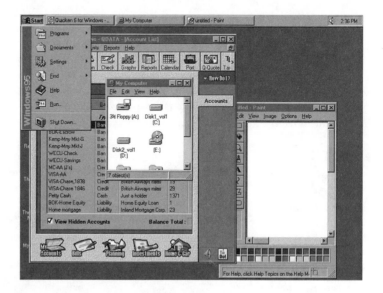

TIME SAVER

When working on a wide spreadsheet or document, you may want as much screen width as you can get. Therefore, you would want the taskbar placed at the bottom or top of your screen when working with such programs. When working with graphics, you usually need more vertical screen space, so you could move the taskbar to either side of the screen when working within a graphics program.

Task 4.1: Move Your Taskbar

Step 1: Description

The taskbar is easy to drag to any of the four edges of your screen. Simply drag the taskbar to the new location. When dragging the taskbar, you'll have to position the mouse pointer over a blank spot in the taskbar, such as between two buttons or to the right of the Start button if no other windows are open.

4

Step 2: Action

1. Find a blank spot on your taskbar and point to the spot with the mouse cursor. Be sure that you are pointing within the taskbar and not over a button on the taskbar.
2. Click and hold the mouse button while dragging the taskbar to another edge of the screen. As you drag the mouse, an outline of the taskbar moves with the mouse.
3. Release the mouse button to anchor the taskbar at its new position.

Step 3: Review

The taskbar does not have to stay at the bottom of your screen. If you like, drag the taskbar to another location. You may want to place the taskbar at one location for one program and move the taskbar for another program later. You can move the taskbar any time, even after you've started one or more programs. If you share a computer with another user, have your Network Administrator set up a user profile for both of you. When you log on (see Hour 1), your Windows 95 session's taskbar will appear where you last left it no matter where the other user moved the taskbar before you logged on.

The Taskbar Properties Menu

In the previous hour, you learned that a right mouse button click (or the left button click if you've set up your mouse for left-handed operation) often displays a context-sensitive menu of options available to you. The taskbar is one such location where the right mouse button brings up a helpful menu, called the *taskbar properties menu.* You can use it to change the appearance and performance of the taskbar and the windows controlled by the taskbar. After finding a blank spot on your taskbar, clicking the right mouse button brings up the context-sensitive taskbar properties menu shown in Figure 4.4.

CAUTION

> Do not click the right mouse button over one of the taskbar programs unless you want to activate that button's program or window (known as bringing the program into *focus*). For example, suppose you load these three programs: a word processor, a spreadsheet, and a database. The taskbar will list each program's taskbar button. If you are typing with the word processor and decide that you want to change the taskbar's properties through the right mouse button's taskbar menu, *don't* click the right mouse button when the mouse pointer points to the database or spreadsheet button. If you do, Windows 95 will give that program's window the focus and will display a menu that controls the size and location of the window—not at all what you had in mind.

Figure 4.4.

A click of the right mouse button on a blank space on the taskbar displays a context-sensitive menu.

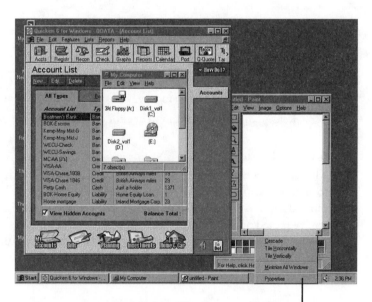

The taskbar Properties menu _____

The taskbar properties menu is not necessarily a menu you'll want to display often. Most users play around with different taskbar and window settings for a while until they find preferences that suit them best. Thereafter, those users may rarely use the taskbar properties menu.

3.1 ▶
Step Up

Whenever you wanted to change the performance of Windows 3.1, you would often have to step through a series of program groups and menus. The right mouse button's context-sensitive help offers tremendous shortcut power when you want to perform common maintenance tasks within Windows 95.

The first three menu options are important when you want to work with more than one open window. These three menu options offer three ways of arranging your open windows so they are more manageable. If you open two or more windows at once, perhaps by running several programs, all those windows can be difficult to manage individually. You could maximize each window and display only one window at a time. There are many reasons, however, to keep more than one window open and displayed at the same time, such as when you want to copy data from one window to another. (Hour 5, "Cruise with Documents and Windows" explains how to copy between windows.)

JUST A MINUTE

Most users feel that a 17-inch monitor (or larger) is necessary to work effectively between two or more open windows on the screen at once.

4

Tiling Windows

When you want to see more than one open window at a time, the taskbar properties menu gives you tools that provide quick management of those windows so you do not have to size and place each window individually. Figure 4.5 shows how too many windows open at the same time can be confusing. You'll see in the Task section that follows how to use the taskbar properties menu to straighten up such a mess.

Figure 4.5.

Too many open windows can quickly cause disorganization.

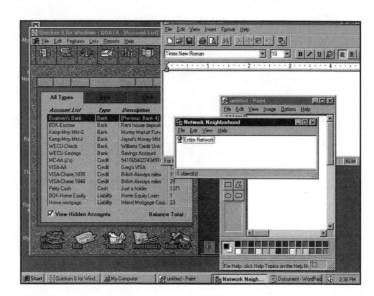

Task 4.2: Organizing Multiple Windows

Step 1: Description

The taskbar properties menu provides a way to organize several open windows with the click of a mouse. There are three ways to organize the windows: You can cascade them, vertically tile them, or horizontally tile them.

Step 2: Action

1. Click the My Computer icon to open the My Computer window.

2. Click the Recycle Bin icon to open that window as well. Although you may not understand the Recycle Bin until Hour 6, "Explore the Windows 95 System," the open window will show the effects of the taskbar's properties menu.

3. Display the Start menu and select the **H**elp option. Shortly, you'll see a help window open up. Again, this window is just to put more on your desktop to work with.

4. Now that you've opened three windows, ask Windows 95 to organize those windows for you. Display the taskbar's properties menu by right-clicking the mouse button after pointing to a blank spot on the taskbar.

5. Select the first menu item labeled **C**ascade. Windows 95 instantly organizes your windows into the cascaded series of windows shown in Figure 4.6.

Figure 4.6.
The windows are now more manageable.

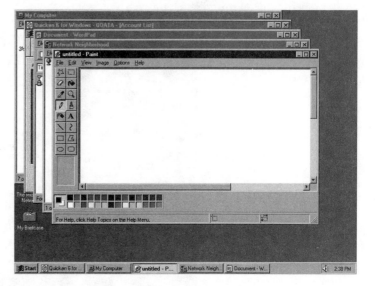

Notice that the title bar of *all* open windows appears on the Windows 95 desktop area. When you want to bring any of the hidden windows into focus, click that window's title bar, and the window will rise to the top of the stack of the screen's windows. The cascading effect always gives you the ability to switch between windows. As long as any part of a hidden window is peeking out from under another, you can bring that hidden window into focus by clicking the mouse button on that hidden window's title bar.

6. Sometimes, you need to see the contents of two or more windows at the same time. Windows 95 lets you *tile* the open windows so you can see the actual body of each open window. Windows 95 supports two kinds of tiling methods: horizontal tiling and vertical tiling. Display the taskbar's properties menu and select Tile **H**orizontally. Windows 95 will properly resize each of the three open windows as shown in Figure 4.7.

4

Figure 4.7.

*The windows
are now tiled
horizontally.*

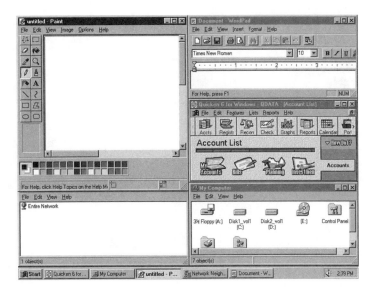

CAUTION

Your windows may differ in size and placement depending on your
monitor size and graphics card settings.

At first glance, the tiling may seem too limiting to you. After all, to fit those three
open windows on the screen at the same time, Windows 95 cannot show you a *lot*
of any one of the windows. Keep in mind that all the window resizing and moving
tools that you learned about in the previous hour work even after you've tiled
windows. Therefore, you can move the Help window towards the top of the screen,
after tiling the windows, if you want to see more of that window. (Scroll bars
automatically appear in tiled windows if the contents of the window consumes
more space than can be displayed at once.)

7. The vertical tiling method produces side-by-side windows that are fairly thin but
   offer yet another kind of open window display. Select Tile **V**ertically and Windows
   95 will reformat the screen to look something like Figure 4.8.

8. After changing the look of your open windows by using the taskbar properties
   menu, you can revert the windows to their previous state through the taskbar
   properties menu as well. Now that you've vertically tiled the open windows, you
   can restore the original placement of the windows by selecting **U**ndo Tile.

4

Figure 4.8.

*The windows
are now tiled
vertically.*

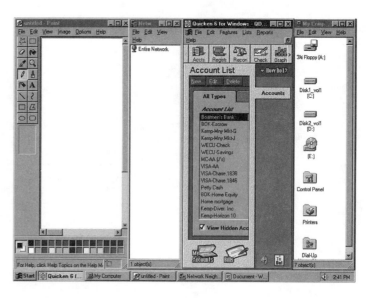

9. The **M**inimize All Windows taskbar properties menu option *attempts* to minimize all open windows at the same time. The problem with the **M**inimize All Windows option is that not all windows can be minimized. Therefore, the option minimizes only those windows that have a minimize button (most do). For example, the Help window that you opened does not have a minimize button, so if you attempt to minimize all the open windows on your screen, Windows 95 will minimize all the windows and leave the Help window. If you want to shut Windows 95 down quickly, you can minimize all windows, and then select **S**hutdown as described in Hour 1. Don't minimize the windows now, however, as you'll need them open for the next task.

JUST A MINUTE

No matter how you tile or cascade the windows, each window's mini-mize, maximize, and restore buttons all work as usual. Therefore, you can maximize a cascaded window at any time by clicking that window's maximize button.

Step 3: Review

You can use the taskbar's properties menu to control the appearance of the open windows on your screen. The nice thing about using the taskbar to manage open windows is that you don't have to size and place each window individually. Instead, leave the hard work to Windows 95 when you want to see a tiled or cascaded series of windows at one time.

4

Working with Taskbar Properties

The taskbar properties menu not only controls the appearance and performance of open windows, the taskbar properties menu also controls the appearance and performance of the taskbar itself. The Properties menu option displays the Taskbar Properties tabbed dialog box shown in Figure 4.9. With the Taskbar Properties dialog box, you can change the way the taskbar appears and performs, and you also can change the contents of the Start menu.

Figure 4.9.

You can change the taskbar's appearance and performance by using the Taskbar Properties dialog box.

JUST A MINUTE

In Hour 8, "Manage Your Desktop," you'll learn how to use the Taskbar Properties dialog box to change the contents of the Start menu.

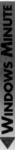

Using Dialog Boxes

You saw your first tabbed dialog box in the previous hour when you changed the mouse cursor (Figure 3.7). Tabbed dialog boxes are often called *property sheets*. Before you can understand a *tabbed* dialog box, you should know what a standard untabbed dialog box is all about.

When Windows 95 needs one or more items of information from you, you may see a special window called a *dialog box* on your screen. A dialog box captures all kinds of information that Windows 95 needs. Windows 95 might put command buttons, option buttons, checkmarks, text boxes, or other kinds of controls, all together inside a dialog box. You can choose to respond to one or more of those controls depending on the information you want to provide at the time. When you click the dialog box's OK button, Windows 95 closes the dialog box and your dialog box settings go into effect.

JUST A MINUTE

In addition to the OK button, some dialog boxes have an **A**pply button. Generally, these dialog boxes change a Windows 95 setting such as the font size. If you click **A**pply, Windows 95 puts your dialog box settings into effect but does not close the dialog box. Therefore, you can see the results of your dialog box settings without getting rid of the dialog box.

When Windows 95 displays a tabbed dialog box, it is offering you more than one dialog box at the same time. Instead of displaying two or more dialog boxes on the screen at the same time, the tabs give you a way to select just which dialog box you want to respond to. You can even respond to one dialog box and then click another tab and that tab's dialog box then appears so that you can respond to it, too, if you desire. Windows 95 will often put an OK command button on a dialog box that you can press when you are finished responding to the dialog box's controls.

Task 4.3: Using the Taskbar Properties Dialog Box

Step 1: Description

The Taskbar Properties dialog box accepts from you information that controls the way the taskbar appears on the screen. You can allow (or disallow) windows to overlap the taskbar if those windows are large enough to do so, you can eliminate the clock from the taskbar, and you can even minimize the taskbar so that it does not appear until you need it. (Normally the taskbar appears no matter what else you have displayed on the Windows 95 screen, as you've already seen.)

Step 2: Action

1. With the three windows still open on your screen from the previous task, display the taskbar properties menu once again by right-clicking the mouse button on the taskbar.

2. Select the P**r**operties command to display the tabbed Taskbar Properties dialog box shown in Figure 4.9.

3. The first checkmark option, Always on **t**op, is checked normally because Windows 95 normally sets the taskbar to be displayed at all times. The taskbar is most helpful when it is on the screen, right? The only problem with the taskbar's being on the screen at all times is that one complete row of the screen is consumed by the taskbar instead of by your own windows. Uncheck the option by clicking over the checkmark or anywhere on the words beside it. The graphic inside the dialog box actually changes when you remove the checkmark to show a window overlapping the clock in the taskbar.

4

4. Click the OK command button to see the results of the unchecked option. (If you clicked the **A**pply command button, Windows 95 would have changed the taskbar immediately while still displaying the dialog box.)

5. Display the Taskbar Properties dialog box again. Check the **A**uto hide option and click the OK button. Where did the taskbar go?

6. The taskbar is now out of sight and out of the way. The taskbar hasn't gone far—point the mouse cursor to the bottom of the screen and the taskbar will reappear. You can now have your taskbar and hide it, too!

TIME SAVER

If you display the Taskbar Properties dialog box but decide that you don't want to make any changes after all, click the Cancel command button and Windows 95 will remove the Taskbar Properties dialog box and leave the taskbar unchanged.

7. Although only a little of the taskbar is still showing, you can display the Taskbar Properties dialog box once again and check the Always on **t**op option and uncheck the **A**uto hide option.

8. The third checkmark option controls how the Start menu's icons are displayed. Normally, this option is unchecked. If you want to save some screen room when you display the Start menu, you can request small icons, and the Start menu will consume less screen space. If you uncheck the last option labeled Show **C**lock, the clock will go away from the taskbar after clicking the OK command button on the dialog box. Figure 4.10 shows both the Start menu with small icons and the taskbar without a clock.

4

JUST A MINUTE

You'll learn what that speaker icon is at the right of the taskbar in Hour 20, "Multimedia Is Really Here."

9. Display the Taskbar Properties tabbed dialog box once again and set the checkmark options to your desired values. Before clicking the OK command button, click the tab labeled Start Menu Programs (at the top of the dialog box). You'll see the second dialog box, which is shown in Figure 4.11.

Figure 4.10.

The change in the screen's appearance after shrinking the Start menu's icons and removing the taskbar clock.

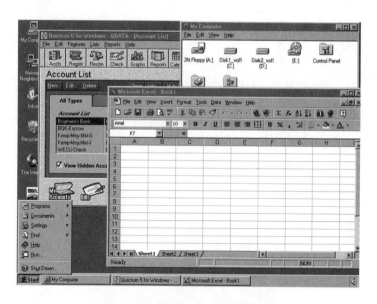

Figure 4.11.

The second dialog box appearing from behind the taskbar options.

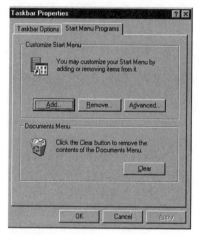

The second dialog box lets you change the appearance of the Start menu. Since you have yet to really learn what the default Start menu is all about, we'll save the discussion of this dialog box until Hour 8, "Manage Your Desktop."

The second half of this dialog box controls the contents of the Start menu's Documents command. Again, we'll save the discussion of this part of the dialog box also until later (Hour 5, "Cruise with Documents and Windows").

10. Click the Cancel command button to close the dialog box and return to the regular Windows 95 desktop. Close all windows that are now open by clicking the Close button in the window's upper-right corner.

Step 3: Review

There are several ways to change the taskbar's properties and performances through the taskbar properties menu. The menu appears when you click the right mouse button. The menu contains commands to modify the appearance of all of the following:

- ☐ The open windows on the screen
- ☐ The taskbar
- ☐ The Start menu's commands

Sizing the Taskbar

What happens if you open a number of windows by starting several programs? The single-line taskbar fills up very quickly with buttons and icons and descriptions that represent those open windows. Figure 4.12 shows such a taskbar. If you're doing a lot of work, the taskbar gets squeezed for space. However, you can solve that problem rather easily.

Figure 4.12.

The taskbar needs more room.

Just as you can resize a window, you also can resize the taskbar. When you enlarge the taskbar, it can more comfortably hold several buttons for open windows, and the descriptions on those buttons can be longer. Figure 4.13 shows the same taskbar as the one shown in Figure 4.12. This time, the taskbar is larger, and you can better tell by the descriptions on the taskbar buttons what each program is.

Figure 4.13.

The taskbar now has more breathing room.

CAUTION

You can change the height of the taskbar from one to several rows. The taskbar can consume up to half your screen space. Keep in mind, however, that the more space you devote to the taskbar, the less space you'll have for your application windows. The taskbar is there to help you do your real work, so don't make it too large, or you won't have screen space for the rest of your work.

Task 4.4: Resizing the Taskbar

Step 1: Description

If you need to expand (or shrink) the taskbar, you can drag the top of the taskbar up the screen until it reaches the middle of the Windows 95 desktop. The taskbar then has more room for more open window buttons and descriptions. Of course, if you've moved the taskbar to one of the other edges of the screen, you'll drag the inward-most edge of the taskbar towards the middle of the screen to increase the size of the taskbar. If you want to shrink the taskbar, you can reverse the dragging until the taskbar is as small as you want it to be.

Step 2: Action

1. Move the mouse cursor to the top edge of the taskbar. The cursor will change to a bidirectional resizing arrow that looks like the window resizing cursor shape you saw in Hour 2.

2. Drag the taskbar toward the center of the screen. As you drag the taskbar, Windows 95 expands it one taskbar row at a time until you complete the dragging operation.

3. Release the mouse button and you'll see the resulting (and larger) taskbar with more room for descriptions and open window buttons.

4. You can leave the taskbar at its present size or shrink the taskbar back down again by dragging the top edge of the taskbar toward the outer edge of the screen.

TIME SAVER

> If you drag the top of the taskbar all the way down to the bottom of your screen, the taskbar goes away. By shrinking the taskbar in this way, you shortcut the procedure needed to hide the taskbar. In the previous section, you learned how to hide the taskbar by first displaying the taskbar properties menu and then displaying and selecting from the Taskbar Properties dialog box. It is easier to shrink the taskbar with the mouse than by using the dialog box to hide the taskbar. To bring the taskbar into view, move the mouse to the bottom of the screen until the mouse cursor changes to bidirectional arrow. Drag the arrow up the screen and the taskbar will appear.

Step 3: Review

When you need more room for the taskbar, drag the taskbar's edge until the taskbar is the size you need. You can expand or shrink the taskbar by dragging the taskbar's innermost edge with the mouse.

4

Starting Programs with Start

The Start menu offers an extremely simple way for you to start the programs on your computer. Two or three clicks start virtually any program on your disk drive. The **P**rograms command on the Start menu launches your programs. To start a program you only need to display the menu that contains that program and then click the program's name or icon.

Task 4.5: Starting Solitaire

Step 1: Description

Microsoft gives you a Windows 95-based version of the Solitaire card game. Solitaire is considered an *accessory* program. Accessory programs are programs Microsoft included with Windows 95 which fall under several categories, such as multimedia programs, text editors, and games such as Solitaire. Between the four major parts of this book, you'll learn how to control the Solitaire game, as well as other fun programs that you get with Windows 95. For this hour, you'll learn how to start and stop Solitaire.

Step 2: Action

1. Display the Start menu.
2. Select the **P**rograms command. A cascaded menu will appear next to the Start menu. Your computer is unique and a different set of commands might appear here. Figure 4.14 shows the screen from a computer with a lot of program folders displayed by the **P**rograms command.

Figure 4.14.

You may have a list of several programs on your system.

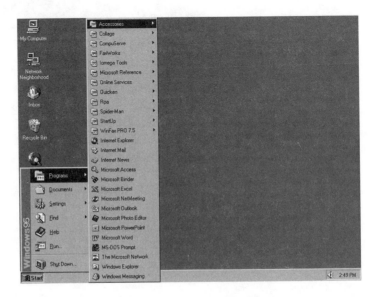

Each of these items in the second menu represents either a program or a folder of programs. When you buy a program such as a word processor, the word processor usually comes with more than *just* a word processor. The word processor might come with several related programs that help you manage the word processor environment. The word processor folder would open to yet another window (you can tell by the presence of an arrow at the right of the word processor's folder) which would then list all the related programs in that folder.

3. Select the Accessories command to display the programs in the Accessories folder. Search down until you see the Games menu. Open the Games to see the Solitaire game (look for an opening pack of cards).

4. Click the Solitaire game. You'll see the opening Solitaire screen, shown in Figure 4.15.

Figure 4.15.

Get ready to have fun!

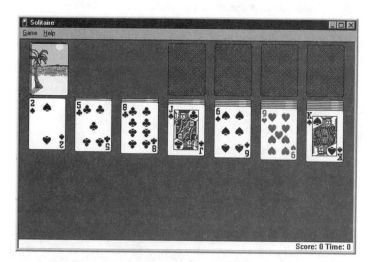

JUST A MINUTE

Your Solitaire screen may differ slightly from the one in the figure because your default card deck may be set to have a different picture backing.

5. There's no time to play right now! This hour's closing in quickly. Therefore, terminate the solitaire program by clicking the Close button (the button with the X as you learned in the previous hour). Solitaire goes away and you'll be back to the regular Windows 95 desktop.

4

Step 3: Review

The **P**rograms command launches any and all programs on your system. Depending on the way your programs are set up and because many Windows 95 programs are stored in folders, you may have to display one or more menus to access individual programs that you want to execute.

How did all those programs get on the Start menu? If you upgraded from a previous version of Windows, the Windows 95 installation program automatically updated your programs so they appear on the Start menu.

If you didn't upgrade from a previous Windows version, your Start menu may not have many items. Only those programs that come with Windows 95 will appear. To add other programs on your system, if you have other programs, you'll have to install those programs all over again using Windows 95. (Read the program's Windows installation instructions to see how to install the program.) When you reinstall the program, Windows 95 adds the program to the Start menu.

In the future, Windows 95 will add more and more programs to the Start menu's series of menus as you install programs. Therefore, you don't need to worry about adding programs to the Start menu because Windows 95 does the work for you as you install each program.

4

Using the Run Command

In addition to the Start menu's **P**rograms command, you can use another method to start programs that aren't set up on the **P**rograms' cascade of menus. The **R**un command on the Start menu provides a way for you to execute specific programs.

CAUTION

Before using the **R**un command, you must understand the basics of disk drive names (such as C: and D:) and pathnames of files (such as `c:\WORD\DEC97`). You must also know the exact name of the program you want to run. Most newcomers to Windows 95 stay away from the **R**un command for good reason: **R**un requires a fairly comprehensive level of understanding of the underlying program you are trying to start. Many Windows 95 users will work inside Windows 95 for years and never need the **R**un command because Windows 95 programs install their own icons on the Start menu.

Reaching Your Files

A *pathname* is the exact computer system location of a file. The document and folder concept in Windows 95 makes working with paths much easier than before Windows 95 came along. Most often, you will specify pathnames visually by clicking folder icons instead of typing long pathnames as you had to do before Windows 95.

The folders in Windows 95 are more technically known as *directories* as explained in Hour 2, "Tour Windows 95 Now." A directory is just a collection of files and other directories. In file listings, Windows 95 often displays a folder icon with a name to represent a directory that holds other files. Directories also can hold subdirectories so the location of a file, the file's *path*, may be deep within several nested directories on a disk or CD-ROM drive.

A full pathname begins with a disk drive name followed by a colon (:), followed by a backslash (\). If the file resides in the disk drive's top directory (the *root directory*), you then type the filename. If, however, the file resides in a directory, you must list the directory after the backslash. If the file resides in several nested directories, you must list each directory in order, from the outermost directory to the innermost directory, and separate each directory name with a backslash. Both of the following are full pathnames to specific files:

```
c:\autoexec.bat
d:\Sherry\WordProc\Home\Insure\Fire and Casualty
```

The first filename is autoexec.bat located in the root directory. The second filename is Fire and Casualty located within a series of nested directories.

Windows 95's icon folder concept makes specifying long pathnames almost obsolete. Aren't you glad? Clicking folders to open them is much easier than typing the long streams of characters that often represent pathnames.

The Start menu's **Run** command mirrors the **File | Run** command in Windows 3.1. Generally, you used the **File | Run** command to install programs in Windows 3.1. You'll install programs in Windows 95 using one of two methods. Often, if the program is on a CD-ROM, the first time you insert the CD-ROM in the caddy the installation program starts *automatically* (depending on how the program was written).

Also, an Add/Remove Programs icon in the My Computer window walks you through the installation of new programs. Just as a novice user would, you may have to read the software's installation guide to find the best way to install the program. If the program was specifically written for Windows 95, the Add/Remove Programs icon located in the My Computer window's Control Panel will walk you through an appropriate installation procedure.

4

Task 4.6: Running with Run

Step 1: Description

The Start menu's **R**un command offers a tedious way to execute any program on your computer. If you want to run a program that would not properly set up in Windows 95 (perhaps the program is an old DOS-based program), you'll have to execute the program using the **R**un command. This task executes the Solitaire program by using **R**un.

Step 2: Action

1. Display the Start menu and select the **R**un command. Windows 95 displays the dialog box shown in Figure 4.16.

Figure 4.16.

You can run programs directly from the Start menu.

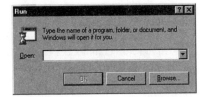

There may or may not be text next to the **O**pen text prompt. Windows 95 needs to know the exact name and path of the program you want to open (and run).

Almost all users install Windows 95 on drive C. This is where it gets tricky... some people choose to install Windows 95 on a drive different from C. If your Windows 95 system is installed on another drive, substitute your drive name for the C: listed in the subsequent steps.

2. Type the following *exactly* as you see it (using either uppercase or lowercase letters):

```
C:\WINDOWS\SOL
```

The Solitaire game is normally installed to the Windows directory on drive C. The name of the program is SOL.EXE. To execute any program with an .EXE filename extension, you'll only need to type the first part of the filename such as SOL. If Solitaire does not start, you may have typed the line incorrectly. Try again and be sure that you use *backslashes* and not *forward* slashes. (UNIX users, take note!)

3. Once you get Solitaire to load and run, close the program and return to the Windows 95 desktop. The instructions in Time-Out 1 explain more about the Solitaire game if you have trouble starting the game or need the rules on how to play.

Step 3: Review

You may be one of the lucky few who never needs the **R**un command. Nevertheless there are many programs on the market that Windows 95 cannot execute in its environment. Using **R**un, you can execute any program on your computer as long as you know the program's pathname and filename.

TIME SAVER

> Hour 5's chapter ("Cruise with Documents and Windows") explains how Windows 95 supports a strong document concept. You'll learn that Windows 95 is data-driven more than program driven. Here's a quick preview: If you type a *data file* (such as a Microsoft Word document) instead of a program name with the Start menu's **R**un command, Windows 95 automatically starts the program needed to work with that data file and loads the data file for you. Therefore, you worry less about your programs and you can concentrate more on your data. In addition, if you use the Internet, you can type an Internet address (often called a *URL*) at the **R**un command's prompt and Windows 95 automatically starts your Internet browser and takes you to the Web site you entered.

Summary

This hour concentrated mostly on the taskbar. The taskbar gives you a play-by-play status of the open windows on your system. As you open and close windows, the taskbar updates with new buttons to show what's happening at all times. If you start more than one program, you can switch between those programs as easily as you switch between cable TV shows: Click a button on the taskbar.

There are several adjustments you can make to the taskbar. You can move and resize the taskbar. You can determine whether the taskbar appears or not. You can remove the clock on the taskbar if you want the space. The taskbar includes a context-sensitive menu that lets you modify all these settings and more.

The taskbar works along with the Start menu to start and control the programs running on your system. Use the **P**rograms command on the Start menu to start programs with a total of two or three mouse clicks. Although you can use the **R**un command to start programs, the **P**rograms command is easier as long as the program is set up properly in Windows 95.

4

Workshop

Term Review

accessory programs   Programs that Microsoft included with Windows 95 which fall under several categories such as multimedia programs, text editors, and games such as Solitaire.

cascade   The effect of neatly stacking all open windows on the screen so that each window's title bar appears.

dialog box   A special window in which you can enter information needed by Windows 95.

tabbed dialog box   Two or more cascaded dialog boxes appearing on the screen at the same time.

taskbar properties menu   The menu that appears when you click the right mouse button over an empty spot on the taskbar. You can control the performance and appearance of the taskbar and Windows 95 through the taskbar properties menu.

Taskbar Properties tabbed dialog box   A tabbed dialog box that appears when you select the Properties command on the taskbar properties menu. The Taskbar Properties tabbed dialog box lets you modify the appearance and performance of the taskbar and the Start menu.

tiling   The effect of placing all open windows on the screen so that the body of each window appears next to, above, or below, the other windows.

URL   The address of an Internet Web site. URL is an acronym for *Uniform Resource Locator.*

Q&A

Q Why would I use the taskbar properties menu to organize my open windows when I can do the same thing manually?

A The taskbar properties menu gives you the ability to adjust the appearance of your screen's open windows with one mouse click. If you select a cascading window scheme, Windows 95 ensures that all open window title bars appear on the screen with the most recently opened window as the front window of focus. You can bring one of the hidden windows into focus by clicking the window's title bar. If, instead, you select the horizontal or vertical tiling options, Windows 95 displays a little bit of every open window on top of each other or side-by-side.

If you normally work in only one window at a time, you won't use the taskbar properties menu to organize windows. However, you may use the taskbar properties menu to change the appearance of the taskbar itself.

Q How can I use the taskbar properties menu to change the appearance or performance of the taskbar?

A The taskbar is set by default to appear, no matter what else is on your screen. Microsoft thought it best to keep the taskbar on the screen so that you can switch between programs and adjust the Windows 95 performance easily. However, to maximize the screen space and clear away as much as possible, you can change the taskbar's performance so that on-screen windows cover the taskbar giving you an additional line for the open window. In addition to letting open windows cover the taskbar, you can select that Windows 95 always hide the taskbar completely, showing you the taskbar only when you point to the bottom of the screen with the mouse cursor. If you increase the size of the taskbar you can still hide it. The increased size will appear when you show the taskbar, but the taskbar will not be in the way when hidden.

The taskbar properties menu also controls the size of the Start menu's icons so you can decrease the width of the Start menu if you prefer. You also can eliminate (or add) the clock from the taskbar so that the taskbar has room for another window's button.

Q What are tabbed dialog boxes?

A A dialog box is a special window that appears when Windows 95 needs several kinds of answers from you. A dialog box might contain command buttons, option buttons, checkmark boxes, text prompts, and other kinds of controls used by Windows 95 to gather information from the user.

Windows 95 displays a tabbed dialog box when more information is needed than will comfortably (or logically) fit within a single dialog box. By displaying a series of cascaded tabbed dialog boxes, with each tab acting like a file folder's descriptive label, you can select whichever dialog box you want to look at and answer. The bottom line is that a tabbed dialog box gives Windows 95 the ability to offer several sets of dialog boxes in the space of a single dialog box. The Windows 95 dialog boxes are often called *property sheets* because each of the tabbed sheets represents a set of properties you can set for a unique situation.

4

Q Help! My taskbar has fallen and I can't get my Start menu up! What did I do and how can I fix it?

A You've changed the options in the Taskbar Properties dialog box to hide the taskbar. The taskbar is not gone for long, however. To see the taskbar again, all you need to do is point to the very bottom of the screen with the mouse, and the taskbar appears once again.

Q I've opened a lot of windows. How can I get more room on my taskbar to see more buttons?

A You can drag the innermost edge of the taskbar to expand the taskbar so that more open window buttons and icons fit within the taskbar comfortably.

4

Hour 5

Cruise with Documents and Windows

Whereas Windows 3.1 began to pioneer the idea that documents should be the user's focus rather than the programs that work on the documents, Windows 95 extends that document concept more fully by integrating it into the heart of the operating environment. The document concept is the centerpiece of Windows 95's power.

This hour explains some of the ways you manage the documents on your system. Windows 95 enables you to find the documents you need when you want them. The files you create and use with programs (the *documents* in the Windows 95 environment) are more important than the programs themselves because those files are the results of your labor. Windows 95 gives you the tools to access those document files when you need them. After all, when you work on your computer, you run programs to create documents, load documents, change documents, erase documents, move data between documents, and store documents. Rarely do you run programs without doing work with a document (except to play games!).

When I wrote this book's first edition, I debated at length with reviewers who thought a chapter on the Windows 95 document concept was unneeded. After winning the debate, I've since received letters from readers who told me they never fully understood Windows 95's underlying document-centered concept until this chapter put things into perspective for them. You will not learn about just Windows 95 documents here; in addition, you'll master Clipboard and Windows 95 view skills that you can use throughout Windows 95.

The highlights of this hour include:

☐ Why the document concept is so important to Windows 95

☐ How to open documents using both an old and new interface

☐ How the right mouse click makes document management a snap

☐ What the copy, cut, and paste operations do to ease your work with documents

☐ Where you can find single-click document retrieval in the Start menu

The Document Concept

When you write a letter in a word processor, you store that letter as a document file on the disk. Most computer users have little trouble understanding that the data from their word processors are known as documents. There is hardly a user in existence today who does not use some kind of word processor in addition to the other programs on the system.

A Windows 95 user should think of a *document* as being far more than just a word processed document. All of the following are documents:

☐ Sound files

☐ Graphic images

☐ Database datafiles

☐ Spreadsheets

☐ Programs

At first glance, it may seem strange that a program or sound file is a document. In several instances, Windows 95 treats programs as data documents. When you use Windows 95 to arrange files in the folders on your disk drive, Windows 95 considers programs to be documents that contain data and unique filenames.

TIME SAVER

Think of a document as being any file on your computer's disk drive. A collection of Windows 95 documents, therefore, goes into a folder. As you learned in the previous hour, Windows 95 folders often represent directories of disk files.

The rest of this hour explains how the Windows 95 tools help you manage, move, load, and store document files on your system. As computer disk drives get larger and larger you'll need more help managing those disk drives and their contents. The Windows 95's document-centered design gives you the help you need to wade through tons of files by mimicking file cabinet actions when you work with files on your disk.

3.1 ▶
Step Up
Windows 95 supports long filenames (files that don't have to conform to the old 8-letter name and 3-letter extension requirement). To take advantage of long filenames you'll have to use dialog boxes written specifically for Windows 95 as explained in the next section.

Opening Documents

When you want to work with a document file, no matter what kind of file it is, you'll need to open that file. *Open* is the Windows term for loading a document file from the disk drive and using the file in a program. Perhaps the easiest example is a document file you open with a word processor in order to make changes to the document.

There are three common ways to open documents:

☐ Use the Windows 3.1 Open dialog box

☐ Use the Windows 95 Open dialog box

☐ Use the Documents menu

It may sound strange to be discussing the Windows 3.1 dialog box in a Windows 95 book. Actually, this hour will not spend a lot of time with the Windows 3.1 Open dialog box, but some time is needed. For a few years, programs that you run using Windows 95 will have been written for the Windows 3.1 environment. Even though you use Windows 95 to run those programs, they still have the properties of a Windows 3.1 program, including the same file-opening procedures.

3.1 ▶
Step Up
The Windows 3.1 Open dialog box is fairly simple, and your first impression of the Windows 95 Open dialog box may be that it is more involved and thus more complicated. After you get used to the Windows 95 Open dialog box (as well as the other common dialog boxes such as the Save and Print dialog boxes), you'll see that Windows 95's dialog boxes are much more powerful than were those in Windows 3.1 and are just as easy to use. As with most of the Windows 95 environment, "different" does not imply more difficult.

When using a program written for the Windows 3.1 environment inside Windows 95, such as Microsoft's Word 6 for Windows word processor, you select **File** | **O**pen from the program's menu bar to inform the program that you want to load a document into memory and work on that document. If you are just now switching to the Windows 95 environment from 3.1, you probably still use Word 6 for Windows as your word processor. Figure 5.1 shows the Open dialog box supported by several Windows 3.1 programs when you open a document file.

Figure 5.1.

An Open dialog box originally written for Windows 3.1.

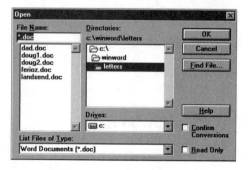

TIME SAVER

Ctrl+O is the accelerator keystroke for the File | Open command in all Windows 95-compatible programs.

Anytime you need to specify a document to open, you must tell Windows 95 the document's filename and the location of that file on the disk (the pathname). Some programs also request additional information such as the type of file. The Windows 3.1 Open dialog box always contains a text prompt where you can enter the filename. You'll also see a scrollable list from which you can select a filename with the mouse.

Another scrollable list appears where you can select the proper pathname where the document is located. The disk drive list always appears as a dropdown listbox. Other information, such as file types, also appears in dropdown listboxes in many Open dialog boxes.

An Open dialog box will always have an OK command button and a Cancel command button. Clicking OK after specifying the filename and location information opens the file. Pressing Cancel closes the dialog box without opening the file. Optionally, some Open dialog boxes contain Help command buttons and other buttons as the application requires.

Dropdown Listboxes

A *dropdown listbox* is a special Windows control that works like a scrolling list but consumes much less screen space. Figure 5.2 shows the same Open dialog box shown in Figure 5.1 except the file type dropdown listbox is open, showing a list of file types.

Figure 5.2.
The dropdown listbox is now open for the user to select a value.

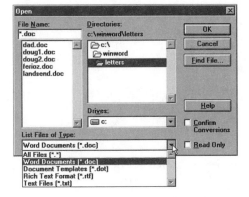

Unlike other kinds of listboxes such as the filename list in the two figures, a dropdown listbox normally consumes only a single line in a dialog box. When the user clicks the down arrow at the right of the dropdown listbox, Windows 95 displays the list of choices. Once the you select one of the choices, the dropdown listbox closes again to give room back to the rest of the dialog box.

Task 5.1: Opening Documents with a Windows 3.1 Open Dialog

Step 1: Description

Not everybody using this book will have a Windows 3.1 Open dialog available for practice. If you are a new computer user having just purchased your computer and software, you may have software that was all written for Windows 95. In that case, your programs will use the new (and improved) Windows 95 version of the Open dialog box, and you can skip this task for now. Be warned, however, that you're *bound* to run across a program eventually that still uses this document-opening dialog box so you should be familiar with it.

5

This task describes how you might use the Microsoft Word 6 for Windows Open dialog box to open a document, called LETTER.DOC, stored on drive D. The document is stored in the directory named MYFILES. You may not have Word for Windows; even if you do, you probably don't have a directory named MYFILES with a file named LETTER.DOC, so just read along and use Figures 5.1 and 5.2 as your guides as you read through this task.

Step 2: Action

1. Select **File | O**pen from the Word for Windows menu bar to display the Open dialog box. (Windows 95 applications also use **File | O**pen to open document file dialog boxes.)

   You could specify the LETTER.DOC file several ways. The most straightforward method, but the one that requires the most typing, is for you to type the entire disk, pathname, and filename at the File **N**ame prompt (you would enter `d:\myfiles\letter.doc`). When typing the path and filenames, you can use uppercase, lowercase, or a combination of both. Instead of typing the complete file specification, it is usually easier, faster, and more reliable to use the mouse to select the file as done next.

2. To avoid typing the pathname of an existing file, select the proper disk drive first by displaying the Dri**v**es dropdown list. To display the list, click the arrow to the right of the dropdown listbox.

3. When the list of available drives drops down, you must point to the drive D and click the mouse button. The dropdown listbox then closes back up and drive D is selected.

CAUTION

> Again, this is theory-only task for you. Even if you have Word for Windows you will not have a file named LETTER.DOC in a directory named MYFILES.

4. Select the MYFILES directory in the **D**irectories list box. Once you select the drive and directory, the File **N**ame list will contain a scrolling list of all files in that directory. You could now select the LETTER.DOC file and press the OK command button to open that file.

JUST A MINUTE

> Always remember that Windows 95 calls directories *folders* and files *documents*. The folder concept makes selecting files using Windows 95 Open dialog boxes easier than having to select from lists of directories as you have to do with Windows 3.1 Open dialog boxes.

5

Step 3: Review

Although you may not use Word 6 for Windows, keep in mind the importance of mastering the older style Windows 3.1 Open dialog boxes. Whenever you use a program inside Windows 95 that was not specifically written for Windows 95 (there are still many in use out there!), you'll run across this same kind of dialog box.

As a productive computer user you must focus on documents because documents hold the work that you create with the programs that you run. When you need access to a document and you've started a program in Windows 95, you'll be loading those documents through Open dialog boxes like the one shown in this section.

Over time, as more and more software vendors update their software to be fully compatible with Windows 95, you'll see the new Windows 95 Open dialog box shown in Figure 5.3. The Windows 95 Open dialog offers more document control than the older Open dialogs provided.

Figure 5.3.

Opening a file in Windows 95.

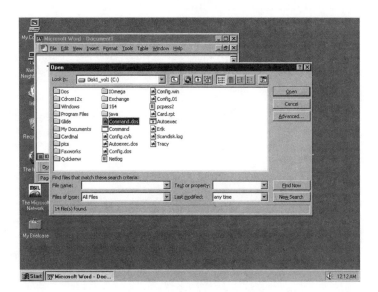

When you want to work with a file using a program written specifically for Windows 95, you'll get the Windows 95 Open dialog box when you enter the **File | O**pen command in the application. No matter what kind of document you are opening (text, multimedia, or graphic), the **File | O**pen command produces this common Windows 95 Open dialog box.

TIME SAVER

By using this standard Open dialog box, all Windows 95 applications will be easier for you to master. You have to learn only one Open dialog box to know how all of the Windows 95 Open dialog boxes operate.

Task 5.2: Using the Windows 95 Open Dialog Box

Step 1: Description

This task will be available to *all* readers (not just those using Word 6 for Windows version 3.1) because Windows 95 comes with several accessory programs written specifically for Windows 95 that you can try out. This task uses the WordPad program found in the Accessories folder.

WordPad is a simple word processor that recognizes the several document file *formats*. The supported formats mean that you can quickly look at and edit files of several types of documents, including Microsoft Write, Microsoft Word for Windows, text files, and *RTF* files. RTF stands for Rich Text Files and refers to an industry-standard document file format. You'll need to open only one program (WordPad) to view and make simple edits to document files consisting of any these file types.

You don't have to be a master at WordPad to follow this task. Every Windows 95 installation gets a copy of WordPad so you should be able to follow this task. The purpose of this task is to familiarize you with the appearance and use of the Windows 95 Open dialog box because you will see this dialog box so often as you work with Windows 95. You will also get more experience with the Start button's cascading menus as well.

Step 2: Action

1. Click the Start menu.
2. Point to the **P**rograms command. The next layer of menus will appear next to the Start menu.
3. Point to the Accessories folder. The Accessories folder is probably at the top of the menu because it comes early in the alphabetized list of choices that you'll see. The icon next to the label for Accessories indicates that it is a folder and not a program that runs as soon as you click that command.
4. Locate the WordPad icon on the Accessories menu. Next to the label for WordPad is a notepad icon, not a folder icon. This means that selecting the WordPad command will start a program rather than open another folder's menu.

5

5. When Windows 95 opens the WordPad program window, your screen will look something like the one in Figure 5.4. Now that you're using a Windows 95 program, you can see the Windows 95 version of the Open dialog box.

Figure 5.4.

The WordPad program window is now open.

6. Select **File | O**pen from the menu bar at the top of the WordPad program. The Windows 95 Open dialog box appears just like the one in Figure 5.3. The folders and files that you see inside the window will differ from the figure's depending on the files installed on your computer system.

    All Open dialog boxes initially open to the currently active folder which will usually be the Windows folder. The Windows folder contains additional folders and files.

    WordPad can open several types of files. The default file type that WordPad opens is a Word for Windows file. The problem is that no Word for Windows files usually reside in the Windows directory. To open a file of a different type so that you can see a list of files, click the dropdown listbox arrow next to the dropdown listbox labeled Files of **t**ype.

7. Select the Text Documents (*.txt) item from the list by clicking that choice. The *.txt indicates that the last four characters of the file (the *file extension*) will contain the letters .txt. The asterisk is a *wildcard character* that stands for any one or more characters that come before the extension.

5

Once you change the file type request, WordPad displays a list of folders along with any files in the Windows folders that end in the .txt extension. Your screen will look something like the one in Figure 5.5. If your Windows folder contains a large number of additional folders and files, Windows 95 provides scroll bars so you can scroll through the choices.

Figure 5.5.

Viewing text files that you can now open.

3.1 ▶
Step Up

In a way, file extensions are slowly being phased out of Windows. Due to the long filenames that Windows 95 supports and the ease of election provided by the folder concept, the extension may not be needed as frequently. Windows 95 displays an icon that identifies the file type instead of the file extension. For example, Word 6 files appear in file listings with a Word 6 icon instead of the .DOC extension.

8. Double-click on the document named Readme. (Readme's full filename is Readme.txt, but the .txt extension does not show.) If the Readme document does not appear in the list of documents, choose another document. Don't choose another folder, however, or you might have trouble finding a text file to open. The Readme.txt document file opens inside the editing area of WordPad. The Open dialog box disappears until you need it again.

5

The text documents you see in the Windows folder were copied to your disk drive when you installed WordPad. Don't make changes to any document that you load here because you may need the information in the file. Keep WordPad loaded for the next task.

JUST A MINUTE

WordPad does not, by default, display filename extensions. There is no reason to show the .txt extension because the file type that you chose earlier requested only files that end with the characters .txt.

TIME SAVER

If you cannot find a file you're trying to open, click All Documents to display all document files in the folder instead of the default documents only.

Step 3: Review

The Windows 95 Open dialog box that you've seen so far works a lot like the Windows 3.1 dialog box. The reason you're having to spend so much time in this hour with the Open dialog boxes is that you have to know how to access the documents you need.

There is more than meets the eye, however, with the Windows 95 Open dialog boxes! Underneath the Open dialog box lies a tremendous amount of hidden power as the next section shows.

5

Advanced Open Dialogs

The Open dialog box contains a large number of features that go far beyond the act of simply opening a file. When you display an Open dialog box you might decide you need to do something other than open a document file at that point. You might see the list of folders and document files before you and decide to rename a file, copy a file, or delete a file, before actually opening one of the files in the list.

Step Up   In Windows 3.1, you would have to change from the File Manager to DOS before performing many of the actions that the Windows 95 Open dialog box allows.

There are several tasks listed below which, by example, demonstrate many of the actions you can perform using the Open dialog box.

Task 5.3: Changing Folders Using Open

TASK

Step 1: Description

If the Open dialog box does not open to the folder you want, you can easily change to a different folder anywhere on the disk. You also can change to another disk drive and open a file there just by clicking the mouse.

Step 2: Action

1. With WordPad still loaded, select the **File | O**pen command once again to display the Open dialog box.

2. The Open dialog box displays a list of folders, if any exist in the default directory, as well as files that match the selected file type. If you want to open a file in one of the folders instead of a file that already appears in the dialog box, double-click the folder to open that folder and display its contents which you then can open.

   Double-click the Help folder to open it and you'll see one file named License. (In the Help folder, there is only one file that ends in the .txt extension, which is what the Open file type is still set to.)

3. Instead of opening the License file, point to the icon at the right of the Look **in** text prompt. The icon is a picture of a folder with a bent arrow on the folder. The icon is part of the Open dialog box's *toolbar* which is very common in Windows 95 dialog boxes and programs. A toolbar contains a list of icons that instantly execute pushbutton commands. Before clicking the icon, hold the cursor over the folder for a moment and Windows 95 displays a description of the icon's purpose as shown in Figure 5.6.

5

Figure 5.6.
*Get ready to back
up one directory.*

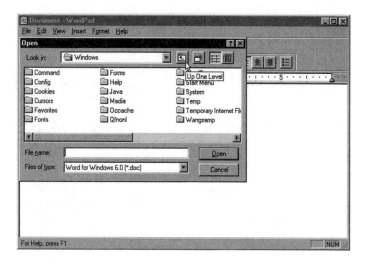

When you search through folders on your disk, you'll often open folders such as the Help folder and decide that you want to go back to the previous set of folders. The icon you now point to moves the Open dialog box back to the previous set of folders. Click the icon now to see the original list.

The Up One Level toolbar button really moves the Open view back to the parent directory of the directory being viewed. The Up One Level button moves you back up through folder levels quickly.

The Backspace key is the shortcut accelerator key for the Up One Level icon. Instead of pushing the icon you only need to press Backspace.

TIME SAVER

4. If you want to search your computer system for a document not located in the Windows folder (or inside any of the folders *within* the Windows folder), click open the Look in dropdown listbox. The Look in dropdown listbox then displays

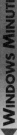

WINDOWS MINUTE

5

an overview of every aspect of your computer that contains documents: other hard disks, floppy disks, and CD-ROM drives.

JUST A MINUTE

> If you work on a network, you'll also see networked locations appear in the dropdown listbox. If you work on the Internet, you'll even see Internet location access (such as FTP sites)! Remember that Windows 95 does not limit your desktop access to your own personal computer but seamlessly integrates outside computers.

5. Click the row with the C: icon in the dropdown list and the open dialog box displays a list of top-level folders and documents that reside on drive C. (There may be many folders depending on your computer.)

   If you click the drive A: icon (assuming there's a disk in your diskette drive), the Open dialog box displays a list of documents and folders on the floppy disk.

6. Go back to the Windows folder (which probably resides on drive C) to prepare for the next task. You may have to scroll the window to the right to see the folder labeled Windows. Double-click the Windows folder to open it and display its contents.

Step 3: Review

The Open dialog box gives you the ability to find documents located anywhere in your computer system. When you view the contents of folders within folders, the Up One Level icon takes you to the parent folder.

TIME SAVER

> If you know the exact filename and location of the document you want to open, you can bypass the mouse clicks and type the full pathname in the File **n**ame text box prompt and click the OK button (or press Enter) to open that document. Given Windows 95's powerful Open dialog box and considering the extremely long filenames that Windows 95 supports, most users will enjoy the benefit of zeroing-in on the file using the mouse instead of typing complete path and document names such as these:
>
> ```
> c:\winword\docs\balance.doc
> a:\Note for James
> ```

5

Task 5.4: Detailing the List of Files

Step 1: Description

If you want to display document information with more detail than by name and location only, the Open dialog box's Details icon (the fourth icon on the toolbar, indented in Figure 5.7) changes the view of the documents and files in the Open dialog box.

Figure 5.7.

You can look at more document detail by clicking the Details icon.

Details icon

Step 2: Action

1. With the Open dialog box still open to the Windows folder, click the Details icon. The list of folders and files changes format to provide additional information about each (see Figure 5.7).

   The Name column holds the name of the item, the Type column tells you whether the item is a folder or text document (there are other document types as well, such as programs, sound files, and images), and the Modified column lists the date and time that someone last modified (changed or created) the item.

2. The long filenames available to users of Windows 95 means that the Name column can hold fairly long names. If you want to adjust the size of any of the three columns, point the mouse to a dividing line between any of the three column names. The mouse cursor changes shape and you can drag or shrink the size of the column. Adjust the Name column now so it extends farther to the right to hold longer document names. Figure 5.8 shows the name column after extending it considerably to the right.

TASK

5

Figure 5.8.

The column sizes in the detailed view are adjustable.

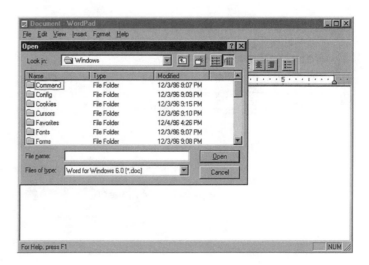

3. The drawback to the detail showing in the Open dialog box is that the Open dialog box cannot display as many documents at one time—the extra information takes up space otherwise consumed by the document icons. To change the detailed view back to the icon view (called the *list* view), click the List icon on the toolbar. (It is the second icon from the right, which you can verify by positioning the mouse cursor there for a moment until the description appears.)

Step 3: Review

There are two different views of the documents in an Open dialog box. You can look at the list view and see the folders and documents displayed as icons. If you request a detailed view, Windows 95 displays the folders' and documents' sizes, types, and last-modified information as well.

Task 5.5: Creating a New Folder

Step 1: Description

If you decide to create a new set of documents that logically go together, such as your holiday letters and birthday greetings for each year, consider putting those documents in their own folder. Instead of wading through a huge list, you can find specific documents more easily by clicking on their folder. This displays only those documents when you want to work with them. The toolbar's Create New Folder icon creates new folders for you.

Instead of using the File Manager or DOS to create a new directory, the Create New Folder icon creates a new directory instantly anytime you view a Windows 95 Open dialog box.

5

Step 2: Action

1. Click the Create New Folder icon (the third icon from the right on the Open dialog box's toolbar). Windows 95 creates a new folder and names that folder New Folder as shown in Figure 5.9.

Figure 5.9.

Create a new folder with one mouse click.

The newly created folder

2. The name New Folder is not a great name. To rename the folder to something more appropriate, click over the New Folder's name once and Windows 95 surrounds the name with an editing box.

3. Type the name My Holidays and press Enter. Instantly Windows 95 changes the name of the folder to My Holidays.

Step 3: Review

Adding new folders for new document groups is as easy as clicking a toolbar icon and typing a name for the new folder. Of course if you double-click on a new folder there will be no contents inside. Once you create the new folder, you can then copy, move, or save related documents in that folder when you're ready to do so.

Task 5.6: Manage Documents with a Right Mouse-Click

Step 1: Description

After you display the Open dialog box you can point to any folder or document and click the right mouse button to perform several actions on the document that you might want to do. Here are the things you can do with documents:

☐ Select the document

☐ Play sound documents or open graphic documents

☐ Print the document

☐ Copy the file to a diskette

☐ Cut or copy selected text to the Windows 95 Clipboard

☐ Create a shortcut access to the file so you can later open the file without using the Open dialog box

☐ Delete the document

☐ Rename the document

☐ Change the document's system attributes

A right click over a folder's name produces a menu that lets you perform these same actions as well as start the Windows 95 Explorer program (described in the next hour) or search the disk for other files and folders.

The following task walks you through many of these right-click actions.

Step 2: Action

1. Point to the Readme document and click the right mouse button. The document menu opens up to the right of the document as shown in Figure 5.10.

Figure 5.10.

The right mouse displays the document menu.

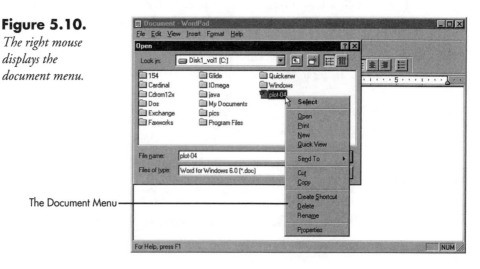

The Document Menu

5

In Task 5.2, you opened the Readme document by double-clicking the document. The Select command performs the same function as double-clicking a document name. The **O**pen command will always attempt to examine the document's native format and open the document with an appropriate program while still keeping WordPad active. For text files, the second command is **O**pen, but if you click the right mouse button while pointing to a sound file, the second command will be Play. For now, don't select either command.

JUST A MINUTE

You'll learn all about the printing of documents in the Hour 15, "Increase Printing Power."

2. Find a blank formatted disk. Insert the disk in drive A. Click the right mouse button over the Readme document and select the Se**n**d To command. The disk drive will appear when you select Se**n**d To. When you select the disk drive, Windows 95 begins sending an exact copy of the Readme.txt document to the disk in drive A. Windows 95 graphically displays the sending of the document to drive A, as shown in Figure 5.11.

Figure 5.11.

Windows 95 entertains you while copying documents.

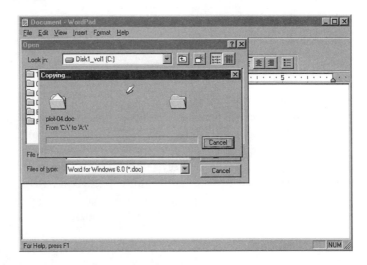

JUST A MINUTE

If you attempt to copy a document over another one that already exists with the same name, Windows 95 warns you that you are about to overwrite the existing document.

3.1 ▶
Step Up   The overwrite warnings in Windows 95 are much more informative than in Windows 3.1. Windows 95 displays the date, time, and file size of each file (the target and the source file of the copy) to help you decide whether or not you want to overwrite the file on the floppy drive.

3. Point to the Readme document and click the right mouse button. Select **D**elete. Windows 95 displays the message box shown in Figure 5.12. *Don't* choose **Y**es because you need to keep the Readme document in your Windows directory.

Figure 5.12.

The Recycle Bin holds deleted documents for a while.

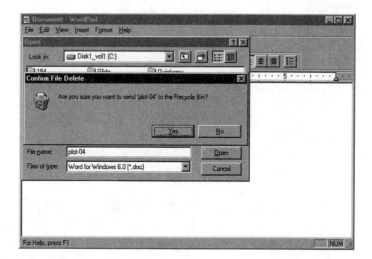

The Recycle Bin is a special location inside Windows 95 that holds the documents you delete. In previous versions of Windows, deleted documents were difficult (and often impossible) to recover. Windows 95 gives you one last chance to recover deleted documents. When you delete a document file of any type, Windows 95 sends that file to the Recycle Bin. The documents are then out of your way but not really deleted permanently until you empty the Recycle Bin. You'll learn all about the Recycle Bin in the next hour. For now, remember that you can delete documents directly from any Open dialog box.

TIME SAVER
▼

The File | Save and File | Save As menu commands in Windows 95-compatible programs also display dialog boxes that act just like the Open dialog box. All of the right-mouse click commands described here are also available in those dialog boxes.

4. Click the No command button because you should not delete the Readme document.

5. It's extremely easy to rename a document. Click the right mouse button to display the document's menu and select Rename. Windows 95 highlights the name, and you can edit or completely change the name to something else. Type NewName and press Enter to change the name.

CAUTION

Do not supply an extension when you rename the document file. For example, if you renamed the Readme document (that is really named Readme.txt) to NewName.txt, the document would actually be named NewName.txt.txt! About the only way to rename a document and its extension is through the Windows Explorer program described in the next hour. If you or someone else has set up your Windows 95 system to display filename extensions in file listings (as described in the next hour's chapter), you will be able to rename the full filename including the extension.

6. Try this: Close the Open dialog box by pressing Esc. Move the mouse pointer to an area of the document list where no folder or document appears and click the right mouse button. A new menu appears, as shown in Figure 5.13.

Figure 5.13.

You can undo the renaming of a file.

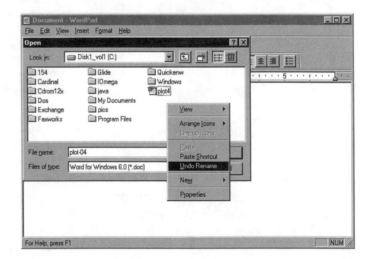

The **Undo Rename** command reverses the previous renaming of the document. Select **Undo Rename** and the NewName document reverts to its original name of Readme.

TIME SAVER

> The **Undo Rename** remembers a long list of past names. For example, if you change a document's name three times in a row, then select **Undo Rename** three times, Windows 95 reverts the name to its first and original name!

7. Select the right-click's **Pr**operties command. Windows 95 displays the Properties window shown in Figure 5.14.

Figure 5.14.
Changing the attributes of a document.

The Properties window not only describes the folder or document in detail but also lets you specify *attributes* of the file. Table 5.1 describes the attributes that you can set for documents and folders. The Readme document's Archive checkmark is checked because you've recently changed the file (renamed it and then reversed the renaming) since your last file backup. If you routinely back up your files, and you should, the archive property determines whether the document has been backed up in its current form or not. (See Hour 19, "Back Up and Squeeze Disk Space.") The Readme document is neither read-only, a system file, nor a hidden file, so none of those attribute options are checked.

5

Step 3: Review

This task covered the most important commands in the Open dialog box's right-click document menu. This menu differs slightly depending on the kind of document you click over (folder, sound, graphic, program, text, word processor document, and so on), but the fundamental menu of commands stays the same and works the way this task described. If you want to make copies of files on the hard disk or move the file to a different location, you'll want to master the techniques described in the next task.

> You'll learn about the Create **S**hortcut command in the next hour.

JUST A MINUTE

Table 5.1. Document file attributes.

Attribute	Description
Read-only	When checked, you can read the file but not modify or delete it.
Archive	When checked, the file has been modified since the most recent backup was made.
Hidden	When checked, the file cannot be seen from normal directory listings.
System	When checked, the file is a protected class of files most generally used by the operating system. (System files are often hidden as well.)

5

Task 5.7: Copy and Move Documents

Step 1: Description

The document's right-click menu offers advanced copying and moving of files. The *Clipboard* is the go-between for all Windows 95 copy, cut, paste, and move operations. When you want to copy a file from one place to another, you can place a copy of the file on the Windows 95 Clipboard. When you do, the file is on the Clipboard and out of your way, until you go to where you want the file copied. You'll then paste the file to the new location, in effect copying from the Clipboard to the new location. When you copy a file to another location, the file remains in its original location and a copy is made elsewhere.

JUST A MINUTE

The Clipboard holds one file at a time. If you copy a document to the Clipboard, a subsequent copy will overwrite the first copy.

TIME SAVER

If you want to copy a file to a disk, use the Send To command explained in Task 5.6 because the Send To command is easier to use than copying to a disk.

When you move a file from one location to another, Windows 95 first performs a *cut* operation. This means that Windows 95 deletes the file from its current location and sends the file to the Clipboard (overwriting whatever was on the Clipboard). When you find the location you want to move the file to, Windows 95 copies the Clipboard's contents to the new location (such as a different folder or disk drive).

The Clipboard

In a way, the Clipboard is like a short-term Recycle Bin. The Recycle Bin holds all deleted files until you are ready to remove them permanently. The Clipboard holds deleted (or copied) documents and pieces of documents, but only until you send something else to the Clipboard or until you exit Windows 95 and turn off your computer. In Hour 12, "Clip and Save," you'll learn how to view the contents of the Clipboard and how to work with specific text on the Clipboard itself.

Step 2: Action

1. Right-click over the Readme document.
2. Select the Copy command. Windows 95 sends a complete copy of the document to the Clipboard. The Clipboard keeps the document until you replace the Clipboard's contents with something else or until you exit Windows 95. Therefore, you can send the Clipboard document to several subsequent locations.
3. Right-click over the System folder located in the Open dialog box (System is a folder within the Windows folder). The System folder's menu appears with the Paste command. Windows 95 knows that something is on the Clipboard (a copy of the Readme document), and you can send a copy of Readme to the System folder

5

by clicking the **P**aste command. Don't paste the Readme document into the System folder, however, unless you then open System and remove the document file. There is no need to have two copies of Readme on your disk.

4. Right-click once again over the Readme document. This time, select Cu**t** instead of **C**opy. Windows 95 erases the document file from the Windows folder and places the file on the Clipboard.

JUST A MINUTE

> The copy, cut, and paste operations all get their names from the paper equivalents of copying, cutting, and pasting scraps of paper.

CAUTION

> Windows 95 keeps the name of the document in place until you paste the document elsewhere. The name is misleading because the name makes you think the document is still in the Windows folder. A ghost outline of an icon appears where the document's icon originally appeared. As long as the name still appears in the Windows folder, you *can* still open the file and do things with the file, but as soon as you paste the Clipboard contents somewhere else, the file goes away permanently from the Windows folder.

5. Right-click over the Config folder. As soon as you do, the Readme document leaves the Windows folder and is copied from the Clipboard to the Config folder. If you want to double-click the Config folder to see that Readme is there, go ahead and do so now, but click the Up One Level icon once you see that Readme is there to return to the Windows folder.

6. Windows 95 is as safe as possible. If you change your mind *after* a copy or cut operation, you can always reverse the operation! Right-click over the Config folder and the pop-up menu contains the command **U**ndo Paste. Select **U**ndo Paste and Windows 95 reverses the move and sends the file back to the Windows folder where it was before the move.

TIME SAVER

> Here's a *much faster way* to move a document to another folder listed in the Open dialog box: Drag the document to the folder! Try it by dragging the Readme document over to the Config folder. An outline of the Readme document travels with the mouse cursor as shown in Figure 5.15. When

you point to the Config folder, let up on the mouse button and the Readme document moves from the Windows folder to the Config folder (the name goes away from the Windows folder). Want it back again? Right-click the mouse and select **U**ndo Move. Windows 95 always lets you undo moves no matter how you made the move.

Figure 5.15.

Drag and drop makes moving documents simple.

Moving the document ——

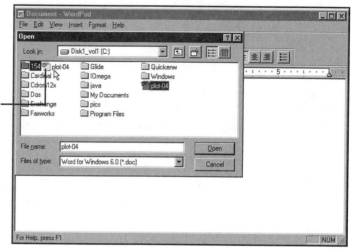

TIME SAVER

If you want to use the drag-and-drop shortcut method for *copying* documents, hold down the Ctrl key while dragging the document to the other folder. The key combination is easy if you remember that both *copy* and *CTRL* begin with the same letter. As you drag to copy an item, Windows 95 displays a plus sign at the bottom of the icon to indicate that you are copying and not moving. To cancel a copy you've started, drag the item back to its original location before releasing your mouse button or press ESC before releasing your mouse button.

CAUTION

You cannot drag an item such as a document to just anywhere. Windows 95 changes the mouse cursor to a circle with a slash through it (the international "Do Not" symbol) when you drag the document over any area of the screen that cannot accept that document.

5

7. Sometimes, you may need a document for a program outside of the program you're currently working in. You can place a document onto the Windows 95 desktop. Select the Readme document and copy the document to the Clipboard by right-clicking Readme and selecting **C**opy. (You also can use drag-and-drop if you want. Hold down Ctrl and drag the Readme document out of the Open box and continue with Step 8.)

8. Move the cursor to the Windows 95 desktop to an area of the wallpaper that has no icon on it. Click the right mouse button to display a menu and select **P**aste. (If you are dragging the Readme document, release the mouse button as soon as the mouse cursor appears in the area of the wallpaper that you select.) As Figure 5.16 shows, even the wallpaper can hold documents.

Figure 5.16.

Putting items onto the desktop itself.

The desktop now holds a copy of the document

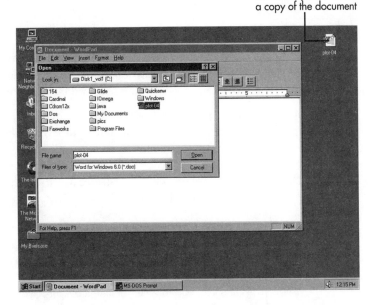

Step Up

The Windows 3.1 desktop could only hold program groups, not individual files or portions of files. The Windows 95 desktop acts somewhat like a secondary and visual Clipboard where you can store items. The desktop is actually more like a bulletin board where you can pin items such as documents until you need them at a later time.

To copy or move the wallpaper document, use the right click menu or drag the document with the mouse as explained earlier in this hour.

JUST A MINUTE

When you delete a desktop document, the document goes to the Recycle Bin. You can retrieve the document later if you wish, or delete the bin, as the next hour explains. Once you've deleted a desktop document, a right mouse click over the wallpaper displays an **U**ndo Delete command. Use it to put the document right back on the wallpaper if you change your mind.

9. Delete the Readme document from the wallpaper at this time. To delete the document, you can use the right mouse click and select Delete or simply click on the Readme icon and press the Del shortcut key on the keyboard.

Placing Documents on the Desktop

The items you place on the desktop, whether by copying or by moving, stay on the desktop until you remove the item from the desktop. Even after shutting down Windows 95 and turning off your computer, the desktop item will be there when you return.

Although you shouldn't put too many documents out on the desktop, which would cause clutter, you may want to work with a document in several different programs over a period of a few days. By putting the document on the desktop, it is always easily available to any application that's running. Of course, if you run an application in a maximized window, you'll have to shrink the window to some degree to retrieve the document because you have to see the desktop to copy and move the items on it.

TIME SAVER

Instead of moving the Readme document by dragging with the left mouse button, repeat this task by dragging the Readme document to the wallpaper with the *right* mouse button (reverse this for a left-handed mouse). When you position the document over the wallpaper and release the right mouse button, Windows 95 displays the menu shown in Figure 5.17. The **M**ove Here and **C**opy Here commands give you the choice of a move or copy, or you can cancel the operation altogether, if you change your mind. (The shortcuts to these procedures are explained in the next hour.)

5

Figure 5.17.
The choice is yours regarding the document's drag operation.

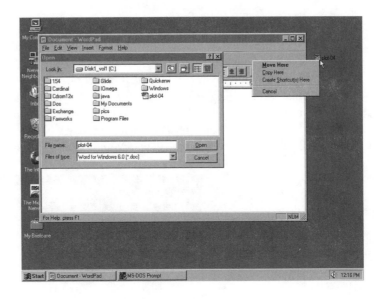

Step 3: Review

Managing documents often involves moving or sending copies of those documents from one location to another. Perhaps you want to work with a document in two or more applications. If so, you can copy that document into each application's folder.

Windows 95 supports a complete set of menu-driven cut, copy, and paste commands from the right mouse click. With these commands, you can copy or move files from one place to another. If you can see the target location of the copy or move, such as another window's folder on the screen or the desktop, use the mouse to copy or move the document and save time.

Task 5.8: Copy and Move Pieces of Documents

Step 1: Description

In addition to copying or moving documents of all types, you'll often need to copy or move pieces of documents, such as a paragraph of text or sections of art, from one document to another. Several programs that you use, such as word processors and spreadsheets, enable you to copy or move specific pieces of documents. As long as those programs are written for Windows 95, the techniques for copying and moving are the same. Therefore, master these techniques now, and you'll already know how to perform these functions in almost every program you run.

Step 2: Action

1. Open the Readme document inside the WordPad program by double-clicking the Readme document.

2. Find the location in the document that reads Microsoft Windows 95 and select that text by dragging the mouse from the beginning of the text to the end of the text before releasing the mouse. Your screen should look something like the one in Figure 5.18. (Your WordPad document may look slightly different from the figure's, depending on the date of your Windows 95 installation.)

Figure 5.18.

*Text is now
selected.*

The selected text ———

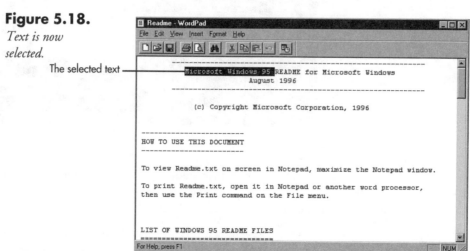

How To Select Text

If you've never selected text before, you do so with the mouse. Windows 95 must always know exactly what text you want to copy or move when working with portions of documents. To select text, find the upper-left corner of the text that you want to select and click the left mouse button to begin selecting. Then drag the mouse to the right and continue dragging the mouse down if the text you wish to highlight will span more than one line. Select text until all the text you want to cut or copy is highlighted. When you let up on the mouse button, Windows 95 ends the selection of text. (You may also select text by holding down the Shift key and pressing one of the arrow keys.)

3. Click the right mouse button while pointing to the selected text. Among the commands you'll find the familiar Cut, Copy, and Paste. In addition to copying or cutting an entire document to the Clipboard, as you did in previous tasks, you also can cut or copy only portions of the text.

5

4. Once you cut or copy the text to the Clipboard, you can paste that text in another place inside the currently open document. You also can open a different document and paste the text there. Select **C**opy from the menu to send the selected text to the Clipboard.

TIME SAVER

The shortcut to copying the text to a new location is to drag the selected text to a different location. After the dragging of the text, Windows 95 will put a copy of the text wherever you release the mouse button.

One of the most interesting things you can do with the desktop is paste the selected text to the desktop as you did previously with an entire document. The selected text lying on the desktop is known as a *scrap*. You can later copy or move that scrap of text to another document.

5. Point to a blank area of the desktop and paste the text there. Windows 95 displays an icon that shows a document with a selected scrap of text. The icon's title is made from the program that produced the scrap (in this case Microsoft's own WordPad), the type of file (document), the word Scrap, and the first few letters of the scrap.

6. Click over the scrap lying on the desktop. Press Del to send the scrap to the Recycle Bin and clean the desktop back up.

7. You are now through with WordPad for now. Select **F**ile | E**x**it from the menu. If WordPad asks if you want to save changes that you might have made to the document, answer no by clicking the No command button.

Step 3: Review

This task showed you that you can copy or cut selected portions of a document using many of the same tools that you used earlier for entire documents. When you copy a portion of a document to the desktop, that portion is known as a scrap. The scrap's icon description describes the scrap and displays a few characters from the scrap.

Step Up

In Hour 14, "Activate DOS-Based Applications," you'll learn how to copy, cut, and paste data from or to a DOS program. Windows 3.1 did not support DOS-based copy, cut, and move operations as well as Windows 95 does.

The Documents Menu

The document concept is so vital to Windows 95 users that Microsoft added a **D**ocuments command to the Start menu itself. When studying how people use Windows 95, Microsoft found that people often refer to the same few documents over and over. For example, you might work on a report for several days in a row before you are finished with it. The report might also contain several tables and graphs from other sources such as a spreadsheet program or a drawing program.

When you select the **D**ocuments command, Windows 95 displays a menu of several recent documents such as the menu shown in Figure 5.19. The next task shows how to access and use the Start menu's **D**ocuments command.

Figure 5.19.

Quickly return to a document from the Start menu.

Recently used document names

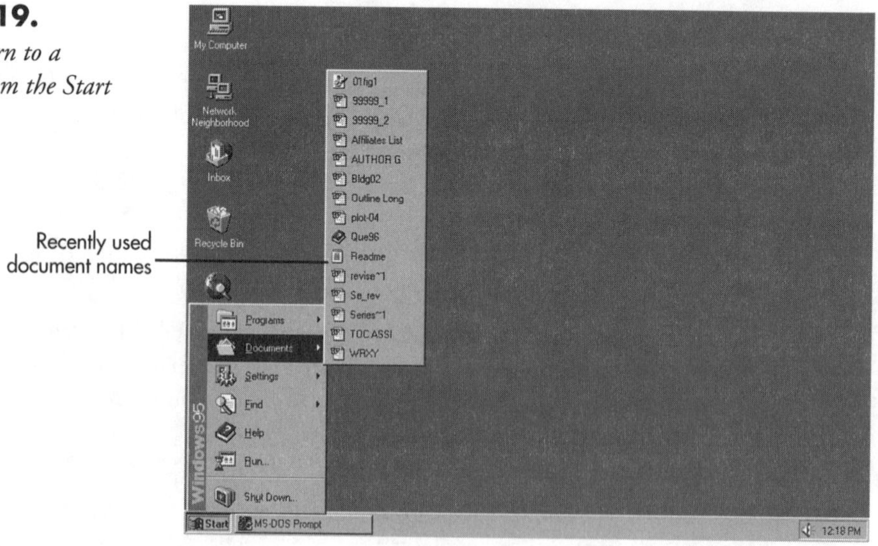

Task 5.9: Opening Documents from the Documents Menu

Step 1: Description

When you select a document from the Start menu's Documents list, Windows 95 analyzes the document to determine the best method of opening that file. If you select a graphics file, Windows 95 opens an appropriate graphics program so you can view and edit the open graphics document (see Hour 11, "Paint a Picture"). If you select a text file, Windows 95 uses

5

either Notepad or WordPad, depending on the size of the file. There are several other document file associations that Windows 95 makes to determine the best way of opening the file you want.

TIME SAVER

> When you need to make changes to a document, why not go directly to that document and let Windows 95 figure out the best way of opening the document? That's exactly what you do when you open documents using the **D**ocuments command. Instead of locating and running the correct program, and *then* opening the document to edit it, you can select your document directly, if that document appears on the Documents menu. Then, Windows 95 figures out the best program to run to enable you to look at and edit the document.

Step 2: Action

1. Click the Start button on the taskbar to open the Start menu.

2. Select **Documents**. The list of recently accessed documents appears.

3. Select the Readme document. Windows 95 loads the Readme document into the Notepad program. Notepad is a simple text editor that works with small text files. Notepad cannot work with as many document types as WordPad can.

CAUTION

> Don't get confused! Although this hour earlier used WordPad to open the Readme document, Windows 95 opens the document inside the Notepad editor because Notepad is more efficient, as you'll learn in Hour 10, "Compose Using Writing Tools." If the text document is too large to fit inside Notepad, Windows 95 opens the file in WordPad.

4. Once Windows 95 starts the program, you can do whatever you want with the document. For now, select **File | Exit** to exit Notepad.

These kinds of file associations are also available in Windows 3.1, but only from the File Manager.

Step 3: Review

The Start menu's **Documents** command gives you double-click access to your documents. A click on the menu, and then on the document you want, instantly starts the program associated with the file's type, and you can go to work on that document.

TIME SAVER

> If the Documents menu gets too large, you can empty it. Select **S**ettings from the Start menu and select **T**askbar (as you did in the previous hour). Click the tabbed dialog box labeled Start Menu Programs. The bottom half of the dialog box contains a single command button labeled Clear with which you can completely erase all the documents on your Documents menu.

Summary

This hour showed you how important the document concept is to Windows 95. Although previous versions of Windows supported a document concept, Windows 95 takes the concept to an extreme by making the focus of all disk file operations a document-related focus. Although you view a list of files when opening or saving data, the icons and menu commands available to you act as if you are working with paper documents that you can copy or move from one place to another. Windows 95 extends the document concept even further to include all kinds of files including programs, graphics, sound, and multimedia files.

When managing the documents inside Windows 95, you've got to master the Windows 3.1 version of the Open dialog box, as well as the Windows 95 version. The Windows 95 Open dialog box supports several additional commands as well as the right click menu that appears when you right click over a folder or document.

When you want extremely quick access to a document that you've been working on recently, select that document from the Documents menu. Windows 95 determines the best program to use to open the file and starts that program for you.

Workshop

Term Review

Clipboard An area of Windows 95 that holds documents or parts of documents. The Clipboard can hold any kind of document including text, sound, and graphic images.

copy The process of sending a copy of an item such as a document or part of a document to the Clipboard. From the Clipboard you can place the item elsewhere, in effect making a copy of the item in at least two places on your computer system.

5

cut   The process of removing an item, such as a document or part of a document, from somewhere in your computer system. The removed item goes to the Clipboard. From the Clipboard you can place the item elsewhere, in effect moving the item.

file extension   The end part of some filenames including a period followed by one to three characters. By giving some files the same filename extension you can group them together so that, using wildcards, you can work with those files as a collection. All major applications support their own filename extension. For example, WordPad likes to use the Word for Windows standard .DOC filename extension at the end of all documents you open with WordPad. You can select a different filename extension in WordPad if you prefer to work with a different type of document.

formats   Different files are stored on the disk differently depending on the nature of the file. The format is the nature of the file that determines if the file is a graphic, text, or program file.

kilobyte   Approximately 1,000 characters of storage. See also **KB**.

KB   The abbreviation for *kilobyte*. *8KB* refers to approximately 8,000 characters of storage.

paste   The process of sending the contents of the Clipboard to another area of the computer system such as to a specific folder or to the Windows 95 desktop.

Recycle Bin   A special location in Windows 95 that temporarily holds all the files that you delete. Until you empty the Recycle Bin, you can recover the deleted files just as you can remove trash from your office trashcan until the can's contents get taken away by the janitor.

RTF   Stands for *Rich Text Format* and refers to a universal file format that many different programs support. The RTF format differs from a straight text file format because RTF files can contain text encoded with special effects such as boldfacing and underlining.

scrap   A selected portion from a document that you send to the desktop.

toolbar   This area of a window contains a list of icons that instantly execute push-button commands. Many Windows 95 applications and dialog boxes contain toolbars that make issuing commands easier for you.

wildcard character   When you want to refer to more than one file, you can often use a * or ? wildcard character. The * substitutes for zero or more characters in a filename and the ? substitutes for one character. Therefore, *.txt refers to all files whose names end in the .txt filename extension, whereas month?.txt refers only to those files that match the pattern month1.txt, month2.txt, montha.txt, month$.txt, and so on.

5

Q&A

Q Why do I need to master Windows 3.1 dialog boxes?

A For a long time to come, you'll use programs with Windows 95 that were written for the Windows 3.1 environment. Even though you'll be running those programs under Windows 95, the dialog boxes that you see when you open or save documents will take on the simple and less-powerful old style of dialog boxes.

Q Why should the document concept be so important to me when using Windows 95?

A Windows 95 is a document-centered operating environment. The Microsoft programmers realized when they designed Windows 95 that your focus should *not* be on the programs that you run, but on the data that your programs produce. Today's programs don't just produce text documents. They also produce graphics, sound, and compressed data that take on all kinds of different formats.

Once you master the management of documents you will have mastered the management of your own data files. You'll often want to share document files between different Windows 95 programs, and the document concept makes this file-sharing possible.

The document is so vital to the operation of Windows 95 that you'll find a Documents command on the Start menu.

Q Why would I want to cut or paste entire files?

A By cutting and pasting files, using the Clipboard as the go-between, you can perform copying or moving of files. Perhaps you need to move a file from one folder to another or from one disk to another. You'll first cut that file from its original location. When you cut a file, that file goes directly to the Windows 95 Clipboard awaiting your next command. When you copy a file, the file also goes to the Clipboard, but it stays in its original location as well. Once you send the file to the Clipboard by either means, you are free to paste the file elsewhere.

As a bonus, Windows 95 gives you the ability to use the mouse to drag-and-drop files from one location to another.

Q Why would I want to cut or paste specific sections of documents?

A Word processors have been able to copy, cut, and paste sections of text since their inception. Windows performs these functions on a global scale across files and applications. Sometimes you don't want a copy of an entire file, but only a word, sentence, or paragraph from that file. The selected text copy, cut, and paste operations work almost exactly like their document counterparts.

If you paste scraps of text onto the Windows 95 desktop, those scraps will remain on the desktop where you can retrieve them at another time.

5

Q What's the difference between the Clipboard and the Recycle Bin?

A The Clipboard is a temporary holding place for selected text and documents that you copy and cut. The Recycle Bin receives all documents that you delete. Before the Recycle Bin concept, you would find it difficult to recover deleted document files. With Windows 95, when you delete a document, it goes away from its current location, but Windows 95 saves the document in the Recycle Bin until you empty the Recycle Bin, as described in the next hour.

Both the Clipboard and the Recycle Bin can hold all types of documents.

Q Why use the Documents menu when I can open document files with File | Open from within my programs?

A The Documents menu is much quicker. Provided that a document's filename and icon appear on the Documents menu (and the name *will* appear if you've recently worked on that document and have not yet cleared the contents of the Documents menu), you can click on that document name, and Windows 95 starts the program needed to view and edit it. Without the Documents menu, you would have to start the program and then, in a second step, open the document you want to view and edit.

5

Hour 6

Explore the Windows 95 System

Windows 95 includes a comprehensive program that you might use every time you turn on your computer. The Windows 95 Explorer graphically displays your entire computer system in a hierarchical tree structure. With Explorer, you have access to everything inside your computer (and outside if you are networked). Even though the My Computer window also displays all the devices in your computer, Explorer can do so inside a single window whereas you must open separate windows for each device to see the contents of devices within the My Computer window. The advantage of the single window is that you have much more freedom to manage files, folders, icons, and even electronic mail using a single Explorer window.

This hour demonstrates the Windows 95 Explorer and shows you its ins and outs. You have already mastered some of Explorer's commands in the previous hour because Explorer uses some of the same copy and move techniques that Open dialog boxes use. Explorer goes far beyond the capabilities of dialog boxes, however, by letting you manipulate all of your computer's software and hardware. Once you've learned about Explorer, the hour wraps up by showing you some time- and disk-saving features of Windows 95.

The highlights of this hour include:

☐ How to change the various displays of the Windows 95 Explorer

☐ Why Explorer makes managing your computer painless

☐ Where to go when you want to find documents quickly

☐ What "shortcuts" are all about

☐ How to use the Recycle Bin

Hello, Windows 95 Explorer!

You'll find the Windows Explorer program listed on the Start menu's second cascaded menu. Click the Start button now to display the Start menu. Select **P**rograms, and then select Windows Explorer. The Explorer window will open up to look like the one shown in Figure 6.1. Figure 6.1 shows the Explorer screen fully maximized, but you can run Explorer in a smaller window if you want something else to appear on your screen as well.

Figure 6.1.

Explorer's opening window.

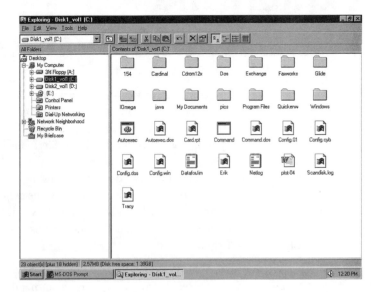

6

JUST A MINUTE

Your Explorer screen may look slightly different depending on your Windows 95 configuration. You'll see how to change your view of Explorer in the next task.

TIME SAVER

Quickly start Explorer by right-clicking over the Start menu and selecting Explore from the pop-up menu that appears.

The left side of the Explorer screen contains a hierarchical overview of your computer system. Click the vertical scroll bar on the left window, if there is one, to see the rest of the hierarchical system tree.

JUST A MINUTE

If a folder icon appears with a plus sign to the left of it, as the Windows folder does, that folder contains additional folders. Folder icons without the plus sign contain only documents (as you learned in Hour 5, "Cruise with Documents and Windows," a Windows 95 document might be any kind of file, including programs that you can run), but not additional folders. When you open a folder and display its contents, the plus sign changes to a minus sign, as you'll see in the first task.

The right window contains a pictorial overview of the contents of whichever device or folder that you select in the left window. The overview might contain large or small icons depending on the view you click. As you select different items in the left window, the right window changes to reflect your changes. Task 6.1 guides you through an initial exploration of Explorer.

Step Up

Did you ever use the full capabilities of the Windows 3.1 Program Manager and File Manager? Rarely do people, even experts, know or use all the capabilities in those programs. The two utility programs are simply too cumbersome to use all of their power.

The document architecture of Windows 95 goes a long way toward simplifying the things you could have done, but often did not do, in Program Manager. The Windows 95 Explorer makes working with the Windows 3.1 File Manager seem like working with a rock tablet and chisel. The Explorer is not just a disk and file manager but a complete system manager.

6

Instead of getting a single view of a single disk, Explorer continuously maps out your entire computer system so you can easily work with multiple hardware devices. The Windows 95 Explorer is not even limited to directories and files, but displays folders, including your networked folders, as well as online Microsoft Network and Internet services.

Task 6.1: Changing Explorer's View

Step 1: Description

This task teaches you how to adjust Explorer's display to see the Explorer screen in different ways. As you use Explorer, you may change the display to offer the best option for the information you're looking for at the time.

This task assumes that you've already started Explorer as requested in the previous section.

TIME SAVER

> There are several ways to do the very same things in Windows 95. You can start Explorer by right-clicking over the My Computer icon.

Step 2: Action

1. Scroll the left window pane until you see the icon for drive C in the window.

2. If you see a plus sign next to your C: icon in the left window (you may have to scroll the window's scroll bar to see the C: icon), click the plus sign to display the contents of drive C. The plus becomes a minus sign, and the left window opens the C: icon showing the list of folders and documents on drive C. Click the drive's minus sign again to close the window. Click once more to turn the plus to a minus and watch the right window. As you change between these two views of drive C (detailed and overview), watch the right window change.

JUST A MINUTE

> Notice that the right window does not change as you click the C: icon in the left window. The reason is that the right window always displays the contents of whatever you highlight in the left window. Whether or not the C: icon is open (with a minus sign) or closed (with a plus sign), the C: icon is highlighted. The right window displays that selected drive C's highest level folders and documents. If you were to click on one of those documents *on* drive C, the right window would then update to show the contents of that folder (don't click on a folder just yet).

6

3. Click on the highest level in the left window labeled Desktop, and Windows 95 displays the contents of your desktop in the right window. See Figure 6.2.

Figure 6.2.

You can view the desktop contents in the Explorer.

4. Click on the C: icon to display the contents of drive C. Depending on the contents and size of your drive C, the right window may contain a few or several document files.

5. Press Alt+V to open the **V**iew menu on the menu bar. Select **T**oolbar to display the toolbar of icons that appears right below the menu bar.

CAUTION

Your toolbar may already be on your Explorer screen. If so, selecting **V**iew I **T**oolbar will make the toolbar go away. Select **V**iew I **T**oolbar until you see the toolbar. A checkmark will appear next to **T**oolbar on the View menu.

The dropdown listbox at the left of the toolbar gives you a third access tool for swapping between devices, folders, and files on your computer. If you ever detail too much information than will fit in the left window, the dropdown listbox keeps the list smaller and more manageable, always giving you more of a high-level overview of your computer system.

Figure 6.3 shows the toolbar with its icons labeled. The toolbar offers push-button access to many commands that are on the Explorer menus.

6

Figure 6.3.

The toolbar makes common tasks easier.

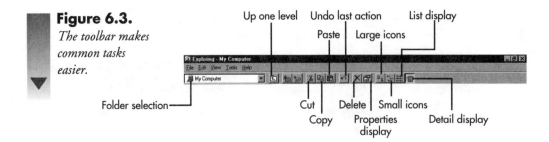

6. Display the **V**iew menu once again. The La**r**ge Icons window (the default display view) consumes most of the right window. Therefore, select **V**iew | **Sm**all Icons to gather more room in the right window. The **V**iew | **Sm**all Icons command shrinks the size of the icons to show more items at once in the right window.

7. Select **V**iew | **L**ist. Windows 95 Explorer retains the small icon sizes and displays the items by type of item (folders first and then documents).

8. Select **V**iew | **D**etails. Windows 95 Explorer displays the items in a detailed format that describes the name, type, and modified date of each item as shown in Figure 6.4.

Figure 6.4.

Sometimes you want more detail about the Explorer items.

As with the Open dialog box detailed lists, you can adjust the column widths of the three detailed columns in the right window by dragging the column title dividers with the mouse.

6

Click over Name, the title of the first detailed column in the right window. Watch the window's contents change as you then click over Type. Explorer sorts the display to appear in alphabetical order by type. Click the Modified column, and Explorer displays the items in reverse date order from most recent to the oldest. If you click any column twice in a row, Windows 95 sorts the column in reverse order.

9. If you want to see more of one of Explorer's windows, you can drag the vertical dividing line that falls between the two windows to the left or right. For example, if you want the left window to be smaller to make room for more large icons, drag the center column to the left and release the mouse when the left window is as small as you need it to be. (Remember that the mouse cursor changes shape when you place it at the proper position on the dividing column.)

Explorer will not update the display every time you resize a window. Therefore, if you enlarge the right window, Explorer does not automatically rearrange the right window's icons to fill up the newly enlarged space. The **V**iew | **R**efresh command will adjust the icons to fill the space evenly. Therefore, you'll almost always want to select **V**iew | **R**efresh after modifying Explorer's window sizes. Figure 6.5 shows an Explorer screen with a small left window.

Figure 6.5.
Adjust the Explorer window sizes if you need more room.

JUST A MINUTE

If you make the left or right window too small (such as this figure's left window is), Windows 95 adds a horizontal scroll bar to the small window so you can scroll its contents back and forth to see what's highlighted or to select another item.

10. The Explorer environment is always updating itself to reflect your current actions. Therefore, the right-click menu commands change depending on whether you select a text document, folder, sound document, graphic document, disk drive, or network drive. Click over a folder and click the right mouse button to see the menu that appears. Now, click the right mouse button over a document file, and you'll see a slightly different menu. The actions you might want to perform on a document are often different from the actions you might want to perform on a folder, and the menu reflects those differences. The right-click's pop-up menus are context-sensitive, so they contain only the options you can use at the time.

JUST A MINUTE

> When viewing your system and its folders inside Explorer, all of the techniques that you learned in the previous hour's discussion on Open dialog boxes apply for Explorer as well. For example, you can open a folder by double-clicking it, and then return to the previous (parent) folder by clicking the Up One Level icon on the Explorer's taskbar.

11. Many users will use Explorer to copy files to and from diskette drives and other kinds of drives such as networked drives. In the previous hour, you learned how to copy and move individual files, and as you see here, the same techniques apply inside Explorer.

Now that you're accustomed to copying and moving individual files, Explorer makes it easy to copy and move *multiple* files at once. Often, you want to put one or more files on a diskette to take to your home computer for weekend overtime (sure, you *want* to do that a lot!).

To select more than one document at a time, hold down the Ctrl key while clicking over each document that you want to select. You can even select folders as well as documents. When you select a folder and other document files to copy to a disk, for example, Windows 95 copies all of the document files *within* the folder, as well as the other document files you've selected, to the disk. Figure 6.6 shows an Explorer screen with several document files and a folder selected. The **File | Send To** command is about to send those files to the diskette in drive A.

6

Figure 6.6.
Select multiple documents and folders if you need to copy several at a time.

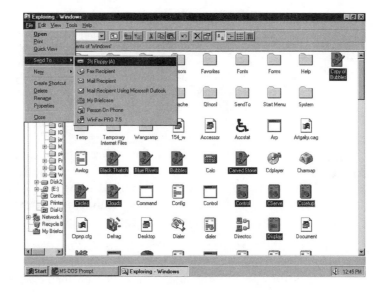

TIME SAVER

If you want to select all but one or two documents and folders inside a window, first Ctrl-click on the one or two that you *don't* want to select (which selects those) and choose **E**dit | **I**nvert Selection to reverse the selection. All the items that were not selected will now be selected, and the one or two that were selected are not selected anymore.

Step 3: Review

The Explorer windows give you both high-level and detailed overviews of your computer system and the computer's files. Explorer offers two windows for two different views: A computer-level view and a folder view, if you need one. Clicking on folder icons inside either window opens those folders and gives you a view of more documents and folders deeper within your computer system.

Once you display documents and folders, you are free to copy, move, delete, and rename those items as you learned to do in the previous hour inside the Open dialog boxes.

CAUTION

> You cannot select parts of a document to copy or move inside Explorer as you could do with Open dialog boxes. Remember that once you open a document using a program, such as a spreadsheet, you see the contents of that document. The text selection commands you learned in the previous hour selected text only from documents you had already opened; you cannot do that inside Explorer.

Step Up

The File Manager's windows displayed only a single disk drive at a time. Therefore, when you wanted to copy or move a file from one directory on one disk to another directory on a different disk, you had to open two windows using the File Manager non-intuitive menu. Then you had to select the two directories on the two disks, and *then* issue the command to copy or move.

The strength of Explorer is that your *entire computer system* appears in the left window at all times. When you want to drag a document or folder to a different directory on a completely different drive (or even to another computer on the network if you are connected to a network), the target disk drive always appears in the left window. As long as you've clicked the disk drive's plus sign to display that disk's directories, you can drop a file into that directory from elsewhere in the system.

The Explorer Options

Explorer supports various display options for the items inside its windows. As you'll recall from previous hours, Windows 95 supports the use of filename extensions. The **V**iew | **O**ptions command displays tabbed dialog boxes that let you control the items in the Explorer display.

Step Up

Windows 95 often uses filename extensions as a means of registering file types. Although two files of different types can have the same extension, the extension is often a clue as to the purpose of the file.

Task 6.2: Changing Explorer's Options

TASK

Step 1: Description

Different users require different output from the Explorer program. There are types of documents that you simply don't need to display during normal work inside Explorer. The system files are good examples of files that the typical user does not need to see.

In addition, the actual location of the file, known as the path, does not always match the system of embedded folders. (See Hour 4, "Take Windows 95 to Task," for more information on pathnames.) In other words, a document may be located inside two embedded folders shown with the Explorer display, but the actual file might be embedded three levels deep on your hard disk. The system of folders—but not always—matches the system of directories on your disk. If you need to know exactly where folders and documents are located on your disk drive, you can request that Explorer display the full pathname of those folders and documents.

Step 2: Action

1. Select the **View | O**ptions command to display the Options tabbed dialog box shown in Figure 6.7.

Figure 6.7.

The Options dialog box determines the appearance of Explorer.

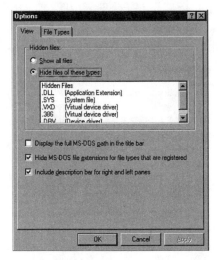

2. You can click either the **S**how all files option or the Hide files of these **t**ypes option to determine whether you want to see all types of documents in the Explorer windows. The types shown in the scrolling listbox are generally system-related files used internally by Windows 95 to keep track of system resources and inter-program communications.

3. If you click Display the full MS-DOS **p**ath in the title bar, Explorer displays a full pathname of selected documents in the *title bar* (the area above the right window's display that describes what you are viewing) every time you select one of the items in the left window.

4. The next option is Hide MS-DOS file **e**xtensions for file types that are registered. Windows 95 comes installed with several types of files already *registered,* and you may never need to register additional types. Registered files are files that Windows 95 recognizes by their filename extensions.

When you register a file type (as described in the next task), you tell Windows 95 the program for all files with that extension to associate to. Once registered, when you double-click that file's icon, Windows 95 starts the program you've associated with that file. For example, when you double-click a file with a .CDA extension, Windows 95 starts the CD Player application because CD Player is the application associated to all files that end in the .CDA extension.

TIME SAVER

If you are familiar with MS-DOS and filenames, you might feel more comfortable if you display the file extensions on the Explorer screen documents. Hiding the extensions reduces clutter in the right window, but with the extension, you can determine the exact name of the file when you need the exact name.

CAUTION

If you hide filename extensions in Explorer, Windows 95 hides those extensions in almost every other file listing. For example, if you hide Explorer's extension display, you will no longer see extensions in WordPad's Open dialog boxes. You won't even see them in applications that you purchase in addition to Windows 95 applications, such as Microsoft Excel.

5. Clicking the Include **d**escription bar for right and left panes turns on or off the display of the title bar. Windows 95 is inconsistent here; in the middle of the dialog box Windows 95 calls the title bar a *title bar,* and Windows 95 calls the title bar a *description bar* here. Nevertheless, getting rid of the title bar's display gives you additional room in the Explorer windows but removes the title bar's description for selected items.

Step 3: Review

If you don't like the way Explorer displays information, you can probably change the display. Explorer's options let you determine how documents appear, how large their windows are, and whether or not filename extensions should appear.

Task 6.3: Registering File Types

TASK

Step 1: Description

As the previous hour explained, Windows 95 makes the document, rather than the program, the focus of everything you do. When you want to edit a graphic image, you ought to be able to click on that image instead of starting a graphics program, and then loading the image from there. By registering file types, and the file's extension, you teach Windows 95 how to work with all files of that extension.

Suppose that someone designs a new graphics format after you begin using Windows 95. The format increases the computer's graphic compression ability and lets you store huge graphics files in a small amount of space. Suppose these compressed graphic files have an extension of .CPR and the program that displays those graphics is called Compress Graphics. You can associate the .CPR filename extension to the Compress Graphics program name so that when you click on any file whose extension is .CPR, even if that extension is not showing in the Explorer window, Windows 95 knows to start the Compress Graphics program and automatically loads the image you double-clicked.

This task shows you how to view and change any associations that currently reside on your system.

CAUTION

> You are probably better off *not* changing any file associations at this time. The only reason to change a current association is if you install a program you like that works with a certain type of file better than one already registered for that type. Most Windows 95 installation programs automatically register their file types when you install the programs. Therefore, this task is more informative than active so you can better understand the purpose of file associations.

Step 2: Action

1. Select the **View** | **O**ptions tabbed dialog box again if you don't have the dialog still showing from the previous task.

2. Click the tab marked File Types. You'll see the File Types dialog box shown in Figure 6.8.

Figure 6.8.

*The File Types
dialog box where
you register file
types.*

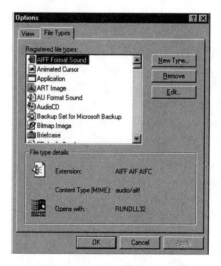

3. Click the item in the scrollable listbox labeled CD Audio Track. In the File type details portion of the dialog box you'll see that the extension associated with this file type name is .CDA and that CDPLAYER is the name of the program that automatically starts when you double-click any file with this .CDA extension. The icon you see also serves to identify the file type.

JUST A MINUTE

> When double-clicking a file to start that file's associated program, the file's extension does not have to show on the screen. Remember that many users hide the display of filename extensions when using Windows 95.

4. Click the Edit command button to see more information on .CDA file types. You'll see an additional dialog box, called the Edit File Type dialog box, appear. Figure 6.9 shows the Edit File Type dialog box.

6

Figure 6.9.

The Edit File Type dialog box controls the details of file associations.

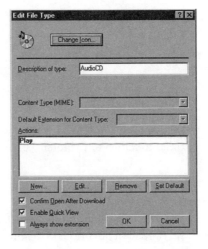

Here is where you select or change icons associated with registered file types. Every .CDA file appearing in Explorer (or in the Open dialog box displays) will have the same icon. You could select a different icon if you want (don't do so now). The **D**escription of type prompt displays a description of the file type for reference purposes. The **A**ctions describe the first thing the program must do. Given the screen shown in Figure 6.9 (your screen should not be too different), the .CDA files have an icon that contains a compact disc over a document, the description of this file type is *CD Audio track*, and the first thing the CDPLAYER program will do automatically, upon loading itself after you double-click a .CDA file, is execute the Play command. This plays the .CDA song file you've selected.

Each application has its own way of working with files. For example, a word processor would more than likely open a file so you could edit the file, but a song file, such as one stored on disk as a copy of a CD audio track, is usually played and not edited.

5. Click the **E**dit command button to see the lowest-level of detail available for file type associations. You'll see the Editing action dialog box shown in Figure 6.10 appear.

Figure 6.10.

The lowest level of detail available when you associate a file type.

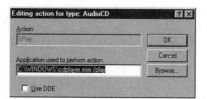

6. Now that you've seen what's involved with registering file types, press the Esc key three times to return to Explorer. Leave Explorer loaded for the next task.

Step 3: Review

The file type registration is fairly complex. Rarely will you have to associate files with applications because the application's installation program should register its file types automatically. You might be curious as to how Windows 95 "knows" how to open programs when you click over those programs' document files, however, so you may want to return to the File Types dialog box once in a while to study various file associations as you've done here for the .CDA audio file types.

JUST A MINUTE

Want to know what those song files are all about? The fourth part of this book, entitled "Into the Nighttime," describes the multimedia capabilities of Windows 95, including the CD Player program and audio files stored on your system.

Finding Information

These days, computers are powerful. Not only are they powerful but they hold *lots* of information, and wading through that information looking for something can be daunting. Windows 95 offers a powerful find feature, available both through Windows 95 Explorer, and on the Start menu, that searches your computer for files and folders that you are looking for.

JUST A MINUTE

The **F**ind system hunts for files and folders across networks, hard disks, floppy disks, CD-ROM drives, and even Microsoft's online service called *Microsoft Network*. This hour describes how to look for documents and folders on the disks and CD-ROM drives only, because that's where you'll be using **F**ind most of the time.

6

Task 6.4: Using Find

Step 1: Description

The **Find** command locates files that meet a search criteria. You can search an entire disk for a specific file or for a document that contains a certain word or phrase.

Have you used the Windows 3.1 File Manager to search for files? As you might expect, Windows 95 offers a more powerful tool for searching through documents and folders.

If you know a partial filename, you can find all files that contain that partial filename. If you want to search for a file that you modified two days ago, you can find all files with modified dates that fall on that day. You can even save searches that you perform often so you don't have to create the search criteria each time you need to search.

Step 2: Action

1. Display the **Tools** menu on the Explorer menu bar.

2. Select **Find**.

3. When the next menu appears, select **Files** or folders. The Find dialog box appears as shown in Figure 6.11.

Figure 6.11.

The Find dialog box searches across drives for specific documents and folders.

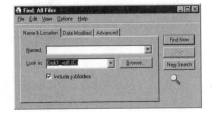

4. Leave the **Named** prompt empty. If you wanted to narrow the search down to specific documents and folders that meet a certain wildcard criteria, such as Acctg*, you could type this name search pattern here.

5. Type c:\WINDOWS in the **Look in** prompt. You are going to scan drive C's Windows folder looking for specific files.

CAUTION

> If your Windows folder is located on a different drive, type that drive's letter instead of c, or open the **Look** in dropdown listbox and select the drive and folder.

6

6. Leave the checkmark next to the Include subfolders option. Find searches the Windows folder as well as all folders within the Windows folder.

7. Click the Date Modified tab to display the Date Modified dialog box shown in Figure 6.12. Leave the All files option marked. If you wanted to limit your search to specific dates, the Find all files created or modified option lets you search only for files modified between a beginning and ending date or within the last few days or months.

Figure 6.12.

You can narrow the search to specific dates.

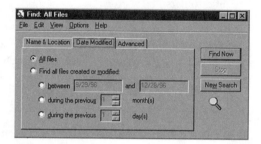

8. Click the Advanced tab to display the Advanced dialog box.

9. Open the Of type dropdown listbox, shown in Figure 6.13, to display a list of file types. These file types are actually descriptions for file types. (In the previous task you learned how to add descriptions for file types.) If you want to search for files of a certain type, such as for Microsoft Word 6 for Windows documents only, you can select that file type from the list, and Find ignores all files that don't match that selected type.

Figure 6.13.

Search through specific file types with the Advanced dialog box.

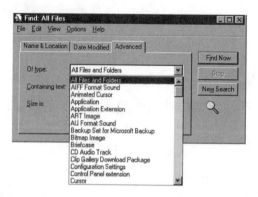

JUST A MINUTE

For this task keep All Files and Folders selected to perform a search across every file in the Windows folder.

10. Type wind at the **C**ontaining text prompt. You are directing Find to find all files in the Windows folder that contain the text *wind.* The value *wind* is called the *search string* (the string of characters that you want to search for).

11. With these options selected, Find will search for files of any size. However, you could narrow the search criteria even further by limiting the search to files of at least or at most (depending on your selection in the **S**ize is dropdown listbox) a specific number of kilobytes.

12. Click the **F**ind Now command button and wait a bit while Windows 95 scans your disk drive. The search may take a while depending on the speed of your computer and the number of files in your Windows folder.

TIME SAVER

During a long search you can click any button on the taskbar to start or switch to another program. The file search can continue in the background while you write a letter to someone or play a game.

13. When the search completes, the Find dialog box lists the files that meet your search criteria in the bottom portion of the Find dialog box. If there are several files that meet the criteria, Windows 95 displays vertical scroll bars so you can scroll through the list of choices.

   The list contains not only the document file's name, but also the folder the document's located in, the size of the document, the type of file, and the date and time the file was last modified.

14. If you select **F**ile | **S**ave Search, Windows 95 sends the find results and search criteria to an icon located on the desktop, where the results will be available for you at a later time, if you want to work with the list after closing Explorer.

15. Select **F**ile | **C**lose to close the dialog box.

TIME SAVER

Remember that the Start menu contains a Find command that displays the Find dialog box. The Start menu's Find command is available to you even when you're not using Explorer. You can both left-click and right-click the Start button to access the Find dialog box.

Step 3: Review

The searching capability of Windows 95 finds documents and folders on your system that match certain criteria that you provide. You can search for documents by name or by a search string. If you want to limit the search to specific modified date ranges you can do so.

Where Do the Deleted Files Go?

When you delete files using dialog boxes or Explorer, you now know that those files go to the Recycle Bin. Once in the Recycle Bin, those files are out of your way and deleted in every respect except one: They are not really deleted! Those files are gone from their original location, but they stay in the Recycle Bin until you empty the Recycle Bin.

Periodically, you'll want to check the Recycle Bin for files that you can erase completely from your hard disk. The following task explains the Recycle Bin in more detail.

TIME SAVER

> The Recycle Bin icon changes from an overflowing bin to an empty one when you empty the Recycle Bin. Therefore, you can tell at a glance whether or not your Recycle Bin is empty.

Task 6.5: Using the Recycle Bin

Step 1: Description

The Recycle Bin appears on your Windows 95 desktop. Any time you want to view or delete items from the Recycle Bin, display your desktop and access the Recycle Bin icon.

TIME SAVER

> If your desktop is completely covered up with running applications, you don't have to close those applications to see the desktop. Minimize your application windows until you can see the Recycle Bin on the desktop. If you want to quickly minimize your desktop open windows, right-click the taskbar and select **M**inimize All Windows.

Step 2: Action

1. Display your desktop by minimizing any open windows you may have on the screen.

2. Double-click the Recycle Bin icon. The Recycle Bin window opens up to one like the window shown in Figure 6.14.

6

Figure 6.14.

The Recycle Bin lists deleted files that you can recover.

Name	Original Location	Date Deleted	Type	Size
EGYPTALK	C:\My Documents	12/28/96 12:51 PM	Microsoft Word Doc...	19KB
ERRATA~1	C:\My Documents	12/28/96 12:51 PM	Microsoft Word Doc...	12KB
Fax for Janna-Luxor	C:\My Documents	12/28/96 12:51 PM	Microsoft Word Doc...	13KB
Fax order for A. Ca..	C:\My Documents	12/28/96 12:51 PM	Microsoft Word Doc...	19KB
GARYDISK	C:\My Documents	12/28/96 12:51 PM	Microsoft Word Doc...	17KB
CANYON	C:\WINDOWS\ME...	12/28/96 12:51 PM	MIDI Sequence	21KB
CHIMES	C:\WINDOWS\ME...	12/28/96 12:51 PM	Wave Sound	16KB
CHORD	C:\WINDOWS\ME...	12/28/96 12:51 PM	Wave Sound	25KB
DING	C:\WINDOWS\ME...	12/28/96 12:51 PM	Wave Sound	12KB
Bach's Brandenbu...	C:\WINDOWS\ME...	12/28/96 12:51 PM	MIDI Sequence	142KB
Beethoven's 5th S...	C:\WINDOWS\ME...	12/28/96 12:51 PM	MIDI Sequence	91KB
Beethoven's Fur El..	C:\WINDOWS\ME...	12/28/96 12:51 PM	MIDI Sequence	21KB
In the Hall of the ...	C:\WINDOWS\ME...	12/28/96 12:51 PM	MIDI Sequence	38KB
Jungle Asterisk	C:\WINDOWS\ME...	12/28/96 12:51 PM	Wave Sound	88KB
Jungle Close	C:\WINDOWS\ME...	12/28/96 12:51 PM	Wave Sound	141KB
Jungle Critical Stop	C:\WINDOWS\ME...	12/28/96 12:51 PM	Wave Sound	172KB
Jungle Default	C:\WINDOWS\ME...	12/28/96 12:51 PM	Wave Sound	138KB
Jungle Open	C:\WINDOWS\ME...	12/28/96 12:51 PM	Wave Sound	127KB
PASSPORT	C:\WINDOWS\ME...	12/28/96 12:51 PM	MIDI Sequence	23KB
GOTODLG.FRM	C:\WINDOWS\WA...	12/28/96 12:52 PM	FRM File	4KB
IMGSAMP.FRM	C:\WINDOWS\WA...	12/28/96 12:52 PM	FRM File	42KB
IMGSAMPL.VBP	C:\WINDOWS\WA...	12/28/96 12:52 PM	VBP File	2KB

31 object(s)   1.36MB

3. If you've been following along in this book so far, you should have one or two files already in the Recycle Bin. There may be many more, depending on what has taken place on your system. You'll recognize the format of the Recycle Bin's column headings; you can adjust the width of the columns by dragging the column separators with your mouse.

JUST A MINUTE

If you've deleted portions of a file (the scraps), the Name column contains the first few characters from that deleted text.

4. The bottom of the Recycle Bin contains the total number of *bytes* (characters) the deleted files consume on your disk. In other words, if you were to empty the entire contents of the Recycle Bin in Figure 6.14, you would add a total of 303 kilobytes of free space to your computer system. Look at your Recycle Bin's *status bar* (the bar of information at the bottom of dialog boxes), to see how much free space you could regain by emptying your Recycle Bin.

6

CAUTION

The Recycle Bin dialog box contains *all* deleted files on your system—*not* just the deleted files on one of your disk drives.

5. Most of the Recycle Bin dialog box's menu bar commands are identical to the commands on Open dialog boxes and the Explorer. There is even a Recycle Bin toolbar that you might want to display if you plan to work a lot with the Recycle Bin. (You can display the toolbar with **View | Toolbar**.) When you select an item (or more than one item using a Ctrl+click), the menu commands apply to that selected item.

6. Double-click one of the Recycle Bin's items to display a Properties dialog box for that item. It tells you additional information about the deleted item, such as the date you created and deleted the item. Figure 6.15 shows a Properties dialog box. If you wanted to delete only that selected item, you could do so. If you selected more than one item, you could delete them also.

Figure 6.15.

You may display the properties of any selected item.

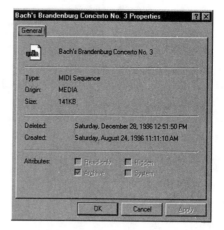

7. Perhaps the most important menu command is File | Empty Recycle Bin. This command empties the entire Recycle Bin. You can select this command now, if there is nothing in your Recycle Bin that you think you'll need later.

8. Select **File | Close** to close the Recycle Bin dialog box.

TIME SAVER

Select **V**iew to look at a Recycle Bin document if you want to verify the contents before deleting the document.

JUST A MINUTE

Using a dialog box, Windows 95 asks once more if you are sure you want to empty the Recycle Bin. This precaution ensures that you don't inadvertently erase files that you might really need.

6 ▼

Step 3: Review

The Recycle Bin lets you delete files without really removing those files from your disk. All deleted files go to the Recycle Bin. Those files are not truly deleted from your disk until you empty the file from the Recycle Bin. You can empty a single selected file, several selected files, or the entire Recycle Bin.

CAUTION

Remember that the Recycle Bin does not hold files you delete from the MS-DOS prompt. When you use MS-DOS to delete a file, Windows 95 erases the file as soon as you issue the command. Unlike the MS-DOS that came with earlier versions of Windows, Windows 95's MS-DOS does not include an UNDELETE command. Make sure you want to delete a file when you issue the MS-DOS DEL or ERASE commands.

Making Windows 95 Easier

There are numerous ways to make Windows 95 easier for your day-to-day work. Three often confusing time-saving techniques are

- ☐ Changing the Start menu
- ☐ Adding single-key access to programs
- ☐ Shortcuts

It's not that these three time-saving techniques are difficult to understand, but they are difficult to set up. Once you set them up, though, these three techniques make life easier for the Windows 95 user. Once you create single-key access to a program, or a shortcut, or change the Start menu, those time-savers stay in effect, making work inside Windows 95 much more efficient.

Task 6.6: Adding Time-Savers

Step 1: Description

The time-savers described in this task may not be for everyone, but they often help users of Windows 95. You'll have to experiment with the techniques until you find the ones that help you the most.

Step 2: Action

1. You can add programs to the Start menu by displaying the Start menu and selecting Settings.

6

TASK

2. Select **T**askbar from the **S**ettings menu.

3. The tabbed Taskbar Properties dialog box appears that you learned about in the last hour. Click the Start Menu Programs tab to display the Start Menu Programs dialog box shown in Figure 6.16.

Figure 6.16.

Add or remove programs from the Start menu here.

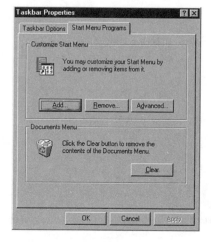

4. Suppose that you want to put the Windows 95 Calculator program (normally found on the Accessories menu) on the Start menu. You would click the **A**dd menu button to display the Create Shortcut dialog box shown in Figure 6.17.

Figure 6.17.

Use the Create Shortcut dialog box to add a specific program to the Start menu.

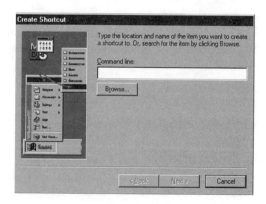

CAUTION

6

Before adding programs to the Start menu, you must know the command and location of the program you are adding. If you do not know the path to the program, you can use the **B**rowse command button to search the computer for the program.

5. Type c:\windows\calc.exe at the **C**ommand line text prompt. If your version of Windows 95 resides on a drive other than C, change the prompt accordingly. The Windows 95 calculator program's exact filename is calc.exe, and the program is stored in the Windows 95 directory (folder), which is usually named windows.

6. Click Next to move to the next screen in the dialog box. Figure 6.18 shows the dialog box that appears.

Figure 6.18.

You must tell
Windows 95 where
to store the shortcut.

7. The Select Program Folder tells Windows 95 where to place the icon and program labeled Calc. If you want to place the program on the Start menu, double-click Start Menu at the top of the scrolling listbox. (If you prefer to have the calculator appear in a menu that cascades off from the Start menu, select a folder and double-click over the folder.) In the Select Program Folder dialog box each folder represents a menu.

8. Once you select a location for the shortcut, Windows 95 displays one last dialog box asking for a name that will appear as that program's title on the menu. Leave the Calc title if you're following along on this example.

9. Click the Finish command button to finish the process. When the dialog box goes away, the Taskbar Properties dialog box reappears.

10. Close the Taskbar Properties dialog box by clicking OK.

11. Display the Start menu. As shown in Figure 6.19, the Start menu contains the calculator program that is now only two clicks away at any time.

CAUTION

Don't change the Start menu too dramatically until you are comfortable with Windows 95. The Start menu is probably best left alone in its current helpful state until you get more acquainted with Windows 95. If you share a computer with others, you could confuse your co-workers if you change the Start menu too much.

Figure 6.19.
*You can now access
the calculator
quickly within
Windows 95.*

Shortcuts

The name *shortcut* has a double-meaning in Windows 95—one of the reasons that this task's time-savers can get confusing.

A shortcut is actually better termed an *alias file*. When you create a shortcut—whether that shortcut is a shortcut menu command, such as having the calculator now on the Start menu bar, or whether that shortcut is a shortcut you create in Open dialog boxes or through Explorer—Windows 95 does not make a copy of the calculator program in every location where you place the icon. Windows 95 actually creates a *link* to that program, called a *shortcut* in Windows 95 terminology, that points to the program on your disk wherever its location may be.

If you were to right-click over a document or folder in Explorer's right window, you would see the Create **S**hortcut command that creates a shortcut to the document or folder you are pointing at. Windows 95 creates a new icon and title (the title begins with Shortcut to_) but does not actually create a copy of the item. Instead, Windows 95 creates a link to that item. The link reduces disk space taken up by multiple copies of the same files. You may create a shortcut even to a networked item that resides on a different computer altogether; the networked shortcut appears to exist on your own computer's desktop or menu, while it actually resides on the other machine.

12. Delete the Calculator program from the Start menu (you can add it later if you really want it there) by selecting **S**ettings | **T**askbar from the Start menu, selecting the Start Menu Programs tab, and clicking the **R**emove command button. Instead of the Create Shortcut dialog box, the Select Program Folder box appears next. Double-Click the Programs folder under the Start Menu icon, as highlighted in Figure 6.18.

13. Select the Calc icon and click the Remove command button to remove the calculator program from the Start menu, and return to the Start Menu Programs tabbed dialog box.

6

14. Press the Advanced command button. Windows 95 starts the Explorer program.

15. If you click the programs folder, Explorer displays the items in the Start menu's first set of cascaded menus as shown in Figure 6.20.

Figure 6.20.

Explorer starts so that you can add a single-key quick access to any program.

16. Open the Accessories folder to view the contents of the Accessories group. Remember that you're viewing contents of the Accessories menu that cascades from the Start menu. You'll see the Calculator icon appear in this folder group.

17. Right-click over the Calculator icon to display a menu.

18. Select Properties to display the Calculator program's Properties tabbed dialog box.

19. Click the Shortcut tab to display the dialog box shown in Figure 6.21.

20. Press Alt+K to move the cursor to the Shortcut key text prompt. Type the letter C at the prompt. Windows 95 changes the C to Ctrl + Alt + C on the screen. Ctrl+Alt+C is now the shortcut for the Calculator program. If you run a program that uses a shortcut key you've added to Windows 95, the program's shortcut key takes precedence over the Windows 95 shortcut key.

21. Click the OK command button to close the dialog box.

22. Select File | Close to exit Explorer.

Whenever you press Ctrl+Alt+C, Windows 95 starts the calculator program. This single-key shortcut (actually a simultaneous three-key shortcut) enables you to start programs instantly, from virtually anywhere in the Windows 95 system, without having to locate the program's menu or icon.

Figure 6.21.

You can now add a single-key shortcut that will start the calculator program.

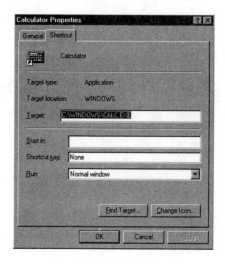

Step 3: Review

You can now add a shortcut to the Start menu, to any of Start's cascaded menus, to the desktop, and even a single-key shortcut to the programs you use most often. Although it may not always be obvious how to create shortcuts, each of the ones presented in this section helps you get started faster with the programs that you want to run.

Just wait until you get to Hour 8's chapter! Hour 8 explains a faster way to add programs to your Start menu. As you'll learn throughout this book, Windows 95 typically gives you many ways to do different jobs. The taskbar at the bottom of your screen provides many shortcuts as Hour 8, "Manage Your Desktop," explains.

Summary

This hour showed you how to use the Explorer to search your computer system for documents and folders, as well as how to manage the computer system using a uniform interface for all your storage devices. Copying and moving among folders and documents are painless functions when you use Explorer's two-window interface. You can display the item to be moved in the right window and drag that item to any device listed in the left window. It is also inside Explorer that you associate file types to programs so that you can click a document and run the appropriate program that works with that particular type of document.

Not only can Explorer help you manage your system, it also helps you locate information quickly. By using the Find command in Explorer (also available from the Start menu), you can search for files based on the file name, contents, size, and date last modified.

6

There are three shortcuts that help you access your programs. You can add a shortcut to the desktop, to the Start menu system, and even to the keyboard to start programs quickly.

Workshop

Term Review

byte   One character of storage.

Explorer   A powerful system-listing application that gives you both high-level and detailed descriptions of your computer system and the files on the system.

Microsoft Network   An online service available from Microsoft.

registered   A file is registered when you've associated an application with that file's extension.

search string   A string of one or more characters, such as a filename, that you want to search for.

shortcut   When you create a shortcut by adding programs to the Start menu or by creating shortcuts within Explorer or within Open dialog boxes, Windows 95 creates a link (the *shortcut*) to that item instead of wasting disk space with two separate files that have the same contents.

status bar   A message area at the bottom of a window that updates to show you what is happening at any given moment. For example, when you click over a menu item, the status bar tells you what that menu item will do.

title bar   A location above many Windows 95 windows (such as the Explorer right-hand window) that describes the documents you are currently viewing.

Q&A

Q Why does it seem as if much of the Explorer functions are available elsewhere, such as in the My Computer window and in Open dialog boxes?

A You can find *many* of Explorer's capabilities elsewhere. Windows 95 is known for giving you the tools that you need where you need them. Many other operating environments, including previous versions of Windows, put their tools in one place, which made you hunt for the proper program tool when you needed to do something such as move a file.

Windows 95 makes its tools available to you from a variety of locations because you'll often need to perform the same tasks while doing a wide range of activities.

6

Q **Why would I use Windows Explorer to copy or move files when I can do the same thing from the Open dialog boxes as I learned in the previous hour?**

A Don't confuse the ability to copy and move files within dialog boxes with that same ability within Explorer. It is true that you can copy and move from either. The one you decide to use depends on your current Windows 95 activity. For example, if you are in the middle of using a word processor, opening, and saving documents, you might decide to copy or move a file from one location to another. You might as well display the Open dialog box to do that. If, however, you are not working on a Windows 95 application, but want to copy or change files around, start Explorer from the desktop and use Explorer to handle the task. In addition, you cannot move or copy files between hardware devices in Open dialog boxes, but you can with Explorer.

Q **Do files that I delete, but have yet to empty from the Recycle Bin, still consume disk space?**

A Certainly. The Recycle Bin *must* keep the entire file intact or you would not be able to recover it from the Recycle Bin if you needed the file again. Although files in the Recycle Bin consume disk space, they are retrievable at any time until you empty the Recycle Bin.

Only after emptying the Recycle Bin, does Windows 95 physically delete the file from your disk. Once it is gone from the Recycle Bin, you cannot recover the file. If you get short on disk space, the first thing you should do is search the Recycle Bin for any and all files there that you can delete.

Q **I'm confused; are there *three* kinds of shortcuts?**

A There are three versions of shortcuts in Windows 95. You can add a single-key shortcut key to any program. When you press Ctrl+Alt and that key at the same time, Windows 95 starts that program. You could be working in Explorer, at the desktop, or in virtually any other program, but when you press that shortcut keystroke, Windows 95 starts the program you've assigned to that shortcut key.

When you right-click over a document or folder and select the Create **S**hortcut command, Windows 95 creates a shortcut to the item, which is really an alias name that knows the location of the original document or folder, but that acts like a copy of the item.

When you add items to the Start menu (or any menu cascading out from the Start menu), you must create a shortcut to that item because you don't want a copy of the same program all over your disk drive. Therefore, the menu command will be a shortcut to the program that, once you select that menu item, finds the program on the disk drive and starts the program.

6

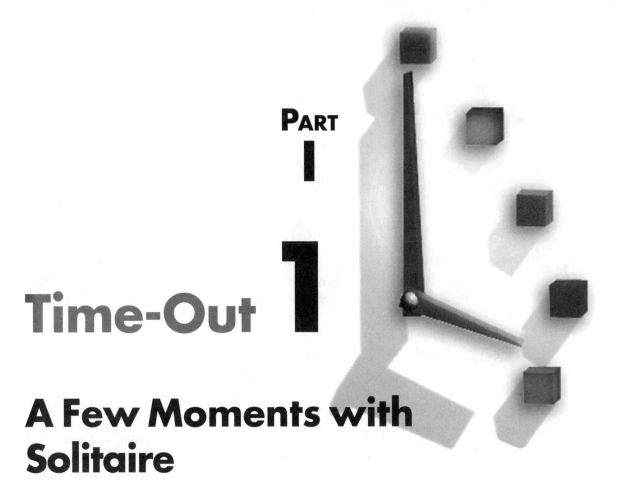

Time-Out 1

A Few Moments with Solitaire

People use Windows 95 to help them get their work done. Windows 95 is not an end unto itself; when you use Windows 95, you use it to launch programs and manage documents. To be proficient with Windows 95 means that you are proficient at starting programs, using the mouse, selecting from Windows 95-style menus, as well as performing many other tasks that improve the way you work with your computer.

On Your Mark...

If Windows 95 is for serious computing, then why are we wasting time with games?

Between each of this book's four major sections is a time-out from your 24-hour tutorial. You'll have fun with Windows 95 during these time-outs. The reason for these time-outs is three-fold:

☐ If you are new to the Windows 95 environment, there is no better or faster way to improve your mouse and keyboard skills than with games or other recreational computer activities.

☐ Over time, you will run across these programs that come with Windows 95 and wonder what they're all about. These time-outs will satisfy your curiosity ahead of time.

☐ The time-outs are really fun!

These time-outs are not heavy and long. The time-outs simply get you started running the program and give you overviews of the programs' operations.

JUST A MINUTE

Once you get started, you can access the programs' online help to get detailed help, if you need it. You'll probably need little help, though, because these programs are easy to use.

Get Set...

Follow these steps to start the Solitaire game:

1. Click the Start button to display the Start menu.
2. Select the **Programs** command to display the top-level menu of programs on your computer.
3. Select the Accessories command to display the Accessories menu.
4. Open the Games menu and select Solitaire. Windows 95 loads and runs the Solitaire game. Your screen will look something like the screen in Figure T1.1.
5. Your screen will contain a different set of dealt cards because Windows 95 Solitaire deals a different hand every time the program begins. Also, your cards may have a different backing than the card backs shown in Figure T1.1. If so, go ahead and change the card backs to match the figure because the card back is animated; during play, the sun sometimes makes a face at you to divert your attention.

1

Figure T1.1.

The Solitaire game that you can play during your time-out.

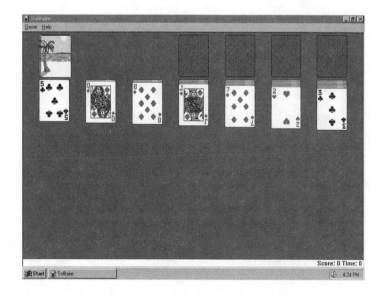

Select **G**ame | De**c**k to display the list of card back choices shown in Figure T1.2. Double-click over the palm tree back, and the playing screen returns with the new palm tree backing.

Figure T1.2.

The Select Card Back box offers you a variety of card styles.

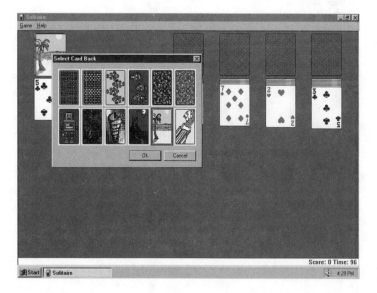

Go!

You can now start the game. The purpose of Solitaire is to place all of the cards in the four blank areas in the upper-right area of the screen. These four stacks are called the *suit stacks* because each area will eventually hold a stack of cards from the same suit.

You must build the suit stacks from Ace (the *low card*) to the King (the *high card*). Once you've sent all 52 cards from the rest of the screen to the suit stacks, you win the game and see an animated card dance. (Winning is not easy and requires both luck and skill.)

If an Ace appears anywhere on the screen, at any time, you can double-click that Ace to send the Ace to start a new suit stack. Once you send an Ace you can then send a two, three, and so on, until you build the entire suit in each stack. Whenever you see the next card from any of the suit stacks, you can double-click that card to put the card on the stack. In Figure T1.1, there are no Aces showing so you cannot put a card on a suit stack yet. You'll have to begin rearranging and displaying cards in the lower portion of the screen to find cards to send to the suit stack.

TIME SAVER

You also can drag the card from the lower area of the screen to the suit stack. After playing Solitaire for a while, you'll be a pro at dragging with the mouse.

Before building on a suit stack, you've got to find cards on the screen that go there. The seven stacks of cards, called the *row stacks,* that you see in the middle of the screen build downward. Row stacks are made from high cards to low cards and alternate from red to black. In other words, you always can place a red 8 on a black 9, and you always can place a black Queen on a red King.

If you can drag and drop a card on any of the seven row stacks to another stack, you should do so. For example, study Figure T1.1. The 2 of hearts (a red card) can be dragged to the 3 of clubs (a black card). Dragging the red 2 to the black 3 produces the screen shown in Figure T1.3.

1

Figure T1.3.

A row stack is beginning to grow.

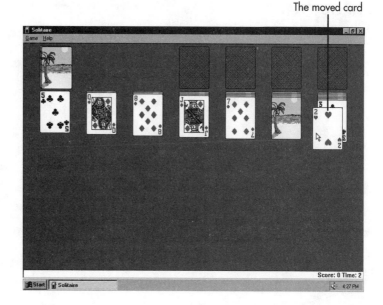

The moved card

There are cards left but still face down where the 10 of hearts originally resided. Click on the hidden row stack to uncover the next card. If the card is an Ace, you can place that Ace on a suit stack as described earlier. If the card can go on a row stack, you can drag the card there. If nothing can be done with the card at this time, look elsewhere for a card.

TIME SAVER

You can move more than one card from one row stack to another. For example, in Figure T1.4, the entire third row stack of shown cards can go to the fourth stack because a red 3 of diamonds (the 3's suit) can go to a 4 of spades (a black card). Therefore, you can click and drag the 3, which drags *all other cards below the 3*, to the 4's row stack.

Figure T1.4.

You can move entire row stacks to other stacks.

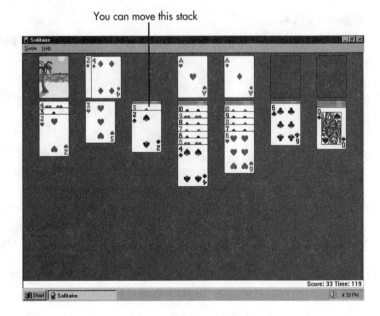

After you've rearranged and built the row stacks (and possibly added cards to the suit stack) as far as you can with the displayed cards, you'll have to deal from the deck in the upper-left corner. Click the deck to deal cards.

CAUTION

Solitaire always deals three cards at a time, as is the standard Solitaire rule. You can change the number of cards dealt through the **O**ptions menu if you want to change the way you play the game.

If you can place the card showing on top of the three dealt cards on a suit stack or a row stack, you can drag the card to that location. If you can do nothing with the dealt card, you'll have to deal again. Once you deal all the cards, you can deal once again by clicking on the deal stack twice. Solitaire monitors all your moves to ensure that you don't place the wrong card somewhere. If you attempt to move a card where it does not belong, Solitaire will move the card back.

The game continues until you complete all four suit stacks, or until you run through all the dealt cards without being able to drag one to another stack. Solitaire keeps track of a score in the lower-right corner as you play your cards. The faster you win a game, the higher the score.

PART

II

Accessories in the Afternoon

Hour

Hour 7

A Call for Help

This hour shows you how to help yourself! That is, how to help yourself find help when using Windows 95. Although this book is *really* all you'll ever need to use Windows 95 effectively (self-promotion was never one of the author's weak points!), when you get confused, Windows 95 offers a good set of online tools that you can access to find out how to accomplish a specific task.

If you've used previous versions of Windows, there are parts of the Windows 95 screens that may be confusing due to the Windows 95 implementation differences. The Windows 95 online help system lets you point to an item on the screen and request specific help on that item.

The highlights of this hour include:

- [ ] Why Windows 95 includes online help
- [ ] How to access the help system
- [ ] What Roving Help is all about
- [ ] When to use the help system to display the Welcome Screen

Introducing Help

Even Windows 95 experts need help now and then with Windows 95. Windows 95 is simply too vast, despite its simple appearance and clean desktop, for users to know everything about the system. Windows 95 includes a powerful *online* help system. Because it is online, the help system is available whenever you need it. For example, if you are working with Explorer and forget how to send a document to the disk, you can search the online help system for the words *send to* and Windows 95 gives you advice on how to locate and use the Send To command.

There is a tremendous number of ways you can request help while working in Windows 95. There is also a tremendous number of places from which you can get help. This hour focuses on the most common ways that you'll use online help and also offers tips along the way. The next task explains how to access the top-level online help features.

JUST A MINUTE

To use every help feature available to you in Windows 95, you'll need Internet access. Microsoft keeps up-to-date helpful advice on the Web. In addition, some help is available on all Windows 95 installations, but you'll need your Windows 95 CD-ROM to access the Windows 95 Tour described in this hour.

Task 7.1: Accessing Help from the Start Menu

Step 1: Description

The taskbar is always available to you no matter what else you are doing in Windows 95. Even if you've hidden the taskbar behind a running program, the taskbar is available as soon as you point the mouse to the bottom of the screen. You'll find a **Help** command on the taskbar's Start menu. The **Help** command displays the online help's primary dialog boxes that enable you to access the help system.

Step 2: Action

1. Click the Start button to display the Start menu.

2. Select **Help** to request online help. After a brief pause, you will see the Help tabbed dialog box, shown in Figure 7.1.

   The dialog box shown in Figure 7.1 shows the initial Help command's screen, with the first tabbed dialog box selected. Task 7.2 explains how you access this dialog box's help information.

7

Figure 7.1.

The Help Contents dialog box displayed from the Start menu.

CAUTION

> Depending on the date of your Windows 95 release, you may see a slightly different screen.

3. Actually, your help dialog box might look different from the one in Figure 7.1 because, depending on your system's recent usage, another tab might be selected in the dialog box. Also, another one of the three tabbed dialog boxes may be selected when you issue the **H**elp command from the Start menu.

Figure 7.2 shows the dialog box that appears if the second tab, labeled Index, is selected when you see the Help screen. If you do not see this dialog box now, click the Index tab to display the Index dialog box.

Figure 7.2.

The Index dialog box.

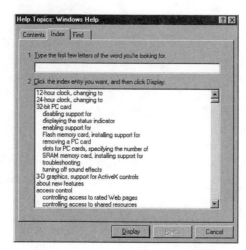

Task 7.4 explains how to use the Index dialog box's helpful information.

4. If you click the third tab, labeled Find, you may get the help dialog box shown in Figure 7.3 or you may get a dialog box labeled Find Setup Wizard, shown in Figure 7.4.

Figure 7.3.

The Find dialog box.

Figure 7.4.

The Find Setup Wizard dialog box.

If you see the Find Setup Wizard dialog box, you will have to execute the wizard to create a table of contents for the Find dialog box. Accept the default wizard values as you follow the wizard screens to build the Find contents. After a brief pause, Windows 95 displays the Find dialog box, shown in Figure 7.3. Task 7.5 explains how to use the Find dialog box when looking for online help.

7

5. Click the first tab, labeled Contents, to prepare for the next task.

TIME SAVER

Increase your help text's font size if you have difficulty reading the help windows. Right-click over the help window and select **O**ptions from the pop-up menu. Click Tab to display the Tab dialog box, and select a font size option. When you close the dialog box, your help windows will display their text in the new font size.

Wizards in Help

A *wizard* is a Windows 95 routine that guides you through a process of some kind. The wizard that executes when you first select the Find help dialog box builds a table of contents for the Find searches. You can build a small online help database (the default recommended choice) or a large online help database that will offer a more complete base of online help but will consume a tremendous amount of your disk space. Rarely will a Windows 95 user need to take up so much disk space as the maximized help database would take.

The reason that you may not see the wizard's screens is that someone else may have already run the wizard and built the help database for you.

Step 3: Review

The Start menu contains a **H**elp command that displays a tabbed dialog box of online help information. The first time you use the online help system, Windows 95 will have to build a table of contents for the Find dialog box. If you are using Windows 95's help system for the first time, you'll probably have to follow the wizard's instructions to build the table of contents.

Task 7.2: Using the Contents Help Dialog Box

Step 1: Description

The Contents dialog box portion of the Start menu's **H**elp command offers an overview of the Windows 95 environment. You may want to scan through the Contents dialog box, but you already know enough Windows 95 that much of the information will be repetitious for you.

JUST A MINUTE

Your version of the Contents dialog box may differ from the one shown in this task, depending on the date of your Windows 95 system.

7

Step 2: Action

1. The first help item in the Contents dialog box—Windows, the Web, and You—
   starts the Windows 95 Internet Explorer application, shown in Figure 7.5. If
   you've got Internet access, you can log into the Internet and read the online
   Windows 95 help on Microsoft's Web site. The site includes documentation not
   available at the time Microsoft created your Windows 95 CD-ROM. In addition,
   the site includes help with maximizing your use of Windows 95 and the Internet.

Figure 7.5.

*Learning about
Windows 95 on
Microsoft's Web site.*

2. The second item in the Contents dialog box starts a 10-minute tour of Windows
   95. Generally, you'll need a CD-ROM drive on your computer, and the Windows
   95 distribution CD-ROM must be in the drive. When you click on the item
   labeled "Tour: Ten minutes to using Windows," the tour will begin, and after a
   brief pause, you will see the tour control screen, shown in Figure 7.6.

   If you want to take a break and watch the Windows 95 tour, do so now. Click the
   Exit button to return to the Contents dialog box when you finish. If you installed
   the tour option when you installed Windows 95, you will not need the CD-ROM.

3. The remaining items on the Contents dialog box are marked with book icons. If
   you double-click an item next to a book, the book opens up and additional topics
   appear (like a folder that opens to show other documents and folders). Click the
   topic labeled How To, and you'll see a long list (scrollable with the vertical scroll
   bar to the right of the window) of topics from which you can choose.

7

Figure 7.6.

Beginning to take a tour of Windows 95.

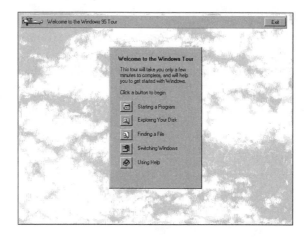

TIME SAVER

If you double-click on an open book icon, that topic (and the book) closes and the sub-topics disappear. The closed and open books work like the collapsed and expanded Explorer folders that display plus and minus signs to show their open and closed states. (Refer to Hour 6 for more details.)

4. Keep clicking on the topics (opening each book icon) until you see an icon next to a topic that contains a question mark sitting on a document. When you click on one of these document icons, Windows 95 will display a help screen like the one shown in Figure 7.7.

Figure 7.7.

A Windows 95 help topic.

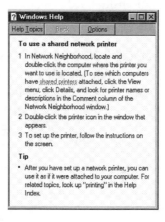

The small help topic dialog boxes stay on your screen even when you switch to other tasks. Therefore, if you want help on a topic such as moving a file, you can first display the help topic related to file moving, and then start Explorer. The help topic will remain on the screen while you use Explorer.

> You can move and resize a help topic dialog box just as you can other kinds of windows.

JUST A MINUTE

When a help topic's dialog box contains green underlined text, that text is a *cross-referenced help topic*. You can click on the text to display a description of its topic. The help topic dialog box remains on the screen while you read the underlined text's cross-reference.

5. Most help topic dialog boxes contain buttons labeled Related Topics. When you click this button, Windows 95 displays a list of cross-referenced topics that, when you click on one of them, display a different dialog box containing a description of that related topic.

Step Up

The help screens in Windows 3.1 generally consumed large windows. Often, when you maximized a help window you *still* could not read all the help text in the window at once.

Windows 95's help screens are much more manageable. Microsoft wrote the Windows 95 help screens to be smaller and more numerous than Windows 3.1's help screens. Therefore, when you display a help topic in Windows 95, that topic usually takes only a small window that measures, at most, a quarter of your screen. The small size of the help topic screens lets you keep that screen displayed over other programs without the help window getting in your way.

Step 3: Review

The Contents dialog box offers an overview of tasks that you might want to perform while working in Windows 95. When using the Contents dialog box, your goal (unless you want to take the Windows 95 tour) is to find the topic you want help with and display that topic's dialog box. From the topic dialog box you can look at cross-referenced help items and related topics.

7

Task 7.3: Traverse Help Topic Dialog Boxes

TASK

Step 1: Description

Rarely do you view one help topic dialog box at a time. Typically, you'll get help on a topic, and then decide that you want help on another topic. You'll use the help topic dialog box command buttons to move back and forth between other help dialog boxes.

Step 2: Action

1. Figure 7.8 shows a help dialog box with three command buttons at the top of the box labeled Help **T**opics, **B**ack, and **O**ptions. (Small command buttons also appear on the help page itself so you can link to other help topics.)

Figure 7.8.

Help topic dialog boxes appear with command buttons.

2. If you click the Help **T**opics command button, Windows 95 displays the Contents dialog box once again.

3. If you need to select several related help topics in succession, each topic will appear in its own dialog box. You can back up one topic at a time by clicking the **B**ack command button.

4. The **O**ptions command button displays a menu of commands you can use to change the way you use the help system. If you select the **A**nnotate command, Windows 95 displays a miniature text editor on which you can type notes that Windows 95 will attach to the help topic.

   Subsequently, when you display that annotated help dialog box, you'll see a paper clip icon at the top which indicates that there is an annotated reference available when you want to read it. Click the paper clip to read, change, or delete the annotation.

5. The Copy command sends the dialog box's help text to the Windows 95 Clipboard. From there, you can later paste it into another area.

6. The **P**rint Topic command prints the contents of the help dialog box. A Print dialog box will appear. Print dialog boxes are explained in Hour 15, "Increase Printing Power."

7. There are three font sizes: small, normal (the default), and large. You can change the font size by selecting **O**ption | **F**ont from the help topic dialog box. By making a help topic dialog box's font smaller, you can display more help in a smaller dialog box.

8. The next command on the **O**ptions menu determines whether or not the help menu stays on the screen on top of all other windows when you change to a different task. As mentioned earlier in this hour, the help dialog box always stays on the screen. You can change this default behavior by modifying the value of the **K**eep Help on Top command on the **O**ptions menu.

9. The last command on the **O**ptions menu changes the help topic dialog box colors to the Windows 95 system colors so that the information inside the help dialog boxes matches the colors of your regular Windows 95 windows. Ordinarily, the help topics display is a pale shade of yellow, simulating the yellow sticky notes you can attach to papers around the house or office.

10. If you've been following along and viewing the menu commands so far, close the help topic dialog box now. You can press Esc to close the dialog box quickly.

TIME SAVER

All of the **O**ptions menu commands are available if you right-click the mouse button over the help topic dialog box.

Step 3: Review

The command buttons at the top of the help topics contain extra power that lets you maneuver back and forth within the help system, as well as change the appearance of the help that you request.

Task 7.4: Using the Index Help Dialog Box

Step 1: Description

When you want Windows 95 to find a specific topic in the online help system, click the tabbed dialog box labeled Index. Windows 95 displays the Index dialog box. Here you can ask the online help system to search for topics for you. (You had to find your own topics when using the Contents help system.)

All three of the online help system's tabbed dialog boxes eventually display their helpful advice using the same set of small dialog boxes. The help method that you decide to use depends greatly on how you want to approach that topic. If you want to find help on a specific topic, you are better off looking for that topic in the Index or Find tabbed dialog box rather than the Contents dialog box.

JUST A MINUTE   The Index dialog box (described in this task) searches for help when you enter topics to search for. Windows 95 searches only help dialog box titles. If you want to search all of the help system's actual text, use the Find tabbed dialog box described in Task 7.5.

Step 2: Action

1. When you want Windows 95 to find help for you, display the Index dialog box and type the first few letters of the help topic that you wish to find. For this example, type mov. As you type mov in section 1, Windows 95 narrows the possible help topics matches in the list under section 2. Windows 95 displays all titles that begin with the letters mov, as shown in Figure 7.9.

Figure 7.9.

Make Windows 95 look for a topic for you in the index of help titles.

Type the search phrase

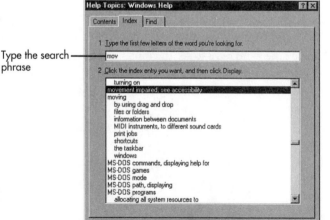

2. Most of the time you will not need to finish typing the search phrase. As soon as you type two or three characters, Windows 95 narrows the list of help topics close to the one you want help with. If you want help with moving files and folders, the typed letters mov get the list in Index dialog box's lower section close to the topic entitled "moving files or folders".

3. If the topic you double-click over (in the lower section) appears in two or more help topic dialog boxes, Windows 95 displays yet another dialog box with every title that contains that topic. Select the topic you want help on, and Windows 95 displays the matching dialog box with the helpful information at your disposal. This is a good way to see several related topics at a glance.

Step 3: Review

The Index tabbed dialog box searches through all the help topic titles, looking for the subject you want to find. Whereas the Contents dialog box requires that you scan through all the help topics looking for the subject you want, the Index dialog box searches every help title for your word or phrase, and displays the resulting dialog boxes when you click over the listed topics.

Task 7.5: Using the Find Help Dialog Box

Step 1: Description

The Find tabbed dialog box searches through all the help text on your system, looking for a specific word or phrase that you type.

Step 2: Action

1. Click the Find tabbed help dialog box to display the dialog box on your screen.

2. At the prompt labeled "**T**ype the word(s) that you want to find," type the complete word or phrase that you want the help system to search for. Basically, the Find dialog box's interface is similar to that of the Index search described in the previous task. Once you find a topic, you can double-click it and then display its dialog box.

3. Type the word move to see the topics update in the second and third scrolling listboxes in the dialog box. A large scrolling list of help topics that contain the letters move appears in the lower window, as shown in Figure 7.10.

7

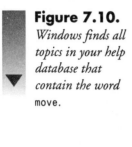

Figure 7.10.
*Windows finds all
topics in your help
database that
contain the word*
move.

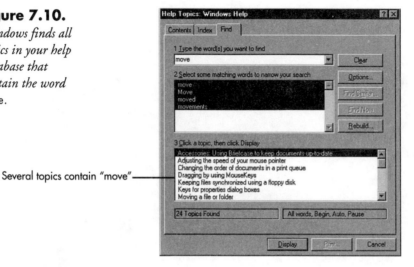

Several topics contain "move" ———

Narrowing the Search

The Find search dialog box finds every occurrence of your search word or phrase that resides in the help system's text. (Actually the amount of text searched depends on whether you built the index using a maximum database size or a minimum database size, the default, when you first displayed the help system.)

The Find dialog box is often not as accurate as the Index dialog box search, because Find searches a larger body of text than does the Index dialog box, described in the previous task. Therefore, you'll find that the word move appears in many different topics, as shown in the lower window's huge scrolling list of topics.

Since the word moved also contains the letters move, Windows 95 incorrectly lists all topics containing the letters moved as well as move. To get rid of the topics containing moved and movements, hold down the Ctrl key and click over the words moved and movement in the middle window to *deselect* those topics. When you deselect a selected topic, the highlight goes away and that topic is no longer selected. You've now ensured that only those topics that contain the word move appear in the Find dialog box of search topics.

4. Scroll through the list of choices in the bottom window and double-click any of them to display that topic's help dialog box. This dialog box works like the other help dialog boxes described earlier in this hour.

5. Notice the list of command buttons to the right of the Find dialog box. Clear erases all the help topics so you can look for another. The **O**ptions command button displays the Find Options dialog box, shown in Figure 7.11.

Figure 7.11.

Describe how you want Windows 95 to find your help topics.

The Find Options dialog box describes how you want Windows 95 to find the information, based on your search word or phrase. You can request that Windows 95 search all the words in any order (the default) or at least one word that you type. If you click the first option, Windows 95 would only find help topics that contain the phrase my computer, if you were to enter that phrase as a search topic. If, however, you clicked the second option, Windows 95 would find all help topics that contain either the word my *or* the word computer.

There are additional options you can click as you become more acquainted with Windows 95. For now, press Esc or click Cancel to close the Find Options dialog box.

6. After you use the help system for a while, you may decide that you want more detail when hunting for specific items. You may find that the minimized database that the wizard set up when you first displayed the Find dialog box is not detailed enough. You can rebuild the help database by clicking the **R**ebuild command button and rerunning the help database build wizard once again, this time selecting the maximized database size. Do this now only if you have ample disk space (four or more megabytes free).

7. Click the Cancel command button to close the Find dialog box.

Step 3: Review

The Find dialog box searches across all your help topic dialog boxes. Whereas the Index dialog box searches strictly through the help topic titles, the Find dialog box searches the body of the help topic text, looking for any and all topics that contain your key search word or phrase.

7

Roving Help

Sometimes you'll be in the middle of a dialog box working inside Windows 95 when you spot a command button or a control that you do not understand. Look in the upper-right corner of the window for a question mark on a command button. If you find such a command button, you've found Windows 95's *Roving Help* command button and cursor (sometimes called *Pop-up Help*).

Whereas a help search on that dialog box would produce a description of the entire dialog box, the Roving Help lets you narrow the focus and request help on a specific item on the screen. Not all dialog boxes or screens inside Windows 95 contain the Roving Help feature, so look for the question mark command button, to the left of the window minimizing and resizing buttons, in the upper-right corner of whatever window you're working on.

Task 7.6: Using the Roving Help Feature

Step 1: Description

As long as a dialog box contains the command button with a question mark on it, you can request Roving Help for the items on your screen.

Step 2: Action

1. Display the help screen once again by selecting **H**elp on the Start menu.
2. Click the Contents tabbed dialog box once again (refer to Figure 7.1). In the upper-right corner of the dialog box, you'll see the Roving Help command button and its question mark.
3. Suppose you forget what the large listbox of topics in the center of the screen is for. Click the question mark command button once, and the cursor changes to a question mark that follows the mouse cursor as you move the mouse.
4. Point the question mark mouse cursor to the list of topics in the middle of the screen and click the mouse button. Windows 95 displays a popup description box, shown in Figure 7.12, that describes the topic list and what you are to do with it.
5. Press Esc to get rid of the roving description box and return to the regular Contents screen.
6. There's another way to produce the Roving Help. Point the regular mouse cursor over the item. Right-click now over the list of topics in the middle of the Contents screen. Windows 95 displays a popup description box that contains a one line menu with the command **W**hat's This? in the menu.
7. Click on the **W**hat's This? command, and the same roving description box appears that's shown in Figure 7.12.

Figure 7.12.
The Roving Help helps you when you point to a place on the screen.

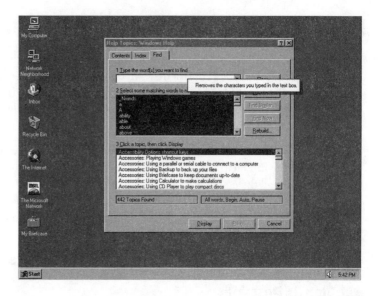

JUST A MINUTE

The Roving Help is also known as *context-sensitive help*. Windows 95 looks at what you are currently doing when you request help and displays help that matches the context of your current actions.

Step 3: Review

The Roving Help feature of Windows 95 comes in handy if you forget what to do when displaying a dialog box or when working in a Windows 95 application. Click on the question mark icon and then click over the control that you want help with. Windows 95 then looks at the control that you clicked and displays helpful advice and a description for that control.

TIME SAVER

The F1 function key is the shortcut access key for the Roving Help. When displaying a dialog box, you often can press F1 to get a helpful description of what you can do next.

7

I Want My Welcome Screen Tips!

Do you still see a Welcome Screen when you start Windows 95? Hour 1, "What's Windows 95 All About?," described the Welcome Screen and explained how the Welcome Screen provides you with tips every time you start Windows 95. It also told you how to get rid of the Welcome Screen but *not* how to get the Welcome Screen back! The next task finally shows you how to get the Welcome Screen back again so it appears every time you start Windows 95.

Task 7.7: Adding the Welcome Screen to Windows 95 Start-Up

Step 1: Description

The reason you're learning how to add the Welcome Screen in this hour is that Windows 95 requires that you use the help system to add a Welcome Screen. In this instance, the help topic does not just describe helpful advice but actually does work for you.

Step 2: Action

1. Select the **H**elp command from the Start menu.
2. Click the Index tab to display the Index dialog box (shown in Figure 7.2).
3. In the top input prompt, type `Welcome`. When you type `Welcome`, Windows 95 highlights the Welcome Screen, seen in the lower window.
4. Double-click the selected topic and you'll see the help topic dialog box shown in Figure 7.13.

Figure 7.13.

This help topic dialog box displays the Welcome Screen.

5. Read through the dialog box text. Do you see the command button with the crooked arrow inside the text? Click over that command button. After a brief pause, Windows 95 displays a Welcome Screen with a helpful tip.

7

6. If you want to see the Welcome Screen every time you start Windows 95, be sure to check (by clicking) the option at the bottom of the screen labeled Show this Welcome Screen next time you start Windows.

7. You can now close the Welcome Screen. Each time you restart Windows 95, the Welcome Screen will appear.

8. Close the help topic dialog box.

Step 3: Review

The help system often does work for you. When you see a command button inside a help topic dialog box, you can often click that command button to accomplish a task. In this task, you learned how to add back the Welcome Screen every time you start Windows 95.

TIME SAVER

> Some versions of Windows 95 provide a Tip Tour option on the Accessories menu. You can display the Welcome Screen and run the Windows 95 tour from this option. If you do not see this menu option, you'll have to initiate the Welcome Screen from the help system, as described in this task.

Summary

This hour showed you how to access the powerful help features of Windows 95. When you have a question about Windows 95, you can ask Windows 95 itself for help. There are several ways to access the helpful dialog boxes about a variety of topics. The most common method of getting detailed help is to select the **Help** command from the Start menu.

The **Help** command displays a help tabbed dialog box containing three different help search screens. The first, the Contents dialog box, displays an overview of Windows 95 in a book-like form that you read at your leisure. In addition, the Contents dialog box can start a ten-minute tour of Windows 95 if you have a CD-ROM with the Windows 95 system. (The tour requires heavy use of graphics and sound, so Windows 95 needs the storage capacity found on the CD.) You can also get on-line help if you have Internet access.

There are two ways to search for help using the help tabbed dialog boxes. If you select the Index dialog box, Windows 95 searches the help topic titles for the word or phrase that you need help with. If you display the Find dialog box, Windows 95 searches the help topics themselves for the word or phrase you're hunting for.

The roving context-sensitive help feature is nice because it lets you click over an item, such as a control in a dialog box, and Windows 95 displays help on that item. Usually, the Roving Help displays a description as well as advice on what you can do to make the control work for you.

7

Workshop

Term Review

context-sensitive help   Refers to the capability of Windows 95 to look at what actions you are currently performing (the *context*) and display help that explains how to complete those actions.

cross-referenced help topic   Green underlined text inside help dialog boxes that displays definitions when you click them.

deselect   The process of reversing a selected item so that item is no longer selected. Usually when you deselect an item, the highlight around the item disappears.

online   Information that is available interactively as you use Windows 95.

Roving Help   Windows 95 lets you point to items on dialog boxes and click the window's question mark command button to get help about that item. You also can display this Roving Help by right-clicking over an item to see a description of that item and learn the commands you can perform.

wizard   A step-by-step process that leads you through the execution of a Windows 95 task. Many Windows 95 programs, such as Microsoft Word for Windows, include specific wizards of their own.

Q&A

Q There are so many kinds of help available; which one should I use?

A The method of help that you access depends on the task you're trying to accomplish. Generally, there are several ways to get help on the same topic. If you want help on a procedure such as moving files, you can probably find related topics grouped together in the Contents dialog box. There, you will find topics, grouped by subject, which you can browse.

If you want to search the help system for *all* topics related to the one you want, such as changing icons on folders and documents, you will probably want to search the Index or Find dialog boxes. The Index dialog box searches topic titles for key words that you specify. The Find dialog box searches the text itself for the topic you want to find. The Find dialog box can locate more help topics than the Index dialog box can.

When you see a Windows 95 control or menu command that you do not understand, click the question mark icon in the upper-right corner, and then point and click over the item you want help with to get specific help about the screen.

Finally, if you cannot find help on a topic, especially if you want help with the Windows 95 Internet interface, check out Microsoft's Web site for help.

Q When would I want to build a maximized search database?

A If you have plenty of free disk space (at least 4MB), you can build a maximized search database so your Find dialog box searches across much more text than would otherwise be the case for minimized database builds.

Rarely will you search for topics that you cannot find easily with the smaller minimized database. Keep in mind that your searches will be more sluggish if you search across a maximized database of search topics, but the search will be more thorough. The index that the wizard builds is an index of key search words and phrases that Windows 95 searches when you subsequently select the Find dialog box.

Q Is Roving Help always available?

A Sadly, the Roving Help system is not always available. When you want to know how to perform a task, such as copying a file, you'll probably have to issue the **Help** command on the Start menu and search for your topic.

The Roving Help is a great tool to use when you want a description of a screen element. For example, when displaying a dialog box, you can display the Roving Help cursor to find out what commands the controls on the dialog box perform.

7

Hour 8

Manage Your Desktop

This hour is a little different from the other hours. Instead of studying a single central aspect of Windows 95, such as Explorer, this hour contains a *potpourri* of desktop management tips and procedures that improve the way you use the Windows 95 environment. Whereas the previous hours have studied topics in depth, this hour offers advice that you may want to use while you work within Windows 95.

One area this hour explores is screen savers. Windows 95 comes with several screen saver designs and you can purchase and download additional screen savers. Screen savers not only provide something for your computer to do while it is idle, but they offer security features as well.

This hour also offers a collection of tips that simply help make your use of Windows 95 even easier than it would otherwise be. For example, you learned how to modify the Start menu in Hour 6, "Explore the Windows 95 System," through the important **S**ettings menu on the Start menu. In addition to going through the **S**ettings menu, you also can use the mouse to drag programs to the Start menu without displaying a single menu!

Start Windows 95 and walk through this hour, trying the shortcuts and advice, and decide which topics suit your needs best. Now that you've mastered the major Windows 95 tools such as Explorer and the **S**ettings menu, you are ready to streamline the way that you use Windows 95.

The highlights of this hour include:

- ☐ Why screen savers improve the use of your computer's idle time
- ☐ How screen savers add security while you are away from your computer
- ☐ Where to double-click when you need to change the computer's time or date
- ☐ When to let Windows 95 arrange the desktop icons for you
- ☐ How to use the mouse to add programs to your Start menu
- ☐ What to do when you get tired of your Windows 95 colors

SOS: Save Our Screens!

Want to know an insider's computer industry secret? Here it is: Screen savers really don't save many screens these days. In the past, computer monitors, especially the monochrome green-letters-on-black kind, would *burn in* characters when left on too long without being used. In other words, if you left the monitor on for a long time and did not type anything, the characters on the monitor would begin to leave character trails that stayed on the monitor even after you turned it off.

To combat character burn-in, programmers began to write *screen savers* that blanked the screen or displayed moving characters and pictures. The blank screens had no burn-in problems, and the moving text never stayed in one place long enough to burn into the monitor. The screen savers would kick into effect after a predetermined length of non-use. Therefore, if you walked away from your computer, the screen saver would begin after a few minutes. Upon returning, you could press any key to restore the computer screen to its original state where you left it.

Almost everybody has heard of screen savers these days. Computer software stores contain shelf after shelf of screen saver programs. There are screen savers that display pictures of your favorite television characters. There are screen savers with cartoons. There are screen savers that continuously draw geometric and 3D designs. Microsoft designed Windows 95 to include several screen savers also. Therefore, you don't have to buy a screen saver because if you have Windows 95, you already have an assortment of them to choose from.

Getting back to that industry secret: Today's monitors don't have the burn-in problem that previous monitors had. Screen savers aren't needed. Why, during an age when they are not needed, are screen savers more popular than ever before? The answer is simple: Screen savers

8

are fun! Screen savers greet you with designs and animated cartoons when you'd otherwise look at a boring screen. It's *cool* to use a screen saver.

TIME SAVER

If you think that you might want to try one of the store-bought screen savers, first try one from Windows 95 to see if you like screen savers. Some people decide they don't like them once they begin using screen savers.

CAUTION

Screen savers aren't just for fun and games so don't rule them out before you've looked at them! Even though you may not care for screen savers (as I just mentioned, not everybody likes them), the Windows 95 screen savers offer an added benefit not found in many other screen savers: The Windows 95 screen saver provides password protection. If you need to walk away from your screen for a while but you want to leave your computer running, you can select a password for the screen saver. Once the screen saver begins, a user has to enter the correct password to use your computer. This ensures that payroll and other departments can safely leave their computers, without fear that somebody will see confidential information.

Task 8.1: Setting Up a Screen Saver

Step 1: Description

TASK

Windows 95 contains several screen savers from which you can choose. Through the Screen Saver dialog box you can set up a blanking screen saver or one that moves text and graphics on the screen. You control the length of time the monitor is idle before the screen saver begins.

Step 2: Action

1. Click the right mouse button over the Windows 95 wallpaper. The display menu appears.

JUST A MINUTE

If you are working in Windows 95 now, using a word processor or other program, you may not see the wallpaper. Minimize your current window so that you can see the wallpaper and right-click over the wallpaper

2. Select the Properties command. The Display Properties tabbed dialog box shown in Figure 8.1 appears.

Figure 8.1.

The Properties command displays the Display Properties tabbed dialog box.

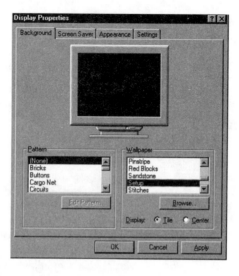

JUST A MINUTE

The Display Properties tabbed dialog box is the same dialog box you selected in Hour 2 to change your Windows 95 wallpaper. Therefore, if you don't currently use wallpaper (see the blank desktop background on Figure 8.1), your screen may differ slightly from the one in Figure 8.1.

3. Click the tab labeled Screen Saver. Windows 95 displays the dialog box shown in Figure 8.2.

Figure 8.2.

The Screen Saver dialog box controls the screen saver's timing and selection.

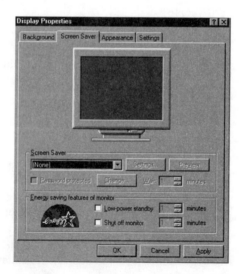

8

Depending on your attached hardware, the bottom portion of the Screen Saver dialog box may or may not be grayed out as is the figure's. If your monitor is designed to be *Energy Star*-compliant, the lower dialog box settings will be available to you. You'll be able to adjust these options to save energy. The Energy Star controls work independently and override any screen saver settings you might use.

4. The dropdown listbox, directly below the **S**creen Saver prompt, that you display when you click the down arrow contains a list of Windows 95 screen savers. Click the box now to see the list. When (None) is selected, no screen saver will be active on your system.

5. If you select Blank Screen (the item in the dropdown list directly after (None)), Windows 95 uses a blank screen for the screen saver. When the screen saver activates, the screen will go blank, and a keypress (or password if you set up a password) returns the screen to its original state.

   The remaining screen savers are more fun than a blank screen saver. Click any one of the remaining screen savers in the list now (such as Flying Windows), and Windows 95 gives you a preview of it on the little monitor inside the dialog box as shown in Figure 8.3.

Figure 8.3.

You may preview any of the screen savers.

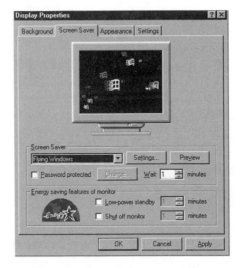

6. The animated screen savers can move fairly fast. If you want to adjust their speed, click the Settings button. In some cases, you also can adjust the number of animated items that appear on the screen saver screen.

7. The Preview button lets you view, full-screen, the screen saver if you want a better preview than the small screen inside the dialog box provides. Click Preview to see the actual screen saver in action. Press any key or move the mouse to terminate the screen saver preview and return to the dialog box.

8. The **W**ait prompt determines how many minutes your computer must remain idle for the screen saver to activate itself. By pressing Alt+W (the shortcut key combination for the **W**ait prompt), you can enter a new minute value or click the up and down arrow keys to change to a new minute value.

> Task 8.2 explains how to use the password option with the screen saver.

JUST A MINUTE

9. When you click the OK command button at the bottom of the dialog box, Windows 95 activates the screen-saver program. The screen saver remains active in all future Windows 95 sessions until you change it again using the Screen Saver dialog box.

10. The screen saver operates in the background but never shows itself, even on the taskbar of program buttons, until your computer sits idle for the specified minute time value. Don't touch the keyboard or mouse for the waiting time period, and you'll see the screen saver go into action. Press any key (or move the mouse) to return to the desktop.

Step 3: Review

Screen savers are easy to set. A right mouse-click on your desktop and selecting Properties from the resulting menu will activate the Display Properties tabbed dialog box where you can launch a screen saver. Not only can you control which screen saver is used, but you also can control the number of idle minutes the screen saver requires before activating. You can control the speed of animated screen savers as well.

> If you don't want a screen saver, select (None) in the screen saver's dialog box.

TIME SAVER

Task 8.2: Securing Your Screen Saver

Step 1: Description

Using the Display Properties box, you can add a password to any of the Windows 95 screen savers including the blank screen saver. Once the screen saver executes, it requires a password before relinquishing control to you or anyone else who wants to use your computer.

8

Step 2: Action

1. Display the Display Properties tabbed dialog box once again by right-clicking over your screen's wallpaper and selecting **P**roperties.

2. Click the Screen Saver tab to see the Screen Saver dialog box.

3. Click the **P**assword protected checkmark prompt.

4. Press the **C**hange button. You must tell Windows 95 the password it will require before releasing a screen saver. The Change Password dialog box, like the one in Figure 8.4, opens.

Figure 8.4.

*Tell Windows 95
the secret screen
saver password.*

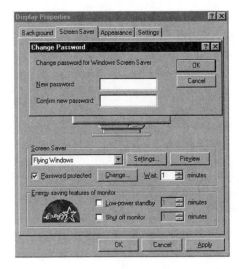

5. Windows 95 requires that you type the password twice. The password appears on the screen as asterisks, as you type, so that no one looking over your shoulder can read your password. Due to the asterisk protection, Windows 95 asks that you enter the password twice to ensure that you make no mistakes as you type the new password. Type the same password at both prompts on the screen.

6. Press the OK command button. Now when Windows 95 starts the screen saver, you will have to enter the password to use the computer.

CAUTION

The screen-saver password does *not* guarantee total computer security. Someone can reboot your computer and use the computer's files. The password-protected screen saver does, however, keep people from looking at the work you were performing before you left the computer idle.

Step 3: Review

The password lets you protect your computer's screen from view by others. By setting a password, you ensure that people cannot stop the screen saver to look at what you were doing with the computer before the screen saver took effect.

Check the Time

A clock showing the current time appears at the right of your taskbar. (The clock's position may differ depending on where you moved your taskbar.) In addition to the time, your computer and Windows 95 also keeps track of the date.

There are several reasons why you may want to change the computer's time and date settings. Perhaps you've moved to a different part of the world and need to change the computer's clock. Perhaps your computer contains a time and date memory kept current with a battery that has gone bad. Perhaps the person who set up your computer simply didn't know the right time or date when he or she installed Windows 95. Whatever the reason for setting the time and date, you'll see here that these settings are simple to adjust.

JUST A MINUTE

Windows 95 uses the international settings, found by double-clicking the Regional Settings icon in the Control Panel, to format all date and time values displayed from within Windows 95. Therefore, the selected country in the Windows 95 international settings determines the appearance of all time and date values.

As you saw in Hour 2, "Tour Windows 95 Now," the Control Panel contains many of your system's hardware and software settings. You can change your computer's date and time settings by double-clicking the Date/Time icon inside the Control Panel. There's a better way, though, a much faster and easier way, as Task 8.3 describes.

Task 8.3: Changing the Time and Date with the Mouse

Step 1: Description

The taskbar itself gives you access to the time and date settings of your computer. You can double-click on the taskbar clock to display the time and date modification dialog box.

JUST A MINUTE

If you don't see the time on your taskbar, select the **S**ettings | **T**askbar command on the Start menu and check the Show **C**lock option.

Step 2: Action

1. Double-click your taskbar's clock. Windows 95 displays the Date/Time Properties tabbed dialog box shown in Figure 8.5.

Figure 8.5.

A double-click displays this Date/ Time Properties dialog box.

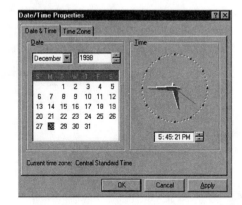

8

2. This is the easiest clock you'll ever have to set! The up and down controls let you change the month or year. If you click on a day inside the month, the date instantly changes to that date.

3. Click over the hour, minute, or second to change the time. If you highlight the hour (by dragging the mouse cursor over it), the minute, or the second, then click either the up or down arrow next to the time. That highlighted value increases or decreases by one unit. As you change the time value, the analog clock face changes also.

4. When you are done modifying the date or time, click the OK command button to close the dialog box, and the taskbar's time reflects your changes. You can now turn off your computer, and the computer's new settings will still be in effect (up to the second) when you turn on the computer again.

5. Windows 95 is smart and can handle time zones easily. If you display the Date/ Time Properties dialog box and click the Time Zone tab, Windows 95 displays the time zone dialog box shown in Figure 8.6.

   The time zone currently in effect is highlighted on the global world map. If you want to set a different time zone, you either can drag the map's highlighted time zone line left or right, or click the dropdown listbox arrow to display the world's time zones. The listbox contains a list of every possible time zone in the world.

Figure 8.6.
Change the time zone visually or using a dropdown listbox.

TIME SAVER

Not all time zones respect daylight saving time. For example, if you live in Indiana, you don't have to change your clocks every six months because you don't follow daylight saving time. For those who don't want Windows 95 to adjust for daylight saving, uncheck the option at the bottom of the screen.

6. Once you select the proper time zone and daylight saving time setting, click the OK command button to close the dialog box, and the settings will then take effect.

Step 3: Review

Changing the date and time requires double-clicking over the time on your taskbar. The tabbed dialog box that appears lets you change the time, the date, and the time zone. If you want Windows 95 to update the clock every daylight saving time period, you can check an option to have Windows 95 do just that.

JUST A MINUTE

If your computer adjusts the clock due to daylight savings time, Windows 95 lets you know about the change with a dialog box the first time you use Windows 95 after the change.

Arrange Those Icons

Over time, you could place many icons on your desktop. A clean desktop keeps the clutter down, so you don't want to place too many items on the desktop at any one time. You might,

8

however, using the copy and paste tools discussed so far in this book, want to put your most popular programs out on the desktop (created as a shortcut) so the programs are always there when you want to double-click their icons.

TIME SAVER

> As you learned in Hour 6, "Explore the Windows 95 System," you can place your most commonly used programs on the desktop by copying the icons and creating a shortcut to the icon programs. If you do this, you then don't have to display the Start menu and click through a series of cascaded menus when you want to execute that program.

Once you place a lot of icons on the desktop, you may get a cluttered screen, such as the one shown in Figure 8.7. Windows 95 supplies tools that can help align those icons better and make your desktop look a little more professional, as Task 8.4 explains.

Figure 8.7.

Numerous icons can clutter the Windows 95 desktop.

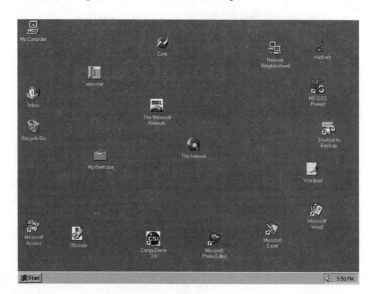

Task 8.4: Arranging Your Desktop Icons

Step 1: Description

Your desktop can get cluttered. When it does, use the right mouse button's desktop menu to put order back in your icons.

TASK

Step 2: Action

1. Close or minimize any open windows to get a clear view at your desktop.

2. Point to the desktop with the mouse cursor and click the right mouse button to display the desktop menu. The first two commands, Arrange Icons and Line up Icons, manage your desktop icons. The first command, Arrange Icons, produces the following set of commands:

By **N**ame

By **T**ype

By Size

By **D**ate

Auto Arrange

The first four of these commands determine how you want Windows 95 to arrange the icons. If you want the icons in alphabetical order, for example, you would select the by **N**ame command. The second command arranges the icons by the file type they represent (executable program, document, and so on). The third command arranges the icons by size from smallest to largest. The fourth command arranges the icons in date order using the date of their last modification.

Figure 8.8 shows the result of ordering icons in Figure 8.7 by name. See if you can spot a problem.

Figure 8.8.

The icons almost appear in alphabetical order.

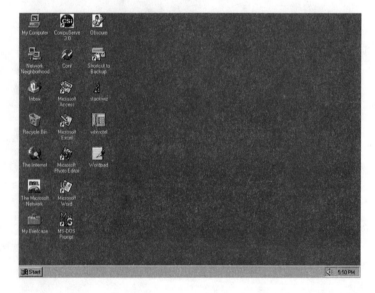

8

8

Windows 95 puts its own icons at the head of the list. Therefore, icons such as My Computer, Inbox, Recycle Bin, Network Manager, and The Microsoft Network (you may not have all these Windows 95 icons on your desktop) always will come before your own icons. Windows 95 then arranges the remaining icons in alphabetical order as shown in Figure 8.8.

The **A**uto Arrange command is really an option, not a command, that you can check on and off. Windows 95 puts a checkmark next to the **A**uto Arrange command on the right-click menu when you choose **A**uto Arrange. Thereafter, no matter what order you select for the icons, Windows 95 keeps the icons arranged in your order, but in straight and organized columns. If, for example, the **A**uto Arrange option were checked in Figure 8.8, when you attempted to drag one of the icons out of the alignment to the far right edge of the screen, Windows 95 would snap that icon right back into the columns of icons on the screen.

TIME SAVER

> The **A**uto Arrange option keeps you from having to adjust icons manually, putting them in aligned order every time you add a new icon to the desktop or remove an icon from the desktop.

3. Click your **A**uto Arrange option now. Your desktop icons will arrange themselves into rows and columns.

4. Click the by **N**ame command to put your non-Windows 95 icons in alphabetical order.

5. The Lin**e** up Icons command organizes your icons into straight columns and rows but does not group them together. Suppose, for example, that you want a few icons in the upper-right corner of the desktop and a few in the lower-right corner. You can move the icon groups to those corners, and then select Lin**e** up Icons to put those icons in rows and columns while still maintaining their locations on the screen.

JUST A MINUTE

> The **A**uto Arrange option, when checked, always overrides any attempt to order icons in groups using Lin**e** up Icons.

Figure 8.9 shows how you can create organized groups of icons using Lin**e** up Icons after dragging the icons to their approximate locations within the groups on the screen.

Figure 8.9.
*Use the Line up
Icons command to
create organized
groups of icons.*

Step 3: Review

By right-clicking over your desktop you can use the Windows 95 tools to place your icons
in an organized order. You can organize the icons and keep them organized if you want to
leave the work up to Windows 95; the **A**uto Arrange option ensures that icons go into a table
of rows and columns as soon as you add an icon. If you delete an icon from the desktop, the
others rearrange automatically also. If you want more control, you can turn off the **A**uto
Arrange option and use the Lin**e** up Icons command to organize your icons into related
groups on the desktop.

TIME SAVER

Remember that you can delete an icon from the desktop by right-clicking
over that icon and selecting the **D**elete command. If you select more than
one icon (by holding Ctrl while clicking the left mouse button) before
clicking the right mouse button over one of the selected icons, Windows
95 deletes all of the selected icons in one action.

The Neatest Tip Yet!

Want to add programs to the Start menu quickly? Hour 6 taught you how to access the
powerful **S**ettings | **T**askbar dialog boxes with which you can modify the way the taskbar
behaves. The **S**ettings | **T**askbar dialog boxes include several options that let you rearrange
the Start menu and add or remove programs to and from the Start menu.

8

If all you want to do is add programs, such as the calculator program, to the Start menu, you don't need the Settings | Taskbar dialog boxes, as Task 8.5 explains.

Task 8.5: Quickly Adding Programs to the Start Menu

Step 1: Description

After starting Explorer, opening the My Computer icon, or displaying a Windows 95 Open dialog box, drag the program's icon to the Start button. Windows 95 instantly adds that program to the Start menu. Earlier you saw how to add the Windows 95 Calculator program to the Start menu. This task offers you a faster way to add programs by showing you how to drop the calculator program onto the Start button.

Step 2: Action

1. Start Explorer.

2. Click on the Windows folder to display the Windows directory.

3. Scroll the right window until you see the calculator icon appear with the name Calc beneath the icon.

JUST A MINUTE

> If you've turned on the display of filename extensions, the full name of the Calculator program is `Calc.exe`.

4. Drag the calculator icon to the Start button. Drag the icon slowly. As the icon passes over certain parts of your screen, such as the dividing lines between windows, you'll see the icon change to a circle with a slash through it (the international "Do not" sign), but the icon reappears when you drag the cursor to the Start button.

5. Release the icon over the Start button. Click the button to display the Start menu. As Figure 8.10 shows, your Start button will now include the calculator program that you can start directly from the first level of the Start menu.

6. If you've been following this task, you may or may not want the calculator program to remain on the Start menu. If not, select Settings | Taskbar and follow the steps to remove the program as described in Hour 6.

Figure 8.10.
*The calculator
program is now
part of the Start
menu.*

Step 3: Review

From an Open dialog box, the Explorer screen, or the My Computer icon, you can add programs to the Start menu with a simple mouse drag. Don't add too many programs to the Start menu, though, or you'll clutter the Start menu too much. Keep only your special and frequently used programs on the Start menu.

CAUTION

Unfortunately, Windows 95 offers no short way to remove programs from the Start menu. You'll have to return to Hour 6's chapter and remove the program from the Start menu within the Settings dialog box explained there.

Paint Windows 95

Windows 95 offers several color schemes for you to select. Microsoft designed several color schemes that work well together. Depending on your taste, you can choose from conservative to very wild colors.

The color schemes that you can select have nothing to do with the colors of icons, wallpaper, or screen savers on your system. The color schemes determine the color for various system-wide items such as screen title bars, window backgrounds, and dialog box controls.

Task 8.6: Changing the Color Scheme

Step 1: Description

By selecting from various color schemes, you can determine the colors Windows 95 uses for common system-level items such as window controls. The Control Panel contains a Display icon that you use to change the color of your Windows 95 installation.

8

Step 2: Action

1. Select Control Panel from the Start menu's Settings menu.
2. Double-click the Display icon. The Display Properties tabbed dialog box appears.

TIME SAVER

> To display the Display Properties tabbed dialog box quickly right-click over the wallpaper and select Properties.

3. Click the Appearance tab to display the Appearance dialog box shown in Figure 8.11.

Figure 8.11.

Change system colors using the Appearance dialog box.

4. If you want to take the time, you can change the colors of every item on the Windows 95 screen including dialog boxes, window borders, and title bars. However, it's much easier to pick a color scheme from the list of the many choices that Microsoft supplies.

   In the Appearance dialog box, the top half contains the selected color scheme. If you select a different color scheme, you'll see that scheme's color appear at the top of the dialog box. For example, suppose you're taking your powerful color laptop to Egypt to write with while cruising down the Nile River. Open the dropdown listbox labeled Scheme and select Desert from the list. Instantly, the top half of your dialog box changes colors to a Desert scheme. Now you can compute like a true Egyptian!

5. The color scheme of your Windows 95 installation does not instantly change. You're still in the process of selecting colors at this point. If you don't like the desert color scheme, try another. As a matter of fact, try **all** of them to find one you really like.

TIME SAVER

> There are some color schemes that include the additional benefit of large text sizes. As Figure 8.12 illustrates, you can select a color scheme that makes window text easier to see by enlarging the character size of the Windows 95 characters when they appear in dialog boxes and title bars.

Figure 8.12.

You can change not only system colors but also common Windows 95 character sizes.

6. When you find a color scheme that you really like, click the OK command button to close the dialog box and change the color scheme to your selected colors. You can now begin working with the new color scheme; as soon as you open a window you'll see the difference.

Step 3: Review

The Control Panel contains a display icon that enables you to change the color scheme of your Windows 95 installation. Once you change the colors and, optionally, the font size, all standard Windows 95 displays, such as windows, borders, and title bars, will reflect the new colors.

8

TIME SAVER

Although Microsoft Plus! is an add-on program you must purchase separately from Windows 95, Plus! offers several additional color schemes as well as entire desktop *themes* that let you add personality to your Windows 95 desktop.

As you change your color scheme, feel free to change the Windows 95 display font as well. By default, Windows 95 displays icons and window titles and messages in the MS-DOS Sans Serif font. From the Appearance dialog box, you can select a different font for almost every kind of text Windows 95 displays.

Summary

This hour took a brief detour from the style of surrounding hours. In this hour, you caught a glimpse of some tips and desktop-management tools that may help you work inside Windows 95 more effectively. After completing the first part of this book, you already have a good foundation of the tools that are available to you as a Windows 95 user. Now that you've become more comfortable with these aspects of Windows 95, you'll appreciate some of this hour's time-saving tips.

Windows 95 is misleading in one respect: It is extremely easy to use. Both novices and advanced users seem to enjoy Windows 95. It remains simple and free of clutter so beginners don't get confused by having to deal with too many things at once. Windows 95 also contains powerful options and tools so that advanced users can always find a different way of accomplishing tasks that take longer using other operating environments.

In this hour, you learned how to improve your computer's idle time by setting up a screen saver. By password-protecting that screen saver, you can add security to your system so you can safely leave for a few minutes without exiting the program you're working in.

There are many timesaving features inside Windows 95. You now know how to change the computer's time, date, screen colors, and even how to add programs to the Start menu with just the mouse. These timesaving features help both the novice and the advanced user utilize Windows 95 more fully.

Workshop

Term Review

burn-in Characters left on older computer monitors begin to burn into the monitor, leaving their outlines even after the monitor's power is turned off.

Energy Star A name applied to monitors that comply with environmental guidelines that limit the use of continuous power applied to your monitor.

screen saver A program that waits in the background and executes only if you stop using your computer for a while. The screen saver either blanks your screen or displays moving text and graphics. Screen savers have, in the past, helped eliminate burn-in problems.

Q&A

Q **In the second hour I learned how to change the wallpaper. How does the wallpaper pattern differ from the screen saver pattern? Are they the same thing?**

A The wallpaper is your *desktop's background*. You always see the wallpaper when you first start Windows 95 and when you minimize or close programs you are using within Windows 95. You will never see the screen saver unless you quit working on your computer for a few minutes and the screen saver begins running.

The screen saver must be a moving pattern (or be completely blank) to accomplish the goal of a screen saver. A screen saver is primarily a running program that keeps the screen's characters from getting burned into the screen's phosphorus. The burn-in problem is not too common today, so a secondary goal of a screen saver is to display an animated and often fun screen during your computer's idle times.

Q **I do serious work. Why would I want a screen saver?**

A The screen saver probably will not help your monitor if you have a modern monitor because modern monitors don't have burn-in problems. If you don't like the fancy animated screen saver screens that come with Windows 95 or that are for sale in software stores, you shouldn't activate the screen saver for entertainment purposes.

Depending on the nature of your computing, however, as well as the level of security at which you operate, you may want to activate a password-protected screen saver for precautionary reasons. When you leave your computer, you can activate the screen saver so that, upon returning, you must enter a predetermined password to work with the computer once again. The password-protected screen saver keeps others from snooping into your computer's files.

8

8

Q How do I adjust my computer's clock when daylight saving time occurs?

A You don't have to do anything when daylight saving time occurs, as long as you've checked the daylight saving time option in the Date/Time Properties dialog box. When you check this option, Windows 95 monitors the calendar and adjusts your computer's time appropriately. If you live in an area that does not follow daylight saving time, be sure to leave the option unchecked so your computer won't change the clock every six months.

Q Why would I want to group my desktop icons into several areas of the screen?

A Suppose you copy icons that represent documents you often use to the desktop. In addition, you also copy several games that you like to play to the desktop. You can't play games all the time, so you decide to place your word processor's icon as well as your spreadsheet's icon to the desktop, too.

These three groups of icons logically fall into these categories:

Documents

Games

Programs

In addition to the three categories you've created, Windows 95 always likes to display some of its own program icons on the desktop, such as the My Computer icon and possibly The Microsoft Network icon if you're set up to use the online network service. If you use Auto Arrange, Windows 95 puts all these icons together at the left of your screen. If, instead, you put all your games in one corner, all your programs in another corner, and all your documents in yet another corner, you could select the Line up Icons command to put these groups of icons into rows and columns *but still keep their approximate placement on the screen.* The rows and columns ensure that the icons look neat (it's almost impossible to drag icons into rows and columns), but you maintain your icon groups as well.

Part V

Hour 9

Put the Calculator to Work

This book has done some work already with the calculator program by adding or removing that program to and from the Start menu. In case you are curious as to how to use this accessory application, this hour explains how to use the calculator. The calculator program performs both simple mathematical and advanced scientific calculations.

You will find the calculator program in the Accessories menu. (Of course, if you left the calculator on your Start menu, you don't have to hunt very far for it.) The calculator was around in previous versions of Windows. Windows 95 supplies updated versions of the calculator that take advantage of the new look and feel of Windows 95.

The calculator program exemplifies the desktop analogy that Windows 95 tries to emulate. After all, most desktops have a calculator, right? This hour teaches you how to use the electronic versions of a calculator. If you add more desktop tools, such as the Microsoft Outlook program that comes with Microsoft Office 97, you can supplement the calculator program with a calendar and note file as well.

The highlights of this hour include:

- ☐ Why you may want to choose one of the two calculator versions offered by Windows 95

☐ When to use the keyboard for calculations and when to use the mouse

☐ How to use the Clipboard to transfer calculator results into the application you're using

☐ Computing statistics with the calculator program

If you've used the Windows 3.1 calculator program, you'll see that very little has changed in the way you use the Windows 95 equivalent program.

JUST A MINUTE

> The calculator program is one of several programs, including the Clipboard viewer, Notepad, and WordPad programs, that you'll find on the Windows 95 Accessories menu. Subsequent chapters explain how to use these additional programs.

Step Up   If you upgraded from Windows 3.1 to Windows 95, you'll also find the Windows 3.1 Calendar and Cardfile programs on your Accessories menu.

Calculate with Success

Calculators have gotten smaller over the years. The early calculators were bulky and did no more than modern-day, solar-powered calculators. Windows 95 changes all that; when you use Windows 95, you go back to using a big desktop computer to do your math homework and checkbook organizing!

Seriously, the presence of a Windows 95 calculator program provides you with all kinds of computing benefits. Throughout a working day, you use your computer constantly, writing letters, printing bills, and building presentations. As you work, you often need to make a quick calculation and, if you're like this author, your calculator is probably covered up beneath papers stacked a foot high. Once you start the Windows 95 calculator, it is *never* farther away than the taskbar.

Step Up   Windows 95 lets you run an almost unlimited number of programs at the same time. As you are probably painfully aware, Windows 3.1, although in theory was supposed to run many programs at once, ran into memory problems after you started just a handful of programs. After working in Windows 3.1 for any length of time, starting and stopping programs, your memory limits could even be exceeded by starting as few as two programs at the same time.

9

Windows 95 does have a memory limit, but that limit is a more practical limit than the capacity of Windows 3.1. You certainly cannot start 40 programs at the same time and expect to have plenty of memory for 40 more, but there's enough memory space for you to run the calculator in addition to your other day-to-day programs.

TIME SAVER

The calculator program actually contains *two* calculators, a *standard calculator* and a *scientific calculator*. Most people will need the standard calculator that provides all the common mathematical operations required for day-to-day business affairs. The scientific calculator contains additional operations, such as statistical and trigonometric operations. The default calculator that appears when you first start the calculator program is the standard calculator.

Tasks 9.1 and 9.2 walk you through the use of the Windows 95 calculators. Even if you've used other computer popup-windowed calculator programs, you should follow along with Task 9.1 to see how the Windows 95 calculator program works.

Task 9.1: Using the Standard Calculator

Step 1: Description

The Windows 95 standard calculator provides full-featured calculator functions. When you use the calculator program, you can sell your own desktop calculator at your next yard sale. Windows 95 even lets you copy and paste the calculator results directly into your own applications.

JUST A MINUTE

The basic usage of both the standard and scientific calculators is identical. Therefore, once you master this task you'll have already mastered much of the scientific calculator's operation.

Step 2: Action

1. Start the Windows 95 calculator. If you followed the tasks in previous hours, the calculator program may still be on your Start menu. If not, display the Start menu, select the **P**rograms command, display the Accessories menu, and click on calculator to start it. The calculator that you will see appears in Figure 9.1. If you see a calculator window with many more buttons than the figure's, select **V**iew | Standard to work with the non-scientific calculator.

Figure 9.1.

The Windows 95 calculator program goes beyond a pocket calculator.

CAUTION

The calculator program does not let you maximize the window or resize the window. You can only minimize the calculator program to a taskbar button. If you need to move the calculator window you can do that, too.

2. To steal from an old cliché, it doesn't take a rocket scientist to use the standard calculator. Obviously the Windows 95 calculator performs standard addition, subtraction, multiplication, and division. Table 9.1 lists all the math capabilities of the calculator and describes each.

JUST A MINUTE

All of the calculator operations produce *running totals*, meaning that you can continuously apply operations, such as addition to the running total in the calculator's display.

Table 9.1. The Windows 95 standard calculator operations.

Button	Keyboard	Operation	Description
/	/	divide	Performs division
*	Shift+*	multiply	Performs multiplication
−	−	minus	Performs subtraction
+	Shift++	add	Performs addition
sqrt	Shift+@	square root	Calculates the square root
%	Shift+%	percent	Converts multiplication products to their percentage equivalent
1/x	r	reciprocal	Calculates the reciprocal of values
=	=, Enter	equal	Displays the result of the current operation

Button	Keyboard	Operation	Description
+/–	F9	sign change	Reverses the positive or negative sign of the displayed value
Back	Backspace	edits display	Removes the last digit of the value you've entered into the calculator
CE	Delete	clears display	Clears the display of its current number
C	Esc	clears total	Completely erases the running total from the calculator's display
MC	Ctrl+L	clears memory	Clears the calculator's stored memory value
MR	Ctrl+R	returns memory	Recalls the value stored in memory and displays that value in the calculator's window
MS	Ctrl+M	stores memory	Stores the displayed value in the calculator's memory
M+	Ctrl+P	adds to memory	Adds the displayed value to the calculator's memory

CAUTION

> Be careful when using the calculator's keyboard equivalents. As you can see from Table 9.1, for instance, the C key does *not* clear the total (Esc does), even though C appears on the calculator's button to clear the total.

3. Click over the numbers 1, then 2, then 3. As you click, the numbers appear inside the display.

4. Click the multiplication sign (the asterisk).

5. Click the 2.

6. Click the equals sign, and the calculator displays the result of 246.

7. Click C to clear the display.

8. The mouse is great for many things, but the mouse will only slow you down when using the calculator. Turn on the Num Lock feature of your keyboard. Most keyboards have a Num Lock indicator light that lights up when Num Lock is turned on.

Repeat the previous operation by typing the number 123 on your keypad. Press the asterisk. Type 2 on the keypad. Press the equal sign. The result, 246, appears as expected. As you can see, the keyboard is a quicker way to enter numbers and math operators. Press the Esc key (the shortcut key that clears the display).

The Backspace key erases any character that you type incorrectly.

TIME SAVER

9. As Table 9.1 describes, the percent key produces a percentage only as a result of multiplication. Therefore, you can compute a percentage of a number by multiplying it by the percent figure. Suppose that you want to know how much 35 percent of 4000 is.

   Type 4000 and then press the asterisk. Type 35 followed by the percent key (Shift+5 on the keyboard). The value 1400 appears, as shown in Figure 9.2. The result: 1400 is 35 percent of 4000. (The word *of* in a math problem is a sure sign that you must multiply by a percentage. Calculating 35 percent *of* 4000 implies that you need to multiply 4000 by 35 percent.)

Figure 9.2.

The Windows 95 calculator makes calculating percentages simple.

10. Most of the calculator's operators are *binary operators*, which means they work on two values. The square root and the reciprocal keys work on single numbers. (These are known as *unary operators*.) Press Esc to clear the display and type 64. Click the square root key or press the Shift+@ key to see the square root of 64, which is 8. (8 times 8 is 64.)

    With the 8 still showing (remember that the calculator makes running totals, which means your next operation can work on the values produced by the previous operation), press the reciprocal key. The reciprocal key contains an *X*, which represents the number in the display. Therefore, if 8 is showing, the reciprocal key produces the value 1/8 or .125. Often the reciprocal key is useful for calculating stock quote values. Stocks are often priced in 8ths or 16ths of dollars.

9

11. When you want to negate the number in the display, click the +/– key. Suppose that you want to subtract the display's current value, .125, from 6.875. Although you could clear the display and perform the subtraction, it's faster to negate the .125 by clicking the +/– key, thus producing – .125. Then press the plus sign, and then enter 6.875 and press the equal sign.

12. Some calculators have multiple memories. Unfortunately, the Windows 95 calculator has only a single memory. To store a value in the memory, click the MS key (or press Ctrl+M). Click MS now to store the display's value of 6.75.

The calculator displays a letter M above the four memory keys when you store a value in the memory.

TIME SAVER

13. Whenever you want the memory value back in the display, click MR. For now, click the C to clear the calculator's display, enter the number 10.25, and press the minus sign. Now click MR to display the memory value, 6.75, that you stored in the previous step. The memory store kept you from having to enter the 6.75 a second time. Press the equal sign to see the result.

   If you want to store a running total, click the M+ button every time you want to add the display's value to the memory. Click MC when you want to erase the memory contents completely. The M goes away from the memory indicator box when you clear the memory.

14. When you want to switch over from your application to the calculator to perform a calculation, and then enter the result of that calculation elsewhere such as in your word processor, select **Edit | Copy** (Ctrl+C) to copy the value to the Clipboard. When you switch back to the other Windows 95 application, you'll be able to paste the value into that application. You can also reverse the process by copying (or cutting) values to the clipboard from another application and then pasting that value into the calculator's display with **Edit | Paste** (Ctrl+V), where you then can perform a math operation on the value.

   Leave the calculator window open for the next task.

Step 3: Review

The standard calculator performs all the operations that most Windows 95 users will need most of the time. The interface is simple and allows the use of a mouse or keyboard to enter the values. Perhaps most people will find that the keypad offers the easiest interface to the calculator as long as the Num Lock key is active.

Task 9.2: Using the Scientific Calculator

TASK

Step 1: Description

The second Windows 95 calculator, the scientific calculator, supports many more advanced mathematical operations. Despite its added power, the scientific calculator operates almost identically to the standard calculator. The standard keys and memory are identical in both calculators.

Step 2: Action

1. To see the scientific calculator, select **View | S**cientific. Windows 95 displays the scientific calculator shown in Figure 9.3.

Figure 9.3.

The Windows 95 scientific calculator provides advanced operations.

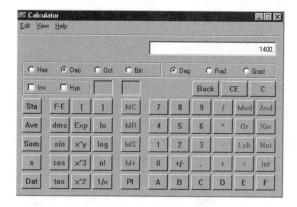

TIME SAVER

If you are using either calculator and, in the middle of a calculation, you decide that you want the functionality of the other calculator, you can switch views to the other calculator, and Windows 95 saves the value of the display when you see the next calculator.

Obviously, the scientific calculator offers more keys, operators, and indicators than does the standard calculator. Table 9.2 lists the additional operators and actions supported by the scientific calculator.

9

Table 9.2. The Windows 95 scientific calculator operations.

Button	Keyboard	Operation	Description
Sta	Ctrl+S	statistics box	Opens the statistics box
Ave	Ctrl+A	mean	Computes the mean average of the values in the statistics box
Sum	Ctrl+T	sum or sum of squares	Computes the sum of the values in the statistics box, the sum of the squares, if you select the Inv option first
s	Ctrl+D	std deviation	Computes the standard deviation of the statistics with a population parameter of n—1 or a population parameter of n if you click Inv first (n is an abbreviation for the number of items in the series)
Dat	Ins	adds to statistics box	Adds the displayed value to the statistics box F-Ev scientific notation. Turns displayed *decimal* (base 10) numbers into their scientific notation equivalents and back again
dms	m	deg/min/sec	Converts the display into degrees, minutes, and seconds as long as the displayed value is in degrees. If you need to convert the displayed value to degrees, click Inv first
sin	s	sine	Computes the sine of the display
cos	o	cosine	Computes the cosine of the display
tan	t	tangent	Computes the tangent of the display
(	shift+(	parentheses	Starts a new level of parentheses (25 levels are possible)
)	shift+)	parentheses	Closes the previous level of parentheses
Exp	x	Scientific entry	Lets you enter decimal numbers in scientific notation

continues

9

Table 9.2. continued

Button	Keyboard	Operation	Description
x^y	y	x raised to a power	Computes the value of x (the display) raised to the y power (the next value you enter)
x^3	shift+#	cube	Multiplies the display by itself three times
x^2	shift+@	square	Multiplies the display by itself
ln	☐	natural log	Calculates the natural logarithm
log	l	common log	Calculates the common logarithm
n!	shift+!	factorial	Calculates the factorial of the displayed number
PI	p	PI	Displays the value of the mathematical PI
Mod	shift+%	modulus	Computes the integer remainder
Or	shift+|	bitwise OR	Returns the bit-by-bit, OR operation of the integer value in the display
And	shift+&	bitwise AND	Returns the bit-by-bit AND operation of the integer value in the display
Xor	shift+^	bitwise XOR	Returns the bit-by-bit XOR operation of the integer value in the display
Lsh	shift+<	left bit shift	Shifts the bits of the integer value in the display (you can perform a right bit shift by clicking Inv first)
Not	shift+~	bitwise invert	Reverses the bits in the displayed integer value
Int	;	integer conversion	Converts the displayed value to an integer (truncates the fractional portion)
A - F	A - F	high hex values	Lets you enter *hexadecimal* (base 16) values from 10 through 15
F-E	v	Scientific notation	Turns scientific notation on and off

9

Button	Keyboard	Operation	Description
Hex	F5	convert to hex	Converts the display to a hexadecimal integer
Dec	F6	convert to decimal	Converts the display to a decimal integer
Oct	F7	convert to octal	Converts the display to an *octal* integer
Bin	F8	convert to binary	Converts the display to a *binary* integer
Inv	i	inverse function	Inverts many of the operations
Hyp	h	hyperbolic	Sets up the sine, cosine, and tangent operations for a one-time hyperbolic calculation
Deg	F2	degrees	Displays the result in degrees
Rad	F3	radians	Displays the result in radians
Grad	F4	gradients	Displays the result in gradients
Dword	F2	32-bit word	Displays full 32-bit values
Word	F3	16-bit word	Displays 16-bit values
Byte	F4	8-bit word	Displays 8-bit values

The keys Ave, Sum, s, and Dat work only if you click the Sta first.

JUST A MINUTE

2. Obviously, this hour is not going into each of these scientific operations. To explain their purpose would be teaching you advanced math and not Windows 95.

   Actually, if you have a need for these operations you already understand their use. The only new interface that you need to master to use these advanced operations is the statistical interface. To compute a mean or standard deviation, you must work with several values at a time (a *series*). The Statistics Box contains the series of values as you enter them because the calculator's display shows only a single line at a time.

Make sure that the Dec option is chosen and click C to clear the display of any values that might be in the calculator. Enter the value of 15. Click Sta, and the calculator displays the statistics display. The box is empty right now, but you'll fill it up as you go. Click the Dat key to add the value of 15 to the Statistics Box and return to the calculator so you can enter more values.

3. Enter 45 and click Sta, and then Dat.

4. Enter 65 and click Sta, and then Dat.

5. Enter 20 and click Sta. Your screen should look like the one in Figure 9.4. The calculator has yet to add the 20 to the series list, but as soon as you press Dat (do so now) the calculator will add the 20 to the series. Sta simply shows the Statistics Box dialog box.

Figure 9.4.

The Statistics Box keeps track of your series of values.

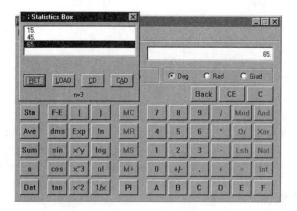

6. Click Sta and then Ave to see the average mean.

7. Click Sum to display the sum of the Statistics Box. You don't have to show the Statistics Box before clicking the four statistical buttons as long as you've entered a series of values.

8. Click Inv and then s to see the standard deviation with a population parameter of n–1.

JUST A MINUTE

Windows 95 adds vertical scroll bars to the statistics box if the box contains more than four values.

9

The Statistics Box

The Statistics Box contains four command buttons labeled **RET**, **LOAD**, **CD**, and **CAD**. The **RET** button returns you to the calculator's screen by minimizing the Statistics Box. The **LOAD** button sends the selected value from the series to the calculator's display. **CD** removes the selected value from the series. **CAD** removes all values from the series.

In addition, the calculator always displays the number in the current series (the value of n) at the bottom of the Statistics Box. If you already entered the value of 20, your screen shows $n = 4$.

8. Just for grins, why not try changing the base of a number. Clear the Statistics Box by pressing Sta and clicking **CAD**.

9. Click the calculator's C key to clear the display.

10. Enter the number 197.

11. Click the Hex option to see that the calculator changes the value to the hexadecimal number C5. (Hexadecimal numbers, or hex numbers for short, sometimes contain the letters A through F.)

12. Click the Oct option to see the calculator change the value to base 8.

13. Click the Bin option to see the calculator change the value to base 2 (base 2 numbers consist of 1s and 0s only). Figure 9.5 shows the calculator program displaying a binary result.

Figure 9.5.

Binary values consist of 1s and 0s.

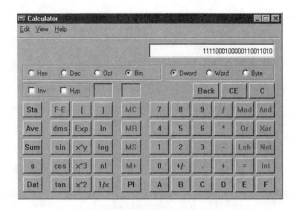

14. Click the Dec option to see the calculator change the value back once again to the familiar decimal (base 10) value of 197. If you understand all these bases, you're probably a computer pro.

JUST A MINUTE

> C and C++ programmers will recognize the need for the bitwise operators. This book does not describe those operators.

15. Close the calculator's window.

Step 3: Review

The scientific calculator requires more mathematical knowledge to use. The calculator itself is not difficult to use, but understanding some of the math can be. To use the calculator fully, you must master the Statistics Box. The Statistics Box contains a series of values on which you can calculate statistical results.

Summary

This hour showed you one of the most useful accessory programs, the calculator program, along with its advantages over its real-world desktop equivalent. The calculator program attempts to be more available on your Windows 95 desktop than its physical counterparts are to your own desk. Windows 95 contains two versions of a calculator: a scientific calculator and a standard calculator that performs more common operations.

Workshop

Term Review

binary   The base-2 numbering system.

binary operators   Operators that work on two values such as the addition and subtraction operators.

decimal   The base-10 numbering system.

hexadecimal   The base-16 numbering system.

n   The number of entries in a statistical series.

octal   The base-8 numbering system.

running total   The Windows 95 calculator operations, such as addition and subtraction, keep operating on the calculator's running display. For example, if the display contains the value 87 and you press the plus sign, and then press 5, the calculator adds the 5 to the 87 and produces the sum of 92. If you press the plus sign again and enter another value, the calculator adds that number to the 92 producing a continuous running total. The running total continues until you clear the display or close the calculator program.

9

scientific calculator   A Windows 95 calculator that supports trigonometric, scientific, and number-conversion operations.

series   A set of values on which you perform statistical operations.

standard calculator   A Windows 95 calculator that performs common mathematical operations.

statistics box   A box that holds your entered series of statistical values. (The calculator's display can hold only a single value at a time.)

unary operators   Operators that work on single values such as square root.

Q&A

Q Why would I ever need the scientific calculator?

A If the standard calculator does not perform all the math you need, you must use the scientific calculator. Even many business applications, such as financial analysis, require the use of advanced mathematical, statistical, and trigonometric operations, such as the average, standard deviation, and the factorial.

If you like to go to Vegas you'll use the factorial key a lot when computing odds at games of chance also. See, math doesn't have to be boring!

TIME SAVER

Q What is the Statistics Box for?

A The Statistics Box holds more than one value, whereas the calculator's display can hold only a single value at a time. When you must compute statistical measurements based on a series of numbers, you'll need a place to store that series of numbers. The Statistics Box is such a place.

By using the Statistics Box's four command buttons, you'll be able to manage the values in the Statistics Box. Once you build a series of numbers in the Statistics Box, you can click the various statistical operations to make calculations based on the series.

Hour 10

Compose Using Writing Tools

For many people, this hour contains a review of procedures they already know. The Notepad and WordPad programs that appear on your Accessories menu are simple editing programs that accept your text as input and create documents. The WordPad program does not contain all the features of a word processor, such as Microsoft Word for Windows 6; WordPad does, however, contain many formatting features and can accept documents created in several word processing programs. WordPad accepts any document created by Word for Windows 6, as well as documents created in other word processors that can save the documents in RTF (*Rich Text Format* as defined in Hour 4, "Take Windows 95 to Task"), or in the text format.

Before looking at WordPad, this hour explores the Notepad program. Notepad loads more quickly than WordPad (or virtually any word processor) and takes less memory, but it has less functionality than WordPad. Notepad handles only text files up to the size of 64KB (approximately 64,000 bytes of memory). Therefore, Notepad holds about 60 pages of single-spaced text. Notepad works only with text files, so if you have to work with text files, you don't have to select from among various document file types as you have to do with WordPad.

JUST A MINUTE

Notepad and WordPad are actually *text editors* and not word processors because they do not contain the powerful formatting abilities available in word processors.

The highlights of this hour include:

☐ When to use Notepad and when to use WordPad

☐ How to edit text within the Notepad environment

☐ How to edit and format text within the WordPad environment

☐ Why the Print Preview feature can save you time and paper costs

Notice the Notepad

When you start Notepad from the Accessories menu, the Notepad program window opens as shown in Figure 10.1. You can resize and maximize the window. The Notepad window contains both horizontal and vertical scroll bars, so Notepad can create documents that are larger than the window's width and height.

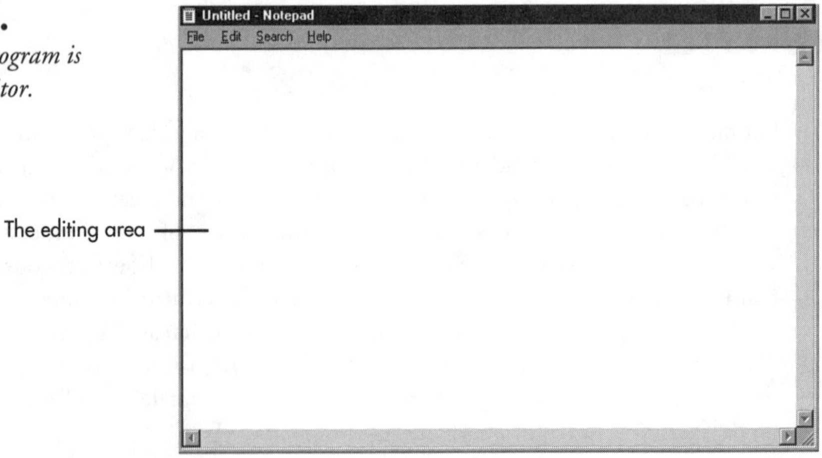

Figure 10.1.

The Notepad program is a simple text editor.

The editing area ———

10

TIME SAVER

If you have not used a word processor before, or if you have not used a Windows-based word processor before, Notepad and WordPad provide great introductions to word processors. You can get the basics of data-entry using Notepad, and then add the formatting capabilities of WordPad before tackling a comprehensive word processor program such as Word for Windows.

All of the typical text-entry control keys, such as Backspace, the cursor-movement arrow keys, the Enter key, the Del(ete), the PageUp and PageDown keys, operate normally on the text you type inside the Notepad window. In addition to the usual keys, the following keys control the text-entry as well:

10

Ctrl+Left Arrow	Moves the cursor to the beginning of the previous word in the document.
Ctrl+Right Arrow	Moves the cursor to the beginning of the next word in the document.
Home	Moves the cursor to the beginning of the current line.
End	Moves the cursor to the end of the current line.
Ctrl+Home	Moves the cursor to the beginning of the document's first line.
Ctrl+End	Moves the cursor to the end of the document's last line.

JUST A MINUTE

These same keys are available in WordPad also. Therefore, if you learn the keys in Notepad, you'll already know them when you work with WordPad.

Task 10.1: A First Look at Notepad

TASK

Step 1: Description

This task loads a text file from the Windows 95 directory into Notepad. Once you load the file, you can then practice changing the file and using the keyboard editing tools.

Step 2: Action

1. Select **File | Open**. You'll see the familiar (familiar after Hour 5, "Cruise with Documents and Windows") Windows 95 Open dialog box.

2. Display the contents of the Windows folder (usually located on drive C) by double-clicking on the Windows folder. By default, Notepad expects to open text document files with filename extensions of .TXT, so when you see an Open dialog box, the only documents you see in the list are text documents and folders.

3. Double-click the document named Readme.txt (you may not see the extension, depending on the settings of your Explorer Options). The TYItents of your Windows 95's Readme.txt document file might differ from the figure's.

JUST A MINUTE

If you want to see filename extensions or hide them, you must set the appropriate option using the Explorer program's **V**iew | **O**ption command, as described in Hour 6, "Explore the Windows 95 System." The Explorer setting determines how all Windows 95 Open dialog boxes display filename extensions.

When Notepad loads the file, your Notepad window should look similar to the one in Figure 10.2.

Figure 10.2.

Notepad now has a document loaded in memory.

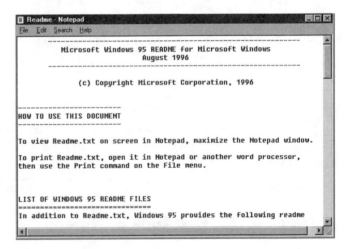

CAUTION

If you maximized the Notepad window, resize the window so that the size fills only the center of the screen. The smaller window gives you more practice scrolling using the scroll bars. Remember, too, that your version of Windows 95 might differ slightly from this book's version meaning that the actual contents of your Readme.txt text document might be different from the one shown here.

10

4. Click the scroll bars and use the cursor-movement keys described earlier to practice navigating through text documents.

TIME SAVER

> You can move the mouse to any position where you want the text cursor and click the mouse button to move the text cursor instantly to that location.

5. Press Ctrl+End to place the cursor at the very end of the document.

6. Type these words: This is the end of the Readme.txt document.

7. Press Enter to position the cursor at the start of the next line.

8. Press the Up Arrow to move the cursor to the beginning of the line you just added.

9. Press the Ctrl+Right Arrow key until the text cursor rests just before the letter *t* in the third word (*the*) on the line. Type the word really and press the spacebar. Notice that Notepad shifts the entire line to the right to make room for the new word.

CAUTION

> Notepad does not support an *overtype* mode as do most word processors, including WordPad. Notepad only works in *insert* mode which means that each character you type, when that character precedes others on the line, shifts all other characters to the right to make room for the new character. Overtype mode, when available in other programs such as WordPad, means that new characters always overwrite existing characters on a line.

10. Press Backspace twice. As you press Backspace, Notepad backs up the cursor, erases as it backs up, and shifts the remaining characters to the left to close up the space caused by the deleted characters.

11. Press Ctrl+Z. Ctrl+Z is the shortcut key for **Edit** | **Undo**. The **Undo** command reverses the most recent edit. Notice that your two deleted characters return.

12. When you want to delete an entire word, or a group of words, you might be better off selecting the text first with the mouse. Drag the mouse cursor over the beginning of the selected text and release the mouse after highlighting the selected text.

    Select the entire word really, plus the space at the end of the word, as shown in Figure 10.3.

Figure 10.3.

Select words with the mouse or keyboard.

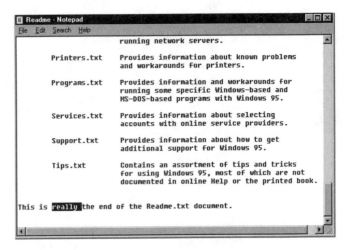

TIME SAVER

You can select text by holding down the Shift key and pressing the arrow keys. Holding down a Shift key while pressing *both* Ctrl and a left or right arrow key selects an entire word at a time. Holding down the Shift key plus an up or down arrow highlights the previous or subsequent lines.

13. After you select text (you can select multiple paragraphs at the same time if you need to work with that much text at once), you can copy the text to the Clipboard, cut the text from the document and send that cut text to the Clipboard, or delete the text without using the Clipboard. All of these commands are available from the Edit menu.

    Press Del to delete the selected text.

TIME SAVER

You can select the entire text document at once by choosing the **E**dit | Select **A**ll command.

14. Add to the end of the line. Press the End key to move the cursor to the end of the line. Press the Spacebar and type this text: Now is the time to finish.

    If you've worked with word processors, you may have expected the text to *wrap* when the cursor got to the end of the window. Notepad does not automatically wrap text to the next line at the edge of the window. There is a way to force the text to wrap at the edge of the window. Select the **E**dit | **W**ord Wrap command and watch your screen. Notepad reformats the entire file so that no line is hidden by the right edge of the screen. Notepad removes the horizontal scroll bar when the Word Wrap is turned on because there is no text to the right to require scrolling.

10

15. Without Word Wrap turned on, the Notepad program wraps text to the next line only when you press Enter. Turn off Word Wrap (by selecting **Edit** | **W**ord Wrap once again) to put the Readme.txt file back to its original margins. The line you typed at the end of the file, as well as many of the other lines in the file, will now span past the right edge of the screen.

16. Press Ctrl+End to move the cursor to the end of the document file.

17. Type this: Today is, and then press the Spacebar to put a space after is.

18. Press F5. F5 is the shortcut key for the **Edit** | **Time/D**ate command. Notepad places the time and date at the cursor's position as shown in Figure 10.4.

Figure 10.4.

Notepad can insert the time and date at the cursor's position.

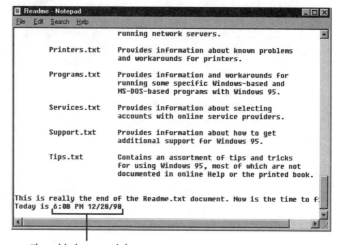

The added time and date

10

If you want only the time or the date, you can insert the full time and date and delete the unwanted portion.

TIME SAVER

Here is a strange feature of Notepad: If you ever type the word .LOG (notice the initial period) at the top of a Notepad text document and then save the document, every subsequent time that you open the document, Notepad appends the current time and date to the end of the file. You can use this feature to keep a log file using Notepad.

19. Display the **S**earch menu. Select **F**ind. Notepad displays the Find dialog box shown in Figure 10.5. You can look for specific text. If you want Notepad to search for the text you enter and match only the text that exactly matches the uppercase and lowercase characters of your search text, click the Match **c**ase option. If you want Notepad to search up from the cursor's current position (something you would want if, as is now the case, the cursor appears at the end of the file) select **U**p and Notepad searches from the current cursor position to the start of the file. By default, Notepad searches down in the file and stops the search at the end of the document.

Figure 10.5.

Notepad can search for specific text within the document.

Type Windows and click the **U**p option to locate the previous occurrence of the word. Press **F**ind Next to start the search. When Notepad finds matching text, it displays the Find dialog box once again and you can continue searching.

20. If you want to save the document text you created, select **F**ile | **S**ave. Don't save the Readme.txt file, however, because you made changes to the document that shouldn't appear in the file. Select **F**ile | E**x**it to exit the program. When Windows 95 informs you that you may want to save the changes you made to the file, Click the No command button.

Step 3: Review

Notepad offers a simple text editing tool for text files. Although Notepad provides only fundamental editing features, you can quickly load Notepad and work with text files whether or not you want those files created with Word Wrap.

TIME SAVER

If you are a programmer, you can use Notepad as a quick editor for programs. Turn off the Word Wrap feature so that Notepad does not automatically wrap at a window's edge. Notepad always opens and saves document files in the standard text format, just as most language compilers require.

10

WordPad Works Well with Words

The WordPad program is more than a text editor, but slightly less than a word processor. WordPad offers a large assortment of editing and formatting tools that go beyond the power of Notepad. Whereas Notepad edited, loaded, and saved only text documents, WordPad edits, loads, and saves documents in all the following formats:

☐ Word for Windows

☐ Windows Write (the word processor available in Windows 3.1)

☐ Text documents

☐ RTF documents

☐ Text documents—MS-DOS format

As a result, when you open an RTF or Write or Word for Windows 6 document that contains formatting, such as underlining and boldfaced characters, WordPad retains those special formatting features in the document. (Notepad does not have this capability.)

WordPad supports all the standard editing keys described for Notepad in the previous sections. In addition, WordPad contains a toolbar that you can display to help you access common commands more easily. WordPad also supports the uses of a Ruler and format bar that help you work with WordPad's advanced editing features.

3.1 ▶
Step Up   The WordPad editor is a full 32-bit application. That means Microsoft programmers wrote WordPad to take advantage of all of the internal and external features of Windows 95.

Task 10.2: Working with WordPad

Step 1: Description

The WordPad program contains features for the novice as well as for advanced power-users. If you have no other word processor on your system, you can use WordPad to produce virtually any kind of document that you need. This task leads you through the basic steps for using WordPad and its features.

Step 2: Action

1. Start the WordPad program from the Accessories menu. You'll see the WordPad screen shown in Figure 10.6.

Figure 10.6.

WordPad offers many word processing features.

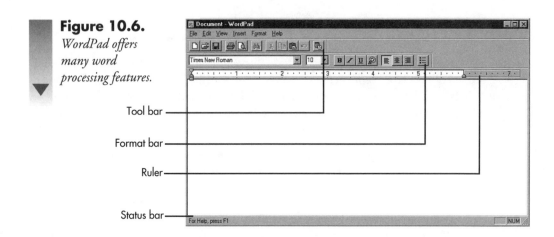

Tool bar

Format bar

Ruler

Status bar

JUST A MINUTE

Your WordPad screen may not look exactly like the one in Figure 10.6. Use the **V**iew menu to checkmark each of the first four commands: **T**oolbar, **F**ormat Bar, **R**uler, and **S**tatus Bar, so that you display each of these four optional tools.

2. For this task you'll practice entering and formatting text. Type the following text: A large line.

3. Select all three words by highlighting them with the mouse or keyboard.

4. Click the first format bar button with the letter B. The text stays selected but something changes; the text becomes boldfaced. You can press an arrow key to get rid of the highlight and see the boldfaced text.

5. Select the three words once again. Click the second format bar button with the letter *I*. WordPad italicizes the text. Now click the third format bar button with the letter U. WordPad instantly underlines the selected text. Keep the text highlighted for the next step.

6. By default WordPad selects a *font* (a typestyle) named *Times New Roman*. You can see the font name directly below the format bar. The font's size, in *points* (a point is 1/72 inch), appears to the right of the font name (the default font size is 10 points).

   You can change both the font and the font size by clicking the dropdown lists in which each appears. When you select text, then select a font name, WordPad changes the font of the selected text to the new font name style. After selecting the text, display the font name list by clicking the dropdown listbox's arrow and select a font name. If you have the *Comic Sans MS*, use that font to correspond to the next figure in this book. If you do not have that font name, select another font name that sounds interesting.

10

Open the point size dropdown listbox and select 22 (you can type this number directly into the listbox if you want to). As soon as you do, you can see the results of your boldfaced, underlined, italicized, large-sized text displayed using the font name you selected. Press the left or right arrow key to remove the selection. Figure 10.7 shows what your WordPad window should look like.

Figure 10.7.

The text is formatted to your exact specifications.

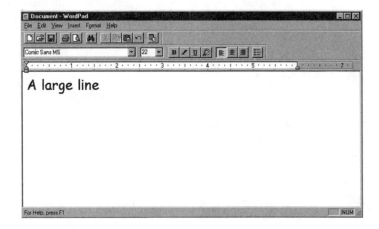

WordPad applied all of the previous formatting on the three words because you selected those words before you changed the formatting. If you select only a single word, WordPad formats only that selected word and leaves all the other words alone.

CAUTION

> Don't overdo the formatting of text! If you make text too fancy, it becomes cluttered, and your words will lose their meaning amidst all the italics, underlines, and font styles. Don't mix more than two or three font styles on the same page. Use italics, boldfacing, and underlining only for emphasis when needed for certain words and titles.

7. Press Enter. Click the B, *I*, and U format bar buttons and return the font name to *Times New Roman*. Lower the font size to 10. Type the following: My name is and press the spacebar. If you do not like the font size, click the down arrow to the right of the font name list and select a different size.

8. Suppose you want to italicize your name. If you now click the format bar for italics, *all subsequent text that you type will be italicized.* Click the italics format bar button now and type your first name. The name will be italicized, but the other text is not italicized.

9. Click the italics format bar button once again and continue typing on the same line. Type this: and I like to use WordPad.

10. As you can see, you don't have to select text to apply special formatting to text. Before you type text that you want to format, select the proper format command and then type the text. WordPad then formats the text, using the format styles you've selected, as you type that text. When you want to revert to the previous unformatted style (such as when you no longer want italics) change the style and keep typing.

Font Controls

Ctrl+B, Ctrl+I, and Ctrl+U are the shortcut keys for clicking the **B**, *I*, and U format bar buttons. You can also change the formatting of text characters by selecting F**o**rmat | **F**ont. WordPad displays a Font dialog box, shown in Figure 10.8, on which you can apply several formatting styles.

As you change the style, the Font dialog box's Sample area shows you a sample of text formatted to the specifications you provide. When you close the Font dialog box, WordPad formats subsequent text according to the Font dialog box settings.

Figure 10.8.

The Font dialog box provides all formatting specifications in a single place.

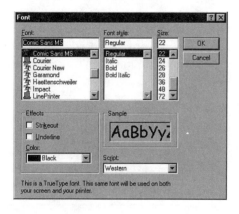

11. The Ruler indicates where your text will appear on the printed page when you print the document. (This book's printer discussion is saved for Hour 15, "Increase Printing Power.") The screen's text measurements will differ from the printed document's measurements because of differences in screen sizes and video *resolution* (the amount of clarity your video adapter and screen can provide). Each number on the Ruler represents an inch (or a centimeter if your computer is set up for a metric setting).

10

As you type you can watch the Ruler to see where the text will appear once you print the document. If you select the Format | Paragraph command, WordPad displays the Paragraph dialog box in which you can set left and right indentations for individual paragraphs (either highlighted paragraphs or the paragraph that contains the cursor when you select the Format | Paragraph command).

Display the Paragraph dialog box now, but leave the values at their default settings. Once you've read through the dialog box press Esc to close the dialog box.

12. If you want to set tab stops, do so by first selecting the Format | Tabs command, and then displaying the Tabs dialog box shown in Figure 10.9.

Figure 10.9.

You can add one or more tab stops to a document's Ruler bar.

10

If you know the exact Ruler measurement of the tab stop you want to create, type that number at the top of the Tabs dialog box and click the Set command button. The Tabs dialog box holds a list of tab stops as you add them. You can clear a tab stop by highlighting the tab stop value and clicking Clear. When you've set the tab stops, click the OK command button to return to the document.

> You can place tab stops quickly by double-clicking over the Ruler at the exact location of the tab stop you want.

TIME SAVER

13. Maximize the size of your WordPad window. Type the following poem; press Enter at the end of each line:

```
Some day soon I will be
A Windows 95 master totally.
So that when I work at my PC
Windows 95 will obey only me.
```

14. Select the entire paragraph so the paragraph is completely highlighted.

15. Click the Center format bar button (the third button from the right that displays the message Center, when you hold the mouse pointer over the button for two seconds). WordPad automatically centers your paragraph on the page. The Ruler determines the centering measurements.

16. Click the Align Right format bar button (the second format bar button from the right). WordPad aligns the poem against the right margin. These formatting buttons adjust the alignment of your WordPad paragraphs. By default, WordPad aligns all of your paragraphs against the left margin.

TIME SAVER

> The center alignment format bar button is useful for centering titles at the top of documents.

The Format | Paragraph dialog box contains a dropdown listbox that offers these three alignment choices in case you don't have the format bar displayed, but you still want to align text. Change the alignment back to the left edge of the screen.

JUST A MINUTE

> A *paragraph* is actually any line or group of lines that end with an Enter keypress.

17. Click the Color format bar button (see Figure 10.10) to display the color-selection listbox shown in Figure 10.10.

Figure 10.10.

Apply color to selected text with the Color format bar button.

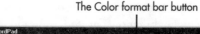

The Color format bar button

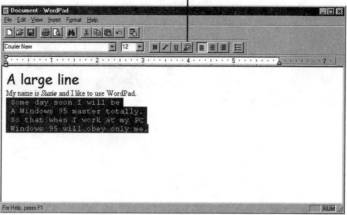

If you select a color, WordPad sets all selected text to that color. If there is no selected text, then all subsequent text that you type from the text cursor's current position will be that color, until you change the color once again.

10

18. Move the cursor to the end of the poem you just typed. Press Enter twice to add a blank line after the poem.

19. Click the far-right format bar button. This is the Bullets format bar button. When you want to create a list of bulleted items, you can first click the Bullets button to get WordPad's help with the bullets. (The format bar button offers a shortcut for the Format | **B**ullet Style menu command.)

    Type three song titles, pressing Enter at the end of each line. When you press Enter, WordPad produces another bullet to the left of the new line. After the third song title, click the Bullets format bar button once again to end the list of bulleted items. Your screen should look something like the screen in Figure 10.11.

Figure 10.11.
WordPad makes adding a bulleted list of items easy.

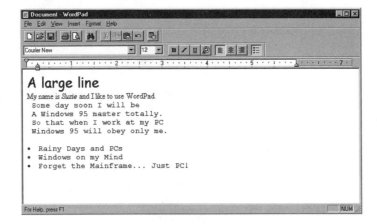

TIME SAVER

> To revert a bulleted list back to regular lines of text, select the list and then click the Bullets format bar button.

20. All of the usual Clipboard editing features, such as Copy, Cut, and Paste, work inside WordPad. Also the **E**dit menu contains Find and Replace commands that let you locate and even globally replace text.

    Suppose that you write a 10-page letter to a Joe MacDonald and then you find out that Joe spells his last name *McDonald*. You could edit the document by hand deleting the *a* inside every *MacDonald*. An easier method would be to select the **E**dit | **R**eplace command to display the Replace dialog box (display this dialog box now). You could type MacDonald at the Fi**n**d what prompt and McDonald at the Re**p**lace with prompt. You could then have WordPad replace each individual occurrence of the name, one at a time, by clicking the **F**ind Next button or you can click Replace **A**ll to request that WordPad make all the replacements for you. For now, press Esc to close the Replace dialog box.

21. WordPad supports an **E**dit | **U**ndo command (Ctrl+Z is the shortcut). You can undo your most recent edit or format command. Many of the menu bar commands are contained on the toolbar buttons as well. Take a moment to run your mouse cursor over each toolbar button for a couple of seconds to see what each button represents. (The toolbar is the row of buttons above the font name dropdown listbox, as opposed to the format bar at the right of the font name dropdown listbox. See Figure 10.6.)

22. Perhaps one of the most helpful features of WordPad is the *Print Preview* feature. Select **F**ile | Print Preview to see a full-page *thumbnail sketch* of how your entire document's page will look when you print the document. If your document is more than one page, press PageDown to see a preview of the subsequent pages. Figure 10.12 shows a sample Print Preview of the document you're now creating.

Figure 10.12.

The Print Preview feature illustrates how your printed document will look.

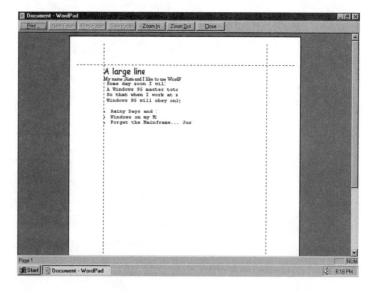

The Print Preview command buttons all work with the preview (printing the document or changing the way the preview appears on the screen). If you want to zero-in on certain parts of the Print Preview, you can move the cursor over that area of the preview. WordPad changes the cursor's shape to a magnifying glass, and when you press Enter, WordPad expands the size of the preview so that you can read the text.

10

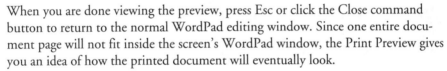

When you are done viewing the preview, press Esc or click the Close command button to return to the normal WordPad editing window. Since one entire document page will not fit inside the screen's WordPad window, the Print Preview gives you an idea of how the printed document will eventually look.

23. Select **F**ile | **Ex**it to leave WordPad for now. Don't save the document you created in this hour.

Step 3: Review

You've now used just about all of WordPad's major features. The commands and tips you now know will get you through the creation of almost any document you want to create using WordPad. Once you type the document and format the document the way you want it, use the Print Preview command before printing the document to get a idea of how the printed output will look. If there is a formatting problem in your document, you can catch the problem during the preview instead of printing output that you'll have to correct and reprint.

TIME SAVER

As with most Windows 95 programs, you can start multiple instances of WordPad. For example, you could start three copies of WordPad and run all three inside their own windows at the same time. Also, the taskbar will contain buttons for all three. With three open windows, you can easily move and copy text between the documents you are editing.

Summary

This hour discussed the two editors of Windows 95: Notepad and WordPad. Notepad creates and edits small text files. Using Notepad you can perform simple editing tasks on documents that have no special formatting in them.

If you want more formatting power, the WordPad program acts almost as powerfully as many word processors on the market. You can format text, display a Print Preview, and control the text placement on a Ruler line. The WordPad program also edits documents created with Word for Windows 6 or other word processor programs.

Even if you don't have a word processor yet, these two programs will get you through many hours of tedious editing.

Workshop

Term Review

32-bit application   A program written to take advantage of the Windows 95 interface and to integrate easily with other Windows 95 application programs.

font   A specific typestyle. Fonts have names that distinguish them from one another. Some fonts are fancy and others are plain. Choose a font style that best serves the idea your words need to convey.

home position   The upper-left position of a document or of a window.

insert mode   Newly typed text shifts the existing text to the right.

overtype mode   Newly typed text overwrites existing text.

point   A measurement of 1/72 of an inch (72 points equals one inch). Most computer on-screen and printed text measures from 9 to 12 points in size.

Print Preview   A full-screen representation of how your document will look when you print the document.

resolution   A measurement that specifies how close together individual screen dots can be. The higher the resolution, the closer together the dots that form characters and graphic images, and the better the picture will be.

text editor   A program that creates document files but offers only primitive formatting and printing functionality.

thumbnail sketch   A small representation that shows the overall layout without showing a lot of detail.

wrap   When an editor or word processor automatically moves the cursor to the start of the next line when the cursor gets to the edge of a window or Ruler margin.

Q&A

Q I have a Windows word processor, so why would I need to use Notepad or WordPad?

A Neither Notepad nor WordPad can match your word processor in skills. Both Notepad and WordPad do, however, take less memory and therefore load faster. Although memory limits are not a constant problem as they were in Windows 3.1, you'll still want to maximize the use of memory and use as little as you need at any one time.

If you want to create or edit simple text document files, your word processor is certainly overkill. In addition, your word processor's automatic word wrap (which is often difficult to turn off in major word processors) will format your text file in a

10

way you probably don't want the file formatted. When you turn off the word wrap in Notepad, using a simple menu command, you won't have to worry about word wrap.

Q I like to create text documents for my programming work and word processed documents for my correspondence. My word processor is great for the correspondence. I can see a programming need for Notepad, but not for my use of WordPad. Am I missing something here?

A You'll probably want to stay with your word processor for your correspondence. Keep in mind, however, that unless your word processor was designed for the Windows 95 environment, its Open dialog boxes (including the related dialog boxes such as the Save and Save As dialog boxes) probably do not support long filenames or the special right-click features of the Windows 95-style Open dialog boxes.

If you need to manage documents much while editing them, you may want to use WordPad for the job once in a while because of the power that WordPad's Open dialog box provides. Remember, too, that WordPad can read and write Word 6 for Windows document files, as well as document files you store in the RTF format. Therefore, you can use your word processor to create files, and then use WordPad when you want to make minor changes to the files without taking the time or memory to load a full-featured word processor.

Q Can WordPad do anything my own word processor cannot do?

A That question cannot be answered here. The answer depends on your word processor's capabilities and whether or not your word processor was written for the Windows 95 environment.

WordPad lets you create multiple instances of itself, which means that you can load more than one WordPad program at the same time and edit different documents in each. Also, the WordPad program supports all the major Windows 95 interface tools, such as the Open dialog boxes (as explained in the previous answer).

Once you become proficient at Windows 95, WordPad supports the use of OLE. OLE stands for *object linking and embedding*, meaning that one application, such as WordPad, can interface to any other Windows 95 application. If you want to, you can embed a WordPad document in the middle of a spreadsheet for textual explanation of your data. When you are working on the spreadsheet, you can click on its copy of the WordPad document. WordPad then automatically starts, and you can edit that document using the WordPad menu and commands, without removing the WordPad document from the spreadsheet or recopying it. You'll get a chance to try OLE in the next hour. Your word processor may not be able to open and edit Word 6 for Windows documents. If not, you can use WordPad, if someone gives you a Word 6 for Windows document that you need to edit or print.

10

Q I don't have a color printer so will I need to use the Color format bar button in WordPad?

A Even if you don't have a color printer, your monitor is probably color. You can apply color to parts of a document that you want to call your own attention to later when editing that document. For example, if you leave some parts of a business report's annual report unfinished, you can color the paragraph that contains the unfinished material in yellow, so you'll later be able to find those locations easily and finish the report.

The Internet provides another reason you may create color documents even if you have no color printer. If you create Web pages from within WordPad, the color will appear on the Web page. By the way, WordPad certainly may not be the best place to create *final* Web pages, but you can use WordPad to generate initial Web pages that you then finish with more comprehensive Web page tools such as Microsoft's Front Page.

Q Why can't I read all the text on the Print Preview?

A The Print Preview feature was not designed to let you read text necessarily. The Print Preview feature simply draws a representation of your document when you print the document on the printer. Instead of printing the document and discovering there is a margin or formatting error, you can often find the errors on the Print Preview screen, so you can correct the problem *before* printing the document.

10

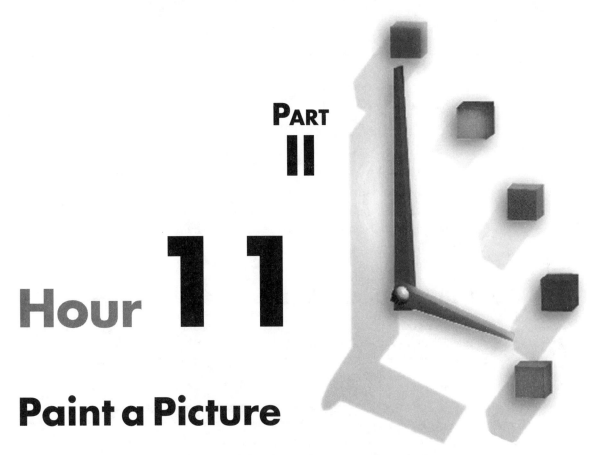

PART

II

Hour 11

Paint a Picture

In the last hour you learned how to use Windows 95's writing tools. In this hour, you learn how to use Windows 95's primary drawing tool. The Windows 95 Paint program is a drawing program. Although Paint won't make you an artist overnight, you can create some fairly sophisticated art using Paint.

Even though Paint has been available since the first version of Windows 95, Microsoft wrote the Windows 95 Paint program from scratch as a 32-bit application that takes advantage of all of the interface features, such as the new Open dialog boxes, available in Windows 95 programs. The pictures that you create with Paint are considered documents so all the document-management tools you've learned so far work with Paint document files as well.

The Paint program provides several kinds of drawing tools with which you can draw lines and geometric shapes. Paint supports color filling and outlining also. One of the most advanced features of Paint, OLE support, lets you embed a Paint picture in the middle of other OLE-compatible documents such as a WordPad document.

Perhaps the best reason to learn Paint: Paint is fun!

The highlights of this hour include:

- [ ] How to navigate Paint's screen
- [ ] What the tool box icons are for
- [ ] When to use the Pencil tool and when to use the geometric tools
- [ ] Where to access the coloring capabilities of Paint
- [ ] How OLE combines two or more products into a single interface that lets you share data and documents between different programs
- [ ] Why graphics are so important in today's world

Learning About Paint's Screen

Paint provides many drawing tools. Before you can use Paint effectively, you must learn how to interact with Paint, and you also must know what each of Paint's tools does. The Paint screen contains five major areas. Figure 11.1 lists each of those five major areas. Table 11.1 describes each area.

Figure 11.1.

The five major areas of the Paint screen.

Menu bar

Tool box

Drawing area

Color box

Status bar

JUST A MINUTE

Paint does not contain a toolbar with buttons as do WordPad and other Windows 95 programs. Paint contains a *tool box* that is the most important area of Paint. It is from the tool box that you select and use drawing tools.

11

Table 11.1. Descriptions of the five areas of Paint's screen.

Area	Description
Drawing area	The drawing appears in the drawing area. When you want to create or modify a drawing, you'll work within this area.
Color box	A list of possible colors you can choose for colorizing your artwork.
Menu bar	The commands that control Paint's operation.
Status bar	Displays important messages and measurements as you use Paint.
Tool box	The vital drawing, painting, and coloring tools with which you create and modify artwork.

There are two scroll bars on the drawing area so that you can scroll to other parts of your drawing. The drawing area is actually as large as a maximized window. If, however, Paint initially displayed the drawing area maximized, you could not access the menu bar or the tool box or read the status bar. Therefore, Paint adds the scroll bars to its drawing area so that you can create drawings that will, when displayed, fill the entire screen.

Task 11.1: Getting to Know Paint

Step 1: Description

This task lets you start Paint and navigate around the screen a bit. The rest of this hour contains several tasks so you can practice Paint and learn Paint's features as you use the program.

Step 2: Action

1. Start the Paint program. Paint is located in the Accessories menu.

2. Maximize the Paint program to full size. Paint is one of the few programs in which you'll almost always want to work in a maximized window. By maximizing the window, you gain the largest drawing area possible.

3. If you do not see the tool box, the status bar, or the color box, display the **V**iew menu and check each of these three important screen areas to ensure that all five areas show as you follow along in this hour.

JUST A MINUTE

When you exit Paint, it saves the screen size and selected viewing options so that when you start Paint the next time, your screen will look like it did when you exited Paint the previous time.

11

TASK

4. Take a look at Figure 11.2. This figure labels each of the tool box *tools*. Each tool contains an icon that illustrates the tool's function. The tools on the tool box comprise your collection of drawing, painting, and coloring tools. When you want to add or modify a picture, you will have to pick the appropriate tool. As you work with Paint in subsequent tasks, you'll want to refer to Figure 11.2 to find the tool named in the task.

Figure 11.2.

The tools on the tool box.

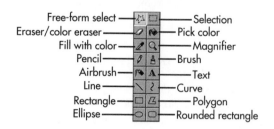

Want to draw a picture? Task 11.2 shows you how!

Step 3: Review

The first thing you should do when starting Paint is maximize the program window. You will often need to have all the areas of the screen showing, especially the tool box. Therefore, once you start Paint for the first time, be sure to display the **View** menu and make sure that the first three **View** menu options are checked.

Task 11.2: Drawing with the Pencil Tool

Step 1: Description

To begin drawing with Paint, select the pencil tool and use the mouse to draw lines on the drawing area. The pencil tool draws lines as you drag the mouse. You can use the color bar to select a line color for the lines and draw more lines of multiple colors.

Step 2: Action

1. Click the pencil tool.

2. Move the mouse cursor over the drawing area, and the cursor changes to a pencil (the same icon that's on the pencil tool).

3. Hold down the mouse button and move your mouse. Move the mouse all around the drawing area. Make all sorts of curves with the mouse. Notice that Paint keeps the pencil within the borders of the drawing area. Figure 11.3 shows what you can do when you really go crazy with the pencil tool.

11

Figure 11.3.

The pencil tool lets you draw with a freehand style.

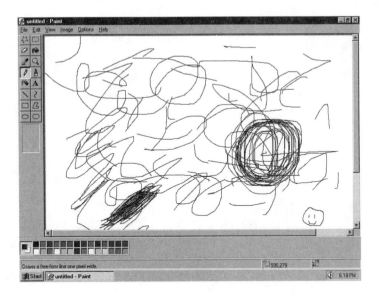

TIME SAVER

Think of clicking the mouse button as being the same as putting the pencil on paper. When you hold down the mouse you can draw on the paper. When you let up with the button (*raise the pencil*), no drawing takes place.

4. The default color for the pencil drawing is black. Click over a different color on the color bar, such as red or green, and draw some more. The new lines will appear in the new color. Select additional colors and draw more lines to pretty the picture even more.

JUST A MINUTE

I said this would be fun, didn't I?

Step 3: Review

The pencil tool is the primary drawing tool for freehand lines and curves. The pencil draws lines in the selected color. The pencil tool draws as you drag the mouse across the drawing area.

TIME SAVER

Every time you change a tool or color or draw a separate line, Paint saves the next group of changes to the drawing area. As with most Windows 95 accessory programs, Paint supports an **E**dit | **U**ndo feature (Ctrl+Z or Alt+Backspace). You can undo up to three previous edit groups. Therefore, if you've just drawn three separate lines, you can remove each of those lines by selecting the **U**ndo command three times.

Task 11.3: Using the Geometric Tools

TASK

Step 1: Description

Drawing with the pencil tool requires patience and skill when you want to draw perfect lines, curves, and shapes. Although the pencil is easy to use, the mouse is not the best freehand drawing device for drawing certain shapes. Paint supplies several tools on the tool box that you can use to draw squares, rectangles, curves, and circles of virtually any shape and size.

Step 2: Action

1. Erase the drawing by selecting **File** | **New**. When Paint displays the dialog box shown in Figure 11.4, click the **No** command button. Paint clears the drawing area so you can start a new document image.

Figure 11.4.

Don't save your first masterpiece.

JUST A MINUTE

If you had loaded and made changes to an existing document image, the dialog box shown in Figure 11.4 would have asked if you wanted to save the changes to that particular file. You haven't saved the image that you created in the previous task, so the dialog box refers to the drawing as *untitled* in the dialog box because the drawing has no document filename.

2. Click the Line tool. Use the Line tool to draw straight lines.

   A straight line is defined by two coordinates: the starting coordinate position and the end coordinate position. In order to draw a line, you must anchor the line's starting position and extend the line to its ending position. Paint automatically

11

WINDOWS MINUTE

draws a straight line from the starting position to the end position. You can draw lines, using the Line tool, in any direction.

Where's the Point?

Paint measures all drawing positions by *coordinates* or *points*. Suppose you draw a single dot in the center of the screen. The smallest dot you can draw is called a *pixel* (coming from the words *picture element*). A coordinate is defined by the number of pixels from the top edge of the screen to a point (your dot) and the number of pixels from the left edge of the screen to a point.

Every dot, line, and shape in the drawing area begins at a specific point and measures a certain number of coordinate points. The way that Paint indicates a dot's position is by a *coordinate pair*, which is two numbers separated by a comma, such as *137,82*. The first number in a coordinate pair represents the number of pixels from the left edge of the drawing area, and the second number represents the number of pixels from the top edge of the drawing area. Every pixel inside the drawing area has its own unique coordinate pair measurement, just as every house has a unique address.

The status bar always displays the starting coordinate position of every dot, line, or shape that you draw. If you draw with one of the geometric tools, the status bar also lists the length (for lines and other shapes) and height (for geometric shapes that have height) of that item, in pixels.

3. Get used to reading coordinate pair numbers in the status bar. Move the mouse around the drawing area (do not press a mouse button yet) and watch the pair of numbers at the right of the status bar change. As mentioned in the Windows Minute, the first number represents the number of pixels from the left edge of the drawing area, and the second number represents the number of pixels from the top of the drawing area.

   Position the mouse cursor at position 118,75 (or as close to that position as you can). This will be the line's *anchor position*. If you were to begin drawing there, the first point in that drawing would begin 118 pixels from the left of the drawing area and 75 pixels from the top edge of the drawing area. Click and hold the mouse button and drag the mouse down and to the right to the point located at 420,245. Figure 11.5 shows the resulting line that should appear on your screen. The Status bar will show where your mouse pointer ends up.

JUST A MINUTE

Don't worry if you cannot place the line at the exact coordinates listed in this hour. Get fairly close and your drawings will look like the figures.

11

Figure 11.5.

You drew a line without pain!

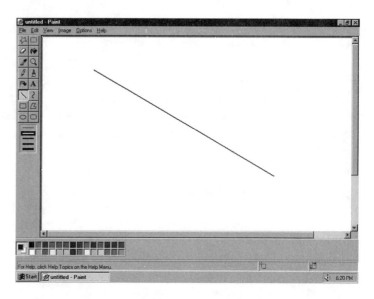

4. Draw two more lines. Remember to anchor the beginning of the line by clicking (and holding) the mouse button before moving the mouse in the direction of the line you want to draw. As you drag the mouse, check out the far left side of the status bar. As you drag the mouse, Paint indicates with a second coordinate pair exactly how far from the line's anchor position (in pixels) the line is.

5. Select a different color and draw another line. Paint draws that line in the new color.

TIME SAVER

Now that you've selected the Line tool, look at the area below the tool box. You'll see five lines, with each line growing thicker than the one before. By clicking on a thick line, the next line you draw with the Line tool appears on the drawing area in the new thickness. You can change the thickness, using this line size list, for any of the geometric shapes.

6. Click over the thickest line in the list of line sizes. Draw a couple of lines to see the thicker lines. If you change colors before drawing, the thicker lines will appear in the new color.

7. The rest of the geometric shapes are as easy to draw as the lines are. Select **File** | **New** to clear the drawing area. Don't save any changes.

8. Click on the Line tool to change the line thickness size to the middle line thickness (the third thickness size).

11

CAUTION

Always change the Line tool's thickness before selecting one of the geometric drawing tools. The Line tool's line size determines the line thickness for all the geometric tools.

9. Select the Rectangle tool. Rectangles, like lines, are determined by their starting anchor position and the rectangle's opposite corner's position. Begin drawing a rectangle at coordinates 190,75. After anchoring the rectangle with the mouse button, drag the mouse until it rests at 385,270. The status line indicator will show 200,200, meaning that the rectangle is 200 pixels by 200 pixels. When you release the mouse you will have drawn a perfect square.

TIME SAVER

Drawing a perfect square is not always easy because you have to pay close attention to the coordinates. Paint offers a better way to draw perfect squares. Hold down the Shift key while dragging the mouse, and the rectangle always appears as a square.

10. The three rectangles below the tool box do **not** represent the line thickness of the rectangles. They determine how Paint draws rectangles. When you click the top rectangle (the default), all of the drawing area that appears beneath the next rectangle that you draw shows through. Therefore, if you draw a rectangle over other pictures, you see the other pictures coming through the inside of the new rectangle. If you click the second rectangle below the tool box, the rectangle's center will overwrite any existing art. As a result, all rectangles you draw will have a blank center, no matter what art the rectangle overwrites. If you select the third rectangle, Paint does not draw a rectangular outline but does draw the interior of the rectangle in the same color you've set for the interior (the default interior color is white).

Keep the first rectangle selected and draw a rectangle from coordinates 120, 35 to 340, 150. The existing rectangle shows through the new one.

Click the second rectangle selection beneath the tool box and draw a rectangle from 40, 145 to 250, 170. This rectangle **overwrites** lines from the other rectangles (the white area is all you see inside the new rectangle) as shown in Figure 11.6.

TIME SAVER

If you want to draw a rectangle in a different color, click the left mouse button over the new color. If you want to fill the *inside* of the rectangle with a different color, click a new color with the *right mouse* button. The two-color pattern shown at the left of the color bar indicates the outline

11

and interior colors of rectangles and other shapes. You can also use the two colors to draw lines. When you anchor and draw a line using the left mouse button, Paint draws the line in the outline color. If, instead, you draw the line using the right mouse button to anchor the line, Paint draws using the interior color.

Figure 11.6.

The rectangle selection deter-mines how the rectangle over-writes other art.

The rectangle selection area

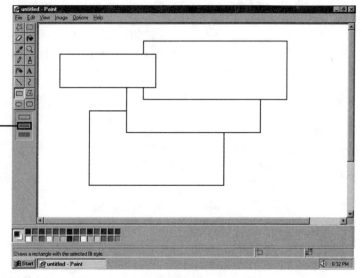

11. Select the third rectangle below the tool box and then select an alternate interior color such as red (using the right mouse button over the color box). Draw a small rectangle from 255, 130 to 330, 210. As shown in Figure 11.7, Paint draws the rectangle, without an outline, overwriting the other rectangles beneath the new one.

12. Now that you understand the rectangle, you also understand the other geometric tools. Click the Ellipse tool to draw ovals (or if you press Shift while dragging, you can draw perfect circles). Click the Rounded Rectangle tool to draw rounded rectangles (or rounded squares if you press Shift while dragging).

    Click the top rectangle selection (to draw see-through shapes) and click the Ellipse to draw circles. Click the Rounded Rectangle tool and draw rounded rectangles. Fill your drawing area with all kinds of shapes to get the feel of the tools.

13. A blank drawing area will help you learn how to use the Polygon and Curve tools, so select **File | New** (don't save) to clear your drawing area.

Figure 11.7.
Including an OLE object inside WordPad.

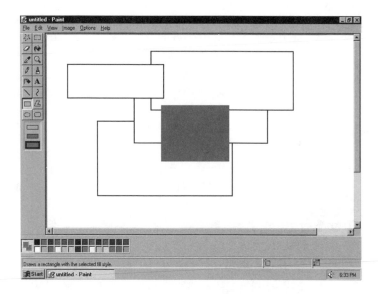

14. Select the Polygon tool. The Polygon is a tool that draws an enclosed figure with as many sides as you want to give the figure. Once you anchor the polygon with the mouse, drag the mouse left or right and click the mouse. Drag the mouse once again to continue the polygon. Every time you want to change directions, click the mouse once more. When you are finished, double-click the mouse, and Paint completes the polygon for you by connecting your final line with the first point you drew. As Figure 11.8 shows, polygons can look fairly wild.

Figure 11.8.
A polygon is an enclosed shape with any number of sides.

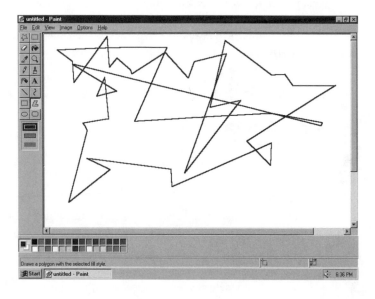

15. Clear your drawing area once again. The Curve tool is one of the neatest but strangest tools in the tool box. Click on the Curve tool (after adjusting the line thickness and color if you wish to do so).

    Draw a straight line by dragging the mouse. Once you release the line, click the mouse button somewhere just outside the line and drag the mouse around in circles. As you drag the mouse, Paint adjusts the curve to follow the mouse. When you see the curve that you want, release the mouse so that Paint can stabilize the curve.

> If you hold Shift while drawing the curve's starting line, Paint draws a perfectly horizontal or vertical line.

TIME SAVER

16. The Eraser/Color Eraser tool erases whatever appears on the drawing area. The Eraser/Color Eraser tool comes in four sizes to give you a small eraser that erases small areas to larger erasers that erase larger areas at one time. When you select the Eraser/Color Eraser tool, you can also select an eraser thickness. (The color you choose has no bearing on the eraser's use.) Select the Eraser/Color Eraser tool now and drag it over parts of your drawing to erase lines you've drawn.

17. Clear your drawing area for the next task.

Step 3: Review

The geometric tools generally require that you select a line width, a drawing style (such as rectangles that hide or don't hide their backgrounds), an exterior and interior color, and then draw the shape. You draw most of the shapes by anchoring their initial position, and then dragging the mouse to extend the shape across the screen. If you make a mistake, you can use the Eraser/Color Eraser tool to correct the problem.

Task 11.4: Colorizing Black and White Art

Step 1: Description

As you learned in Task 11.3, you can add color to drawings while you draw the geometric shapes. Paint also supports several coloring tools that let you add or change colors.

Step 2: Action

1. Draw a black rectangle (with a white center) in the center of your screen.

2. Select the Fill with Color tool. The Fill with Color tool acts like a paint can that you pour onto the drawing area. The selected color fills the drawing area until lines stop the paint flow. The paint stops on a line. Therefore, if you click the Fill with Color tool inside any shape, the shape's interior fills with the selected color.

11

CAUTION

> If you click the Fill with Color tool anywhere on the screen that is not completely enclosed, the paint color will completely fill the drawing area.

3. Click one of the shades of red in the color box.

4. Select the Fill with Color tool.

5. Point to the inside of the rectangle and click the mouse button. Paint fills the interior of the rectangle with the color red.

6. Select a blue color.

7. Click the Fill with Color tool anywhere outside the rectangle. The Fill with Color tool fills the portion of the screen not taken up by the rectangle.

8. The Pick Color tool copies colors from one object to another. Click the Pick Color tool and click over the red interior of the rectangle. Paint instantly changes the mouse cursor to the Fill with Color tool once again because the Fill with Color tool was the tool you used before selecting the Pick Color tool. Click over the outside of the rectangle now and the outside becomes red as well.

JUST A MINUTE

> The Pick Color tool always reverts back to the most recently used tool.

9. Select File | New to start a new drawing.

   The Brush tool acts like a calligraphy pen. When you select the Brush tool, Paint displays the brush selection area beneath the tool box. Figure 11.9 shows the brush selection area that contains the 12 kinds of brushes. When you select a brush shape, Paint uses that shape to brush colors on the drawing area. You can draw with a slanted brush head or a pinpoint brush head.

10. Practice drawing with the various brush shapes. Draw a face with lots of detail; you might draw the next Mona Lisa.

11. Save your face by selecting **File** | **S**ave and enter the name Face. Paint always adds the .BMP extension to your document images. You'll use the face picture in this hour's final task.

11. The Airbrush tool acts like a spray can. Select a color, and then you can spray graffiti all over your drawing area's face. The Airbrush tool has three spray sizes that determine the size of the spray. Clear the drawing area, but don't save the changes, because you don't want to save the graffiti over the face you saved in the previous step.

Figure 11.9.

There are 12 brush shapes you can use.

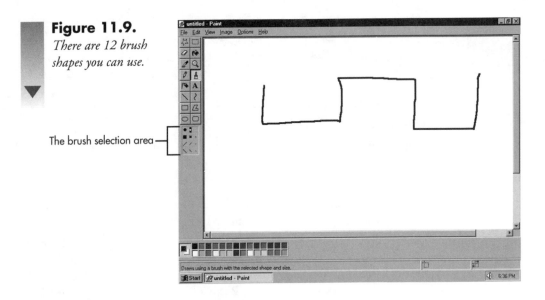

The brush selection area —

Step 3: Review

You can add color while drawing and after completing a drawing. The Fill with Color tool is nice for putting colors within shapes, but you must make sure those shapes are fully enclosed or the paint will overwrite the shape and fill the rest of the drawing area. The Airbrush is fun to use because it acts like a real spray can of paint. By spraying the Airbrush over the drawing area quickly, you can apply a light streak of spray paint. The more slowly you move the Airbrush, the more paint goes on the drawing area making a darker spray.

JUST A MINUTE

Although Paint can only create bitmap files with the .BMP filename extension, the Paint program can read both bitmap and *PC Paintbrush* files. PC Paintbrush filenames end with the PCX filename extension. If you read a PCX file and save the file, Paint saves the file in the bitmap file format.

TIME SAVER

Want to create your own desktop wallpaper? Use Paint! All desktop wallpaper images must appear in the bitmap format with the .BMP extension and those are exactly the kinds of files that Paint creates. Therefore, you can create a bitmap image with your company's logo and use the image for your desktop's wallpaper. See Hour 3, "Understanding the My Computer Window," if you need to review the procedure for changing your desktop wallpaper.

11

TIME SAVER

In addition to the desktop wallpaper, you can also create your own *startup logo*. The startup logo is the logo you see while Windows 95 starts. Create a Paint image and save the image under the name LOGOS.SYS in the Windows directory. Windows 95 will subsequently use this file when you start Windows 95 in the future. You can also display a shutdown graphic image that appears when you shut down Windows 95. Name the shutdown Paint image LOGOW.SYS and you'll see your image when you shut down Windows 95 before you turn off your computer.

Task 11.5: Adding Text to Drawings

Step 1: Description

Drawings often have titles. Graphs often have explanations. Maps often have legends. Pictures that you draw often need text in addition to the graphics that you draw. The Text tool lets you add text using any font and font size available within Windows 95. You can control how the text covers or exposes any art beneath the text. The Text tool works somewhat differently from the drawing tools because you first have to create a text box where you type the text.

Step 2: Action

1. Click the Text tool.
2. Determine approximately how large an area that you want the text box to consume and drag the text frame (the dotted rectangle that appears) until the text frame spans the width and height you want for your text.

If the text frame is not the correct size, you can adjust it later.

JUST A MINUTE

For this task, draw a text frame that's about 165 pixels wide by 80 pixels in height (as described at the right of the status bar). A font dialog box opens, as shown in Figure 11.10.

Figure 11.10.

Paint needs to know the font's name, size, and appearance.

3. For this example, select the Algerian font name, if Algerian is on your system. If you cannot find the Algerian font in the dropdown listbox, select a different font name. Increase the size of the font to 26 points. Do not boldface, italicize, or underline the font.

4. Click the mouse button anywhere within the text frame and type The Rain in Spain. (The Algerian font produces only uppercase letters.)

5. If you want to, you can adjust the font settings. For now, close the Fonts dialog box.

Time Saver

> As long as the text appears inside the text box, you can change the color of the text by clicking over a color in the color box.

6. The first of the two text selection boxes under the tool box lets you change the color of both the text letters and the background within the text box by clicking over a color on the color box with the right mouse button. The second text selection box affects only the text color and lets any art on the background remain visible. As long as the text frame still remains on the screen, you can modify the text frame size (by dragging an edge or corner of the text frame), color, and font information, as well as the text inside the frame.

Click the top text selection box and change both the text and the background colors. Then click anywhere *outside* the text frame. Paint anchors the text in its place, and you can no longer make changes to the text style or size.

Step 3: Review

The text tool requires that you create a text frame first. The text frame lets you select colors and font information for all text appearing inside the text frame. Any other text outside the text frame stays the same.

Task 11.6: Looking at Different Editing Views

Step 1: Description

There are several ways to add the finishing touches to your drawings. The Magnifier tool zooms images so that the pixels are larger and easier to change on an individual scale. If you want to see the drawing maximized to full screen, you can also request that Paint display the drawing without the menu bar and other Paint tool areas so you'll know what the actual figure looks like in its complete expanded size.

11

Step 2: Action

1. With the text still on your drawing area, click the Magnifier tool.

2. The mouse cursor becomes a large square when you move it over the drawing area. Move the mouse cursor to the lower-right portion of your text and click the mouse button. Paint magnifies the area covered by the mouse cursor square so you can edit individual pixels as shown in Figure 11.11. The Thumbnail dialog box shows the magnified area's regular size.

Figure 11.11.

If you need more precision, magnify parts of the drawing.

The four Magnifier tool sizes

TIME SAVER

The Magnifier tool comes in four sizes, which you can choose by selecting a size beneath the tool box before magnifying part of the image.

3. Select the Pencil tool. All of the drawing and geometric tools work while you've magnified part of the drawing, but the pencil tool lets you edit one pixel at a time by clicking the mouse over parts of the screen. Change the color of several pixels. To erase pixels, you can use the Eraser/Color Eraser tool or change the pencil color to the same color as the background.

When you are through editing in the magnified mode, click the Magnifier tool once again, and the drawing reverts to its original size where you can look at your edits from farther out.

Alternate Magnifying Techniques

Select View | Zoom to work with a more powerful magnifying editor. Select the Large Size command to magnify the drawing (use the scroll bars to find the part of the drawing you want to edit). Once you've scrolled to the magnified location that you want to edit, select the View | Zoom | Show Thumbnail command. Paint displays a miniaturized version of the magnified area's full-screen view so that as you make precision adjustments inside the magnified area, you instantly see the results of those pinpoint changes inside the thumbnail inset.

Try editing a portion of your current image using the View | Zoom Large Size command to see the results. Although the screen requires several menu selections to get the thumbnail, you get better feedback than if you only use the Magnifier tool.

5. Paint supports a full-screen view of the drawing area that works a lot like a Print Preview in a text editor or word processor (see Hour 10, "Compose Using Writing Tools"). Select View | View Bitmap (Ctrl+F) to display the entire drawing area on a maximized screen. A mouse click returns you to the normal drawing area size.

6. If you want to copy or delete only a small portion of your drawing area, use the two selection tools (the Free-Form Select and the simple Select tools at the top of the tool box). The selection tools do not draw anything, but they select parts of your drawings. The Select tool selects a rectangular area while the Free-Form Select selects any area you outline by dragging the mouse. Once you select, by dragging an area of your drawing, you can copy, move, or cut that selected part of the drawing area.

7. Clear your drawing area.

TIME SAVER

> If you want to make several copies of part of a drawing, select that drawing part, issue the Edit | Copy command to copy that selected area to the Clipboard, and then issue the Edit | Paste command to paste a copy of the selected drawing to Paint. You then can move the pasted copy to the location where you want the copy.

Step 3: Review

The viewing tools provided by Paint, including the View command on the menu bar, all provide you with different ways to look at your drawing. The Magnifier tool and the Zoom command let you edit the pinpoint pixels of your drawing if you need that much accuracy. Only when you see your drawing in its fully maximized state, do you know exactly how the drawing looks in its entirety.

The Paint Pros Modify Their Art

There are many advanced editing features available inside Paint that you'll want to study once you've mastered the basic drawing tools described in the previous tasks. You already know enough to draw virtually anything you'll ever want to draw; the **I**mage menu, however, contains additional commands that go far beyond the fundamental drawing capabilities offered by the tool box.

The **I**mage | **F**lip/Rotate command lets you rotate the drawing area. The Flip and Rotate dialog box, shown in Figure 11.12, lets you determine whether or not you want to completely reverse the image horizontally, vertically, or by a specific number of degrees.

Figure 11.12.

The Flip and Rotate dialog box controls the direction and amount of rotation.

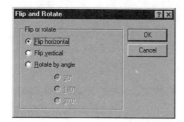

The **I**mage | **S**tretch/Skew command produces a dialog box that lets you stretch the entire drawing area (or the selected area) by a certain number of degrees. By skewing or stretching an image, you can add snowy and wavy special effects to your artwork.

Artists understand better than computer book authors what color inversion is all about. All colors have complementary colors. (The red compliments the blue by telling blue how nice he looks, or something like that!) A complementary color is an offsetting color that is a color's opposite in the color spectrum; white's complement is black, for example. Artists and designers use color charts and color wheels to determine complementary colors when they need to produce offsetting colors in a painting or a room. Paint will complement all colors in the drawing area or within the selected area if you select **I**mage | **I**nvert Colors.

The **I**mage | **A**ttributes menu command lets you change the size of a drawing area. **I**mage | **A**ttributes displays the Attributes dialog box shown in Figure 11.13. The Attributes dialog box determines how large (you specify either in inches, centimeters, or pixels depending on the option you select) you want the drawing area to be. In effect, the Attributes dialog determines the size of your drawing paper. If you want to draw in shades of black and white (as you would do if you were going to print the image on a black and white printer) you would want to create the drawing in black and white and shades of gray, so you'll know on the screen what the drawing will look like when printed.

Figure 11.13.

*The Attributes dialog box
lets you adjust the
drawing area and
measurements.*

The **I**mage | **C**lear Image command works just like the **F**ile | **N**ew command except that **F**ile | **N**ew resets interior and background color selections while **I**mage | **C**lear Image erases the current drawing area without resetting the colors.

One of the most important aspects of the Paint program is its OLE capability. By being OLE-compatible, you can insert images directly into other OLE-compatible programs and edit those images directly from the other program using the Paint menus and tools. Task 11.7 shows you how to work with Paint's OLE capabilities.

Task 11.7: Combining Paint with Other Applications

Step 1: Description

This task embeds the face image into a new WordPad document. WordPad, like most word processors written for the Windows 95 environment, supports OLE, which offers in-place editing of images even when you're not running the Paint program.

Step 2: Action

1. Select **F**ile | **O**pen command and type Face to load the face image you created earlier in this hour.

2. Press the Free-Form Select tool and select the face image. Anchor the mouse immediately above and to the left of the face on the drawing area and drag the selected area down and to the right until you've selected the entire face.

3. Select **E**dit | **C**opy to copy the selected face to the Windows 95 Clipboard. The Clipboard can hold all kinds of documents including art images. Exit the Paint program (by selecting **F**ile | E**x**it).

4. Start the WordPad program. Type the following, and press Enter twice:

   Here is what I look like in the mornings:

5. Select **E**dit | **P**aste (Ctrl+V) to paste the Windows 95 Clipboard (the face image) into the WordPad document at the cursor's position. After a brief pause WordPad displays both your text and image together as shown in Figure 11.14.

   The eight tabs on the face's outline form the image's *resizing handles* with which you can expand or shrink the size of the picture, by dragging a handle with the mouse, while inside WordPad.

TASK

11

Figure 11.14.

You can embed Paint images into WordPad documents.

The embedded image —

6. Press the right arrow to move the text cursor to the right of the image. The resizing handles and frame will disappear.

7. Press Enter to send the cursor to the next line. Type the following text, and press Enter once:

   `I hope I look better by the afternoon!`

8. This combination of text and graphics is impressive, but the OLE capabilities extend even farther. If you want to make changes to the face, double-click over the face's image. WordPad's environment instantly changes, menus and all, so you are instantly working within Paint, and the face image is surrounded by editing borders. You now can make any kind of modification you want using Paint's commands and tools. When you are finished, click over the text area of the document to return to WordPad once again.

Step 3: Review

OLE capabilities mean that you have the ability to perform in-place editing of your Paint images that you embed in textual documents. Both Paint and WordPad support OLE (described in the previous hour), so they both work together to combine text and art.

Summary

This hour taught you how to draw using the Paint program. Paint, a 32-bit application, supports all of the Windows 95 environment, including full OLE support. The drawing tools provided by Paint rival many of the drawing tools supplied in art programs that sell for several hundred dollars.

Paint includes geometric tools that help you draw perfect shapes. You can color the shape outlines, as well as their interiors with Paint's coloring tools. The menu bar provides commands that resize, reshape, invert, and stretch your drawn images. If you want precision editing, you can have it by zeroing in on the fine details of your drawing using the Magnifier tool.

As you become more familiar with Windows 95, especially after you learn how to manage the multimedia power in Part IV, you will learn how to embed all kinds of documents, such as sound and motion pictures, into your WordPad and Paint files. By utilizing the OLE capabilities you learned in this hour, you are mastering the fundamental programming principles that help make your Windows 95 applications work together almost seamlessly.

Workshop

Term Review

anchor position   The starting coordinate pair of lines and other geometric shapes.

coordinate   A pixel position on the screen defined by a coordinate pair.

coordinate pair   A pair of numbers in which the first represents the number of pixels from the left edge of the drawing area of an image, and the second represents the number of pixels from the top edge of the drawing area. In Paint, the coordinates appear on the Status bar.

pixel   Stands for *picture element.* A pixel is the smallest addressable dot on your screen.

point   Another name for *coordinate.*

startup logo   The image you see when Windows 95 loads.

text frame   A rectangular area in which you type or modify the text.

tool box   Paint's collection of drawing, coloring, and painting tools.

tools   The individual drawing, painting, and coloring tools represented by icons on the tool box.

Q&A

Q Will modifying a text frame's colors affect other text that I've already placed on the drawing area?

A No. The text frame encloses a special text area in which you modify only that area's font size, style, and colors. If you anchor text and click outside that text's text frame, you must erase the text and replace it with text that's a different font, size, or color if you want to change text that's outside of a text frame.

Q Why would I want to combine both text and graphics in my word processor?

A Often you'll write reports or send letters that can be spiced up nicely by artwork. One of the most common forms of artwork on letters is a letterhead, used by virtually every business in the world. If you want to write a letter using a letterhead, first create that letterhead logo inside Paint, and then insert that letterhead at the top of every business letter that you write. Your clients will think you pay a professional typesetting company to print your letterheads!

Q I'm no artist, so why should I learn Paint?

A As just stated, there are many applications that combine text and graphics. In the world of communications, which ranges from business to politics, pictures can convey the same meaning as thousands of words can. Graphics catch people's attention more quickly than text. When you combine the details that text provides with the attention-grabbing effect of graphics, you're sure to have an audience.

There are many other graphic reasons to master Paint as well. You might want to use Paint to produce these graphic publications:

☐ Flyers for volunteer or professional organizations

☐ Holiday greetings

☐ Letters that include drawings by the kids

☐ Sale notices for posting on bulletin boards

Perhaps the best reason to learn to use Paint: Hey, as this hour's introduction stated, it's fun!

11

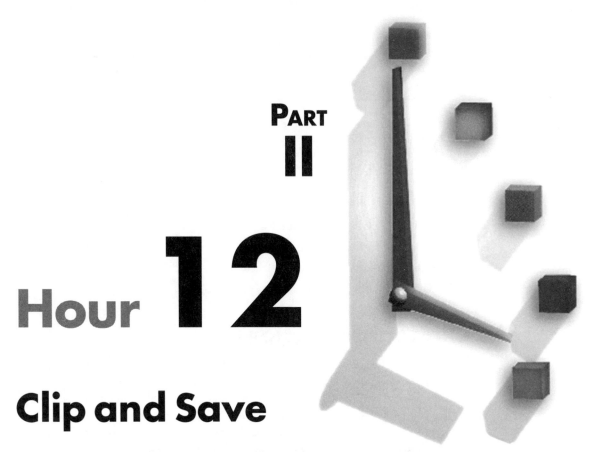

Hour 12

Clip and Save

This hour describes a fundamental Windows 95 tool that you've already used a few times in this book. The Clipboard is the go-between Windows 95 storage location for all kinds of data that you want to transfer between programs. The Windows 95 Clipboard holds text, pictures, sound files, and multimedia presentations.

You will get a little break in this hour. This hour goes fast (because the chapter is fairly short), but the basics you learn here help you with virtually anything you will ever do with Windows 95 in the future. The Clipboard's fundamental use is simple, as you've already seen; the Clipboard holds data until you remove the data or copy new data over the old. Unlike many implementations of a clipboard (many word processors support some form of a clipboard), you can look at and manage the Windows 95 Clipboard through the Clipboard Viewer application.

JUST A MINUTE

Often, small utility programs, such as the Clipboard Viewer that you learn about in this chapter, are called *applets* because these programs are small and don't do much on their own, but support other applications.

The highlights of this hour include:

☐ How to use the Clipboard most effectively

☐ Why former MS-DOS users gain Print Screen advantages in Windows 95

☐ How the Clipboard Viewer helps make Clipboard management easier

☐ The advantages of Clipboard linking

The Clipboard Functions

The Windows 95 Clipboard works with all kinds of Windows 95 programs. Inside virtually any Windows 95 program, you can copy data to the Clipboard, as shown in Figure 12.1. The Clipboard is a section of Windows 95 memory where you can place items that you cut or copy. The contents of the Clipboard stay with the Clipboard even after you paste those contents into another program. For example, in the previous chapter you copied a Paint picture of a face to the Windows 95 Clipboard. Then you started the WordPad text editor and pasted the Clipboard's contents into a text document.

Figure 12.1.

The Windows 95 Clipboard routes data to and from virtually any Windows 95 program.

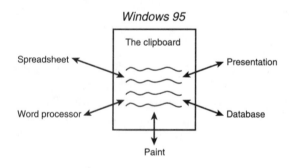

12

Clipboard or Desktop?

The Clipboard is not as permanent as the scraps and shortcuts that you place on the Windows 95 desktop. Suppose that you copy a word processing paragraph of text to the Clipboard and also to the desktop as a scrap. If you exit the word processor and start a spreadsheet program, you can copy from either the Clipboard or from the desktop. If you then copy a group of spreadsheet cells to both the Clipboard and to the desktop as a scrap, the original Clipboard contents will be overwritten by the spreadsheet data, but the desktop will now have *two* scraps. If you shut down Windows 95 and started Windows 95 once again, the Clipboard would be empty, but the desktop would still contain the two scraps.

The desktop always retains scraps until you delete them. The Clipboard is always erased when you exit Windows 95. The Clipboard is also overwritten when you copy something new to it.

Before Windows became the standard operating environment, users worked with the MS-DOS environment. One MS-DOS feature often missed by Windows users is the operation of the Print Screen key. When MS-DOS users pressed PrtSc (spelled out with the full command on some keyboards), an image of the screen went directly to the printer. When Windows 95 users press PrtSc, nothing happens with their printers; instead of going to the printer, an image of the screen goes to the Windows 95 Clipboard. Once on the Clipboard, you can print the screen image only by pasting the Clipboard's contents into Paint or some other program that can handle graphic images.

TIME SAVER

Although Windows 95 requires more work than MS-DOS to print a screen image, the Clipboard offers a much better productivity tool than the direct screen-printing mode that is the only MS-DOS offering. Once it's on the Clipboard, you can paste the screen image into Paint and modify, color, expand, or shrink the image before printing it.

JUST A MINUTE

Screen images are useful for users writing tutorials and presentations. Also, you can print screen images if an unusual message appears on your screen and you want to ask someone else later about the meaning of the message.

12

Task 12.1: Using the Clipboard Functions

Step 1: Description

You've already used the Clipboard, but this task reviews specific Clipboard usage so that you can better understand the need for the Clipboard Viewer that's introduced in the next section.

Step 2: Action

1. Start WordPad.

2. Type the following sentence:

   `The clipboard is one of the handiest tools in Windows 95!`

3. Select the word `clipboard` by highlighting the word with the mouse.

4. Display the **E**dit menu. The **C**opy command (Ctrl+C) copies selected text to the Clipboard. The text that you copy remains in the WordPad document. The Cu**t** command (Ctrl+X) deletes text from WordPad and sends that deleted text to the Clipboard. **P**aste inserts the contents of the Clipboard into the document. Paste **S**pecial inserts the contents of the Clipboard using a special *linking* situation described in the last section of this chapter.

TIME SAVER

> Although the Windows 95 documentation does not discuss these keystrokes, Ctrl+Ins is a shortcut key combination for **C**opy and Shift+Ins is a shortcut key combination for **P**aste. Shift+Del is a shortcut for Cu**t**. Ctrl+Ins, Shift+Ins, and Shift+Del were officially supported in early Windows programs written by and for Microsoft. Many users got used to these keystroke shortcuts so Microsoft products still support the keystrokes today.

5. Point to the selected text and click the right mouse button to see a right-click menu that also contains Cu**t**, **C**opy, and **P**aste commands that work exactly like the **E**dit commands just described. Press Esc to get rid of the right-click menu.

6. Copy the selected word to the Clipboard by pressing Ctrl+C.

7. If you have maximized the WordPad window, resize the window so that you can see the desktop. Click the right mouse button over the desktop and select **P**aste. The scrap with the Clipboard word `clipboard` appears on the desktop. The word is now on the desktop and on the Clipboard (as well as still in the original document) as a scrap.

12

CAUTION

For some strange reason you cannot paste scraps from the Clipboard onto the desktop unless the program where you got those scraps is still open. The desktop seems to be linked to WordPad and other application programs instead of being linked to the Clipboard. Therefore, your Clipboard contents still remain once you exit a program such as WordPad, but you cannot paste the Clipboard onto the desktop once you exit WordPad.

8. Exit WordPad. Don't save the WordPad document.

9. Start the Notepad program.

10. Press Ctrl+V to paste the Clipboard's word onto the Notepad window as shown in Figure 12.2.

Figure 12.2.

The Clipboard might contain a single word or many pages of text.

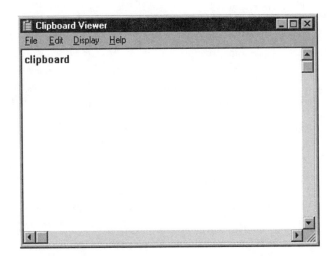

12

11. Exit Notepad. Do not save the file.

12. Restart Windows 95 by selecting the **S**hut down and **R**estart the computer? commands so that Windows 95 restarts fresh.

13. As soon as Windows 95 shuts down before starting up again, Windows 95 removes the word from the Clipboard. When Windows 95 reappears on your screen, you will still see the desktop's scrap because the desktop stays the same between startups. The Clipboard, however, is emptied when you restart Windows 95. If you were to start WordPad, WordPad's **P**aste command would be grayed out because nothing appears on the Clipboard.

14. Now that you've seen the difference between the desktop items and the Clipboard, delete the scrap from the desktop by clicking the right mouse button over the scrap and selecting **D**elete to delete it.

Step 3: Review

This task demonstrated the differences in storage time for the Clipboard and the desktop. Before sending anything else to the Clipboard, you needed to see exactly how volatile the Clipboard is. Don't store long-term data on the Clipboard; instead, store short-term data that you want to paste to a location quickly.

Task 12.2: The Clipboard and the PrtSc Key

Step 1: Description

Here are two ways you can send screen images to the Clipboard:

☐ Press PrtSc to send the entire graphic screen image to the Clipboard.

☐ Press Alt+PrtSc to send only the current window's image to the Clipboard. Therefore, if you have more than one window open on your screen but want to print only one of the windows, click on that window to send the focus to it, and press Alt+PrtSc to save a copy of that window to the Clipboard.

This task demonstrates the actions of both the PrtSc and the Alt+PrtSc keystrokes.

Step 2: Action

1. Start WordPad and Paint.

2. Resize both windows so they both appear on the screen at one time.

3. Press the PrtSc key. The entire screen goes to the Clipboard.

4. If Paint is not the active window, switch to it (by clicking its window or taskbar button).

5. Select **E**dit | **P**aste (Ctrl+V) to paste the Clipboard into Paint. The Clipboard holds the graphic image of the screen, so Paint is the perfect program to work with that image. Figure 12.3 shows Paint's editing area with the screen image inside. If you want to, you can now add text callouts or make other changes to the drawing.

Scroll Paint's editing window to see the entire screen image.

JUST A MINUTE

12

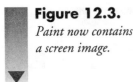

Figure 12.3.

*Paint now contains
a screen image.*

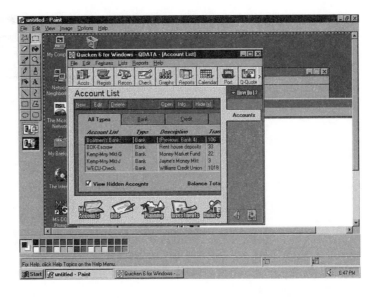

6. Now that the image appears inside Paint, you can print the image with the **File** |
   Print command or save the image to a graphic document.

7. Resize Paint's program window so that you can once again see both the "real"
   WordPad and Paint windows at the same time. It does not matter if the two
   windows overlap. Select **File** | **New** (don't save the image) to clear Paint's editing
   area.

8. Click over the WordPad window or taskbar button to send the focus to the
   WordPad window.

9. Press Alt+PrtSc. Instead of the entire screen, only the WordPad window's image
   goes to the Clipboard.

10. Click over Paint's window to send the focus back to Paint, and then maximize
    Paint's window.

11. Press Ctrl+V to paste the Clipboard's contents into Paint. Maximize the Paint
    window. As Figure 12.4 shows, the Clipboard contained and transferred only the
    WordPad window because you pressed Alt+PrtSc instead of PrtSc.

12

Figure 12.4.

If you press Alt+PrtSc, only the active window's image goes to the Clipboard.

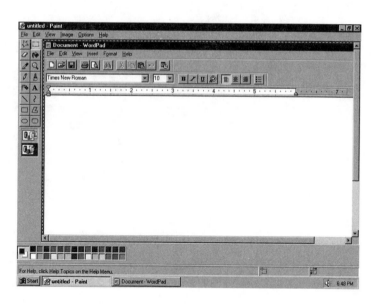

12. Exit both WordPad and Paint without saving either workspace to a file.

Step 3: Review

The PrtSc key sends the entire contents of the screen to the Clipboard. The Alt+PrtSc key combination sends only the currently active window (the window with the focus) to the Clipboard.

The Clipboard Viewer

Windows 95 provides a program called the *Clipboard Viewer* that lets you look at whatever is on the Clipboard. Whereas you have to start Paint to see a graphic image on the Clipboard, or a text editor to see text on the Clipboard, or a sound program to hear sound on the Clipboard, the Clipboard Viewer lets you view the contents of the Clipboard no matter what format the contents take on.

The Clipboard holds whatever you cut or copy to it. Often you'll send one form of data to the Clipboard, such as a Word for Windows 6 paragraph, and then paste that data into a program that requires a different format, such as the Notepad. Windows 95 must be able to distinguish data formats and be able to convert Clipboard contents from one format to another, when applicable, so that your target location (where you'll be pasting those contents) can receive data that was originally generated in a different format. The Clipboard Viewer provides a way to view all available conversion formats of Clipboard data.

12

JUST A MINUTE

Generally, you will not care about the format of data on the Clipboard. Let Windows 95 worry about converting data to a required format. The Clipboard Viewer contains a **D**isplay menu option that lets you look at the conversion formats possible for the data currently on the Clipboard.

One minor drawback to the Clipboard Viewer is that the Clipboard Viewer interface supports only the Windows 3.1 controls such as the Windows 3.1 Open dialog box. Therefore, the Clipboard Viewer does not support long filenames. If you select **File | O**pen within the Clipboard Viewer, Windows 95 squeezes long filenames down to eight characters with a tilde (~) replacing the extra characters in the long filenames.

3.1 ▶
Step Up

Although the Windows 95 Clipboard viewer uses the Windows 3.1 interface, it does, however, access the MS-DOS environment more smoothly than the Windows 3.1 Clipboard. In Windows 3.1, you *could* copy data back and forth between MS-DOS and Windows 3.1, but doing so was a chore. Windows 95 makes the task of copying between MS-DOS and Windows 95 much more easily managed, as you'll see in Hour 14, "Activate DOS-Based Applications."

CAUTION

Depending on the actual release date of your version of Windows 95, your Windows 95 Clipboard may support the new Windows 95 interface, such as the Windows 95 Open dialog boxes explained in Hour 4, "Take Windows 95 to Task."

Task 12.3: Using the Clipboard Viewer

Step 1: Description

TASK

This task explains how to start the Clipboard Viewer and describes some of the Clipboard Viewer capabilities. The Clipboard Viewer's primary purpose is to let you look at the Clipboard whenever you want to know what is there.

JUST A MINUTE

Perhaps the only thing you cannot do with the Clipboard Viewer is print the contents of the Clipboard. If you want to print the contents of the Clipboard, you'll still have to start another program that supports the current Clipboard's contents format and use that program's **File | P**rint command. The Clipboard Viewer's **F**ile menu contains no **P**rint command.

▼

12

Step 2: Action

1. Start the Clipboard Viewer. The Clipboard Viewer resides on the Accessories menu. When you start the Clipboard Viewer you should see the window shown in Figure 12.5.

Figure 12.5.

The Clipboard Viewer displays and saves the contents of the Clipboard.

JUST A MINUTE

If the Clipboard Viewer window is not empty, the Clipboard Viewer will still contain the last contents you sent there (from the previous task, if you're following along). The next item you send to the Clipboard will appear on the Clipboard Viewer's screen.

2. Press the PrtSc key to send a copy of the screen to the Clipboard. The Clipboard Viewer instantly displays the contents of the Clipboard on the Clipboard Viewer window.

3. Maximize the Clipboard Viewer window.

4. Display the **File** menu. The Clipboard Viewer files that you load and save use the .CLP filename extension. Press Esc to close the **File** menu.

5. The **Edit** menu contains a single command, **D**elete (Del), with which you can erase the contents of the Clipboard.

6. The **D**isplay command changes depending on the contents of the Clipboard. If the Clipboard contains a screen print image, as yours does now, your **D**isplay menu contains three commands: **A**uto, **B**itmap, Palette and DIB Bitmap. Generally, you'll leave **A**uto selected. With **A**uto, you let the Clipboard Viewer program

determine the best format for the Clipboard contents. The Clipboard uses this automatic format when pasting the Clipboard contents to other applications. If you want to override the default, you can select a different format.

CAUTION

The Clipboard Viewer rarely, if ever, makes a wrong guess as to the proper format of Clipboard data. Unless you know specifically that the Clipboard is pasting data using an invalid format for the target program, don't change the **D**isplay command from the **A**uto selection.

Use the Clipboard Viewer's **D**isplay menu when the Clipboard contains data that Windows 95 can convert to various formats (most text can be converted to several different formats). Most of the formats will be grayed because the Clipboard Viewer will not let you convert the Clipboard contents to a data format that you cannot see on the screen. (These are internal formats usable by the Clipboard and other programs but not displayable on the screen.)

7. Select **F**ile | E**x**it to terminate the Clipboard Viewer program.

JUST A MINUTE

Even though you exit the Clipboard Viewer, the contents of the Clipboard do not go away. Keep in mind that the Clipboard Viewer and the Clipboard are two different entities. The Clipboard holds whatever Windows 95 data you copy or cut and the Clipboard Viewer lets you view those contents.

12

Step 3: Review

The Clipboard Viewer is a Windows 95 applet program that lets you view, change the format, or delete the contents of the Windows 95 Clipboard. The Clipboard Viewer does not let you print the Clipboard's contents, but you can view the contents without knowing in advance what data format the Clipboard contains.

Linking with Paste Special

Windows 95 supports the use of a Clipboard *link*, which means that when you paste Clipboard contents into a document, Windows 95 sets up a link from one application to another. You saw a similar concept when you worked with an OLE object in the previous chapter.

If the Windows 95 application supports linked objects (not all applications support linked objects), there will be a Paste **S**pecial command on the **E**dit menu when you paste Clipboard data to the application. Once pasted, you can click on that pasted object to edit the object inside the application.

One of the best advantages to using Paste **S**pecial is that some advanced applications support advanced linking so that when data in the first application changes, the pasted data also changes.

Summary

This chapter reviewed the Clipboard so that you could familiarize yourself with the workings of the Clipboard Viewer. The Clipboard Viewer lets you view the contents of the Clipboard no matter what kind of data the Clipboard contains. Not only can you view the contents of the Clipboard, but you can also save the Clipboard to a file and load that file back into the Clipboard Viewer at a later time.

One of the most interesting uses of the Clipboard is for printing the contents of screens. The PrtSc key sends the screen's graphic image to the Clipboard. The Alt+PrtSc keypress sends a graphic image of the selected window to the Clipboard. Using the Clipboard Viewer, you can view the contents of the screen. If you paste the contents of the Clipboard screen into a graphic program such as Paint, you can also print the contents of the screen image.

Without the Clipboard Viewer, you would have to know the format of Clipboard data if you wanted to look at the Clipboard's contents. Depending on the source of the Clipboard data, you may not know exactly what kind of data resides on the Clipboard. The Clipboard Viewer's **D**isplay menu contains a list of all supported formats that you can convert the Clipboard data to.

Workshop

Term Review

applet   A Windows 95 utility program such as the Clipboard Viewer.

Clipboard Viewer   A Windows 95 applet that lets you look at the contents of the Clipboard no matter what kind of data resides on the Clipboard.

link   Pasted Clipboard contents with which Windows 95 keeps an active connection. If you change linked data in its original application, after you have pasted it elsewhere from the Clipboard, the data then also changes inside the other application(s) containing the pasted contents.

12

Q&A

Q Is the Clipboard a file?

A Perhaps the best way to think of the Clipboard is as a section of Windows 95 memory that Windows 95 sets aside to hold one thing at a time. Although Windows 95 might use a file for the Clipboard data, at times, you don't have access to this file directly. By using the Clipboard Viewer, however, you can save the contents of the Clipboard to any file you specify.

Q How can I print the contents of my screen?

A Use PrtScr to send an image of the entire screen to the Clipboard. Once it is on the Clipboard, you can start a graphics program, such as Paint, to receive the contents and print the screen. In addition, you also can save the screen's image to a graphics file using Paint, in case you want to save the image for use in a tutorial or presentation.

Q Why would I ever need the Clipboard Viewer?

A The Clipboard Viewer lets you look at the contents of the Clipboard. It also lets you save the contents of the Clipboard to a data file. Without the Clipboard Viewer, you would have to know the exact format of the Clipboard, and then you would have to start a program that supports that format if you wanted to save or view the contents of the Clipboard.

The Clipboard Viewer lets you look at all the different conversion formats that apply to the current data on the Clipboard. You often can select a conversion format if you want to save the Clipboard contents in a file using a specific format. Most of the time, however, you will use the Clipboard Viewer just for looking at and possibly saving Clipboard contents to a disk file using the default data type.

12

Time-Out 2

Search and Destroy with Minesweeper

In this time-out, you get to throw caution to the wind as you hunt for dangerous mines. *Minesweeper* is a Windows 95 game that's been available in Windows environments for several years. Unlike the Solitaire program that you played in the previous time-out, Minesweeper requires more luck than skill. Minesweeper is also easier to learn than Solitaire, so you'll be detonating mines in no time.

On Your Mark...

The goal of Minesweeper is simple: You set out through a minefield trying to locate the mines before getting blown up. As you'll soon see, the colorful graphics and low-resolution mines make the game much less intense and violent than the description first leads you to believe.

TIME SAVER

> Minesweeper is a fast-paced game. Therefore, if you want something to do while waiting during TV commercials or while sitting in those meetings when you must act as if you're paying attention *and* stay awake at the same time, you can play some quick rounds of Minesweeper to clear the cobwebs and pass the time.

Get Set...

Follow these steps to start the Minesweeper game:

1. Click the Start button to display the Windows 95 Start menu.
2. Select the **P**rograms command to display the top-level menu of programs on your computer.
3. Select the Accessories command to display the Accessories menu, and then display the Games menu.
4. Select Minesweeper from the Games menu. Windows 95 loads and runs the Minesweeper game. Your screen will look something like the screen in Figure T2.1.

Figure T2.1.

Get ready to master the Minesweeper game.

5. For such a simple game, Minesweeper contains several options that you can set. The first thing you should do is reset all the high scores. Minesweeper keeps track of past top scores. A top score is considered to be the best time at which someone has run through the mine field successfully. When it is first installed, Minesweeper

contains the three default top times of 999 seconds for all three levels: beginning, intermediate, and advanced play.

Select **G**ame | Best **T**imes to display the Best Times dialog box. You will need to reset these times so Minesweeper can begin tracking your own best times. Click the Reset Scores button.

6. Choose your personal level of play by displaying the **G**ame menu once again and choosing either **B**eginner, **I**ntermediate, or E**x**pert. Each level of play determines the starting mine field size and the number of mines on the field. The beginning player gets an 8-by-8 grid with 10 mines, the intermediate player gets a 16-by-16 grid with 40 mines, and the expert player gets a 16-by-30 grid with 99 mines.

TIME SAVER

Choose **B**eginner if you don't want to get blown up!

7. The size of the Minesweeper game is adjustable manually, but you cannot adjust the Minesweeper program's window size by dragging the edges of the window, as you can do in most Windows 95 programs. For now, you'll probably want to keep the size of the mine field at 8 by 8 blocks (the beginner level's size). If you want to expand the size of the field, select **G**ame | **C**ustom to display the Custom Field dialog box shown in Figure T2.2. Increase the size of the mine field's height or width by entering new size values.

Figure T2.2.

You can adjust the size of
the mine field.

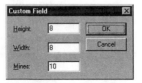

CAUTION

The mine field's smallest possible size is 8 blocks by 8 blocks, and the largest is 24 by 30 blocks. The number of mines you can set ranges from 10 to 667.

Go!

You can now start the game. The purpose of Minesweeper is to locate all mines randomly placed in the mine field without triggering one of the mines. To achieve a top score, you must locate the mines as quickly as possible. Use a combination of lots of luck and some logic to find the mines.

Under each blank square on the mine field is either a mine, a number, or a blank space. To see the contents of the square you click on that square with the mouse.

Start a new game by selecting the **G**ame | **N**ew (F2) option. (You also can click over the happy face to start a new game.) The game proceeds as you click on squares. The first square that you click is only a guess as to whether there is a mine under that square or not. Once you click on the first square successfully (without landing on a mine), you can begin to use logic to determine which remaining squares you can successfully click on. The item under a square determines which of the following things happen:

☐ If a number appears under the square, that number represents the number of mines that appear in the eight connecting boxes that surround the square. For example, if you click on a square that displays a 2, two of the eight squares around the square with the 2 contain mines. Of course, if a number appears in a square that's on the edge of the mine field, there are fewer surrounding squares to worry about.

☐ If a blank appears under a square, the blank indicates there are *no* surrounding mines. In addition, the Minesweeper game will go ahead and clear all squares around the blank, including the squares around connecting blank squares, showing either more blank squares or numbers. Clicking on a blank square is always good because Minesweeper clears part of the mine field for you. A mine never appears in the squares cleared by Minesweeper when you land on a blank square.

☐ If a mine appears, the mine blows up and the game ends. No matter how many squares you have successfully uncovered, you never win a game or make the top scores list if you detonate one of the mines. Minesweeper uncovers all the squares to show you where the rest of the mines were if you blow one up and turns the smiling face to a frowning face.

Every game is different, so you cannot follow along with this book's example play exactly. Nevertheless, consider what happens if, after clicking the upper-left corner square, the mine field in Figure T2.3 results.

Figure T2.3.

*One click tells you a lot
about the mine field.*

The click over the upper-left square produced lots of helpful information. There were no mines under the first square. Also, none of the upper-left corner's surrounding squares had mines on them. Therefore, Minesweeper automatically blanked those surrounding squares, as well as *additional surrounding squares that had either numbers or blanks.*

JUST A MINUTE

> If the first square had a mine under it, the game would now be over, and Minesweeper would have turned over all the game board's mine squares to show you the layout of the mine field. If the first square were touched by *another* square that had a mine, a number indicating the total number of adjoining mine squares would have appeared.

Notice the number 1 located in the top row of Figure T2.3's mine-field layout. One and only one mine is touching that square. Is the mine directly to the right or diagonally down and to the right of the square with the 1? There is not quite enough information to know exactly at this point because the square beneath the 1 has a 2, which indicates *two* mines touch that square, and you don't know where those two mines are.

Actually, the only square that you positively *know* contains a mine is the square that intersects the third column and the fifth row (referred to as "the point 3,5"). The 1 at point 2,4 indicates that a mine touches this square, and there is only one adjoining covered square, the one at 3,5 that touches the 1 at 2,4.

When you know where a mine is, click the *right mouse button* over that mine's location to mark the location. As you locate and mark mines, the mine count in the upper-left corner decreases. The right click produces the flag shown in Figure T2.4. The flag will serve as a reminder so that you don't click over that square again. If you are unsure about a square's mine, right-click the square twice to produce a question mark placeholder that you can change to a flag or space later by right-clicking the mouse.

Figure T2.4.

A right-click produces a
flag when you think you
know where a mine is.

Continue clearing squares until you either hit a mine and lose the game or uncover all squares leaving only the mines flagged or covered. Suppose that you click the square at point 1,3 and there is a mine at that location. Figure T2.5 shows the resulting destruction. Minesweeper uncovers all mine squares and shows you the squares you should have avoided.

Figure T2.5.

Oops! A mine just
blasted.

To start a new game, click the happy face or press F2. Good luck!

PART

III

Windows 95's Evening Out

Hour

Hour 13

Use the HyperTerminal

This hour describes the Windows 95 *HyperTerminal* application. HyperTerminal is an electronic communications program that lets your computer communicate with other computers. HyperTerminal was not available in previous versions of Windows. Microsoft wrote HyperTerminal making thorough use of the 32-bit application environment of Windows 95, so that HyperTerminal can take full advantage of the Windows 95 multitasking capabilities.

This hour explores the HyperTerminal program by showing you how to set up HyperTerminal and connect to online services. Be forewarned: Online communications are fairly technical. Microsoft realized the problems often associated with online access, however, and wrote the HyperTerminal program to eliminate many of the initial setup requirements that often accompany remote computer access.

Many of the more popular online services, such as CompuServe and America Online, provide their own communications software. You don't need a program such as HyperTerminal to connect to CompuServe if you use CompuServe's software. You *can* use HyperTerminal to connect to CompuServe and other services, however, if you don't have or like the service's software. More than likely, you'll use HyperTerminal to connect to bulletin board systems (*BBSs*) and other computers that provide basic online access.

The highlights of this hour include:

- [ ] Why you might want to communicate with remote computers
- [ ] How HyperTerminal makes communicating easier than ever before
- [ ] What safety precautions you need to make when working with remote computers
- [ ] How to upload and download files to and from other computers

Introducing HyperTerminal

The first time you start HyperTerminal, you'll need to provide it with some fundamental information about your modem. Luckily, HyperTerminal makes this one-time setup easy to do.

Before starting HyperTerminal, you need to find a computer to connect to. This computer might belong to a neighbor who is running another version of telecommunications software. The other computer does not even have to be PC-compatible. You will need to find the other computer's phone number and, if the computer is a friend's, make sure that your friend's computer is connected to the phone line when you dial. (Despite the power of Windows 95, Windows 95 has difficulty talking to humans on the other end of a telephone line!)

TIME SAVER

> You can access many local library databases and card catalogs through your computer's modem.

CAUTION

> If you know for a fact that the other computer is running Windows 95, don't use HyperTerminal to talk with that computer. Although HyperTerminal will work, you'll like Windows 95's *dial-up networking feature* described in Hour 22, "Hardware: Big and Small."

13

TIME SAVER

If you want to connect to Microsoft's own dial-up BBS service called Microsoft Network, refer to Appendix C, "The Microsoft Network," for details. Microsoft Network is a full-featured, full-screen, dial-in service that requires a more specialized communications program than HyperTerminal can provide.

Task 13.1: Setting Up HyperTerminal

TASK

Step 1: Description

This task describes how to start HyperTerminal for the first time. Windows 95 does most of the work and recognizes many modem types. The first time that you attempt to start HyperTerminal, Windows 95 will intercept the HyperTerminal program (as shown in this task) and request that you set your first dial-up connection's information before continuing with HyperTerminal.

Step 2: Action

1. Display the Start menu.

2. Select **P**rograms from the Start menu and then display the Accessories menu.

3. Select HyperTerminal from the Accessories menu. Windows 95 opens the HyperTerminal window shown in Figure 13.1. Your HyperTerminal window might differ from Figure 13.1 depending on the number of dial-up systems described by Windows 95 on your computer. Scroll through the window or increase the size to see all the icons. The icon you're interested in now is the one labeled Hypertrm.

Figure 13.1.

The Hyper-Terminal window contains the HyperTerminal program.

13

4. Double-click the icon labeled Hypertrm to start the HyperTerminal program.

   After a brief pause and a quick display of the HyperTerminal copyright notice, Windows 95 displays the screen shown in Figure 13.2.

Figure 13.2.

HyperTerminal knows that you are about to make a connection.

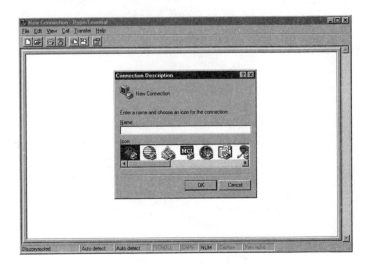

5. HyperTerminal is asking that you assign a name to the computer you're going to connect to and also assign an icon to use for that connection. HyperTerminal tries to work in a way that's best for you. Instead of scrolling through an online listing of computers, phone numbers, and communication parameter settings as most communication programs require, HyperTerminal asks that you give each connection a name that makes sense to *you*, as well as an identifying icon, so that you can recognize this connection later.

   HyperTerminal will add the name and icon to the HyperTerminal window. Therefore, as you add connections, you add icons to the HyperTerminal window. In the future you will just click over the icon inside the HyperTerminal window to dial that connection.

   For the purposes of this book, these tasks are going to connect to CompuServe's text-oriented service. The details of CompuServe are irrelevant to the task at hand because you are going to focus on how the connection is made, instead of the CompuServe details at the other end of the book's computer.

   Type a description for your connection and click on an icon (scroll to find one you like) before clicking the OK command button.

6. HyperTerminal saves your connection name and icon and displays the dialog box shown in Figure 13.3.

13

Figure 13.3.

*Tell Hyper-
Terminal the
connecting
computer's phone
information and
your modem
location.*

Enter the dialing information HyperTerminal needs to connect to the computer
you want to dial. HyperTerminal's **C**ountry code dropdown listbox contains the
country code for almost every country in the world, in case your target computer's
country code differs from the one selected.

Caution

> If you cannot change any of the values in the **C**ountry code, Ar**e**a code,
> or **P**hone number, you've yet to set up your modem. Refer to Hour 22 for
> help with setting up your modem for the first time.

7. Once you enter the dialing values, HyperTerminal displays the verification dialog
   box shown in Figure 13.4. If you need to change any of the values, click the
   appropriate command button to do so.

Figure 13.4.

*HyperTerminal
verifies your
dialing and
modem informa-
tion.*

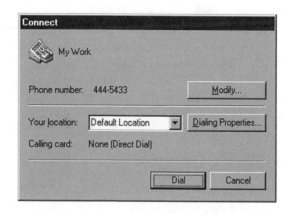

13

> Even if all the verification information is correct, you may want to click the **D**ialing Properties command button to review your telephone properties, such as your calling card information or access number to get an outside line. If you normally dial from home but take your laptop on the road, for example, you may have to enter a value of 9 so that HyperTerminal properly connects to an outside line when dialing from your hotel room. Once you return home, you can clear out the outside line number if needed. To keep things straight, you might want to create separate profiles with their own icons for use at home or away. In addition, if you are dialing a long-distance number, but one that resides inside your own area code, click the option labeled Dial as a long distance call; HyperTerminal will then dial the area code and access number even though the number falls within your own area code. Recently, the phone companies changed long distance dialing within the same area code as the source call; consequently, you must now dial the area code.

8. Click the Dial command button to dial the number. HyperTerminal goes to work connecting to the other computer via the telephone lines. If you don't want to connect right now, click the Cancel command button and HyperTerminal cancels the dialing operation but still keeps track of the connection information.

Step 3: Review

When you want to dial a computer for the first time, HyperTerminal requests that you enter dial-up connection information for that computer. HyperTerminal keeps track of your dial-up connections through a series of *connection profiles*. A connection profile contains a description and a representative icon that you generate when you first set up the target computer's connection. Once you've set up a target computer's connection profile, you can connect to that computer by selecting the profile's icon from the HyperTerminal window. Figure 13.5 shows a HyperTerminal window with three icons. The icon labeled Hypertrm continues to set up new connection profiles. The other two profiles connect to different remote computers.

Secure Yourself

Once you establish a telephone connection with the remote computer and the two computers begin to communicate, your access to that computer is usually limited until you *log on* to the system. Logging on refers to the process of identifying yourself to the remote computer.

13

Figure 13.5.

The HyperTerminal window contains icons for each connection profile.

There are many fee-based remote computer services and many free ones as well. Whether or not you pay, you'll almost always need to set up a *login name* (you'll typically make up a nickname that you'll go by on the remote system) and password. The remote computer can then identify you and enable you to have the access you've paid for or that's available to you.

There are several ways to set up a login name and password the first time you want to use the system. If you're paying for the access, the remote computer's owners may request that you fill out an application or verbally apply over a voice telephone line with your personal and billing information. Some remote computer services let you log in as a new user and then fill out an application online before being allowed to use the rest of the services.

However you set up the initial login name and password, this login procedure guards both you and other users on the system. Each user is known, so any action the user makes on the remote system can be traced, as long as everybody keeps his or her password secret. Your password helps keep others from logging on as you and doing something on your paid time or deleting files in your name.

TIME SAVER

Change your password frequently to make it harder for others to learn it. If your password contains special characters, such as *window^woman*, your password will be very difficult to guess by those who might otherwise be able to decipher "it."

Figure 13.6 shows what a typical CompuServe user sees upon first connecting to CompuServe using HyperTerminal. The user can use none of CompuServe's services until the user identifies himself with a proper login name and password (CompuServe assigns login numbers and not names to new users).

13

Figure 13.6.

You will almost always log into the remote computer.

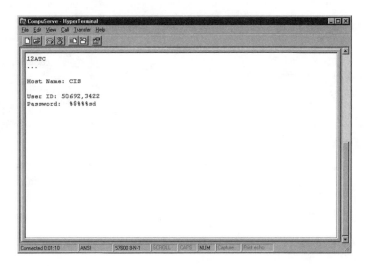

When you finish with a connection, be sure to *log off* by informing the remote computer that you're getting ready to disconnect. There are several ways to log off. Most of the time, you'll type Bye or Exit to log off. After logging off, select **Call | D**isconnect to disconnect your computer from the phone line's signal.

TIME SAVER

> The toolbar contains an icon for disconnecting from remote computers and for connecting to remote computers.

Once you log off, you can dial another connection. You don't have to return to the HyperTerminal window to connect to another computer. You can choose the **File | O**pen menu command to view a list of your connection profiles and connect to another computer. If you want to reconnect once again to the computer where you just logged off, you can do so by clicking the Connect button on the toolbar.

JUST A MINUTE

> If you are connecting to a friend's computer, you may not have to log in. The friend's computer software will determine whether or not you need to identify yourself to the system before using the remote computer from your own computer's keyboard.

13

Some Extra HyperTerminal Features

The HyperTerminal program offers some extra features that make it the program of choice when communicating with Windows 95. With other communications programs, you would have to know much more about the remote computer than you have to know when using HyperTerminal. There are lots of technical terms, such as *baud rate*, that you don't always understand or can't readily obtain from the remote computer, even though your communications program requires that information.

HyperTerminal contains an *auto detect* feature that listens to the remote computer the first time you call it. Windows 95 and HyperTerminal go through a series of beeps and buzzes until HyperTerminal determines exactly how to connect to the remote computer using the best possible *protocol*. (Protocol refers to the technical connection details that must be in place before two computers can communicate with each other.)

Of course, HyperTerminal supports file *downloading* and *uploading*. When you download a file, you receive that file from the remote computer. When you upload a file, you send a file to the remote computer. Here are the steps you'll usually take to download a file from a remote computer:

1. Determine the remote computer's filename for the file you want to download.

2. Instruct the remote computer to send that file to you. The remote computer will want to know which *transfer protocol* you want to use. Here are the transfer protocols supported by HyperTerminal at the time of this writing:

   ☐ 1K Xmodem

   ☐ Xmodem

   ☐ Ymodem

   ☐ Ymodem-G

   ☐ Zmodem

   ☐ Kermit

   You don't have to understand the details behind these transfer protocols—just find a matching transfer protocol in the remote computer's list and select the same transfer protocol on your computer. If all of these choices are available, the Zmodem transfer protocol will probably be the fastest and safest one to use.

3. Click the Receive file button on the toolbar (the second button from the right) or select the **T**ransfer | **R**eceive command from the menu. HyperTerminal displays a dialog box you'll use to type the filename and location for the file once it arrives on your computer, as well as the transfer protocol you are using.

13

4. When you click the **R**eceive command button, HyperTerminal and the remote computer begin communicating, and the file will arrive on your computer. Figure 13.7 shows a file's download in process.

Figure 13.7.

Downloading a file from a remote computer requires matching transfer protocols.

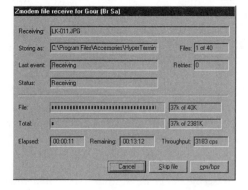

5. Once your computer receives the entire file, the transfer status dialog box goes away and you'll see a message indicating that the file arrived on your computer.

JUST A MINUTE

There is simply no way to give you a step-by-step task that you can practice yourself because each reader will have different access to different remote computers and there is no one site readily available to everyone who reads this book.

To upload a file to a remote computer, you'll basically reverse the process and click the Send toolbar button after telling the remote computer to get ready for the file. Different remote computers receive files in different ways, so you'll have to read the remote computer's online help or call the remote computer's owner for assistance before uploading a file to the computer.

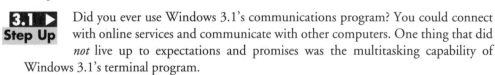

Step Up

Did you ever use Windows 3.1's communications program? You could connect with online services and communicate with other computers. One thing that did *not* live up to expectations and promises was the multitasking capability of Windows 3.1's terminal program.

13

Neither Windows 3.1's terminal program, nor any other communications program running under Windows 3.1, worked well if you also tried to Alt+Tab to another program and download files in the background.

Suppose you started a download using the Windows 3.1 terminal program, and then switched to your database program and attempted to sort a file. More than likely, your communications program stopped downloading during the sorting (the best case), or completely disconnected you from the other computer (a worst case, but common, scenario). Windows 95 promises to eliminate the problems of communicating in the background.

One of the handiest features that people will find in HyperTerminal is the *backscroll buffer*. As you work with the remote computer, your HyperTerminal window will scroll to make room for new text. HyperTerminal keeps track of several screens of your online session in a memory area called the backscroll buffer. The default amount of backscroll buffer HyperTerminal keeps is 500 lines. Therefore, you can look at, by clicking the vertical scroll bars, up to 500 lines of your remote computer session. If you read something earlier on the remote computer that scrolled off the screen before you had a chance to finish reading the text, you can scroll your HyperTerminal screen backwards to look at the text once again.

TIME SAVER

You can adjust the size of the backscroll buffer if you want to increase or decrease the buffer size. Select **F**ile | **Pr**operties and click the tab labeled Settings to see the screen shown in Figure 13.8. You can adjust the number of lines HyperTerminal uses for the backscroll buffer by entering a new value in the center of the dialog box.

Figure 13.8.

You can change the size of the backscroll buffer.

The number of lines saved

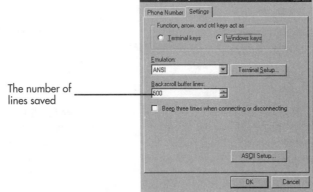

13

If your remote computer requires a special service named *Minitel*, HyperTerminal can often emulate the special Minitel protocols. Select **F**ile | **P**roperties and click the Settings tab. Select Minitel from the **E**mulation list. HyperTermimal changes to support the Minitel services by displaying buttons as shown in Figure 13.9.

Figure 13.9.

HyperTerminal emulates special Minitel services.

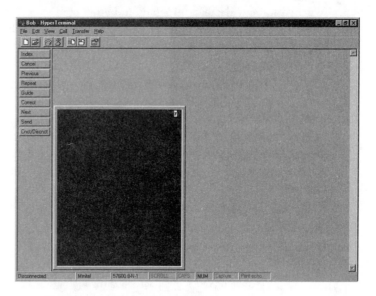

CAUTION

If your remote computer does not require Minitel emulation, don't use the emulation. In addition, some versions of Windows 95 do not supply the Minitel emulation, so you may not be able to access the service if you do not see the emulation in the list.

Summary

This hour introduced you to the world of remote computer communications. The HyperTerminal program lets you connect to other computers, upload and download files, send and receive electronic mail from other users on other computers, and join the online world of computer services such as shopping and banking.

The HyperTerminal works with connection profiles that you set up for each remote computer you want to access. Communicating with a remote computer requires nothing more than a double-click on that computer's icon that you set up. As long as you know the remote computer's phone number, HyperTerminal figures out everything else and starts the connection on the remote computer immediately.

13

Workshop

Term Review

auto detect   HyperTerminal automatically detects the remote computer's technical requirements so you do not have to know anything but the remote computer's telephone number for HyperTerminal to talk to the machine.

backscroll buffer   The memory area, adjustable in size, where HyperTerminal keeps track of previous online screens while you work on a remote computer.

baud rate   A term that describes the speed of computerized telephone communications.

BBS   An acronym for *bulletin board system* that lets you connect your computer, via the phone lines, to exchange electronic mail and files with the BBS's primary computer and other computers connected to the BBS.

connection profile   An individual remote computer site's connection setting information. HyperTerminal keeps track of a remote computer's description, icon, phone number, and modem settings inside each connection profile.

download   The process of receiving a file from a remote computer over the phone lines.

login name   A nickname you go by on a remote computer.

logging off   The process of typing a command that tells the remote computer you are finished using the computer and are ready to exit HyperTerminal or dial a different connection.

logging on   The process of typing an identifying name and password when you first connect to a remote computer to gain access to the remote computer's capabilities.

protocol   The technical connection details that must be in place before two computers can communicate with each other.

remote computer   The computer you are trying to connect to using HyperTerminal.

transfer protocol   A predetermined method of downloading and uploading files. When one computer sends another computer a file, both computers must use the same transfer protocol.

upload   The process of sending a file to a remote computer over the phone lines.

13

Q&A

Q What if I don't know the phone number of the other computer I want to connect to?

A HyperTerminal cannot do much until you do get the other computer's phone number. You must call a support number or find out from the owners of the other computer what telephone number connects your computer to theirs.

Q What if I know the telephone number of the target computer but not technical stuff like the baud rate?

A No problem! HyperTerminal contains new auto detect software technology that automatically detects the target computer's baud rate and other technical connection information. As long as you've supplied the proper phone number, HyperTerminal and the target computer will be able to communicate.

Q What happens if I forget to log off?

A Most of the time, if you disconnect without logging off, the remote computer senses that you've disconnected and will log you off the remote system automatically. In rare cases, you might be charged for several minutes of connect time (assuming you're paying for the remote service) because it could take the remote system a while to figure out that you're no longer connected.

The worst thing that can happen is that, rarely, someone can dial into the remote computer immediately behind you and get access to your account without logging in and without paying for their connect time. Using your ID and password, that user could use the computer on your money, and even destroy files and cause trouble in your name.

It's best to log off before disconnecting, but in those rare cases when you forget, you'll *probably* be okay. There's no guarantee, however, that your account is safe.

13

Hour 14

Activate DOS-Based Applications

Don't believe the media…MS-DOS is not dead! As a matter of fact, Windows 95 empowers MS-DOS applications more than any version of Windows has to date. Not all programs that you run are written for Windows 95 or even for a previous version of Windows. In the past, Windows did not always provide the support that these *MS-DOS programs* required. Sometimes you would need to exit Windows completely to run an MS-DOS program.

Virtually every MS-DOS program will run under Windows 95, including many games that were previously off limits to Windows. In addition to handling memory problems that previously plagued MS-DOS programs running inside the Windows environment, Windows 95 provides modern MS-DOS features that will make you think you're running a new version of MS-DOS.

The highlights of this hour include:

☐ When to open more than one MS-DOS session

☐ How to interpret and use the MS-DOS toolbar

☐ What copy-and-paste communications Windows 95 and MS-DOS programs use

☐ Which MS-DOS Command Properties dialog box controls are important

☐ When to start Windows 95 programs from MS-DOS

☐ How to run MS-DOS programs from within Windows 95

☐ How to start the MS-DOS text editor

MS-DOS and Windows 95

If you want to run an MS-DOS program inside Windows 95, you don't have to start MS-DOS first. You can run the program from the **R**un command on the Start menu (as long as you know the program's path and filename), or you can add the program to one of the Start menu's cascaded menus and click on the program description or program icon.

If you want to load the MS-DOS environment, Windows 95 provides an MS-DOS icon on the Start menu's **P**rograms group. If you click on the MS-DOS icon, the MS-DOS environment runs in a maximized or smaller window (depending on the settings in the **S**ettings | **T**askbar properties dialog box).

In almost every case, Windows 95 provides more free memory for the MS-DOS environment than did previous versions of Windows.

TIME SAVER

> You may start one or more MS-DOS windows! As a result, you can run several MS-DOS programs at one time, and each will run multitasked inside its own window.

Environment Control

In the Windows 95 Sh**u**t Down command's dialog box, there is no command to exit Windows 95. In previous versions of Windows, MS-DOS would be the controlling environment for Windows; Windows 95 is the controlling environment for MS-DOS.

The Shut Down dialog box does provide an option that lets you shut down Windows 95 and start a windowless MS-DOS environment. You would want to enter the MS-DOS environment after shutting down Windows 95, and only when you find one of those rare MS-DOS programs that refuses to run under Windows 95.

14

Task 14.1: Starting an MS-DOS Window

Step 1: Description

This task shows you how to enter the MS-DOS environment from Windows 95. MS-DOS is simply another application to Windows 95, so starting MS-DOS requires no special skills. The MS-DOS environment is known as the *MS-DOS prompt* in Windows 95 because the MS-DOS prompt collects keystrokes as you type them in an MS-DOS window.

JUST A MINUTE

> The MS-DOS window is sometimes called a windowed MS-DOS *VM*, which stands for *Virtual Machine*. Each MS-DOS window acts as if that window contains a separate PC that does not interfere with other MS-DOS VM windows.

Step 2: Action

1. Open the Start menu.
2. Select **P**rograms.
3. Click on the MS-DOS Prompt icon. The MS-DOS window opens as shown in Figure 14.1. Notice that the MS-DOS window contains a toolbar of icon buttons at the top of the window. Previous versions of Windows did not provide a toolbar for MS-DOS windows.

Figure 14.1.

The MS-DOS window acts like any other window in Windows 95.

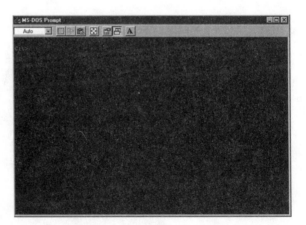

14

JUST A MINUTE

> Your MS-DOS window may appear fully maximized or resized differently from the figure's MS-DOS window.

4. You can maximize MS-DOS windows. Click the maximize button (or double-click the title bar) to produce the maximized MS-DOS window.

JUST A MINUTE

> Although the keystroke is not obvious, you can increase the MS-DOS window to full-screen size by pressing Alt+Enter.

When you increase the MS-DOS window size to full-screen by double-clicking the title bar (or by pressing the Ctrl+Enter shortcut key), the MS-DOS window toolbar disappears.

5. Press Alt+Enter to resize the MS-DOS window.

6. Start yet another MS-DOS window by clicking the MS-DOS prompt's icon on the **P**rograms menu.

7. Start one more MS-DOS window. Previous versions of Windows produced several problems when you opened multiple windows, and you could not properly multitask the MS-DOS windows. Figure 14.2 shows three MS-DOS windows open at one time.

Figure 14.2.

Multiple MS-DOS windows can be open at one time.

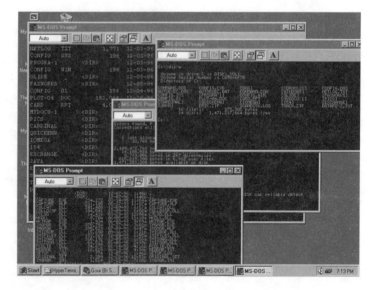

14

8. To close an MS-DOS window, you can click the close button in the upper-right corner (unless the MS-DOS window is maximized, whereby you will see no sizing buttons). You also can type EXIT at the MS-DOS command prompt. You can type the EXIT command using either uppercase or lowercase letters. Close two of the open MS-DOS windows now.

Step 3: Review

The MS-DOS command prompt icon on the **P**rograms menu opens the windowed MS-DOS environment. From the MS-DOS command prompt, you can start MS-DOS programs or issue MS-DOS commands. This task left your Windows 95 environment with one open MS-DOS window. The next task lets you practice using the MS-DOS toolbar at the top of that window.

Task 14.2. The MS-DOS Toolbar

Step 1: Description

This task describes how to use the toolbar that appears on MS-DOS windows. Figure 14.3 shows the toolbar. Previous versions of Windows contained no toolbar. Remember that the toolbar appears only on non-maximized MS-DOS windows. The toolbar is optional, so you can remove the toolbar if you do not want to see it at the top of MS-DOS windows.

Figure 14.3.

The toolbar adds functionality to the MS-DOS window.

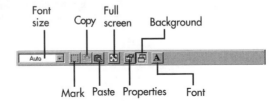

Step 2: Action

1. Click the Font size dropdown listbox button (at the far left of the toolbar) to display a scrollable list of font sizes. The values determine the size, in points, of the text characters on the MS-DOS window. The Auto sizes lets Windows 95 determine the best size of the characters and MS-DOS window. If you select a different font size, the characters inside the window, as well as the window itself, resize to display the new character point size. If the text inside the MS-DOS window is too small to read, you might want to select a larger point size. When you change the font size, Windows 95 resizes the MS-DOS window to show that font more accurately. You can resize MS-DOS windows, but Windows 95 limits the MS-DOS window size to one or two or three sizes, depending on the font size you select.

14

JUST A MINUTE

The double letter **T** next to a font size indicates that the font is a *True Type* font. True Type fonts are generally more readable than non-True Type fonts.

2. The Mark tool on the toolbar lets you mark a section of the MS-DOS window to copy to the Windows 95 Clipboard.

CAUTION

You can copy MS-DOS data to the Clipboard or paste from the Clipboard. You cannot *cut* data from the MS-DOS window.

Issue the DIR command, (for *directory*) at the MS-DOS command prompt to display a directory listing. Once you see the directory listing, click the Mark toolbar button. With your mouse, drag from a point on the MS-DOS window down to a second point creating a highlighted inverted square, such as the highlighted section of the MS-DOS window shown in Figure 14.4.

Figure 14.4.

The highlighted portion of the MS-DOS window is marked for copying.

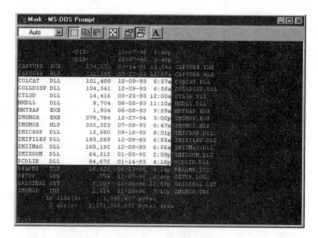

3.1 ▶
Step Up

The Windows 95 version of MS-DOS commands are updated to reflect the new Windows 95 environment. The DIR command works in Windows 95 just as it did in previous versions of Windows and MS-DOS, except you'll see a new column to the right of the listing that contains long filenames for the files in the listing.

14

Windows 95 uses the same internal file structure as previous versions of Windows; when you create a long filename, Windows 95 automatically converts that filename to a unique name that fits within the older naming convention of eight characters with a three-character extension. The DIR command lets you see both the real internal filename and the long filename that you see in Windows 95 dialog boxes.

Another MS-DOS command that you may want to use with long filenames is the COPY command. The following COPY command would never have worked with previous versions of Windows due to the long filenames:

```
COPY "My August sales report" "Old report"
```

(The quotation marks are required when using long filenames that contain embedded spaces.) This command copies the file named My August sales report to a file named Old report so that, at the completion of the copy, two identical files will exist on your computer.

3. Click the Copy toolbar button to send the highlighted MS-DOS data to the Windows 95 Clipboard. As soon as Windows 95 copies the data to the Clipboard, the highlight goes away.

4. To prove that you copied the data to the Clipboard, start WordPad and select **Edit | Paste**. The text you highlighted inside the MS-DOS window now appears inside the WordPad window. Terminate WordPad without saving the file.

JUST A MINUTE

The font used inside the default MS-DOS window is a *non-proportional font*. Therefore, all character columns in the MS-DOS window consume the same width and all align properly into columns of data. Your WordPad's default font might be set up as a *proportional font* so the data, when pasted into WordPad, may not align in perfect columns as the data does when shown in the MS-DOS window. If you paste MS-DOS data into a word processor and the data does not align correctly, change the font of the pasted data to a non-proportional font such as *Courier*.

5. Although you pasted the marked text into WordPad and closed the WordPad application, the data still resides on the Windows 95 Clipboard. To see that, click the Paste toolbar button. Windows 95 pastes the text into the MS-DOS window at the cursor's location.

The MS-DOS command prompt requires specific commands and the data you are pasting probably does not fit within the normal MS-DOS command requirements. Therefore, MS-DOS may issue error messages as the data gets pasted back into the window, but you can safely ignore these messages.

14

6. Click on the Full screen toolbar button to maximize the MS-DOS window to full screen. Issue the DIR command again. A maximized MS-DOS window produces readable text, although the toolbar and Windows 95 taskbar go away until you resize the MS-DOS window once again.

Press Alt+Enter to resize the MS-DOS window to a non-maximized size.

7. Click the Properties toolbar button to display the MS-DOS Prompt Properties tabbed dialog box shown in Figure 14.5.

Figure 14.5.

The MS-DOS Prompt Properties dialog box controls the way MS-DOS starts and performs.

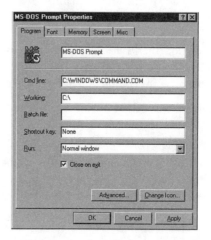

The MS-DOS Prompt Properties tabbed dialog box contains several settings that control the way your MS-DOS windows appear and perform. For example, if you press a shortcut key, such as **D**, at the **S**hortcut key prompt, you will be able to start the MS-DOS window by pressing Ctrl+Alt+D from almost anywhere within the Windows 95 environment.

The **R**un prompt determines how you want the MS-DOS window to appear when you run programs within the window. The dropdown listbox contains these three window size prompts: Normal window, Minimized, and Maximized.

If you want the MS-DOS window to close when an MS-DOS application finishes, make sure that the Close on exit option is checked. Most of the time, you'll want to leave this option checked.

TIME SAVER

Actually, most of the time you'll want to leave *most* of the MS-DOS Prompt Properties tabbed dialog box settings alone. The default settings almost always make MS-DOS windows perform the way you want them to.

14

8. Clicking the **C**hange Icon command button produces the interesting horizontally scrolling dialog box shown in Figure 14.6. If you want a different icon to appear next to the MS-DOS taskbar when running MS-DOS programs, select a different icon from the scrolling list of icons and click OK.

Figure 14.6.

You can change the icon that appears on the taskbar for an MS-DOS window.

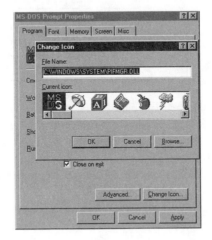

9. The remaining tabbed dialog box options are fairly advanced and are usually set to appropriate values. There are a couple you should know about now, however.

   Click the Screen tab to display a dialog box that controls the way the MS-DOS screen appears to the user. Figure 14.7 shows this dialog box.

Figure 14.7.

The screen options determine how Windows 95 displays the MS-DOS window.

The toolbar can be hidden

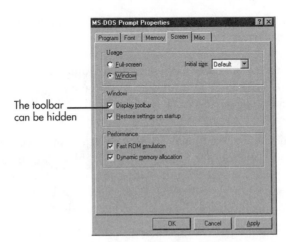

14

If you uncheck the Display toolbar option, Windows 95 does not display the toolbar in the MS-DOS window. If you want the MS-DOS window to appear maximized when Windows 95 first displays the window (you can still resize the maximized window by pressing Alt+Enter), select the **F**ull-screen option.

TIME SAVER

Although you lose some MS-DOS functionality when you remove the toolbar, you gain extra MS-DOS window space that would otherwise be taken up by the toolbar.

10. Click the Misc tab to see another dialog box that controls several miscellaneous MS-DOS window options. You can control whether or not the Windows 95 screen saver is active during the MS-DOS session. Some MS-DOS programs make the Windows 95 screen saver program think that no keyboard action has taken place and will trigger the Windows 95 screen saver, even when you are actively working inside the MS-DOS mode.

You can see how to determine which Windows 95 shortcut keys are active inside MS-DOS. By default, all Windows 95 shortcut keys are active inside the MS-DOS window, and you should not change these without good reason.

Close the tabbed dialog box now that you've reviewed the highlights of the MS-DOS properties.

Step Up   The MS-DOS Command Properties dialog box replaces the need for PIF and many .INI file tweakings that were the bane of Windows 3.1.

11. The Background toolbar button, when clicked, makes your MS-DOS window run in the background, and when clicked again, makes your MS-DOS program run in the foreground. When in the foreground, the MS-DOS program maintains complete control of the computer, and other windows do not multitask at the same time that MS-DOS is running. You would only click the background toolbar button if you had a clock-sensitive MS-DOS application that required heavy system resources.

Click on the Font toolbar button to display the Font dialog box from the MS-DOS Command Prompt. Figure 14.8 shows this dialog box that appears when you click the Font button. The Font dialog box lets you control the size and format of the font used inside the MS-DOS window. (The Font size dropdown listbox discussed earlier controls only the font size, but not the format.)

14

Figure 14.8.

The Font dialog box lets you control the way characters appear inside the MS-DOS window.

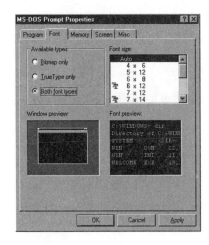

Click the OK command button to get rid of the dialog box. Leave the MS-DOS window open for the next section.

Step 3: Review

The MS-DOS toolbar gives you one-button access to common MS-DOS tasks. You can mark, copy, and paste to and from the Windows 95 Clipboard. You can adjust the screen size and the MS-DOS mode properties so that the MS-DOS session behaves differently. In addition, if you want to use a different font size inside the MS-DOS session, look no further than the help you need to adjust the display font.

CAUTION

> Although you will only rarely find such programs, some older MS-DOS programs and very advanced MS-DOS—based games, will refuse to run if the program detects Windows 95 running. You can fool these programs into running anyway by right-clicking over their Explorer icon, selecting **P**roperties from the pop-up menu, clicking the Program tab, and clicking the option labeled **S**uggest MS-DOS mode as necessary. Although the program *may* still refuse to run because of a memory conflict, most problems will clear up and the program will execute even though Windows 95 is also running.

Wrapping Up the MS-DOS Window

Over time, you'll run across several items in the MS-DOS window that you'll find interesting. Here's something fun you can try: Open the Windows 95 Explorer program and

14

resize the window so you can see both the Explorer window and the MS-DOS window. Find a filename in the Explorer's right window and drag that filename to the MS-DOS prompt. As soon as you release the mouse button, the filename, including its complete drive and pathname, appears at the MS-DOS prompt!

When managing files in the MS-DOS environment, you can drag filenames from Explorer and other Windows 95 Open dialog boxes instead of typing the complete disk, path, and filename. When working inside MS-DOS windows, you can drag the file from the Windows 95 environment, and Windows 95 substitutes the file name at the cursor. Therefore, if you were in the middle of a COPY command, you could drag filenames, from Explorer, to complete the COPY command instead of typing the names.

In addition, Windows 95 has changed the CD command (*Change Directory*). As you may know, the following command moves you up one parent directory level:

```
cd ..
```

If you are buried deep within several levels of directories while in an MS-DOS session, you can add an extra period to the CD command for each directory you want to return to. The following command returns you to three previous parent directory levels:

```
CD ....
```

As always, the following command takes you to the root directory no matter how many directory levels are reside in:

```
cd \
```

Starting Programs in MS-DOS

The MS-DOS window is so fully integrated into Windows 95 that you can execute Windows 95 programs *from the MS-DOS prompt*. Therefore, if you know the filename of a Windows 95 program, you will not have to return to Windows 95, if you're working inside a MS-DOS window, to execute a Windows 95 program.

Although Notepad makes an MS-DOS editor redundant and unnecessary, MS-DOS has supplied a text editor since version 1.0 of MS-DOS. There are many MS-DOS die-hards who still want to edit text files from within the MS-DOS environment.

When the Microsoft programmers wrote Windows 95, they decided to update an old stand-by program, the MS-DOS text editor, to implement the long filenames and to modernize the performance of the program. If you have used an MS-DOS text editor, such as EDIT, you'll feel right at home with the updated version of EDIT (its screen is shown in Figure 14.9).

JUST A MINUTE

This hour does not explain EDIT because the Windows 95 Notepad program replaces EDIT. Notepad, which is explained in Hour 10, "Compose Using Writing Tools," is a Windows 95 program that makes the MS-DOS editor obsolete, except to those who already prefer the older editor.

Figure 14.9.

The Windows 95 text editor, EDIT, supports long filenames and an improved keyboard interface.

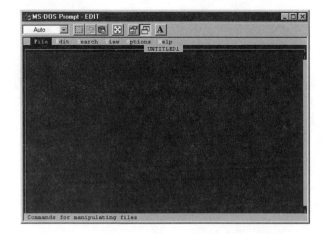

If you want to start MS-DOS in a specific directory, display the MS-DOS Properties dialog box (by clicking the Properties MS-DOS toolbar button); then type the directory's pathname at the option labeled Working.

3.1 ▶
Step Up
If you use DOSKEY (the program that lets you more easily edit past MS-DOS commands), you can make Windows 95 automatically run the DOSKEY program by entering DOSKEY at the Program dialog box's (located inside the Properties dialog box) **B**atch File prompt.

In some cases, an MS-DOS program will refuse to run if you are running a Windows 95 screen saver. Follow these steps to allow the screen saver to work along with such a program:

1. Open Explorer.
2. Locate the MS-DOS program's icon.
3. Right-click over the icon.
4. Select **P**roperties from the icon's menu.
5. Click the Misc tab to display the Misc dialog box shown in Figure 14.10.
6. Click the option labeled **A**llow screen saver.
7. Close the dialog box. The program should now let the screen saver work in conjunction with the MS-DOS program.

14

Figure 14.10.

Letting a screen saver work with an MS-DOS program.

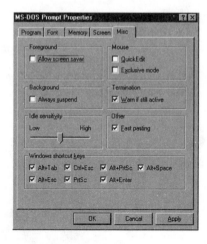

CAUTION

If the screen saver messes things up, uncheck the option described in the previous steps so that the screen saver goes idle whenever that particular MS-DOS program runs.

Summary

This hour focused on the MS-DOS environment inside Windows 95. Although Windows 95 users often work far from the MS-DOS text-based environment of olden days, the MS-DOS environment is still alive and well due to the many programs still in use today that are written for MS-DOS.

Windows 95 supports MS-DOS programs better than any version of Windows has so far. Windows 95 provides more memory for programs, as well as enabling you to open several multitasking MS-DOS programs at one time. In addition, Windows 95 adds a toolbar to MS-DOS windows that makes the management of your MS-DOS windows and programs much easier to work with.

There are people who will work many hours a day with Windows 95 and never need to start the MS-DOS environment. Others still use older MS-DOS programs and current-day games that run only under MS-DOS. Because of the extra memory and runtime support provided by Windows 95, these MS-DOS programs ought to work comfortably inside Windows 95.

Workshop

Term Review

default drive and directory   When you start MS-DOS, the MS-DOS command prompt always contains a disk drive and directory. The disk drive is normally C, and the directory is the root directory called \ (backslash). You can change the default disk or directory by entering a new one at the command prompt.

MS-DOS command prompt   When you open an MS-DOS window, you must issue a command to the MS-DOS environment. The command prompt, usually shown on the screen as `C:\>` indicating the current default drive and directory, accepts your MS-DOS commands as you type the commands.

MS-DOS program   A program written specifically for the MS-DOS environment. MS-DOS programs do not take advantage of the graphical nature of Windows 95.

non-proportional font   A font that contains characters that each consume the same width on the screen or printer.

proportional font   A font that generally makes for a more natural appearance of text. The letters within the text do not all consume the same screen width. For example, the lowercase letter **i** consumes less space than the uppercase **M**.

True Type font   A readable font that appears the same on both the screen and printer.

VM   Stands for *virtual memory* and refers to the concept that each MS-DOS window acts like a separate PC that has access to full memory and other system resources.

Q&A

Q Why would I want to shut Windows 95 down to the MS-DOS environment?

A There are still a handful of rare programs written for the MS-DOS environment that will not run under Windows 95. Microsoft wrote Windows 95 to run most MS-DOS programs, even the ones that previous versions of Windows could not handle. Although the majority of MS-DOS programs work well under Windows 95, the few that do not will run as long as you shut down Windows 95 and restart (via the Shut Down menu command) your computer in the MS-DOS mode.

14

Q When would I want to start more than one MS-DOS window?

A If you want to run two or more MS-DOS programs at once, such as two games, whether or not you are also running Windows 95 programs, the multiple MS-DOS windows let both of the MS-DOS programs work in a multitasking mode. Each window works independently of the other(s).

Q Why would I execute a Windows 95 program from the MS-DOS prompt?

A Users of previous Windows versions found that they often wanted to execute a Windows program from the MS-DOS prompt but, until Windows 95, they were unable to do that. Perhaps you like to use an MS-DOS bookkeeping system and you suddenly want to use a calculator. If you know the Windows 95 calculator's filename, CALC (with the extension .EXE), you can type that filename (precede the filename with the file's disk name and pathname), such as typing `c:\windows\calc`, and the program starts immediately (your MS-DOS window still remains open as well).

Q If I like the Windows 95 Notepad program, is there any need to learn the MS-DOS editor?

A Not really. The MS-DOS editor might be good to use if you're already familiar with previous versions of MS-DOS editors such as MS-DOS 5 and 6's EDIT program. You'll find that Microsoft implemented needed changes to EDIT without changing the fundamental purpose of the MS-DOS text editor.

Hour 15

Increase Printing Power

This hour explains the printing options available to you as a Windows 95 user. The printer is one of those devices that you don't want to think a lot about; you want to print a document within your word processor or from within your spreadsheet program and a few moments later, grab the resulting printed output from the printer. Most of the time, you do not have to think about how Windows 95 relates to your printer.

The reason this hour spends time discussing the printing capabilities of Windows 95 is that once you understand the Windows 95 *printer subsystem* (the internal program that automatically controls all printing from within Windows 95), you will be better equipped to handle advanced printer management. There are times when you may want to print output, but change your mind once you've issued the print command. The printer subsystem lets you rearrange, reroute, and redo printer output before that output gets to the printer.

The highlights of this hour include:

- ☐ When to use the Add Printers Wizard to set up new printers
- ☐ What advantages the print subsystem offers you
- ☐ How to use the Print dialog boxes to route output to a printer
- ☐ How to manage the Print job window's list of printed documents
- ☐ When to defer printing

Introduction to Spooled Printing

When you print documents, Windows 95 automatically starts the printer subsystem. The printer subsystem controls all printing from within Windows 95, whereas the MS-DOS environment sent data directly to the printer when you printed data, Windows 95 *spools* output through the printer subsystem as shown in Figure 15.1. When spooled, the printed output goes to a disk file, managed by the printer subsystem, before being sent directly to the printer.

Figure 15.1.

Windows 95 spools output to the printer subsystem disk file.

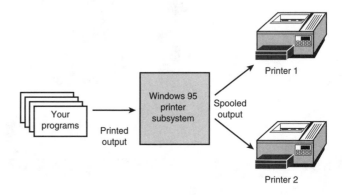

JUST A MINUTE

Every document you print creates a unique *print job* that appears on the spooler. Windows 95 gives you access to these print jobs.

By routing printed output to a spooled disk file instead of sending the output directly to the printer, you can intercept the printed output before that output goes to paper. You therefore have more control over how the output appears on the printer. You also can select which printer receives the output, in case more than one printer is connected to your computer.

Step Up   The Windows 95 printer subsystem is more integrated into Windows 95 than the Windows 3.1 Print Manager. The Windows 95 printer subsystem lets you manage all printing from a special folder labeled Printers.

Setting Up a Printer

If you add a printer to your system, remove a printer from your system, or set up Windows 95 to use a printer for the first time, you'll have to inform Windows 95. Windows 95 helps guide you as you set up printers by giving you the *Add Printer Wizard.*

15

JUST A MINUTE

> As mentioned in Hour 2, a *wizard* is a procedure that Windows 95 guides you through with a series of dialog boxes.

A special Printers folder available from the Start | Settings menu contains all information about your computer's printer hardware. If you have yet to set up a printer, you will have to open the Printers folder and walk through the Add Printer Wizard so that Windows 95 knows exactly which printer to use.

Task 15.1: Using the Add Printer Wizard

TASK

Step 1: Description

Windows 95 needs to know how to format the printed output that you want printed. Almost every printer supports different print functions, and almost every printer requires different kinds of *print codes* that determine how the printer outputs specific characters and character-formatting options. The Add Printer Wizard handles necessary details and asks you appropriate questions that determine how printed output eventually appears.

CAUTION

> If you use a network and you need to set up a network printer in Windows 95, use the Network Neighborhood window and double-click the network printer's icon; you can browse the network to find the printer if the printer's icon does not appear. Then set up the printer following the instructions that appear on the screen.

Step 2: Action

1. Connect your printer to your computer using a printer cable. Most printers connect to the computer's *parallel port.*
2. Click the Start button to display the Start menu.
3. Select **S**ettings | **P**rinters to open the Printers window shown in Figure 15.2.

JUST A MINUTE

> If you have not yet set up any printer, you will see only the Add Printer icon in the Printers window.

The Printers window provides access to all of your printer subsystem capabilities. It is from the Printers window that you can manage and rearrange print jobs that you've started in other Windows 95 applications.

Figure 15.2.
The Printers window controls the setup and operation of printers.

4. The Printers window contains the icon, labeled Add Printer, that starts the Add Printer Wizard. If you've not set up a printer yet, you should double-click over the Add Printer icon now. When you double-click the Add Printer icon, you will see the first screen of the Add Printer Wizard shown in Figure 15.3.

Figure 15.3.
The Add Printer Wizard walks you through the setup of a new printer.

5. Click the Next command button to start the Add Printer Wizard's operation. Select either the **L**ocal printer or the **N**etwork printer.

TIME SAVER

As you walk through a wizard, you can click the Back command button to back up a step and answer any previous prompt differently.

6. A list of printer manufacturers appears in the left scrolling window. Choose a printer manufacturer, such as *Epson* or *HP*, and that manufacturer's printer models appear in the right scrolling window.

   Over time, printer manufacturers update their printers and offer new models. There is no way that Microsoft can predict what a printer manufacturer will do next. Therefore, you may buy a printer that's made after Windows 95 was written. If so, the printer should come with a diskette that you can use to add that printer to Windows 95. If this is your case, click the Have Disk button and follow the instructions on the screen.

15

If your printer *is* in the list, find your printer's model, highlight the model, and click the Next button.

JUST A MINUTE

If you cannot find your printer's exact model, there is probably a printer in the list that closely matches your printer. You may have to check your printer manual for models that are compatible. Choose the printer that most closely matches your printer's model.

TIME SAVER

Microsoft routinely adds new printer makes and models to their list of supported printers. You can often find *printer drivers* (printer description files) for new printers on bulletin board systems, as well as on the Microsoft Network and other major online services.

7. The wizard next needs information about the port that your printer is plugged into. The dialog box shown in Figure 15.4 requests this information.

Figure 15.4.

The Add Printer Wizard needs to know where your printer is.

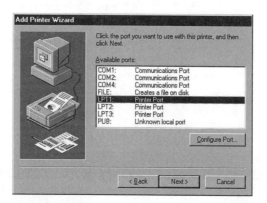

Most of the time, you'll click **Next** to select the default value of the parallel printer port. Perhaps before doing so, you should click the **Configure Port command button. The Configure Port dialog box contains two options. The first option determines if the spooling should apply to MS-DOS programs in addition to Windows 95 programs. The second option determines if you want the printer subsystem to check the port before printing, to make sure that the port is ready for data. Unless you are using special printer hardware that requires extra control, you'll want to leave both these options checked and click the OK command button to return to the wizard.

Select the port where your computer is connected and click the Next command button now.

TIME SAVER

If you want to route an image of the printed output to a disk file, you can select FILE:. Every time you print, Windows 95 will then ask you for the name of a file that you want Windows 95 to use for collecting the printed output. Once it is sent to a file, you can edit the file, view the file, or print the file.

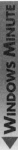

Printer Ports

If you have more than one parallel printer port, you will see at least one additional port listed inside the wizard's listbox. COM1: and COM2: are names for the first two *serial ports* on your computer.

Rarely do today's printers attach to serial ports because these ports are better used for modem and mouse connections. Nevertheless, there are some printers that use the serial ports. The name LPT1: (and possibly LPT2:) refers to the parallel port where most printer cables are connected.

8. When you see the screen shown in Figure 15.5, you can enter the name you want to use for the printer when selecting among printers within Windows 95. If you like the default name, don't change it. If you want a different name, such as Joe's Printer (in case you're setting up a network printer), type the new name. If this is the only printer you are setting up, select **Yes** so that Windows 95 uses the printer automatically every time you print something. If you are setting up a secondary printer, select **No**.

Figure 15.5.

You must tell Windows 95 how to refer to the printer.

9. Click the **N**ext command button to move to the next wizard screen.

10. If you click **Y**es on the next wizard screen, Windows 95 will print a test page on the printer. (Be sure to turn on your printer and make sure it has paper.) By printing a test page, you ensure that Windows 95 properly recognizes the printer. Click the **F**inish command button to complete the wizard.

CAUTION

> Windows 95 rarely has the proper printer setup file on the hard disk. You will probably have to insert a Windows 95 installation diskette or the installation CD-ROM so that Windows 95 can find the proper information for the printer you've selected. Windows 95 prompts you for this extra disk or CD-ROM if needed.

11. Once Windows 95 completes the setup, a new icon with your printer's name appears in the Printers window.

Step 3: Review

Windows 95 must know exactly what kind of printer you have connected to your computer. Depending on the hardware you have, you may have more than one printer physically attached to your computer. If so, you have to run the Add Printer setup wizard for each printer you will print to. When running the Add Printer Wizard, you specify which printer Windows 95 should use for the default printer. Of course, any time you print documents, you can select a printer that differs from the default printer if you want output to go to a secondary printer source. You can also change the default printer by right-clicking over the printer you want to set as the default printer and selecting the Set As Default command from the right-click menu.

TIME SAVER

> If you use your computer for accounting or personal finance, you might have a laser printer for reports and a dot-matrix printer for checks. The default printer will be the printer that you print to most often. If your laser printer is the default printer, you'll have to route output, using the Print dialog box explained in the next section, to the check printer when you want to print checks.

The Print Dialog Box

When you print from an application such as WordPad, you'll see the Print dialog box shown in Figure 15.6. The Print dialog box contains several options from which you can choose. Most of the time, the default option values are appropriate, so you'll simply press Enter to select the OK command button when printing.

Figure 15.6.

The Print dialog box controls the way a print job routes output.

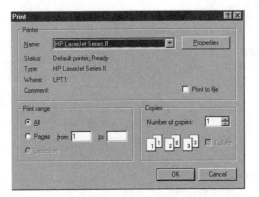

The Print dialog box contains a dropdown listbox of every printer you've added to Windows 95. The default printer will be the printer you've chosen using the Add Printer Wizard's final screen.

TIME SAVER

Even if you have not set up a file-based output device (see Task 15.1's description of the FILE: port), you can route the printer's output to a file by clicking the Print-to-file option. If you want output to go to a physical printer as soon as possible, as is most often the case, leave this option unchecked.

The Print range will be **All** if you want to print all pages. For example, if you are printing 20 pages from a word processor, the **All** option sends all 20 pages to the printer. If you select the **Pages** option, you can enter a starting page number and ending page number to print only a portion of the document.

The Copies section determines how many copies you want to print. The default is one copy, but you can request an additional number of copies. If you enter a number greater than 1, check the **Co**llate option if you want the pages collated (you usually do). If you highlight part of the text before beginning the print process, you can click the **S**election option button to print only the selected text.

15

JUST A MINUTE

There still are many Windows 3.1 programs in existence. They use the Print dialog box shown in Figure 15.7. The options of the Windows 3.1 Print dialog box work just like those in the Windows 95 Print dialog box.

15

Figure 15.7.

You'll probably see Windows 3.1 Print dialog boxes from time to time.

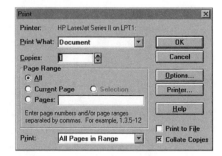

For special print jobs you can click the **P**roperties command button to display a printer Properties dialog box such as the one shown in Figure 15.8. Each printer model supports a different set of options so each printer's Properties dialog box contains different options as well. In the Properties dialog box, you specify the type of paper in the printer's paper tray, the *orientation* (the way the printed output appears on the paper), and the printer resolution (the higher the printer resolution, the better your output looks, but the longer the printer takes to print a single page), among other options that your printer might support.

Figure 15.8.

A printer Properties dialog box controls your printer options.

Keep in mind that the output goes to the print spooler and *not* directly to the printer. The next section explains how you can manage the print spooler.

Caution

Some applications begin printing as soon as you click a printing toolbar button instead of displaying the Print dialog box before beginning to print. Be sure that you understand the way each of your applications handles printing. If you click such a toolbar button several times, you could inadvertently send many copies of output to your printer.

Time Saver

Some print jobs take a while to spool their output to the spool file and, subsequently, to the printer. The taskbar displays a printer icon to the left of the clock during the printing process. If you rest the cursor over the printer icon, Windows 95 displays a roving help box that describes how many jobs are in line to print. If you double-click the print icon, Windows 95 displays the list of all print jobs (the next section describes the window of print jobs). If you right-click over the icon, Windows 95 gives you the choice of displaying a window containing a list of all print jobs or the print jobs for specific printers that are queued up waiting for printed output.

Explorer and Open dialog boxes all display documents, as you've seen already throughout this book. If you want to print a document, such as a bitmap graphic document file, a text document file, or a word processing document file, the right-click menu contains a **P**rint command that automatically prints the selected document (or documents) that you right-click over. The right-click does *not* produce the print dialog box described in this section; rather, Windows 95 automatically prints one copy of the document on the primary default printer.

Just a Minute

Windows 95 cannot print all types of documents. For example, executable programs (such as those ending with the .EXE or .COM extension) are not printable. When you right-click over these non-printable files, the right-click menu does not contain a **P**rint command.

There's yet one more way to print documents that works well in some situations. If you have the My Computer window open or if you are using the Explorer, you can print any printable document by dragging that document to any printer icon inside the Printers window. Windows 95 automatically begins spooling that document to the printer that you drag to.

TIME SAVER

If you copy a printer icon from the Printers window to your desktop (by holding Ctrl and dragging the icon to your desktop), you will eliminate the need to open the Printers window every time you need to access your printer. You can drag files directly to the desktop's icon instead of first having to open the Printers window. In addition, you can access your printer's Properties page by right-clicking over the desktop's printer icon and selecting **P**roperties from the pop-up menu.

15

Managing Print Jobs

When you print one or more documents, from whatever program you print, Windows 95 formats the output into the format required by the Print dialog box's selected printer, and then sends that output to a spool file. Once the output completes, the printer subsystem begins to route the output to the actual printer, as long as your printer is connected and turned on.

Suppose that you want to print several documents to your printer in succession. Although today's printers are fairly fast, the computer's disk drives and memory are much faster than the relative speed of printers. Therefore, you can end up sending several documents to the printer before the first document even finishes printing on paper.

After printing one or more documents, you can open the Printer window and double-click the printer icon that matches the printer you've routed all your output to. A scrolling list of print jobs, such as the one shown in Figure 15.9, appears inside the window.

Figure 15.9.

You can see all the print jobs spooled up, waiting to print.

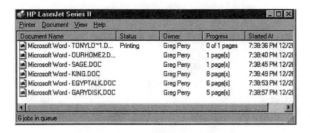

Each line in the window describes one print job. If you've printed three documents, all three documents appear inside the window. The window describes how far along the print job is. The Progress column tells you how many pages of the current print job have been completed. The remaining print jobs await their turn in the list.

3.1 ▶ When you printed under Windows 3.1, it automatically started the Print Manager.
Step Up If you wanted to check on the print jobs, you could switch to the running Print
Manager using Alt+Tab. The printer subsystem used by Windows 95 is more
integrated into the operating environment and does not appear on the taskbar as a separate
program. Therefore, you cannot switch to the print jobs inside Windows 95 using Alt+Tab.
If you want to manage the list of print jobs, you can either click on the printer icon inside
the taskbar or open the Printers folder using the Start menu.

If you want to move one of the print jobs to the top or bottom of the *queue* (the list of print
jobs), you can drag that print job to the top or bottom. Dragging a print job around in the
list changes the priority for that print job. For example, your boss may be waiting over your
shoulder for a report. If you had several jobs waiting to print before your boss showed up, you
could move the boss's print job to the top of the list so it prints next.

Right-clicking over a print job gives you the option of pausing a print job (putting it on hold
until you resume the job) or canceling the print job altogether.

TIME SAVER

> If you select more than one print job by holding down the Ctrl key while
> you select print jobs, you can pause or cancel more than one print job at
> the same time.

Deferred Printing

There are times when you'll print several documents but *not* want those documents to appear
on a printer! Often people carry a laptop with them but not a printer. Even if you don't have
a printer with you, you may create expense reports and other documents that you want to
print as soon as you get back to your office.

Instead of keeping track of each document you want to print later you can go ahead and issue
a *deferred printing* request so that Windows 95 spools the document or documents to the disk
drive in the target printer's image. The printer subsystem will not attempt to send the spooled
data to a printer just yet.

Ordinarily, if you were to print a document to a printer but you had no printer attached to
your computer, Windows 95 would issue the error message shown in Figure 15.10. Although
Windows 95 can spool the output properly and set up a print job for the output, Windows
95 cannot finish the job due to a lack of a printer, and so the dialog box lets you know about
the problem.

15

Figure 15.10.
Windows 95 cannot print to a printer if a printer does not exist.

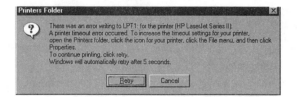

15

JUST A MINUTE

If you do have a printer attached to your computer but you get the error dialog box shown in Figure 15.10, you probably forgot to turn on the printer or turn the printer *online* so that the printer can accept output. You can correct the problem and click **R**etry to restart the printing. If you do not click **R**etry, Windows 95 will automatically retry printing every five seconds.

If you want to defer printing for another time, open the Printers folder and click over the icon that matches the printer you want to defer printing to. Once you highlight the icon, select File | **W**ork Offline. Once you return to your office or plug a printer into the printer port, you can repeat this process to uncheck the **W**ork Offline option. As soon as you set the printer icon back to its normal online status, Windows 95 will begin printing to that printer port.

CAUTION

If your printer icon's **F**ile menu does not have a **W**ork Offline option, you can select P**a**use Printing to achieve the same delayed printing effect. The actual printing will begin when you click P**a**use Printing once more to turn off the pause. The **W**ork Offline option is available only on certain laptop and networked computer configurations.

Separator Pages

If you share a network printer with others, you'll often send print jobs to the printer at approximately the same time as a co-worker. Windows 95 ensures that the first print job to arive prints first, in its entirety, before the second print job, so that you don't have to worry about conflicting and shuffled output. Nevertheless, print jobs can sometimes be time-consuming to separate from a stack of several print jobs that await you and others at the networked printer. Therefore, you might want to designate a *page separator* for the printer. A page separator is a page that prints between print jobs. You can place text or graphics on the page so that the page helps you more easily locate user divisions within a large stack of printer output.

CAUTION

> Windows 95 will print a separator page before each print job. If your printer is rarely used by two or more people at once, you'll always get a separator page before your print job even if yours is the only print job sent to the printer. Therefore, designate a separator page only if you share a printer with other users and often print at the same time as them.

Task 15.2: Designating Separator Pages

Step 1: Description

Separator pages do not have to be fancy. Designate a separator page, as this task demonstrates, if you and others send print jobs to the same printer often.

TIME SAVER

> If you don't use a network printer but you often send several documents to your printer before picking up the output, a separator page will help you find the division between the various print jobs. In other words, separator pages aren't just for networked printers.

Step 2: Action

1. Open your Printers window from the Start menu's **S**ettings option or from the My Computer window.

2. Right-click over the printer on which you want to add separator pages. (You typically have only one or two printer icons in the window.)

3. Select **P**roperties from the pop-up menu to display the Properties page.

4. From the **S**eparator page listbox, select the separator page you want. If you want to use your own file, you can type your file's full pathname and filename or click the **B**rowse button to locate your file.

   The file you use for a separator page must end with the .WMF filename extension. .WMF files are named *Windows metafiles* and you must have access to a program that can create such files before you will be able to supply your own separator pages.

5. Click OK to close the Printers window.

15

Step 3: Review

By setting the separator page option on your printer's Properties sheet, you can designate a separator page that Windows 95 prints before each print job. The separator pages help you separate multiple outputs from one another. When you search through a large printed stack of output, you know you're at a new print job's output when you get to the next separator page.

Summary

This hour explored the printer options you have with Windows 95. Before using a printer for the first time, you must set up the printer using the Add Printer Wizard available inside the Printers folder. Windows 95 supports several hundred makes and models of printers so you'll probably find your printer in the list.

Windows 95 does not send output directly to a printer. Instead, Windows 95 spools output to a disk file and then, once the spooled output is completed, Windows 95 sends the output to a printer. You can defer the printing if you do not have a printer hooked up at the time you issue the print command.

Windows 95 supports more than one connected printer at the same time. If you have two or more printers set up under Windows 95, you can, at the time that you print a document, direct that document to any printer on the system. In addition, if you share a printer with lots of users, you can designate separator pages to make separating the output easier.

Workshop

Term Review

deferred printing The process of issuing print commands but delaying the physical printing of those documents until later. Sometimes deferred printing is called *delayed printing*.

offline A printer is offline when the printer is turned off or on, but not ready to accept output (you might turn the printer offline when you need to feed pages through the printer manually).

online A printer is online when the printer is turned on and ready to accept output.

orientation The position of output on the printed page.

parallel port A connector on your computer where most printer cables plug into.

print codes Special characters that dictate how printers output and format characters.

print jobs   Every document that you print creates a print job on the print spooler.

printer drivers   Small descriptor files that allow Windows 95 to communicate properly with specific printers.

printer subsystem   A program automatically started by Windows 95 that controls the way output appears on the printer.

queue   A list, such as the list of print jobs, that you see in the Printers window when you double-click a printer icon.

separator page   A page that prints before each print job to separate multiple print jobs on an output stack for networked printers.

spooled output   Output that is sent to a disk file before being routed to a printer.

Windows metafile   A special Windows 95 file that ends with the .WMF filename extension. You can use Windows metafiles for separator pages that you create yourself as long as you have a program that can create metafiles with the .WMF filename extension.

Q&A

Q Why should I care how my output gets to the printer?

A There are times when you'll send several documents to the printer and then change your mind about printing one or more of them. As long as the documents haven't printed, you can keep the document from printing by utilizing the printer subsystem available within Windows 95.

   All printer output goes through the print spooler instead of going directly to the printer. The spooler holds all print jobs and controls the order of the print jobs. Once a job is on the spooler's list of documents, you can delete the documents or rearrange their printing priority. If you did not know how Windows 95 spooled printed output, you would not be able to rearrange printer output.

Q Does the spooling of output slow down my printing?

A It's true that your output will not print as fast as it would if the output went directly to the printer. Nevertheless, the decrease in speed is minimal. The advantages you gain by spooling your output more than make up for the delay in printing.

Q When would I set up more than one printer?

A If you have more than one printer connected to your computer, you can choose one printer as the default printer and one as a secondary printer. Windows 95 prints to the default printer unless you override the default and route output to the secondary printer. You have to run the Add Printer Wizard for both printers before you use them the first time so that Windows 95 will know how to format the output.

15

Q **Why does a right-click over some files produce a menu with a Print command while a right-click over others does not?**

A Windows 95 knows that some files are printable and some are not. For example, you could not print a sound file. Executable programs are not printable either. Only document files that contain graphics or text are printable. Therefore, Windows 95 makes sure that the **P**rint command appears only in the right-click menu for document files that Windows 95 can print.

15

Hour 16

Fonts and Viewers

As you now know, Windows 95 is *document-centered*, meaning that Windows 95 manages files as if those files were documents stored inside folders. No matter what kind of information those documents contain, you can view the documents on your screen.

Windows 95 gives you several ways to manage documents. In previous versions of Windows, you would often have to open documents to view their contents because the filename limitations simply didn't let you assign descriptive titles. The long filenames in Windows 95 help eliminate some of this viewing, but there are still many times when you need to look up information in a document.

If you double-click over a document name virtually anywhere within Windows 95, it tries its best to determine the nature of the document and opens a program that displays that document. At times, however, you may not have such a program available. For example, you may work on a desktop or laptop with limited disk space. If you don't have many programs on the computer, how can you view all the spreadsheets, word processor documents, and graphic documents on the computer's disk? The answer is explained this hour.

The highlights of this hour include:

- ☐ What's possible from the Fonts window
- ☐ How to add new fonts to Windows 95
- ☐ How to remove fonts from Windows 95
- ☐ When to use Quick Viewer to look at documents
- ☐ Why the document's orientation often makes a document easier to read
- ☐ How to display a page preview of documents inside the Quick Viewer

Font with Style

Due to the design of documents, the way that Windows 95 displays documents is critical to your viewing of them. The documents must be easy to read. If Windows 95 doesn't automatically display a document in a form that provides for easy viewing, you'll have to change the way the document appears. Perhaps the simplest way to make a document easier to read, no matter what tool you use to view those documents, is by changing the document's *font*. A font is the typeface Windows 95 uses to display a character. If you see two letter *A*'s on the screen and one is larger, more slanted, bolder, fancier, or more scripted, you are looking at two different fonts.

Fonts from the same *font family* contain the same typeface (they look alike) but they come in standard formatting versions such as italicized, boldfaced, and underlined text. Therefore, an italicized font named *Courier* and a boldfaced font named *Courier* both belong to the same font family, even though they look different due to the italicized version of the one and the boldface of the other. A font named *Algerian* and a font named *Symbol,* however, would belong to two different font families; not only do they look different, but they also come in various styles.

Fonts and Typefaces

Before computers were invented, printer experts stored collections of typefaces in their shops. Each typeface contained every letter, number, and special character the printer would need for printed documents. Therefore, the printer might have 50 typefaces in his or her inventory with each of those typefaces containing the same letters, numbers, and special characters but each having a different appearance or size.

WINDOWS MINUTE

16

Windows 95 also contains a collection of typefaces, and those typefaces are stored as fonts on the hard disk. If you want to use a special typeface for a title, you must make sure that Windows 95 contains that typeface in its font collection. If not, you will have to purchase the font and add that font to your system. Software dealers sell numerous font collections. Several fonts come with Windows 95 and with the programs that you use, so you may not even need additional fonts.

The Control Panel contains an icon labeled Fonts from which you can manage, add, and delete fonts from Windows 95's collection of fonts. When you double-click the Control Panel's Fonts icon, Windows 95 opens the Fonts window shown in Figure 16.1. Task 16.1 explains how to manage fonts from the Fonts window.

16

Figure 16.1.
The Fonts window displays your fonts.

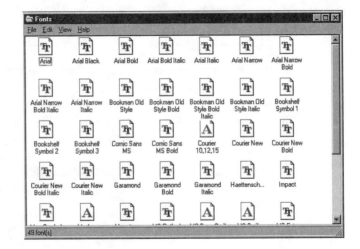

Task 16.1: The Fonts Window

Step 1: Description
This task explains how to access your system's fonts by using the Fonts window. The Fonts window is the control center for the fonts on your system. You can add or remove fonts from this window, as well as learn more about the font details you already have.

TASK

Step 2: Action
1. Open the Control Panel.
2. Double-click over the Fonts icon. Windows 95 opens the Fonts window.

Each icon inside the Fonts window contains information about one specific font on your system. Some fonts are *scaleable,* which means that Windows 95 can display the fonts in one of several different sizes.

JUST A MINUTE

Font sizes are measured in points. A font that is 12 points high is 1/6 inch high, and a font that is 72 points is one inch high.

TIME SAVER

Change the view (using the **V**iew menu command) if you want to display the font information using a different format, such as the detailed or small icon view formats.

3. Double-click any of the icons inside the Fonts window. Windows 95 immediately displays a preview of that font, as shown in Figure 16.2. When you want to create a special letter or flier with a fancy font, you can preview all of the fonts by double-clicking each one until you find one you like. Once you find a font, you can select it from your word processor to enter the text using that font.

Figure 16.2.

Get a preview before selecting a font.

CAUTION

Many fancy fonts are available to you. Don't go overboard, though. Your message is always more important than the font that you use. Make your font's style fit the message, and don't mix more than two or three fonts on a single page. Too many different fonts on a single page make the page look cluttered.

16

4. If you click the **P**rint command button, Windows 95 prints the preview of the font. If you click **D**one (do so now), Windows 95 closes the font's preview window.

5. Another way to gather information about certain kinds of fonts is to right-click over a font and select **P**roperties from the menu that appears. Figure 16.3 shows the resulting tabbed dialog box.

Figure 16.3.

You can view the properties of your fonts.

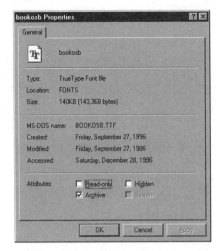

16

JUST A MINUTE

> Not all font property dialog boxes contain two tabbed screens.

The font icons with the letters *TT* are *TrueType* fonts. A TrueType font is a scaleable font that Windows 95 prints using 32-bit technology so it will look as close to typeset characters as possible. The remaining fonts, with the letter *A* or another icon, refer to screen and printer fonts of more limited size ranges than TrueType fonts normally can provide.

TIME SAVER

> Some users prefer to work only with TrueType fonts, due to the rich look associated with them and their scaleability. If you want to view only TrueType fonts in the Fonts window, select **V**iew | **O**ptions and click the TrueType tab. Click the screen's option to display only TrueType fonts.

6. Choose **V**iew | List Fonts By **S**imilarity from the menu. Windows 95 searches through your fonts looking for all other fonts that are similar to a font you choose

from the dropdown listbox and displays the result of that search. Some fonts are very similar, some are somewhat similar, and some are not similar at all.

Figure 16.4 shows a font similarity screen that shows how the other fonts compare to the *Ariel* font.

Figure 16.4.

Find fonts that are similar to other fonts.

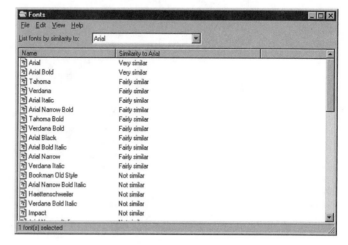

7. Choose **V**iew | La**r**ge Icons to return to the icon view.

8. Check or uncheck **V**iew | **H**ide Variations (Bold, Italic, and so on) depending on whether or not you want to see variations within font families. If the box is unchecked, Windows 95 displays a different icon for each font variation within the same family.

9. When you purchase new fonts, you cannot simply copy those fonts to a directory and expect Windows 95 to know that the fonts are there. When you want to add fonts, you'll probably obtain those fonts on a diskette or CD-ROM. Insert the diskette or CD-ROM and select **F**ile | **I**nstall New Font. Windows 95 displays the Add Fonts dialog box shown in Figure 16.5.

   Select the drive with the new fonts inside the Dri**v**es listbox, and Windows 95 displays a list of fonts from that drive in the upper window. Click on the font you want to install (hold Ctrl and click more than one font if you want to install several fonts) and click the OK command button to install the font to the Windows folder named Fonts.

 10. Close the Fonts window.

16

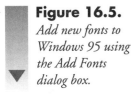

Figure 16.5.

*Add new fonts to
Windows 95 using
the Add Fonts
dialog box.*

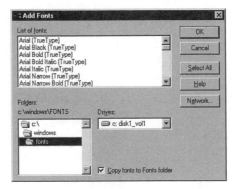

16

JUST A MINUTE

Once you install fonts, they will immediately be available to all your
Windows 95 applications.

Step 3: Review

Windows 95 provides a single location, the Fonts window, where you can view and manage
all the fonts on your system. Due to the graphical and document-centered design of Windows
95, your collection and selection of fonts is vital to making your documents as easy to read
as possible.

Task 16.2: Removing Fonts from Windows 95

TASK

Step 1: Description

Fonts take up a lot of disk space. If disk space is at a premium and if you have lots of fonts
that you rarely or never use, you can follow the steps in this task to remove some of the fonts.
Often, today's word processing and desktop publishing programs add lots of fonts to your
system, and you may not need as many as you have at hand.

Step 2: Action

1. Open the Control Panel.

2. Double-click the Fonts icon.

3. Scroll to the font you want to delete.

4. Click the font that you want to delete; Windows 95 highlights the font. If you hold the Ctrl key while you click, you can select more than one font to delete. Figure 16.6 shows several selected fonts. By selecting several at once, you can remove the fonts with one task instead of removing each one individually.

Figure 16.6.

Select multiple fonts if you want to delete several at once.

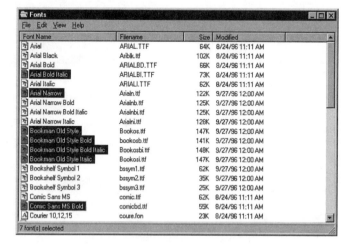

5. Right-click over any highlighted font to display the pop-up menu.

6. Select **D**elete.

7. Click the **Y**es button to confirm the removal.

Step 3: Review

Remove unwanted fonts if you want to save disk space and make your fonts more manageable. The Control Panel's Fonts entry lets you easily select and remove fonts.

Viewing Documents

If you double-click any filename that appears in Explorer or in any file dialog box, you now know that Windows 95 attempts to load and run the program that created the document so that you can view and edit it. Although this feature is a wonderful part of the Windows 95 environment, you may still face a major problem: You may not always have a program that can open that file.

For example, suppose that a friend of yours, a budding artist, gives you a new digital drawing that she wants you to study and critique. You copy the file to your hard disk using Explorer, double-click the file, and, instead of a graphics program that displays the image for your review, you see the dialog box shown in Figure 16.7. Windows 95 needs help! Windows 95 does not recognize the file's type so it displays a scrolling list of programs, hoping that you can find and select a program from the list that will be able to open the file.

Figure 16.7.

Windows 95 does not recognize a file's format.

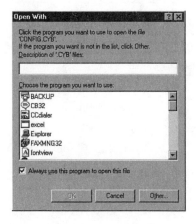

What do you do when you do not have the application needed to view the file? You can either buy a copy of the program you need to look at the file; you can *not* look at the file and tell your friend that you did look at it (you wouldn't tell a fib to a friend); or you can install the Windows 95 *Quick Viewers.*

The standard Windows 95 installation does not include the Windows 95 Quick Viewers, but you can easily install the Control Panel Add/Remove Programs Windows Setup option. The Quick Viewer application is actually a collection of applets that display documents formatted in a variety of formats.

JUST A MINUTE

> Microsoft is asking software developers to add viewers to their Windows 95 programs so the collection of Windows 95 viewers is as current as possible. These programs will link their applications' Quick Viewers to Windows 95's own set.

Table 16.1 contains a list of most of the Windows 95 viewers available in the typical Windows 95 installation. Table 16.1 also contains a list of filename extensions that each Quick Viewer recognizes. (Even if Explorer does not display filename extensions, the Quick Viewer application recognizes the filename extensions and loads the proper viewer dialog box.)

CAUTION

The Quick Viewer application lets you look at files, but you cannot edit those files.

Table 16.1. The available Quick Viewer formats.

Extension	File Type
.ASC	ASCII
.BMP	Windows 95 bitmap
.CDR	CorelDRAW!
.DOC	Word for Windows and WordPerfect
.DRW	Micrographix Draw
.EPS	Encapsulated PostScript
.GIF	CompuServe Graphics Interchange Format
.INF	Setup
.INI	Windows 95 Configuration
.MOD	Multiplan 3, 4.0, and 4.1
.PPT	PowerPoint 4
.PRE	Freelance for Windows
.RLE	Run-Length Encoding bitmap
.RTF	Rich Text Format
.SAM	AMI and AMI Pro
.TIF	TIFF graphics
.TXT	Text
.WB1	Quattro Pro for Windows
.WK1	Lotus 1-2-3 releases 1 and 2
.WK3	Lotus 1-2-3 release 3
.WK4	Lotus 1-2-3 release 4 spreadsheets and charts
.WKS	Lotus 1-2-3 and Microsoft Works release 3
.WMF	Windows metafiles
.WPD	WordPerfect demonstrations
.WPS	Works word processor

16

Extension	File Type
.WQ1	Quattro Pro for MS-DOS
.WQ2	Quattro Pro for MS-DOS release 5
.WRI	Windows 3.*x* Write
.XLC	Excel 4 charts
.XLS	Excel 4 spreadsheets and 5 spreadsheets and charts

Task 16.2: Using the Quick View Viewers

Step 1: Description

This task explains how to use Quick Viewer to look at a document. If you have any application that creates one of the Quick Viewer applications listed in Table 16.1, try to view one of those files. This task uses a standard text file for which you really only need the Notepad text editor to see and edit, but the text file lets you practice using the Quick Viewer.

Step 2: Action

1. Start Explorer.
2. Display the Windows folder in the left window and its contents in the right window.
3. Scroll to the file named Readme (the file's full name is Readme.txt, and you may or may not have set the Explorer's option to hide the filename extension).
4. Right-click the Readme file. You'll see the **Q**uick View command on the menu (as long as you've installed the Quick Viewers).
5. Select the **Q**uick View command. Windows 95 analyzes the Readme file, realizes that the file is a text file and that there is a viewer for text files, and displays the Quick View window.
6. Double-click the title bar to maximize the window. You'll see a window that looks something like the one shown in Figure 16.8.

JUST A MINUTE

> Depending on the date of your Windows 95 release, the text inside the Quick Viewer window may differ slightly from the text in Figure 16.7.

Figure 16.8.

Windows 95 finds the proper way to view a text file.

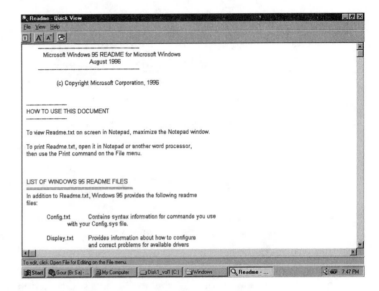

7. Scroll through the file. If you were viewing any type of file from Table 16.1, you would be viewing the text or graphics from that file as if you were working within a program that created those files. For example, Figure 16.9 contains a maximized Quick Viewer window that's displaying an Excel worksheet.

Figure 16.9.

Quick Viewer is displaying an Excel worksheet.

16

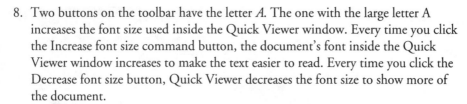

8. Two buttons on the toolbar have the letter *A*. The one with the large letter A increases the font size used inside the Quick Viewer window. Every time you click the Increase font size command button, the document's font inside the Quick Viewer window increases to make the text easier to read. Every time you click the Decrease font size button, Quick Viewer decreases the font size to show more of the document.

   Click one of the font buttons several times to see the effect of the button's font change. Click the other button several times to see the reversal of the font size change.

9. The toolbar contains a Notepad icon at the far left of the toolbar. The Quick Viewer window's toolbar would normally contain whatever icon matches the application that created the file you're viewing. If you click that application's icon, Windows 95 would start that application, so that you could edit that document instead of just viewing that document. (The **File | O**pen File for Editing command also opens that document's application.)

CAUTION

> If you don't have the editing application installed on your computer's disk, you obviously will not be able to edit the document using that secondary application. You will only be able to display the file using the Quick Viewer.

10. Click the **View | P**age View command. Windows 95 displays a page preview of the document similar to the one shown in Figure 16.9.

TIME SAVER

> Click the arrow in the upper-right corner of the page preview to see a preview of the next page. You can scroll back and forth within the previewed document by clicking the arrows in the corner.

11. Click **View | L**andscape to see a *landscape* view of the document. If a document is wide (the Readme text file is not a wide file), landscape view shows how the document looks if displayed across the wide edge of the page. Click **View | L**andscape once again to return to the *portrait* view where the document appears down the page (as a novel's text is often printed).

12. Close the Quick Viewer by selecting **File | Exit**.

Figure 16.10.

Quick Viewer can display a page view.

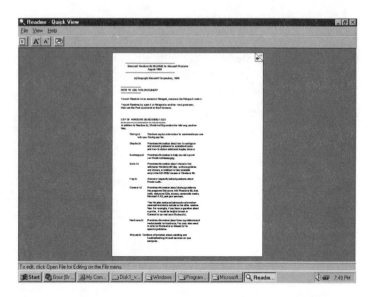

JUST A MINUTE

> The portrait or landscape mode is called the page's *orientation*.

TIME SAVER

> If you want to change the font used in the viewer's display, select **V**iew | **F**ont from the menu.

Step 3: Review

The Quick Viewers are extremely helpful, especially if you work on a laptop or other computer that has limited disk space. The Quick Viewers allow only displaying, not editing, of documents, but the set of Quick Viewers consumes much less disk space than the separate applications themselves.

Summary

This hour discussed the viewing of documents, especially documents that display formatted text. The ease with which you can read text on-screen and in the printed document is often determined by the font used for displaying that text. The Fonts window contains a centralized location from which you can manage all the fonts used by Windows 95. When you purchase new fonts, you'll add those fonts using the Fonts window.

16

When displaying a list of document filenames, a simple right-click on a file produces a menu that lets you quickly view that document using the Windows 95 Quick Viewer. The Quick Viewer application is actually a collection of several individual viewer applications combined into one application. More viewers are being added to Quick Viewer all the time so that future software programs will offer viewers to the Windows 95 collection.

Workshop

16

Term Review

document-centered   The concept that Windows 95 promotes by maintaining that you work with computer's files as if they were documents inside folders in a file cabinet.

font   The typeface used for a document's character display.

font family   Characters that take on the same typeface appearance, but that come in italics, boldfaced, and underlined versions, are all part of the same font family.

landscape view   Shows how the document would look if displayed across the wide edge of the page. Landscape view is helpful for wide documents.

orientation   The way the document appears on the page. The orientation is either the portrait view (vertical) or landscape view (horizontal).

portrait view   Shows how the document would look if displayed down the page, as a novel's text is typically printed.

scaleable   A font is scaleable if Windows 95 can generate characters from the font in more than one size.

TrueType   A scaleable font that Windows 95 prints using 32-bit technology to make text look as close to typeset characters as possible.

viewer   A Windows 95 accessory program with which you can look at documents.

Q&A

Q Why do I need to know how to preview fonts?

A If you are thinking about purchasing new fonts, you will want to display or print a preview of all your current fonts. The preview may show that you have more fonts than you originally thought. You may also want to preview a font before using that font in a word processor or graphics program.

Q I just bought new fonts. What do I do?

A Open the Fonts windows and select **F**ile | **I**nstall New Font to display the Add
Fonts dialog box. Windows 95 must run through a collection and verification
procedure before it recognizes your new fonts. Luckily, this procedure is easy,
thanks to the Add Fonts dialog box. Basically, you'll click on the diskette or
CD-ROM that contains the new fonts, select the font or fonts you want to install,
and click the OK command button to let Windows 95 take care of the rest.

**Q I don't have Microsoft Excel. How can I analyze my office spreadsheets at
home?**

A You don't need Microsoft Excel to look at Excel spreadsheets. All you need is
Windows 95, because it provides the collection of Quick Viewers with which you
can display virtually any type of document.

The Quick Viewer application lets you change the way you view documents. You
can change the font type, the font size, and the orientation (whether or not the
page appears in a landscape or portrait view). If you want to view the overall
document, the Quick Viewers also support the use of a preview mode.

**Q I use Quick Viewer often because it's always there when I right-click over a
document's name. I often decide I want to change the document, and so I
must exit Quick Viewer and start the application that created the document. Is
there a faster way to edit a document from the Quick Viewer window?**

A Yes. Click the first button on the Quick Viewer's toolbar and Windows 95 opens
the document's parent application, and then you can edit the file.

16

Hour 17

Fine-Tune with Advanced System Tools

Windows 95 works well but, like a well-made automobile, you must tune it once in a while to optimize its operation and keep Windows 95 running at top speed. (Who wants a sluggish operating system?) When your operating system slows down, your entire computer system slows down because the operating system controls everything else that happens.

Periodically, you can run tune-up programs that Microsoft provides with Windows 95 to keep your system running smoothly. Most of a system's slowdown is due to the disk drive's mechanical design. The disk, being a mechanical device, can experience problems. The disk's magnetic surface wears down, and files can get lost as a result. Windows 95 can periodically scan your disk looking for trouble spots.

Over time, you create and delete many files. Although the deleted file space is released for other files, your computer's disk drive can become filled with many small holes so that subsequent files stored on the disk must fill those holes resulting in a slowdown (these holes create a *fragmented disk*). Windows 95 can close up these gaps and make larger and contiguous chunks of free disk space available so your files go to and from the disk quickly.

CAUTION

> Disk defragmentation is *not* the same thing as Drive Space which is explained in Hour 19, "Back Up and Squeeze Disk Space."

Not only can your disk cause problems, but memory can produce resource leaks. System Monitor and System Resource Meter are the two memory-analysis programs that can help you detect memory problems and recover lost memory.

The highlights of this hour include:

- [ ] Why ScanDisk can salvage your disk files before you even know they have problems.
- [ ] How the Disk Defragmenter speeds your disk access.
- [ ] How the System Monitor graphically displays several graphs that monitor the system usage statistics.
- [ ] How the Resource Meter appears on the toolbar to display the three primary resource statistics inside Windows 95.

Check the Disk

Windows 95 supplies a program named *ScanDisk* that checks your disk drive for problems and potential problems so that you can avoid future troubles. ScanDisk contains two levels of disk drive inspection: A *standard scan* and a *thorough scan*. The standard scan checks your disk files for errors. The thorough scan checks the files and performs a disk surface test to verify the integrity and safety of disk storage.

JUST A MINUTE

> ScanDisk is just one of the applications inside the folder labeled System Tools that you can install when setting up Windows 95 or when adding programs to Windows 95. Depending on your Windows 95 installation, your System Tools menu might contain one or more of the icons shown in Figure 17.1.

17

Figure 17.1.

The System Tools menu contains several helpful utility applications.

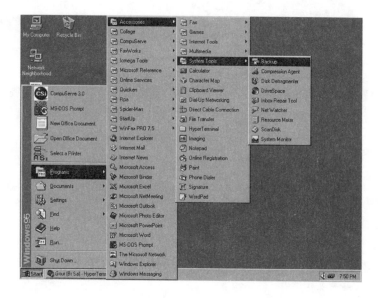

TIME SAVER

Run ScanDisk regularly (perhaps once or twice a week). As with all Windows 95 programs, you can multitask ScanDisk while running another program.

Task 17.1: Check a Disk with ScanDisk

Step 1: Description

This task explains how to use the ScanDisk application. ScanDisk is simple to use and often takes only a few seconds to load and run.

Step 2: Action

1. Display the Start menu.
2. Select the **P**rograms command to display the next cascaded menu.
3. Display the Accessories menu.
4. Display the System Tools menu.
5. Click the ScanDisk menu item. Windows 95 displays the ScanDisk window shown in Figure 17.2.

Figure 17.2.
*The opening
ScanDisk window
for analyzing your
disk drives.*

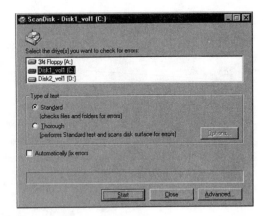

JUST A MINUTE

ScanDisk checks only disk drives, not CD-ROM drives.

6. The Standard option is initially checked by default. To perform a standard
   ScanDisk, press Enter to choose the Start command button now. ScanDisk begins
   its chore of checking your files. The ScanDisk window displays a moving graphics
   bar to show how much time remains in each ScanDisk step, as well as a description
   of each step in the process.

CAUTION

If ScanDisk finds a problem and you've checked the option labeled
Automatically **f**ix errors, ScanDisk attempts to fix any problems it finds
using default repair tools. (You can change the way ScanDisk repairs the
disk by pushing the **A**dvanced command button described toward the end
of this task.)

7. Once ScanDisk finishes, you will see a ScanDisk results window, such as the one
   shown in Figure 17.3.

Figure 17.3.
*ScanDisk reports
its results to you
upon completion of
the disk scan.*

17

The most important line in the results window is the number of bad sectors. Rarely will the number be anything but zero. If bad sectors appear, ScanDisk will attempt to repair them and report the results.

Press Enter to close the results window.

8. Click the **A**dvanced command button. ScanDisk displays the ScanDisk Advanced Options dialog box shown in Figure 17.4. The default values are usually fine, but if you understand disk drive technology and file storage details, you may want to change an option. Click the OK command button to close the dialog box.

Figure 17.4.

The advanced ScanDisk options that you control.

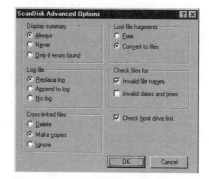

9. Click the **T**horough option and click the **S**tart command button to perform a thorough ScanDisk check. The thorough scan performs a more intense disk check than the standard scan. You'll see the results dialog box when ScanDisk finishes.

Step 3: Review

The ScanDisk program is a dual-leveled disk checking program that searches for disk errors and, optionally, attempts to fix the errors. Run ScanDisk once or twice weekly to make sure your disk is as free from defects as possible.

If you want more control over the ScanDisk process, you can click the **O**ptions button to control these options:

☐ System **a**nd data areas: Scans your entire disk drive including the system areas.

☐ **S**ystem area only: Scans your disk's system areas including the *FAT* (file allocation table, which controls how your files are placed on your disk) and directory.

☐ **D**ata area only: Scans only your programs and data and leaves the system areas unscanned.

Fill in the Holes

The *Disk Defragmenter* is a utility program, available on the System Tools menu, that fills in the gaps on your disks. As you add and delete files, the deleted space leaves free holes around the disk. Over time, your disk response time will slow down as you add or delete document files to and from the disk drive.

Pick Up the Pieces

WINDOWS MINUTE

Windows 95 can store large files on a fragmented disk as long as there is enough total free fragmented space to hold the file. Windows 95 stores the files in linked chunks across the disk drive, filling in fragments and linking them together.

The reason that disk access slows down on a fragmented disk drive is that Windows 95 must jump to each file fragment when retrieving a file. If you run the Disk Defragmenter program often enough (once or twice a month for the average user ought to be enough), Windows 95 keeps the fragments to a minimum and, thus, increases the disk access speed.

TIME SAVER

Some people forget that the Disk Defragmenter helps speed floppy disk drives as well as hard disk drives. As a matter of fact, if you run Disk Defragmenter on floppy disks that you use regularly, you can increase the speed of those floppy disks greatly.

CAUTION

Although the Disk Fragmentation program works well and accurately in most cases, do yourself a favor and back up your system before starting the defragmenting process. Hour 19 explains how to use the Windows 95 Backup program to back up your files.

Task 17.2: Correcting Disk Fragmentation

Step 1: Description

TASK

This task explains how to defragment a disk drive. The task assumes that you'll begin by defragmenting a diskette. If you defragment diskettes, you'll be able to run the Disk Defragmenter program several times (on different diskettes) if you want to.

17

Step 2: Action

1. Display the Start menu.
2. Select the **P**rograms command to display the next cascaded menu.
3. Display the Accessories menu.
4. Display the System Tools menu.
5. Click the Disk Defragmenter menu item. Windows 95 displays the Select Drive window shown in Figure 17.5.

Figure 17.5.

The opening Disk Defragmenter window for analyzing your disk drives.

6. Insert a diskette in your diskette drive.
7. Open the dropdown listbox and select the diskette drive.
8. Click the OK command button to start the defragmentation process. Windows 95 can multitask while defragmenting your disk space, so you can run other programs while Disk Defragmenter runs. At any point during the defragmentation, you can pause Disk Defragmenter or cancel the process. If the diskette is not fragmented, Disk Defragmenter tells you so and asks if you want to run the Disk Defragmenter program on the diskette anyway.
9. When it finishes, Disk Defragmenter lets you know that the fragmentation is complete. Click **Y**es to close the application.

Step 3: Review

The Disk Defragmenter is easy to run regularly because you can run Disk Defragmenter and run other programs at the same time. Disk Defragmenter rearranges information and blank spots on your disk drive, and puts all the data in contiguous disk space and all the empty holes into one large contiguous block. Once defragmented, your disk access will speed up.

Check Your System

Windows 95 contains two programs, System Monitor and the Resource Meter, that monitor your system resources. These applications are extremely advanced for most Windows 95 users because most users don't have to run them and analyze their results.

Windows 95 manages the system and memory *much* better than Windows 3.1 did, and you'll rarely run out of memory or resources when you work inside Windows 95. System Monitor tracks these three items:

- ☐ The *file system*, comprised of disk access statistics
- ☐ The *kernel*, comprised of the CPU's activity, as well as some multitasking activities
- ☐ The *memory manager*, comprised of the various segments of memory that Windows 95 tracks

System Monitor graphically displays one or more of these items and continuously updates the graph to show how your system is being used. You can start the System Monitor and go about your regular Windows 95 work. If the system begins to slow and you want an idea as to which parts of the system are getting the most use, click on the System Monitor on the toolbar to have an idea of your machine's current workload.

The 3.1 Program Manager's **Help** | **About** box displayed a subset of free system resources. The Windows 95 System Monitor program provides a much more complete and accurate analysis of your computer's memory.

When you run the Resource Meter, its program puts a Resource Meter icon next to the clock. You can click the icon to obtain statistics on these items:

- ☐ System resources, which describe the system's resource use percentage
- ☐ User resources, which describe your resource use percentage
- ☐ GDI (*Graphics Device Interface*), which describes your graphics resource use percentage

Task 17.3 demonstrates a simple use of the System Monitor and Resource Meter.

Task 17.3: Checking Resources

Step 1: Description

This task explains how to start System Monitor and Resource Meter. You can use the programs' output to check the efficiency of your computer system.

Step 2: Action

1. Display the Start menu.
2. Select the **P**rograms command to display the next cascaded menu.
3. Display the Accessories menu.
4. Display the System Tools menu.

17

5. Click the System Monitor menu item. Windows 95 displays the System Monitor window. Start another program or two. Click the taskbar to return to the System Monitor graph every so often. As you will see, System Monitor updates its graph, and eventually the graph will fill the window, as shown in Figure 17.6.

Figure 17.6.

The System Monitor screen updates regularly to show your resources.

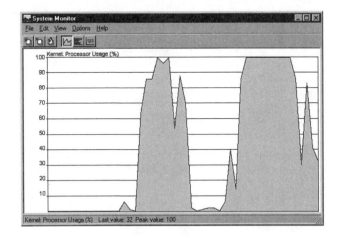

17

JUST A MINUTE

Just a Minute: To show the System Monitor running at extremes, the System Monitor in Figure 17.6 was produced on a fairly slow 486 33-megahertz computer, which had quite a drain on its resources. You can see the high and low extreme peaks in the graph as programs were used, paused, and closed.

6. The default System Monitor displays only the kernel strain. Select **Edit | Add** Item or click the far left button on the toolbar. Click the File System in the left window and highlight every option inside the right window to request that System Monitor update all the file system statistics. Click OK.

7. Select **Edit | Add** Item again to add all the detail items for the Memory Manager. When you click OK, the System Monitor displays several small graphs. Watch the graphs for a moment as they update after they check the resources being analyzed. Your System Monitor window can get full, as Figure 17.7 shows.

TIME SAVER

Click over any of the small graphs. System Monitor describes what the graph means in the status bar at the bottom of the System Monitor window.

Figure 17.7.

The System Monitor can display statistics for several items.

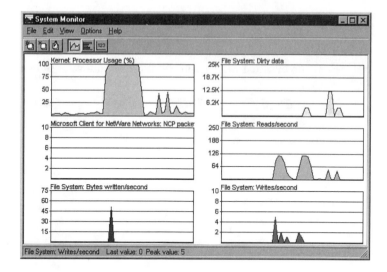

8. Select **File | Exit** to close the System Monitor so you can start the Resource Meter.

9. Display the Start menu.

10. Select the **Programs** command to display the next cascaded menu.

11. Display the Accessories menu.

12. Display the System Tools menu.

13. Click the Resource Meter menu item. Windows 95 displays an opening description dialog box. Read the dialog box and press Enter to close the dialog box.

14. Windows 95 displays the Resource Meter icon to the left of the taskbar clock.

15. Right-click on the Resource Meter icon and select **Details**. Windows 95 displays a graph showing the current resource usage statistics for the three Resource Meter measurements as shown in Figure 17.8.

Figure 17.8.

The Resource Meter window available from the taskbar.

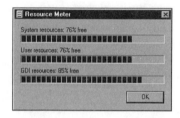

16. As you work in Windows 95, you can check the Resource Meter graphs as often as you want to make sure that you don't get close to running out of resources.

17

17. Right-click the Resource Meter icon and select E**x**it to unload the Resource Meter program.

If you can find a computer running Windows 3.1, start three or four Windows 3.1 programs and select the Windows 3.1's **H**elp | **A**bout dialog box to look at your resources. This number is an average of your total resources, not the three different types shown by Resource Meter. Now start the same three or four programs under Windows 95 and check resources using Resource Meter. You'll be shocked by how much more memory is available under Windows 95.

Step 3: Review

The System Monitor shows one or more graphs, depending on your options, that display usage patterns. The Resource Meter displays a graph of three resource utilizations as you work within Windows 95. If you run graphics- and processor-intensive programs, you can run System Monitor and Resource Meter to see how much of a load you are placing on Windows 95 and the hardware.

Summary

This hour described several system tools you can run to manage and monitor your disk, memory, and other system resources. The ScanDisk program detects errors on the disk drive and attempts to fix as many problems as it is capable of fixing.

The Disk Defragmenter program rearranges your disk files so that all the file space resides in one large block and all the free space is together. This speeds disk drive access and eliminates fragmentation. Run both ScanDisk and Disk Defragmenter every week or two to keep your disk drives as healthy as possible.

The System Monitor and Resource Meter programs work passively to display statistics about your memory, disk, and system usage. Windows 95 handles resources better than previous versions of Windows, but these tools give you two additional ways to monitor the usage.

Workshop

Term Review

Disk Defragmenter   A Windows 95 program that collects and removes blank disk space left from deleted files.

FAT   An abbreviation for file allocation table. Controls the placement of files on your disk.

file system   The collection of disk access routines and memory.

GDI Stands for *Graphics Device Interface* and consists of your graphics resources.

kernel   The CPU's processor routines.

Memory Manager   Controls the various segments of memory that Windows 95 tracks.

standard scan   The quickest ScanDisk version that checks your disk files for errors.

System Monitor   A Windows 95 program that graphically illustrates your computer's resources as you use the computer.

system resources   The amount of CPU, memory, and disk space utilization consumed by Windows 95 and the applications you are running.

thorough scan   The slower, but more thorough, scan that checks the files and performs a disk surface test to verify the integrity and safety of disk storage.

Q&A

Q Should I worry about the advanced ScanDisk options that I don't understand?

A Unfortunately, the advanced ScanDisk options are fairly advanced (that's why they're called *advanced* options!). The details of the options go beyond the scope of this book. Fortunately, you will rarely, if ever, need to modify any of the advanced options. Unless you learn a lot about the disk and the way that Windows 95 stores files on a disk, run ScanDisk using the default options, and you'll virtually always run the proper ScanDisk.

Q I don't know if my disk is fragmented, so do I still run Disk Defragmenter?

A Run Disk Defragmenter whether or not your disk is fragmented. Disk Defragmenter will inform you whether you need to continue if the disk has few or no fragments to collect.

Q How can I use the System Monitor and Resource Meter?

A If you never run more than two or three programs at once, you may *never* need the System Monitor or Resource Meter. Both are necessary if your programs begin to put heavy strains on Windows 95 and the machine.

Multimedia-intensive programs often strain the system's resources. If you attempt to run a multimedia program, as well as one or more additional programs, you'll strain even the fastest of today's computers. The System Monitor and Resource Meter show you where that strain is coming from.

17

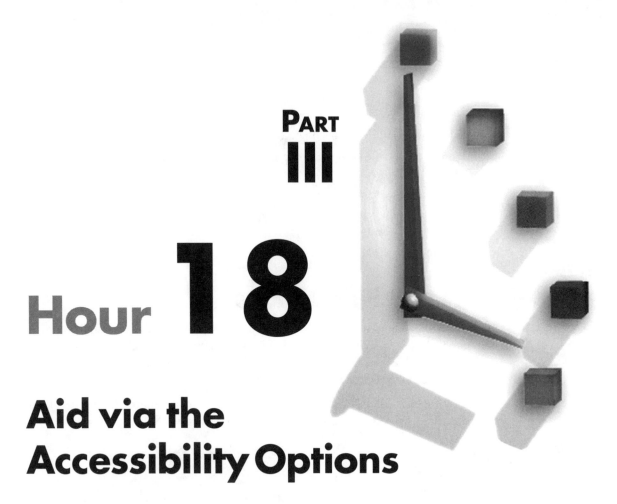

Hour 18

Aid via the Accessibility Options

This hour describes all the Windows 95 tools that provide help for users with special needs. Previous operating environments did not support these kinds of user options. Windows 95's *accessibility options* change the behavior of the keyboard, screen, and speakers so that they operate differently from their default behaviors.

Microsoft set out to design Windows 95 so that everybody could take advantage of the new operating environment. In addition to helping those people who need extra assistance, the accessibility options can also help users who do not normally need special help with their hardware and software. For example, if you have temporarily disconnected your speakers from your computer, you may want to turn on the visual feedback options so that sounds that normally activate the speaker appear on the screen as flashing icons instead.

The highlights of this chapter include:

- ☐ Which accessibility options might benefit you
- ☐ How to change the keyboard's response so that combination keystrokes are easier to type
- ☐ Why visual clues can replace audible signals and alarms
- ☐ Where to set the screen's display so that you read enlarged letters, icons, title bars, and high-contrasting screen colors
- ☐ How to make the keyboard respond as if you were moving and clicking the mouse

The Accessibility Options

The Accessibility Options tabbed dialog box contains settings for the accessibility options that you may want to set up for your Windows 95 environment. All of the accessibility options are available from this dialog box. You can set any or all of the accessibility options from the Accessibility Options tabbed dialog box.

When you double-click the Accessibility Options icon from the Control Panel you will see the Accessibility Properties tabbed dialog box shown in Figure 18.1.

Figure 18.1.

Set one or more accessibility options from this tabbed dialog box.

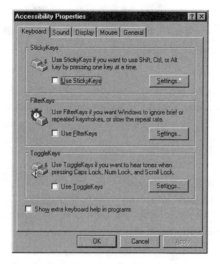

This hour approaches things a little differently from the others. Table 18.1 contains a list of every accessibility option available in Windows 95. The rest of the chapter describes, using the task approach, how to access and use each of these accessibility options.

Table 18.1. The accessibility options.

Option	Description
Accessibility TimeOut	When the computer sits idle for a preset period of time the accessibility options revert to their default state.
Accessibility status	A graphical display of icons that describe which accessibility indicator options are turned on at any given time.
BounceKeys	Keeps users from accidentally producing double keystrokes if they accidentally bounce keys several times in succession.
Customizable	You can change the mouse pointer to make the mouse cursor mouse pointer easier to see. (Hour 3, "Understanding the My Computer Window," explained how to change the mouse cursor.)
FilterKeys	The group of keystroke aids that include RepeatKeys and BounceKeys.
High-contrast	By changing the Windows 95 color scheme to a different color color scheme set, you can make the screen's color contrast more obvious and discernible for people with impaired vision. (Hour 8, "Manage Your Desktop," explained how to change the Windows 95 color schemes.)
High-contrast mode	In addition to offering adjustable high-contrast color schemes, Windows 95 can also ensure that applications adjust themselves to display the highest possible contrast so that visually impaired users will be able to distinguish between background and foreground screen elements.
MouseKeys	Lets you simulate mouse movements and clicks using the keyboard.
RepeatKeys	Users can turn on or off the repetition of keys so that holding down a key does not necessarily repeat that keystroke.
Scaleable user	Each of the system fonts, scroll bars, title bars, and menu interface elements options can be set to a larger size.
SerialKeys	Lets the user use a nonkeyboard input device.
ShowSounds	Provides visual feedback on the screen when applications produce sounds.

18

continues

Table 18.1. continued

Option	Description
SlowKeys	Windows 95 can disregard keystrokes that are not held down for a preset time period. This aids users who often accidentally press keys.
SoundSentry	Sends a visual clue when Windows 95 beeps the speaker (in the case of warning and error message dialog boxes).
StickyKeys	Lets the user press the *modifier keys* (the Shift, Ctrl, or Alt keys) individually instead of having to press them using combined keystrokes. Therefore, the user can press Alt, let up on Alt, and *then* press C instead of combining the two for Alt+C.
ToggleKeys	Sounds a noise on the speaker when the user presses the CapsLock, NumLock, or ScrollLock keys to make them active.

Task 18.1: Controlling the StickyKey Actions

Step 1: Description

Users who need help with the keyboard can set the keyboard options to take advantage of the StickyKeys, FilterKeys, and ToggleKeys options. Once you request the keyboard help, you then can use the modified keyboard to set the other options. This task explains how to set up and use the StickyKeys feature.

Step 2: Action

1. Display the Accessibility Properties tabbed dialog box by opening the Control Panel and double-clicking the Accessibility Options icon.
2. Make sure the tab marked Keyboard is selected.
3. Click the Settings command button inside the StickyKeys section at the top of the dialog box. You'll see the dialog box shown in Figure 18.2.
4. Click the top option to turn on the shortcut key for StickyKeys. Once you set this option, you'll be able to turn on and off the StickyKeys by pressing the Shift key five times.

TIME SAVER

If you share your computer with other users, both you and others can quickly turn on and off the StickyKeys feature by pressing the Shift key five times without having to return to the Control Panel again.

18

Figure 18.2.

The setting available for StickyKeys.

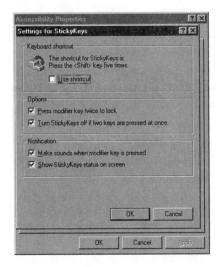

5. If you check **P**ress modifier key twice to lock, Windows 95 will activate the modifier keys if you press any of them twice in a row. For example, instead of having to press the Ctrl key and then P while still holding Ctrl, you will be able to press Ctrl twice to lock the Ctrl key in place, and then press P by itself to simulate the Ctrl+P keystroke. This keystroke locking feature lets users who can type only one keystroke at a time issue combination keystrokes. (Some users must type by pressing the keys with a pencil.)

After turning on StickyKeys, you need to decide how you want the StickyKeys feature turned off. As just mentioned, you can toggle the StickyKeys on and off using a multi-Shift keypress, but there's an even better way. If you check **T**urn StickyKeys off if two keys are pressed at once, the StickyKeys feature stays active as long as you press the modifier keys individually without combining them and their matching keys. In other words, the StickyKeys feature stays on as long as you keep pressing the modifier keys by themselves. If you (or someone else who comes along) press Ctrl+P (or any other modifier keystroke combination) at the same time using a single keypress, Windows 95 turns off the StickyKeys feature.

There are two final options: **M**ake sounds when modifier key is pressed and **S**how StickyKeys status on screen. These options determine whether or not Windows 95 sounds a beep on the speaker when you press a modifier key and whether or not Windows 95 displays a StickyKeys icon next to the taskbar clock when StickyKeys is active. These signals aid users who want audible or visual StickyKeys feedback. The taskbar icon changes when you press a modifier key.

18

For this task, check every option on the **S**ettings screen so you can practice using the StickyKeys feature. Click the OK button to return to the Accessibility Options tabbed dialog box. Don't check the **U**se StickyKeys option now, but click the OK button. If you check the **U**se StickyKeys option, Windows 95 would immediately turn on StickyKeys, but you're going to turn on the feature differently in the next step.

6. Press the Shift key five times. When you do, you'll see a dialog box that reminds you of the StickyKeys feature. Click OK to finish activating StickyKeys. Not only will you then hear an audible sound that indicates StickyKeys is active, but you'll also see an indicator on the taskbar as shown in Figure 18.3.

Figure 18.3.

Windows 95 has activated the StickyKeys feature.

The StickKeys icon

TIME SAVER

If you right-click the taskbar's icon, Windows 95 displays a popup menu from which you can adjust the StickyKeys settings. If you select Show Status **W**indow, Windows 95 displays a popup dialog box on the screen that displays the accessibility options icons using a larger icon size than what appears on the taskbar.

7. Start WordPad by clicking the WordPad icon on the **P**rograms | Accessories menu.

8. Press the Shift key (either the left or right Shift) and release the key. You'll hear an audible signal. You've now locked the Shift key for the next keystroke. Press the A key. An uppercase **A** appears at the cursor's location. You have not locked the Shift key, however. Press the A key again and you'll see a lowercase **a** appear. Press Shift once again, release Shift, and press B to see the uppercase **B** appear. Press B once again to see a lowercase **b** appear.

   You can keep pressing any modifier key, Alt, Ctrl, or Shift, to lock that modifier key before pressing the next key.

9. Now press Shift+A using a normal, single, combination keystroke. Not only will an uppercase **A** appear *but you'll also turn off the StickyKeys feature.* Remember that you earlier checked the option labeled **T**urn StickyKeys off if two keys are pressed at once. Therefore, when you press a normal combination keystroke using one of the modifier keys, Windows 95 turns off StickyKeys.

18

Two users can now share the StickyKeys feature. One can turn on StickyKeys by pressing Shift five times. A second user who does not need StickyKeys does not have to worry about turning off the feature; as soon as the second user presses a combined modifier keystroke as usual, Windows 95 automatically turns off StickyKeys.

CAUTION

> If you find yourself needing to use StickyKeys only occasionally, *don't* check **T**urn StickyKeys off if two keys are pressed at once. Force yourself to turn on and off StickyKeys consciously by pressing Shift five times. If you don't, you'll find yourself inadvertently turning off StickyKeys the first time you combine a modifier key with another key.

Step 3: Review

StickyKeys determines how you want Windows 95 to recognize modifier keys. For users who can only type one keystroke at a time, the StickyKeys feature lets them press and release Alt, Ctrl, or Shift *before* their counterpart keystrokes. Therefore, these users will be able to press Shift, release the Shift, and *then* press the letter that needs to be capitalized.

18

Task 18.2: Controlling FilterKey and ToggleKey Actions

Step 1: Description

Inadvertent errors can occur when users hold keys down too long or press keys using a bouncing motion that often doubles or triples keystrokes. Windows 95 supports the use of FilterKeys to control some of the extra keystrokes that result from certain unintended actions. This task explains how to set up and control FilterKeys.

Step 2: Action

1. Display the Accessibility Properties tabbed dialog box by opening the Control Panel and double-clicking the Accessibility Options icon.

2. Make sure the tab marked Keyboard is selected.

3. Click the Settings command button inside the FilterKeys section of the dialog box. You'll see the dialog box shown in Figure 18.4.

4. Check **U**se Shortcut so that you'll be able to turn on and off the FilterKeys aid by pressing and holding down the right Shift key for eight seconds.

Figure 18.4.

The settings available for FilterKeys.

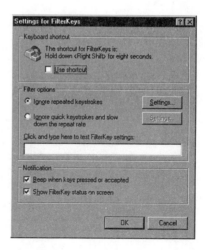

5. The Ignore repeated keystrokes option requests that Windows 95 ignore bounced keys that sometimes result in two or three repeated letters appearing on a line, such as in *theese wooordss*. This option controls the Windows 95 BounceKey feature. Certainly, you don't want Windows 95 to prevent you from typing double letters, because many words, such as *book* and *puppy*, require double letter combinations. Windows 95 initially sets a fairly long pause rate between letters. Therefore, you might want to decrease the time between double keystrokes that Windows 95 recognizes as an error. You can press the Settings command button to change the delay between accidental double keystrokes.

6. The option labeled "Ignore quick keystrokes and slow down the repeat rate" controls the RepeatKeys and SlowKeys features. There may be some users who accidentally press keystrokes from time to time. By checking this option, you can keep Windows 95 from receiving these accidental keystrokes as actual keystrokes; if a key is accidentally held down too long, you'll minimize the repeated keystrokes that would occur.

JUST A MINUTE

The two options described in Steps 5 and 6 are *mutually exclusive*; meaning that you can set either one option or the other. Therefore, you can activate either the BounceKeys feature or you can activate the RepeatKeys and SlowKeys features.

7. If you check Beep when keys are pressed or selected, Windows 95 beeps whenever it recognizes a valid keystroke. If you select Show FilterKey status on screen, Windows 95 displays a stopwatch icon on the taskbar, such as the one shown in Figure 18.5, when the FilterKey option is active. Click OK to close the window.

Figure 18.5.
Windows 95 has activated the FilterKeys feature.

The FilterKeys icon

TIME SAVER

If you right-click the taskbar's icon, Windows 95 displays a popup menu from which you can adjust the FilterKeys settings.

8. If you select the **T**oggleKeys feature, Windows 95 sounds a high beep when you activate the CapsLock, NumLock, or ScrollLock keys and sounds a low beep when you press these keys once again to turn them off. Select the ToggleKeys feature now from the Accessibility Options dialog box. Press CapsLock once to turn on the CapsLock key and you'll hear a high beep. Press CapsLock again to hear the low beep meaning that the second CapsLock keypress deactivated CapsLock.

9. Some Windows 95 programs contain their own accessibility options keyboard features and display on-screen help related to their special keys. If you want to see this help in such programs, check Sho**w** extra keyboard help in programs. Windows 95 will inform all Windows 95 programs you run that you've selected this option, and those programs will respond with appropriate help when available.

Step 3: Review

The keyboard accessibility options change the behavior and functionality of keystrokes. The three modifier keys receive the most attention because they often require a double keypress that some users are not able to perform. The other keyboard accessibility options control accidental keystrokes to keep Windows 95 from recognizing bad keystrokes as valid.

Task 18.3: Controlling the Sound Accessibility Options

Step 1: Description

The Accessibility Options icon's Sound dialog box controls the features of the SoundSentry and ShowSounds accessibility options. These options provide visual feedback that some users require to let them know that certain audible sounds occurred. For instance, if a user cannot always hear the usual warning sounds an application makes when the wrong key is pressed, the user can request that Windows 95 display a visual clue that a sound was made.

Step 2: Action

1. Display the Accessibility Properties tabbed dialog box by opening the Control Panel and double-clicking the Accessibility Options icon.

2. Select the tab marked Sound. You'll see the dialog box shown in Figure 18.6.

Figure 18.6.

The Sound accessibility options dialog box provides visual sound clues.

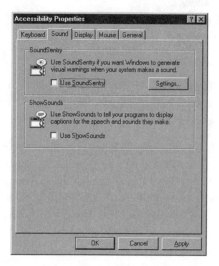

Once you activate the SoundSentry feature, Windows 95 will flash a title bar or another part of the screen when an application makes a sound.

TIME SAVER

You can control which visual clue Windows 95 uses for sounds by clicking the **S**ettings command button to display the SoundSentry dialog box.

3. If you click the **S**howSounds checkbox, Windows 95 turns on the ShowSounds option supported by some Windows 95 programs.

TIME SAVER

The SoundSentry and ShowSounds features can help you if you are hearing impaired, work in a quiet environment where sounds may disrupt others, or work in a noisy environment where you cannot always hear your computer's sounds.

Many applications produce sounds, such as music and speech, that some users cannot hear. By turning on the ShowSounds option, you request that Windows 95 produce visual clues whenever an application sounds from the speaker.

18

If you want to turn on the ShowSounds feature now you can. Click OK to close the dialog box and, if you have some kind of playback device such as a sound card, double-click the Sounds icon inside the Control Panel. Select a sound and click the playback button to hear an audible sound, as well as see a visual representation of that sound.

Step 3: Review

Use the ShowSounds and SoundSentry options when you need visual clues for the sounds that applications produce. This task explained how to turn on and control these features.

Task 18.4: Controlling the Display

Step 1: Description

This task explains how to change the display to increase the contrast Windows 95 uses so that people with vision impairments can see the screen more easily. Windows 95 can change the contrast and letter size, using the high-contrast mode.

Step 2: Action

1. Display the Accessiblity Properties tabbed dialog box by opening the Control Panel and double-clicking the Accessibility Options icon.

2. Select the tab marked Display. You'll see the dialog box shown in Figure 18.7.

Figure 18.7.

The Display accessibility option dialog box provides high-contrast viewing of the screen.

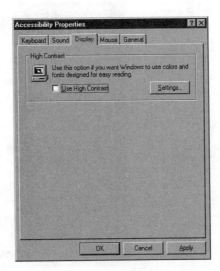

3. Click the **U**se High Contrast option to turn on the high-contrast feature. Windows 95 displays all dialog boxes, menus, and screen colors using a readable and legible display. Although you can click the **S**ettings button to change the high-contrast settings, the default settings often suffice nicely. Windows 95 also turns on the scaleable user interface elements to make icons, title bars, and text easier to read.

JUST A MINUTE

The shortcut key for the high-contrast feature is Left Alt+Left Shift+PrtScr. You can turn the high-contrast feature on or off by pressing Left Alt+Left Shift+PrtScr.

CAUTION

When you use the high-contrast option, Windows 95 increases the size of icons, menus, and screen elements. Although these elements are easier to read by the descriptions beneath icons and on title bars, the terms are often abbreviated because of their large size.

4. Click the OK command button. Windows 95 instantly changes the display to a high-contrast screen such as the one shown in Figure 18.8. The high-contrast mode stays on for subsequent startups of Windows 95.

Figure 18.8.

Windows 95 made this screen more readable using the high-contrast mode.

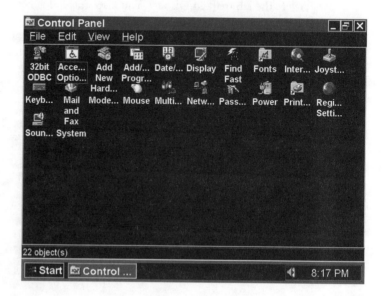

18

Step 3: Review

If you need extra help reading the screen, you can turn on the accessibility options high-contrast option to increase the size of title bars, menus, and other screen elements, as well as to change the color contrast to distinguish between screen elements more easily.

Task 18.5: Controlling the MouseKeys Feature

Step 1: Description

The MouseKeys feature lets you simulate mouse movements and mouse clicks using the numeric keypad on your keyboard. If you have trouble using the mouse or if you sometimes work with a laptop that has no mouse, you may want to turn on the MouseKeys feature.

TIME SAVER

> If your mouse quits working, you can still use Windows 95 effectively by turning on the MouseKeys feature and using the keyboard to simulate mouse movements.

Step 2: Action

1. Display the Accessibility Properties tabbed dialog box by opening the Control Panel and double-clicking the Accessibility Options icon.

2. Select the tab marked Mouse. You'll see the dialog box shown in Figure 18.9.

Figure 18.9.

The Mouse accessibility option dialog box lets you simulate the mouse with keyboard action.

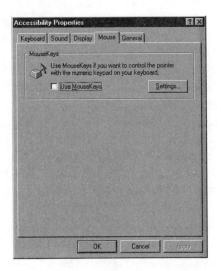

3. If you want to use the keyboard to simulate mouse movements and mouse clicks, click the MouseKeys checkbox, and then click the OK command button. If, before clicking OK, you want to see the setting values for the MouseKeys option, click the **S**ettings button. The MouseKeys settings, shown in Figure 18.10, control the way the keyboard intercepts the mouse actions.

Figure 18.10.

You can change the MouseKeys settings.

Click the **U**se shortcut option to allow for the turning on and off of the MouseKeys feature from the keyboard shortcut (Left Alt+Left Shift+NumLock).

The pointer speed and acceleration options control the keyboard response rate when using the keyboard to simulate mouse movements. You'll probably not need to adjust these default settings. The first option, **H**old down Ctrl to speed up and Shift to slow down, lets you make very large mouse movements by holding Ctrl when using a mouse cursor key and very small mouse movements (for precision) when holding down the Shift key along with a mouse cursor key. Keep this option checked so you can control the mouse speed when you need to.

4. Check O**n** to use the MouseKeys when the NumLock is on, if you want to use NumLock to control both the numeric keypad and the MouseKeys feature at the same time. When on, you'll be able to switch between using the numeric keypad for normal keyboard cursor navigation and using the numeric keypad for MouseKeys operation at the same time. If you set this option to Off, you'll be able to switch between using the numeric keypad for number data-entry and using the numeric keypad for MouseKeys operation at the same time.

Set the option to O**n** if you normally use the numeric keypad for cursor movement and Off if you normally use the numeric keypad for the data-entry of numbers.

5. If you want visual feedback from a taskbar icon that MouseKeys is active, as shown in Figure 18.11, be sure to click the **S**how MouseKey status on-screen option.

Figure 18.11.
Windows 95 has activated the MouseKeys feature.

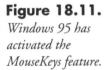

The MouseKeys icon

6. Click the OK command button to close the **S**ettings dialog box, and then click OK again to close the accessibility options dialog box.

7. Press NumLock and then press cursor-movement keys on the numeric keypad to move the mouse cursor. The keypad's number 5 simulates a single mouse click and the plus sign simulates a double-click of the mouse. All other keys on the keypad move the mouse cursor in various directions.

Step 3: Review

The MouseKeys setting converts your numeric keypad to a mouse-controlling keypad when you press the NumLock key. If you have difficulty using the mouse, or if you don't have a working mouse attached to your computer, you can simulate all mouse movements by setting the various MouseKeys options.

Task 18.6: Controlling the Remaining Accessibility Options Features

Step 1: Description

The tab marked General on the Accessibility Options tabbed dialog box controls the remaining accessibility options. You can control the amount of time the accessibility options remain active and the notification of various accessibility options, and you can determine how Windows 95 recognizes a SerialKeys device that you may have attached.

Step 2: Action

1. Display the Accessibility Properties tabbed dialog box by opening the Control Panel and double-clicking the Accessibility Options icon.

2. Select the tab marked General. You'll see the dialog box shown in Figure 18.12.

3. The **m**inutes value determines how long Windows 95 waits before turning off the accessibility options. If you check the option labeled **T**urn off accessibility features after idle, and then enter a **m**inutes value, Windows 95 turns off all accessibility options after the computer has been idle for the specified number of minutes.

   Once set, a user can use the computer's accessibility options and then walk away from the computer to let someone else use the machine. After the specified number of minutes, Windows 95 turns off the accessibility options so that the next person

18

TASK

to use the computer (after the time limit passes) will use the computer with no accessibility options in effect.

Either click off the check mark from this option, or change the **m**inutes value to suit your working environment.

Figure 18.12.

The General accessibility option dialog box provides remaining accessibility optioin controls.

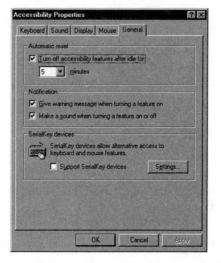

JUST A MINUTE

If you know you will be alternating use of the accessibility options regularly, be sure to check all the shortcut options on each option so that when you return after the idle period, you don't have to go through each menu to turn the accessibility options back on.

4. The Notification section determines whether or not Windows 95 should issue the warning dialog box telling you that an accessibility option is turned on when you press the shortcut key for that option. If you want audible feedback when an accessibility option starts, be sure to check the second Notification option.

5. If you use an alternative input device that attaches to a serial port, check the S**u**pport SerialKey devices option and click the **S**ettings command button to inform Windows 95 which serial port the device is attached to and the baud rate of the device. The alternative input device should contain instructions for the appropriate values.

Step 3: Review

The General section of the accessibility options determines the final settings for the accessibility options. You can control how long the computer is idle before Windows 95 turns off any accessibility options. Also, Windows 95 can notify you of any accessibility options when you click the proper notification options. Finally, you can tell Windows 95 which alternative input devices you use through the SerialKeys options.

Summary

This hour explained how you can control the accessibility options inside Windows 95. Microsoft designed Windows 95 to be accessible to virtually anyone who needs to use a computer, even if that person requires extra help with the keyboard, video display, or mouse.

The primary keyboard accessibility options control the operation of the modifier keys (Alt, Ctrl, and Shift). If you have trouble combining a modifier key with another key, you can request that Windows 95 trap these keystrokes and lock them down when you press them. Other keyboard accessibility options control the repeat rate and help eliminate extra keyboard bounce.

All the accessibility options contain audible and visual clues that tell you when you set or reset these options. The high-contrast display options help improve the screen's visibility. In addition, you can set up the keyboard to control all mouse movements in case you're missing a mouse or cannot use a mouse.

Workshop

Term Review

Accessibility TimeOut   Turns off the accessibility options after a preset period of time.

BounceKeys   Keeps users from producing double-keystrokes if they accidentally bounce keys several times in succession.

FilterKeys   The group of keystroke aids that includes RepeatKeys and BounceKeys.

high-contrast display   A video option that makes your screen more readable by increasing the size of icons, menus, and text, as well as changing screen colors so that the items on the display are as readable as possible.

Modifier keys   The Alt, Ctrl, and Shift keys.

MouseKeys   Lets you simulate mouse movements and clicks using the keyboard's numeric keypad.

mutually exclusive   Two or more Windows 95 controls, such as option buttons, are mutually exclusive if you can set only one option at a time.

18

RepeatKeys   Users can turn on or off the repetition of keys, so that holding down a key does *not* necessarily repeat that keystroke.

Scaleable user interface elements   The text, title bars, and icons enlarge to make them easier to see.

SerialKeys   Lets the user use a nonkeyboard input device.

SlowKeys   Windows 95 can disregard keystrokes that are not held down for a preset time period. This aids users who often accidentally press keys.

ShowSounds   Provides visual feedback on the screen when applications produce sounds.

SoundSentry   Sends a visual clue when Windows 95 beeps the speaker (in the case of warning or error message dialog boxes).

StickyKeys   Lets the user press the Shift, Alt, or Ctrl keys individually instead of having to press them with their combined keystrokes.

ToggleKeys   Sounds a high noise on the speaker if the CapsLock, NumLock, or ScrollLock keys are activated and a low noise when these keys are deactivated.

Q&A

Q How can users who have trouble using the default keyboard interface access the accessibility options?

A All someone has to do is get help the first time by having another user display the Control Panel's Accessibility Options tabbed dialog box. Click the option labeled Use StickyKeys. From that point forward users can activate StickyKeys by pressing either Shift key five times in a row.

Q How can I remember to turn off StickyKeys when my coworker is finished using the StickyKeys feature?

A Make sure the Accessibility Options StickyKeys Settings dialog box has a check next to the option labeled Turn StickyKeys off if two keys are pressed at once. As soon as you press a modifier key in conjunction with any other key, Windows 95 turns off StickyKeys.

Q Can I use the accessibility options if I don't have special physical needs that require accessibility option settings?

A There are times when the accessibility options can benefit all people no matter what their physical needs are. For example, the SoundSentry and ShowSounds features are useful for those who work in noisy environments and cannot always hear the computer's speaker. If you forget your mouse when on the road with a laptop, you can turn on the MouseKeys option to simulate mouse movements and clicks with the keyboard.

18

Time-Out 3

Take Cover...Play Hover!

On Your Mark...

Some people do not think good games can be written for the Windows environment. Until Windows 95, that opinion was somewhat understandable. The number-one-selling computer game for most of 1995 was *DOOM II*—surely you've heard of DOOM II. Perhaps you've even played DOOM II. (Perhaps you'll even *admit* that you've played DOOM II!)

DOOM II does not run under Windows 3.1. Unfortunately, Windows 3.1 was the operating environment of choice for many months after DOOM II was released. Users had to exit Windows 3.1 and return to MS-DOS to run DOOM II. The reason it didn't run under Windows 3.1 was that it displayed never-before-seen, three-dimensional graphics. You, the player, walked through a series of corridors shooting bad people. The sound and graphics required most of a computer's resources, and those resources could not be shared with Windows.

Windows 95 changes everything. If you want to run DOOM II in an MS-DOS window, you can do so. Microsoft wants you to know that you can run games such as DOOM II under Windows 95. Microsoft has a problem, however; Microsoft does not own DOOM II. Therefore, the programmers at Microsoft decided to write a DOOM II-like game that contains more action, sounds, and graphics than DOOM II. The game is called *Hover*.

JUST A MINUTE

> You must have a CD-ROM drive and the CD-ROM version of Windows 95 to run Hover, the game you learn to play in this time-out.

Here is Microsoft's description of Hover:

> *Play a fast-paced game of bumper cars in a huge 3D maze.*

That description doesn't really say much. You have to play the game to see what Hover is really all about. The primary reason to play Hover at least one time, even if you aren't a game-player, is to be stunned by the fast-paced graphics and speed of programs running under Windows 95 that were not possible with previous versions of Windows.

Hover is a game that puts you in a three-dimensional, maze-like environment where you are pitted against an opponent who is trying to capture all three of your red flags while you try to capture all three of your opponent's blue flags. The total score you receive is based on the number of opponent flags you capture and the number of your own flags that you still have at the game's end.

3

Get Set...

Follow these steps to start the Hover game:

1. Find your Windows 95 installation CD-ROM and insert the CD-ROM in your CD-ROM drive.

2. After a brief pause, you'll see the opening Windows 95 CD-ROM logo, as shown in Figure T3.1.

Figure T3.1.

The opening screen for the Windows 95 CD-ROM.

JUST A MINUTE

Depending on the release date of your Windows 95 CD-ROM, your Windows 95 CD-ROM opening screen might look somewhat different from Figure T3.1.

3. The right-hand area of the CD-ROM screen contains several options. Move your mouse over the option labeled Hover! and click the mouse.

   After a brief pause (depending on the speed of your CD-ROM drive), Hover displays an opening dialog box with some initial instructions. Press Enter to close the dialog box, and you'll see Hover's opening screen, as shown in Figure T3.2.

4. There are several options you can set in Hover. For now, accept the default values of the game and click OK.

Figure T3.2.

Hover's opening screen.

5. To familiarize yourself with the Hover screen, move the mouse cursor around the Hover screen and right-click the different parts of the screen. You'll find that the bottom center of the screen comprises the *Map Area*. The Map Area shows an overview of your area (you can magnify the Map Area by pressing the plus-sign key, and you can decrease the magnification by pressing the minus-sign key).

Finish familiarizing yourself with the screen's components by right-clicking over the different areas. Although you won't understand everything that you read yet (you really can't learn the details of Hover until you play the game for awhile), you should get a good feel for the game.

Go!

Now you can start the game. Press F2 (or select **G**ame | **S**tart Game from the menu). When the game starts, use the arrow keys to move forward, backward, left, and right. You'll be moving and bumping around (you're in a bumper car that bounces off many obstacles the car hits) looking for opponent flags to take. To take a flag, just run into the flag and your hovering car will grab the flag. Figure T3.3 shows a game in progress.

Figure T3.3.

*The Hover car bumps
around looking for flags.*

TIME SAVER

There are hot keys you can use to modify the behavior of the Hover car. The letter *A* key is the jump key, which enables you to jump over some obstacles as you move. *S* is the wall key, which leaves a temporary wall behind you to slow down opponents. *D* is the cloaking key, which enables you to hide yourself temporarily from opponents.

There are many options in the game and many strategies you can try. The rest is up to you. Play the game for awhile and then search the help topics so you can improve your game. Good luck!

Part

IV

Into the Nighttime

Hour

Hour **19**

Back Up and Squeeze Disk Space

This hour is for everybody and for nobody! Here's the reason for the paradox: *Everybody* wants more disk space, and *nobody* backs up often enough! This hour attempts to help you get more disk space and back up more often.

Windows 95 also contains a backup program that lets you back up your files. By making regular backups, you help protect your files from accidental erasure later. If a disaster occurs, such as a disk drive failure (often called a *disk crash*), you can restore the backup by copying the files from the backup to a healthy disk drive.

Windows 95 contains the *DriveSpace* technology that compresses disk space by as much as 30 to 100 percent. Therefore, if you have a 200-megabyte disk drive, you can run DriveSpace, and you will have up to *400 megabytes* of space once DriveSpace finishes compressing the drive. DriveSpace compresses both hard disks and floppy disks.

The highlights of this hour include:

☐ Why backing up with Windows 95 Backup is simple to do

☐ When the best times to back up are

☐ Why the different kinds of backup are needed

☐ What precautions you can take to protect your backups

☐ How you can squeeze more data onto your disk drive

Back Up Often

The Windows 95 Backup program is a comprehensive backup program that you can use to save a copy of your disk files. The backup protects you against data loss. If your hard disk breaks down, once you fix or replace it, you will then be able to restore the backup and resume your work. Without the backup, you would have to try to recreate the entire disk drive, which is often impossible, because you will not have a copy of every transaction and document that you've created.

> The Windows 95 Backup program both creates and restores backups.

JUST A MINUTE

Many people back up regularly. Most of these people back up regularly because they once had a disk crash but did not have a backup. (The author is one of those guilty of losing a disk and all the data before learning to back up!) Please don't be one to learn the hard way. Learn to use the Windows 95 Backup program and back up your files regularly.

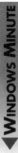

Put It in Reverse—Back Up!

The first time you back up you should back up your entire disk drive. Once you back up the entire disk, you then can make subsequent daily or weekly backups and back up only the files that you've added or changed since the most recent backup.

The Windows 95 Backup program often can compress files while backing them up so that you can back up large disk drives to other disks or tapes that would not normally be able to hold all the data. If you turn on the compression option, the backup should take less time and make the backups easier to do.

The Windows 95 Backup program also lets you select which files you want to back up so that you can make a special backup of a few selected files. Windows 95 Backup can create a *full backup* of your entire disk drive or a *differential backup* (or *incremental backup*), which backs up only the files that have changed since the most recent backup. Backup also lets you direct restored files to a different drive or directory from where they originated.

19

TIME SAVER

Take your home computer's backup files with you to work every day and bring your work's backup files home each night. If a terrible disaster happens at home or at work, such as a fire, you will be able to restore your data, because the backups would not be destroyed.

You must decide which medium you want to store the backup on. The Windows 95 Backup program creates backups on the following types of media:

- ☐ Network disks
- ☐ Hard disks
- ☐ Floppy disks
- ☐ QIC 40, 80, and 3010 tapes

Windows 95 Backup uses the QIC-113 format, which means that Windows 95 Backup can back up and restore onto tapes and other media that have been used by other backup software. Once you make a full backup, especially the very first time, you may also want to run Windows 95 Backup's comparison option to make sure that the backup matches the original data.

JUST A MINUTE

If you use one of the new popular alternatives to hard disks, such as the large capacity removable disks, never fear. The Windows 95 Backup program can easily back up to those disks. During backup, Windows 95 treats the drives as if they are hard disks. You must make sure the disk has a cartridge inside before starting the backup or Windows 95 Backup will not be able to detect the drive.

19

Not only can the Backup program back up your files to tape, but the Backup's **T**ools menu option supplies these common tape drive utilities:

- ☐ **E**rase Tape: Erases the tape in the tape drive so that you have access to all the tape's storage capacity.
- ☐ **F**ormat Tape: Writes the initial tracks needed when you purchase unformatted tapes for your backups.
- ☐ **R**edetect Tape Drive: Finds and configures a tape drive that you recently installed or changed. Generally, a fully plug-and-play–compatible tape drive will not need redetecting.

Task 19.1: Backing Up Your Disk Drive

Step 1: Description

This task explains how to use the Windows 95 Backup program and its major features. This task will describe how to back up a hard disk to floppy disks. Although a tape drive or network drive makes backing up easier than backing up to floppy disks, because you don't have to keep switching diskettes in and out of the drive, most people today still back up to floppy disks.

CAUTION

> Backing up to diskettes can take a **lot** of diskettes! Even if you use Windows 95 Backup's compression option, a large hard disk backup consumes many diskettes. If you have a backup tape drive and want to back up to your tape drive (you should do this if you have the hardware) select your tape drive instead of floppy disks as you follow this task.

Step 2: Action

1. Display the Start menu.
2. Select the **Programs** command to display the next cascaded menu.
3. Display the Accessories menu.
4. Display the System Tools menu.
5. Click the Backup menu item. Windows 95 displays the Backup screen, shown in Figure 19.1.

Figure 19.1.

The opening Backup window for backing up a disk drive.

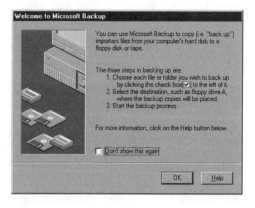

19

The backup screen that you see is a Backup opening screen that describes the backup process. Read the screen to get an overview of the backup process. If this is the last time you want to see the opening screen, click the option at the bottom of the page.

6. Click the OK command button after you finish reading the screen.

7. After a brief pause, Backup displays yet another descriptive window, shown in Figure 19.2. Backup is informing you of the *full system backup file set*. A *backup file set* is a predetermined list of files to back up that you can create. If you back up only a certain group of files on a regular basis, you can create a backup file set that tells Backup to back up only those files. By creating a backup set, you need only to specify the group of files in that set one time. In the future, when you want to back up that same set of files, you will open that backup file set and begin the backup without having to specify all the files again.

Figure 19.2.

The full system backup file set should be your first backup.

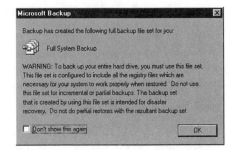

The Windows 95 Backup program supplies you with one backup file set called the full system backup file set. A backup set is a list of files that describes one backup. You can create backup file sets that tell Backup exactly how you want to back up and then select the appropriate backup file set when you want to back up. The Windows 95 Backup program supplies one starting backup file set, the full system backup file set, that instructs Backup to back up your entire hard disk.

The window is suggesting that you use the full system backup file set the first time you back up. This task will use that backup file set to back up your entire hard disk (including programs, data, the registry, and system files including the system files that are normally hidden from your view) to floppy disks. Later, you can create

19

your own backup file sets that describe certain differential backups or backups that will save only a certain set of files or folders.

JUST A MINUTE

If you want to follow this task but not take the time right now to back up your entire hard disk to floppy disks, you'll be able to cancel the backup process once it starts.

8. If you don't want to see Figure 19.2's reminder window, you can check the option at the bottom of the screen to hide future displays of the window.

Click OK now to continue with the backup process.

CAUTION

At this point, you may or may not get a cautionary window telling you either that you do not have a tape drive or that Windows 95 did not detect a tape drive. Backup assumes that you'll want to back up to a tape drive, even though many people have no tape drives. If you have no tape drive, click OK. If you do have one, close the window and exit Backup. Select the Control Panel's Add New Hardware icon to install the tape drive.

9. The Backup program does not start backing up right away because Backup still does not know the kind of backup you want to perform or the type of media to which you want the backup to go.

   Backup displays the window shown in Figure 19.3. The tabs at the top of the window let you select either a backup, restore, or comparison. For this task, you will keep the Backup tab selected. You can look through the two other tabbed windows if you want to learn more about the other tasks Backup can perform. All three tabbed windows work virtually the same, except that the direction of the data flow is reversed using Backup and Restore, and the Compare tabbed dialog box does not back up or restore, but compares a backup to its original set of files to make sure the backup worked.

10. The Backup window contains two panes that work like the Explorer's screen. The window pane on the left describes the storage devices that you may want to back up. The right window pane describes the details of whatever device you select.

    Although you are going to perform a full backup in this task, take a moment for a detour so you can learn something about creating a backup file set.

19

Select drive C by clicking on the square, and wait while Backup collects a list of all files on your drive C. The collection takes a while. Once finished, Backup displays a list of all files and folders from drive C, with a check mark next to each. Backup assumes that you want to back up the entire drive C. If there are folders or files you don't want to back up, uncheck them.

Figure 19.3.

The Backup window where you describe the backup details.

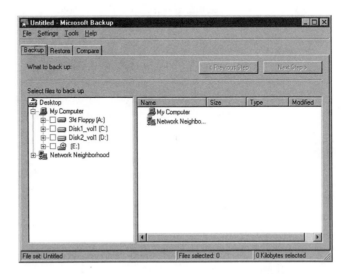

11. Press the Next Step command button so that you can tell Backup what medium you want to use for the backup. Backup displays the screen shown in Figure 19.4.

Figure 19.4.

Tell Backup the backup's destination medium.

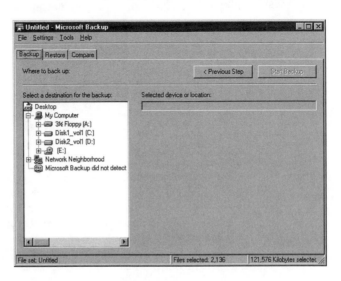

12. Select drive A. Now that Windows 95 Backup knows the files to back up and the destination medium, you can save the backup file set that you've just designed (selected files from drive C backed up to drive A). To do so, select **File** | **Save** and enter a name for the backup file set.

    Instead of backing up just drive C, select the **File** | **Open** File Set command to display the backup file set open dialog box.

13. Select the Full System Backup. Backup then scans your computer and its files, looking for everything to back up, as well as the hardware you can back up to. If you have only one hard disk, the full system backup file set will be the same file selection as you would have if you'd selected all of drive C. If you have several hard disks, the full system backup file set will select every hard disk. Your only job left is to indicate the medium to back up to.

JUST A MINUTE

> When you want to make a differential backup, select **Settings** | **Options** and click on the Backup tabbed dialog box. Click the option labeled Incremental back up of selected files that have changed since the last full back up.

14. Press the Next Step command button and then select drive A for the destination floppy disk (or your tape drive, if you have one).

15. Press the Start Backup command button. Backup displays the Backup Set Label dialog box, shown in Figure 19.5. The *backup set label* is a descriptive name that labels this particular backup. For example, you could name this backup *My first full backup.*

Figure 19.5.

Assign a label to this particular backup.

CAUTION

> **Caution:** If you back up sensitive data, you may want to add a password to the backup so that others will not get your backup files and restore the files onto their system. Before restoring a password-protected backup set, Windows 95 Backup asks the user for the password and refuses to restore without the proper password. Be sure to store your password in a safe place so you can find it (but nobody else can) if you forget the password.

Backup displays a dialog box that illustrates the backup procedure. Your entire hard disk will probably not fit on a single diskette. Backup will ask you to insert the next diskette in drive A after Backup fills the first diskette. If you are backing up to a tape, the entire hard disk may fit on the tape without your intervening at all.

TIME SAVER

Select the **S**ettings | **O**ptions menu and turn on the option Turn on audible prompts in the General tabbed dialog box, so that Backup beeps when you need to insert the next diskette.

16. When Backup finishes (click Cancel if you want to stop the backup early), select File | Exit. Put the backup disks (or tape) in a safe place and label the backup media so you'll know the backup is there.

Step 3: Review

The Windows 95 Backup program contains a complete set of backup, restore, and comparison features. The backup file sets make backing up regularly easy to do, because you can create backup file sets that describe different backup settings and open whatever backup file set you want to use. (The Windows 95 Backup program supplies a full system backup set for you to use when you want to back up all hard disk drives.)

TIME SAVER

The Microsoft Windows 95 add-on product named *Microsoft Plus!* lets you preset a time for backing up your files. You can perform a hands-off backup if you back up to another hard disk or to a network disk drive. (When backing up to floppy disks, you have to be there to change the diskettes.)

Running DriveSpace

The DriveSpace program is easy to run. You only need to run DriveSpace once, because after compressing the disk drive, the disk stays compressed. You also can reverse the DriveSpace compression if you want to, as long as you have enough space on the uncompressed disk drive to hold all your files.

JUST A MINUTE

DriveSpace does no disk defragmentation. Whereas Hour 17, "Fine-Tune with Advanced System Tools," explained how to defragment your disk space, DriveSpace takes the extra step and actually compresses your disk storage to give you almost twice as much room as you had previously.

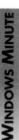

Accessing Compressed Data

Some people mistakenly believe that compressing the disk drive with a program such as DriveSpace slows down disk access. In the majority of cases, a compressed disk drive is as fast or faster than an uncompressed drive.

Mechanical devices are slower than electronic devices. Memory access is much faster than disk access. When Windows 95 accesses a compressed disk drive, it has to retrieve only half as much physical data; Windows 95 then quickly decompresses that data in fast memory. The overall result is faster disk access.

After you compress a disk drive, Windows 95 and your computer act as if you've got more disk space. The free disk statistics will show the extra drive space, and all programs access the disk as if the disk were originally designed to have the extra space.

JUST A MINUTE

DriveSpace uses the same compression technology previously used by MS-DOS 6. If you've already been working with a DoubleSpace or DriveSpace MS-DOS drive, you do not need to convert the drive to Windows 95 or compress the drive again. Once it is compressed, you can squeeze no additional disk space by trying a subsequent compression.

Task 19.2: Compressing Disks Using DriveSpace

Step 1: Description

This task explains how to compress a disk drive using DriveSpace. The disk will be a floppy disk. Once you've compressed a floppy disk drive, you will more fully understand the process and can then compress a hard disk.

CAUTION

You cannot compress a CD-ROM. DriveSpace must be able to write to a device before compressing that device. CD-ROM drives are read-only. (The term *ROM* means *read-only memory*.)

19

When compressing a disk drive, DriveSpace adds a logical disk drive to your system, called the *host drive*. DriveSpace will name the new host drive *H*, or some other name that falls far down anyone's list of disk drives, so that you'll be able to determine which drive is a host drive and which drive is from your list of real disk drives. The host drive will not be compressed, and you will not work with the host drive. DriveSpace and Windows 95 use the host drive to hold descriptive information about the compressed drive. About all you really need to know about the new host drive is that the host is not an actual drive on your system, and Windows 95 uses the host drive to support the DriveSpace compression scheme. All open dialog boxes you see, as well as the My Computer window, will display the host drive now that you've compressed.

Step 2: Action

1. Display the Start menu.
2. Select the **P**rograms command to display the next cascaded menu.
3. Display the Accessories menu.
4. Display the System Tools menu.
5. Click the DriveSpace menu item. Windows 95 displays the DriveSpace window, shown in Figure 19.6.

Figure 19.6.

The opening DriveSpace window for compressing a disk drive.

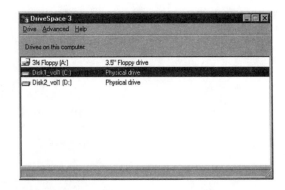

19

JUST A MINUTE

If your computer has additional disk drives, your DriveSpace window will display those additional drives in the list of drives.

6. Insert a formatted diskette in the diskette drive. The diskette can have data on it. The diskette, however, should contain about 30 percent free space. Before you can compress a disk, the disk should contain some free space so that DriveSpace can write some temporary files during the compression process. If the drive does not

have enough free space, DriveSpace will tell you before starting the actual compression, so that you can free some space.

CAUTION

If, while saving a file from an application during a regular work session, you receive an error message telling you that you are out of disk space, you must remove some files from the disk (using Explorer) before there will be room to save the file. If you then want to compress the disk, you will have to copy or move some of the disk's files to another disk drive to free enough space so that DriveSpace can compress the disk. It is always a good idea, when you think a disk is getting full, to check the amount of free space still available, so that you can compress it before it no longer has enough free space for DriveSpace to work.

Obviously, DriveSpace cannot physically make a disk larger, but DriveSpace does make the disk appear larger to Windows 95 and MS-DOS programs.

7. Select the floppy disk drive from the list of drives.

8. Select **D**rive | **C**ompress. DriveSpace analyzes the disk and displays the Compress a Drive dialog box, such as the one shown in Figure 19.7.

Figure 19.7.

The before and after effect of the disk's compression.

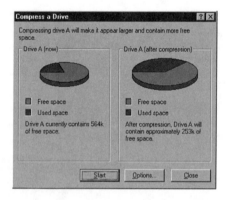

Depending on your disk's contents and original size, you can gain a little or a lot of extra space by the compression. DriveSpace will compress Figure 19.7's diskette only by approximately 310,000 kilobytes, as you can see in the right-hand window, labeled Drive A (after compression).

JUST A MINUTE

If you want to decompress a compressed drive, you would repeat these steps and choose **D**rive | **U**ncompress instead of **D**rive | **C**ompress.

9. Click the **O**ptions command button. Windows 95 displays the Compression Options dialog box, shown in Figure 19.8. The Compression Options dialog box describes the host drive's name (you can select a different name if you want to) and free space (usually there will be no free space). Click the OK command button to close the Compression Options dialog box and return to the Compress a Drive dialog box.

Figure 19.8.

The Compression Options dialog box explains how the compression will operate.

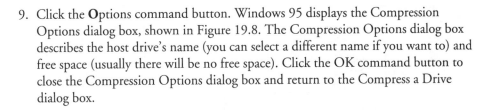

10. Click the **S**tart command button to initiate the drive compression. Before compressing, DriveSpace gives you one last chance to cancel the compression. DriveSpace also offers the option of backing up your files. Although there rarely will be a problem during the compression, it is possible that a power failure during the compression could interrupt the process and cause DriveSpace to corrupt the disk drive (so that the drive would need reformatting). By backing up the drive, you'll ensure that you can return to an uncompressed drive if needed.

JUST A MINUTE

If you choose to back up before completing the drive's compression, DriveSpace will run the Microsoft Backup program, described in the previous section.

19

Once the compression begins, DriveSpace checks the diskette for errors and then compresses the diskette. The compression can take a while. After finishing, DriveSpace displays a completion dialog box. Close the dialog box and look at Explorer's status bar to see the increased disk space available on the diskette.

Step 3: Review

Once you compress a disk drive, Windows 95 recognizes the compressed drive and stores up to 100 percent more data on that drive. There will actually be a second disk added to your drive letters, called the host disk, but you can ignore the host disk, because DriveSpace uses the host disk to store data tables used for accessing the compressed drive.

CAUTION

If you want to format a compressed disk, you must run DriveSpace and select **D**rive | **F**ormat. The Explorer Format command will not format compressed disks. The disk stays compressed during the formatting procedure.

Summary

This hour described the DriveSpace compression program and the Windows 95 Backup program. Both of these programs are new to Windows 95 and take advantage of the Windows 95 32-bit architecture and multitasking capabilities.

The DriveSpace compression program can almost double your disk drive space. By compressing your files and the free file space, you effectively squeeze more data into the same amount of disk space. You can compress both your hard disk drives and floppy disk drives.

The Windows 95 Backup program lets you back up, restore, and compare backups to their original files. The Backup program is the most full-featured backup program that Microsoft has offered. You can create backup file sets that quickly initiate specific backup descriptions. If you purchase a copy of the new Microsoft Plus! program, you can schedule backups so that Windows 95 backs up files while you are away from the computer.

Workshop

Term Review

backup file set   A description that contains a specific list of files that you want to back up. For example, you may have a backup file set that backs up your accounting data files only, as well as a full backup file set that backs up your entire hard disk.

compression   The process of squeezing your disk drive so that almost 100 percent more data fits on a disk.

differential backup   A backup of only the files that have changed since the most recent backup. Also called an *incremental backup*.

disk crash   A disk drive failure.

DriveSpace   The name of the Windows 95 utility program that condenses the disk space so that more data fits on a disk drive.

19

full backup   A complete backup of your entire disk drive.

full system backup file set   A backup file set supplied by Backup that performs a full backup.

host drive   A logical new drive that DriveSpace creates to hold compression information.

incremental backup   See *differential backup.*

media   The types of storage on which you store and back up data. Examples of media would be a diskette, a tape, and paper.

Microsoft Plus!   A Windows 95 add-on product that you can purchase that can automate the backup process (as long as you back up to tape, a network drive, or another hard disk) so that you can request a backup at any time of day or night.

ROM   Stands for *read-only memory* and refers to devices or memory that you can read from, but not write to, delete from, or change.

Q&A

Q How often should I defragment and compress my hard disk?

A You should defragment every week or so. Depending on the amount of file accessing you do, you may need to defragment more or less often. If you notice your disk speed slowing down a bit, you'll often find that Defragment speeds the access process somewhat.

Only compress your disk drive (or each floppy disk) *once.* After the compression, the drive stays compressed. Unless you uncompress the drive, Windows 95 always recognizes the compressed drive.

Q Which kind of backup, a full or differential backup, should I perform?

A The first time you back up you should make a full backup. After you make one full backup, you can make subsequent differential backups of only those files that have changed. Be sure that you save the full backup, however, so that you can restore everything if you need to. If you have a disk failure, you'll restore the entire full backup and then restore each differential backup set of files.

Q Does a full backup take longer than a differential backup?

A Yes. As mentioned in the previous question, first perform one full backup and then, subsequently, you can perform the quicker differential backups.

After you've made several differential backups, you might want to make a full backup once again. By making a full backup every once in a while, you will be able to reuse your differential tapes or disks.

19

Q **Other than full backups which I perform weekly, I want to back up only my three work folders every day. Should I take the time to create a backup file set that describes only those three folders?**

A By all means, you should create a backup file set for those three folders. Although you must take a few moments to create the backup file set the first time, specifying exactly which folders you want to back up, subsequent backups will take less of your time. You'll thereafter only have to select the trio-folder backup file set and start the backup.

19

PART IV

Hour 20

Multimedia Is Really Here

In the early 1990s, several companies, including Microsoft, got together to design a new multimedia standard. There are many ways to implement graphics, motion video, and sound. In fact there are so many ways, virtually every company that was designing multimedia software implemented its multimedia differently from the others. The result was a confused marketplace where many companies' software would not work with very much hardware.

This hour describes the standard that resulted from an industry consortium of software and hardware developers led by Microsoft. As long as you have a computer with the standard hardware, you are certain to be able to run all software that conforms to the multimedia standard.

The availability and compatibility of multimedia hardware and software, combined with the increased power of today's computers and the decreased price associated with that power, make multimedia a reality. Windows 95 continues the tradition that Windows 3.1 started by adding multimedia capabilities never before available. This hour introduces you to Windows 95's multimedia capabilities.

The highlights of this hour include:

☐ What the MPC standard means

☐ How AutoPlay eliminates your usual CD-ROM startup keystrokes

☐ Where to enter the artist, title, and songs for your collection of CDs

☐ Why Windows 95 supports multimedia better than previous versions of Windows

☐ How to control the sound and display of full-motion video

☐ How to turn off AutoPlay temporarily and permanently

The MPC Standard

When Microsoft programmers developed Windows 3.1, they saw the need for an industry-wide multimedia standard. If that standard included Windows 3.1-compatibility, then Microsoft would benefit nicely. The good news for the rest of us is that *we* would also benefit nicely if there were standards in place. We would then know that if we bought a hardware device or software that followed the standard, our investment would be safe because our software would work as expected and fewer conflicts would result.

As computers get faster, multimedia becomes even more important. Thankfully, the industry settled on the *MPC* standard. MPC stands for *Multimedia Personal Computer*. Every software product that is MPC-compatible is known to work as long as you have MPC-compatible hardware.

JUST A MINUTE

> The multimedia consortium has now adopted a more advanced MPC standard called *MPC-3*.

To be MPC-compatible, your computer must be capable of running Windows 95 (it must be already if you've gotten this far) and contain a sound card (SoundBlaster-compatibility is always safe), speakers, a CD-ROM drive, and a microphone. The technical requirements of MPC compatibility used to be more important than they are today because almost every computer with a sound card and CD-ROM sold since 1991 is compatible to the MPC standard.

20

TIME SAVER

Buy multimedia programs with the Windows 95 or Windows 3.1 logo on them because those software products are MPC-compatible.

Windows 95 goes beyond all other operating environments in its support of multimedia services to you as a user. Whether you play games, use motion graphics, or create online presentations, Windows 95 supports your needs and makes your Windows 95-compatible hardware work better with multimedia products than previous versions of Windows did.

Playing with AutoPlay

AutoPlay is a new feature of Windows 95 multimedia capabilities. If you've ever played a game or played an audio CD in your computer's CD-ROM drive, you'll appreciate AutoPlay very much indeed. AutoPlay automatically inspects your audio CD or CD-ROM as soon as you place it in the computer's CD-ROM drive. AutoPlay then does one of three things:

- ☐ Starts the installation on your CD-ROM if the program has yet to be installed
- ☐ Begins the CD-ROM's program if the program already is installed
- ☐ Starts the audio CD player if it is an audio CD

During the development of Windows 95, Microsoft decided that putting a CD-ROM (or audio CD) into the CD-ROM drive almost always meant that you were ready to do something with that CD-ROM. Of course, you could be inserting the CD-ROM in the drive for later use, but that's rare; most of the time when you insert a CD-ROM, you're ready to do something with it right away.

If you took the time to run the Hover game during Time-Out 3 (appearing immediately before this hour), you saw the effects of AutoPlay. As soon as you placed the Windows 95 CD-ROM into the CD-ROM drive, Windows 95 displayed the opening menu screen from which you then played the Hover game.

Now that you've seen AutoPlay used on a CD-ROM (in Time-Out 3), you can see (and hear) the use of AutoPlay using an audio CD in the next task.

JUST A MINUTE

Task 20.1 requires a CD-ROM drive. You must have a CD-ROM drive to be MPC-compatible and, in today's world, you can take advantage of very few multimedia services without a CD-ROM.

20

TIME SAVER

If you want to insert a CD-ROM but want to bypass the AutoPlay feature (perhaps you will want to access the CD-ROM later but insert the disc now), press Shift as you insert the CD-ROM. Keep holding Shift until the CD-ROM light goes out. Windows 95 will not start AutoPlay.

Task 20.1: Using AutoPlay to Play Music from a CD

TASK

Step 1: Description

This task demonstrates the AutoPlay feature as it works on an audio CD. Not only does Windows 95 provide for AutoPlay, but it also supplies all kinds of support for audio CDs and CD-ROMs that may surprise you when you see them.

Step 2: Action

1. Find an audio CD that contains music you like to hear.

2. Place the CD in the CD-ROM drive and close the door or push the CD-ROM drive's insert button to close the CD-ROM drive.

3. Windows 95 immediately recognizes that you've inserted the CD into the CD-ROM *and* begins playing the music! Notice the new CD Player button on the taskbar.

JUST A MINUTE

Depending on the date of your CD's release, something even *more* may happen: you may see a picture of the CD's cover on your screen! If so, move your mouse over the picture and click various parts of the screen to see information about the artist, song lists, the lyrics, and other things.

The feature you are viewing is called *Enhanced CD*, and audio CD makers are going to be adding Enhanced CD support to their audio CDs over time so that you can begin to fully integrate your PC and audio and video capabilities. If the CD you place in the drive does not yet contain the Enhanced CD format, you can still add a title and song list as explained in the rest of this task.

4. Click the CD Player button on the taskbar. Windows 95 displays the CD Player window shown in Figure 20.1.

Figure 20.1.

The CD Player window controls the CD's play.

The CD Player acts like a physical CD player that you can control by pushing the buttons. It displays a Play button (grayed out because your CD is already playing), Pause, Stop, Eject, Previous, and Next track buttons, Previous and Forward time buttons, and an Eject button that you can click when you're done listening to the CD. (Move the cursor over the buttons on the CD Player's window to see a roving help box that describes each button.)

Click the Pause button. Click the Play button. Press Alt+K to move the cursor to the dropdown listbox and click the down arrow button to play a different track on the CD.

TIME SAVER

> You can adjust the volume control by double-clicking the speaker icon on the taskbar. Task 20.2 describes how to adjust the volume.

5. If your CD is not an Enhanced CD, something will be missing because CD Player cannot know who the artist is or what the name of the songs are. *You* must tell CD Player what the artist's name is and what songs are on the song list.

Select **D**isc | **E**dit Play List. CD Player displays the window shown in Figure 20.2.

20

Figure 20.2.

Describe the CD to the CD Player application.

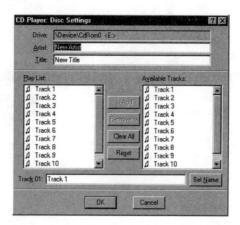

JUST A MINUTE

If you have more than one CD-ROM drive attached to your computer, you can select from among the various drives by clicking the listbox labeled Drive.

6. Find the box your audio CD came in. Type the name of the artist in the text box labeled Artist. Type the artist's last name first, followed by a comma, and then the first name so that you can later compile an alphabetical list of artists.

7. Press Alt+T to enter the title of the CD.

8. There will be a track listed for each song on the CD. Instead of the default titles of *Track 1* and *Track 2*, and so on, you can enter the song titles. Here is the easiest way to do that: Press Alt+K and type the first song title. Press Alt+N to add that title to the track list and enter the second song title. Press Alt+N to add the second title to the track list and enter the third song title. Continue entering all the titles. When you run out of tracks, you will have entered all the songs.

9. The **P**lay List and A**v**ailable Tracks listboxes will now contain the song titles. Don't do so now, but you can later select certain songs from the **P**lay List and click **R**emove to remove those selected songs from the **P**lay List (the song titles will remain in the A**v**ailable Tracks listbox). CD Player only plays those songs listed in the **P**lay list.

The CD Player remembers the artist, title, play list, and track lists by storing the information on your hard disk. Click OK to close the window and return to the CD control window. The window now contains a dropdown listbox from which you can select specific songs you want the CD Player to play.

20

10. Display the various menu commands to see what else the CD Player can do. Display the **O**ptions menu to select **R**andom Order, **C**ontinuous Play, or **I**ntro Play to play the CD randomly, play the CD over and over from the beginning to end, or to play only the first few seconds from each track.

11. Select **O**ptions | **P**references to display the Options Preferences dialog box shown in Figure 20.3. You can control what the CD Player does upon completion of playing a CD, as well as several other items, including the amount of time the **I**ntro Play will play each track's introduction.

Figure 20.3.

You can set various playing options.

12. Click OK to close the window.

13. If you want to enter information about more of your favorite CDs, eject the CD and insert additional CDs to add their descriptions to CD Player's repertoire of CDs.

14. When you're done, eject the CD from the drive and select **D**isc | E**x**it to close the CD Player.

JUST A MINUTE

CD Player recognizes each individual CD once you've entered the CD's detailed information. In other words, you can, a week later, insert a CD into the CD-ROM drive, and if you've entered that CD's information at any time in the past, CD Player will remember the CD and automatically display that CD's descriptive title, artist, and song information.

20

Step 3: Review

The CD Player application not only plays as soon as you insert CDs, but CD Player also keeps track of artists, CD titles, and the CD song lists. After entering a CD's information, CD Player remembers that information. If you insert a CD that CD Player does not recognize, it still plays the CD, and you can subsequently enter the CD's information.

Full-Motion Video

Windows 95 supports full-motion video better than previous versions of Windows did. Windows 95 can display video in a full-screen resolution or smaller windows, if you prefer. The video is smoother than previous Windows versions because of the way Windows 95 handles the playback.

No matter how much Microsoft improves the Windows 95 video playback software, the ultimate quality of video playback depends on your computer's hardware speed. If you notice your video is sluggish, you may have to get a faster computer with a faster CD-ROM drive. Since its release, Windows 95 has included several forms of a video player. Video for Windows was the original video player that played sound and motion from a CD-ROM or a disk file. Newer Windows 95 versions include the Active Movie Control program that more smoothly plays video. You can access either from the Multimedia menu on your Accessories menu.

The Microsoft Video for Windows was formerly distributed as a separate product. If you bought Windows 3.1, you also would have to buy Video for Windows to play full-motion video under Windows 3.1. (Many multimedia products included a licensed version of Video for Windows where you may have purchased your Video for Windows.) Windows 95 automatically includes Video for Windows so you don't have to search for a copy, and software makers don't have to worry about getting a license to include Video for Windows with their products.

Windows 95 uses the *Media Player* application to play video. Media Player is capable of playing all of the following kinds of items stored on the disk:

- ☐ Sound files
- ☐ Microsoft Multimedia Active Movie Player files
- ☐ Video for Windows files
- ☐ MIDI Sequencer files

Most full-motion video clips fall within one of these categories. Rarely do you have to know anything about the details of these files. Windows 95 recognizes the file formats and plays any of them.

Although you saw an example of Windows 95's full-motion video if you looked at the Hover game in Time-Out 3, Task 20.2 demonstrates an even more impressive full-motion video clip that you can play.

20

Task 20.2: Looking at a Full-Motion Multimedia Video

Step 1: Description

This task uses the Windows 95 installation CD-ROM that comes with your system. It demonstrates the full-motion video and sound that Windows 95 supports.

Step 2: Action

1. Locate your Windows 95 installation CD-ROM and insert it into your CD-ROM caddy.

2. After a brief pause, Windows 95 displays the CD-ROM screen that you saw if you ran the Hover game in Time-Out 3.

CAUTION

> If you do not hear a musical sound when the CD-ROM's opening screen appears, you may not have turned on your speakers or the volume control on your sound card could be turned down too low.

3. Click the icon on the right, labeled Cool Video Clips. Depending on the release date of your Windows 95, you'll see a window that contains many, if not all, of the file folders in Figure 20.4.

Figure 20.4.

Choose a video clip to play.

20

TIME SAVER

> When you see document icons that contain a video camera, such as the ones shown in Figure 20.4, those documents are video clips. You can right-click over an icon and select Play or double-click the icon to play the video.

4. Double-click the icon labeled Weezer. You won't believe your eyes and ears! Figure 20.5 shows one shot of the video clip you'll see.

Figure 20.5.

Have a happy day with this video clip.

5. Although the video clip window does not have a maximize button, you can resize the window to full-screen size by dragging the window's edges to the sides of the screen. Resize the window now to suit your viewing preference.

Depending on your video card and monitor's resolution, the video may look better in a smaller window size than a larger size. Use the play and pause buttons at the bottom of the video clip's window. You also can adjust the position of the play by dragging the play meter's indicator left and right.

6. If you want to adjust the volume, you can. Double-click the taskbar's speaker to see the series of volume controls and left and right balance controls shown in Figure 20.6. Depending on the type of multimedia sound you're listening to, you can adjust these volume and balance controls:

Figure 20.6.

You can adjust volume levels for several controls.

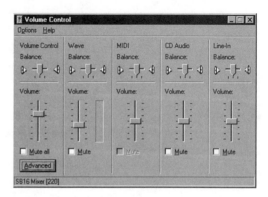

20

1. Volume   Controls the entire system's volume, no matter what is playing.

2. Wave   Controls wavetable sound volume. Wave sounds are realistic sounds unlike FM synthesis, which cheaper sound boards and older PCs use.

3. MIDI   Controls MIDI sound (stands for *Musical Instrument Digital Interface*) that reproduces musical instruments and other sounds.

4. CD   Controls the volume of your audio CDs when played with CD Player.

5. Line-In   Most sound cards contain a line-in port in which you can connect an outside sound source such as a stereo's output.

6. Adjust the volume to a comfortable level and then close the video window after you finish watching the video.

7. Close the Videos window, and then close the Windows 95 installation CD-ROM opening screen's window. You are now finished with the CD-ROM, so you can put the Windows 95 installation CD-ROM away for now.

Step 3: Review

Full-motion video is a lot of fun to see on a computer. For too long, computer graphics have been low quality. Full-motion video requires ample storage space, so most video resides on CD-ROMs that can hold a lot of data. The Windows 95 Media Player application controls all full-motion video, and the volume control window lets you adjust the different kinds of volumes to the best levels.

TIME SAVER

Open the Multimedia icon inside the Control Panel to find a tabbed dialog box that lets you control audio, video, and CD-ROM settings. For example, you can select an option that displays all full-motion video clips full-screen by default.

JUST A MINUTE

Although the technology is still fairly advanced, you soon should begin seeing powerful video-editing hardware and software interfaces for Windows 95. As disks get larger, the capacity to store video clips becomes more cost-effective. In addition, video hardware quality is getting better and less costly every day. The bottom line is that soon you'll be able to send your video camera's tape output to your computer; edit, rearrange, and add special effects to your home movies; and output a final produced and edited film. The new digital video cameras promise to help promote home video editing to a higher level.

20

Task 20.3: Unhooking Windows 95's AutoPlay Feature

TASK

Step 1: Description

You learned earlier in this hour how to bypass the AutoPlay feature when you insert individual CD-ROMs. Windows 95 lets you turn off AutoPlay completely if you do not want to use AutoPlay.

Step 2: Action

1. Display the Start menu.

2. Select Settings | Control Panel.

3. Double-click the System icon.

4. Click the Device Manager tab.

5. Click the plus sign next to your CD-ROM drive; the CD-ROM drive's description appears.

6. Click Properties.

7. Click the Settings tab. Windows 95 displays the Settings dialog box shown in Figure 20.7.

Figure 20.7.

Turn off AutoPlay from the Settings dialog box.

8. Uncheck the option labeled Auto insert notification to turn off AutoPlay. (If you subsequently check this option again, AutoPlay will return.)

9. Click OK to close the Settings dialog box.

20

10. Click OK to close the System dialog box.

11. Close the Control Panel window.

Step 3: Review

Although the AutoPlay feature is helpful, many Windows 95 users choose to turn off AutoPlay because they want to start the CD-ROM at a later time and are inserting the CD-ROM for subsequent use only. The Control Panel's System icon gives you access to the AutoPlay feature.

Summary

This hour described how Windows 95 finally integrated multimedia into the windowed multitasking environment. The multimedia capabilities of Windows 95 are advanced and provide for smooth video and sound. As computer hardware gets faster, Windows 95 will support better multimedia that uses the extra speed.

Windows 95's AutoPlay multimedia feature automatically installs CD-ROM software, loads and runs CD-ROM software, and plays audio CDs as soon as you insert the CD-ROM or CD into its drive. If you like, you can enter a description of the CD's artist, title, and tracks so that when you insert that same CD in the future, Windows 95 recognizes the CD and displays the lists from which you can select specific songs. The new audio CD format named *Enhanced CD* places text and graphics on the audio CDs you purchase at the music store.

Audio is only part of the multimedia glitz. Full-motion video capabilities allow for full-screen viewing of video clips using the Media Player. The video is smoother than previous versions of Windows.

Workshop

Term Review

Active Movie Control   The new Windows 95 video player. If you do not see the Active Movie Control on your Multimedia menu, you can contact Microsoft or check out their Web site at `www.microsoft.com` for an update.

AutoPlay   The ability of Windows 95 to install or start a program from a CD-ROM as soon as you place the CD-ROM in the drive. AutoPlay plays audio CDs as well.

Enhanced CD   A new audio CD standard that puts graphics and text on the same CDs that your stereo plays.

20

FM synthesis   An older sound standard that produces non-realistic computer-generated sounds.

Media Player   The Windows 95 application that plays video clips.

MIDI   Stands for *Musical Instrument Digital Interface* and reproduces musical instruments and other sounds.

MPC   Stands for *Multimedia Personal Computer.* A computer hardware and software standard that has been in effect for several years. It determines the minimum hardware and software requirements for a product to be called a multimedia product that's endorsed by the MPC compliance committee.

MPC-3   A more modern version of the MPC standard that requires a double-speed CD-ROM drive.

Video for Windows   The internal player Windows 95 uses to produce full-motion video on your screen.

Wave   Also called *wavetable.* Sound that produces realistic sounds from your computer's speaker.

Q&A

Q How do I know if my computer is MPC-compatible?

A Your PC's manual should say somewhere if the computer is MPC-compatible or not. Most likely, you have an MPC-compatible computer if you've purchased your computer within the past few years and your computer has a sound card, speakers, a microphone, and a CD-ROM.

Perhaps the easiest way is to work through the two tasks in this hour. Your computer will probably have few or no MPC problems if the tasks work on your computer as described in the text.

Q Why can't I use the CD volume control to adjust a video playing from my CD-ROM drive?

A The volume control labeled CD is useful for controlling audio CDs that you play using the CD Player application. When playing videos, the computer uses one of the other volume controls such as the Wave or MIDI volume control.

Q Why are there so many kinds of sounds (CD, Wave, FM synthesis, and MIDI)?

A The different sounds produce different qualities of audio. Your hardware and software determine the kinds of sound that come out of your computer's speakers. Luckily, you probably won't have to worry about the different sounds because Windows 95 recognizes most sound sources and selects the proper playing software accordingly.

20

PART
IV

Hour 21

The Basics of Sound

This hour extends last hour's multimedia discussion by describing some of the Windows 95 sound features. In the previous hour, you learned how Windows 95 provides support for CD and video sound and graphics. This hour explores the way you can add sounds to typical Windows 95 *events*. An event is a common task you do while using Windows 95. For example, when you open or close a window you'll be able to add a sound to each of those events, making Windows 95 more fun.

Perhaps you've already heard some sounds coming out of your PC's speakers as you've worked with Windows 95. If you like the sounds, you're going to learn here how to add new sounds and change the ones that you want to change. If you don't want the event sounds, you can also eliminate them.

JUST A MINUTE

> The Windows 95 event sounds can help those who are visually impaired. The audio feedback verifies that an event took place, and the sounds can also signal that an error occurred.

In addition to adding sounds provided by Windows 95 and other software, you can record your own sounds using the Sound Recorder application. All you need is a microphone attached to your sound card, and you're ready to turn your computer into a home recording studio.

The highlights of this hour include:

☐ What Windows 95 events are all about

☐ How you can assign sounds to specific events

☐ When predefined sound schemes make sense

☐ How the Sound Recorder acts like a digital tape recorder

☐ What to do if you want to embed a sound file in the middle of a text document

Event Sounds

Some Windows 95 users do not like sounds attached to events, and others do. The event sounds certainly can be obvious, because you can request sounds for all of the following common Windows 95 events:

☐ Dialog box opening and closing

☐ User errors

☐ Starting Windows 95

☐ Exiting Windows 95

☐ Minimizing and maximizing windows

☐ Starting programs

☐ Displaying menus

☐ Displaying help screens

21

You can assign sounds to several more events, in addition to these more common ones. You can even attach sounds to some networking events, such as the appearance of an electronic message.

If you want, you can attach sounds to specific events or use a predetermined set of sounds that comes with Windows 95. The next two tasks describe how to initiate event sounds. Programs written for Windows 95 can access your own sounds; the display of a dialog box from your word processor, then, might produce a sound that you've assigned to that dialog box event.

Task 21.1: Assigning Your Own Event Sounds

Step 1: Description

If you want to assign a specific sound to every Windows 95 event, or just some Windows 95 events, you can do so. There are many kinds of sounds available, and you can, as you familiarize yourself with the available sounds, customize Windows 95 so that anyone within hearing range will know it's *you* using Windows 95 and nobody else.

Step 2: Action

1. Open the Control Panel.
2. Double-click the Sounds icon to open the Sounds Properties dialog box, shown in Figure 21.1.

Figure 21.1.

Specify event sounds with the Sounds Properties dialog box.

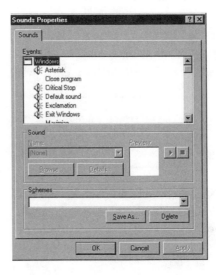

21

3. Scroll through the Events list to see all the events to which you can assign sounds. The events are listed by application. The first application is Windows 95 itself. As you scroll through the list, you'll see specific events listed for Explorer, the Control Panel, and other Windows 95 applications.

   Some of the events may seem cryptic to you, but as you use Windows 95 more, you'll better understand their purposes. For example, the event labeled Exclamation occurs when an application displays a message dialog box with an exclamation mark, indicating an important message that you need to read.

JUST A MINUTE

> The events with a speaker icon next to them have associated sounds. The events without the speaker icons do not have sounds associated with them, but you can add sounds to those, as you'll do in this task.

4. Select the event titled Maximize. You may or may not see a speaker icon next to it.

5. Press Alt+N to move the cursor to the **N**ame dropdown listbox. Open the listbox to see the list of choices. Select Chimes. A large speaker icon appears in the box labeled Preview. Click the Play button to the right of the speaker icon to hear the chimes sound. The chimes will sound whenever you maximize a window. If you want to change an event's sound, highlight the event and double-click the sound. You can always preview the sound by pressing Play.

Step Up

Windows 95 controls the sounds, not individual applications. Therefore, no matter which program you run, even those programs written for Windows 3.1, the chimes will sound whenever you maximize any window.

If you want to select a different sound for the maximizing of windows, go ahead and do so. Finish adding and removing the sounds that you want.

TIME SAVER

> If you see only three or four sounds in the **N**ame list, you may need to run the Windows Setup program (see Appendix C for help) to install additional sounds from the installation disks or CD.

6. Now that you've customized your own Windows 95 sounds, you can save that customized sound by clicking the **S**ave As command button and entering a name for the *sound scheme* (your customized set of Windows 95 sounds) in the Save Scheme As dialog box that appears. Figure 21.2 shows the Save Scheme As dialog box.

21

Figure 21.2.

Save your custom-ized Windows 95 sounds to select them in the future.

7. Close the Sounds dialog box by clicking the OK key and try the sounds out. Open windows, minimize windows, maximize windows, and display message boxes and dialog boxes to hear your sound scheme.

Step 3: Review

The Windows 95 Sound dialog box lets you attach sounds to various system events. If you don't know what a sound sounds like, you can preview the sound by clicking the Play button.

Task 21.2: Using a Predefined Sound Scheme

Step 1: Description

This task shows you how to load a sound scheme that you or someone else has saved. The Windows 95 installation disk supplies you with several predefined sound schemes that are interesting, as you'll hear during this task.

Step 2: Action

1. Open the Control Panel and double-click the Sounds dialog box.

2. Click the arrow next to the Schemes dropdown listbox to display the list of sound schemes currently defined for your system. Figure 21.3 shows one such list.

3. Select the Jungle Sound Scheme. Instead of listening to each sound, using the sound dialog box's preview button, close the Sound dialog box by clicking OK.

4. Minimize (don't close) the Control Panel… Look out, here come the tigers!

5. Display the Start menu, and you'll hear the rattle of snakes.

6. Every menu that you display produces the snake sound.

7. Start a program to hear the program's open sounds of the jungle.

8. Close a program to hear its close sounds.

9. Return to the Sounds dialog box and select the Musical Sound Scheme and try that sound scheme out. You'll enjoy the variety of sounds Microsoft Windows 95 can generate.

21

Figure 21.3.
*Numerous sound
schemes are
available to you.*

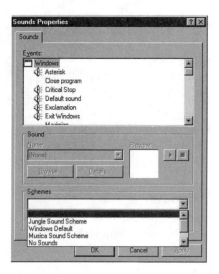

Step 3: Review

By using the predefined sound schemes, you can customize your computing session to fit the mood you're in. Explore the Explorer application using African wild jungle sounds. Have fun writing letters to friends using the melodic sounds of the musical sound schemes.

TIME SAVER

> If you tire of the sounds, select the sound scheme named No Sounds to turn off all system sounds.

Recording Your Own Sounds

As long as you have an MPC-compatible sound card that accepts a microphone, you can record your own sounds for the event sounds, as well as for other programs that use sound. The Sound Recorder saves your voice or sounds as digital document files on the disk. The multimedia capabilities of Windows 95 can play back those digitized sounds.

CAUTION

> Sound files can take a lot of disk space. If you try to record complete songs but you have only two or three free megabytes of disk space, you might run out of disk storage.

21

Remember that Microsoft wrote Windows 95 to be a data processing environment and, in today's world, *data* does not mean just textual and numeric data. Multimedia requires text, numbers, sounds, graphics, and full-motion video. Most of today's Windows 95 word processors let you insert a sound (or even a full-motion video file such as you saw in the previous hour) inside a document. The word processor will place a speaker or some other kind of icon where the sound goes. When the user to whom you give the document double-clicks on the sound icon, the user hears your voice!

Task 21.3: Using the Sound Recorder

Step 1: Description

If you've used a tape recorder or a VCR, you'll have no trouble using the Sound Recorder application. All the play, fast forward, rewind, record, stop, and pause controls appear on the Sound Recorder window, just as many of these same VCR-like controls appear on the Media Player's window, as you saw in the previous hour.

This task introduces you to the Sound Recorder application. You'll record a sound and assign that sound to a Windows 95 event.

Step 2: Action

1. Display the Accessories menu by clicking Start | **P**rograms and traveling to the Accessories menu.
2. Click the Multimedia menu.
3. Select the Sound Recorder menu. Windows 95 opens the Sound Recorder window, shown in Figure 21.4.

Figure 21.4.

Get ready to record your own sound using the Sound Recorder.

4. You'll recognize the familiar rewind, fast forward, play, stop, pause, and record buttons that you know from other recording devices.
5. Get your microphone ready. Turn on the microphone (if it has a switch), put the microphone to your mouth and click the record button. Say the following phrase distinctly and clearly: *I'm a Windows 95 wizard!*

6. As soon as you finish the sentence, click the Stop button. While you recorded the sentence, Sound Recorder displayed the digital wavelength of your voice in the center window.

7. Of course, you now want to hear yourself. Click the rewind button to reset the sound file pointer back to the beginning and click the play button.

8. Perhaps the quality is not what you'd like to hear. As long as you've got ample disk space, you can improve the quality of the recording. Select **Edit | Au**dio Properties. Windows 95 displays the Audio Properties window, shown in Figure 21.5.

Figure 21.5.

You can adjust the quality of the recording.

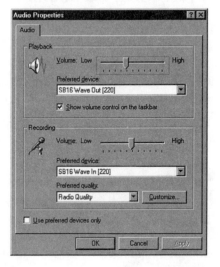

9. Depending on your sound card, the settings listed on your Audio Properties screen may differ from those in Figure 21.5. The important setting for now is the setting listed beneath the Preferred quality dropdown listbox. Click the listbox and select CD Quality. Although your sound files will now consume more disk space, they will sound better.

10. Click the OK command button to return to the Sound Recorder window.

11. Click the rewind button to reset the sound file pointer back to the beginning of the file.

21

12. Click the record button and, following steps 5 and 6's instructions, record the sentence once again.

13. When you rewind and play back the sentence, your voice should now be clearer. If you want to adjust the volume of the playback, you can double-click the taskbar's volume control speaker icon and adjust the volume, using the volume control window.

JUST A MINUTE

There are increasing and decreasing options available on the Sound Recorder's Effects menu, but the volume control window is a better window for adjusting your system sounds.

14. Try adding a special effect. Select Effects | Add Echo and play the sound again. Your sound will appear to be coming from a hole.

15. For fun, select Effects | Reverse, rewind the sound, and play the sound again. The sound comes out backwards! Straighten things out by reversing the sound once more.

16. Select Effects | Increase Speed (by 100%) and replay the sound.

17. Decrease the speed once again and replay the sound to make sure that the sound is now normal.

    You can apply all kinds of special effects and editing actions to sound files that you record. You may also edit songs and sound files from other sources, such as the event sound files. The Edit menu contains instructions for inserting other sounds into your sound files and for removing parts of sound files to shorten sound clips.

    The sound work that you do with Windows 95 is all digitally recorded. Therefore, you can speed up, slow down, reverse, and re-reverse sound files without losing any quality that you'd normally lose if you were dubbing from one standard tape-based recording device to another.

    The File | Open menu lets you load other sound files and edit or change them. For this task, do not load another sound file until you've saved your recording in the next step.

18. Save your file using File | Save. Store the file in the Media folder located within the Window folder if you want your sound recording file to be saved in the same area as Windows 95's system sounds.

21

JUST A MINUTE

Windows 95 stores all sound document files using the .WAV filename extension.

TIME SAVER

For this task, use the Windows Media folder, but if you want to store your files in your own folder, right-click over the Save dialog box's white document area. Select New Folder, and create a new folder for your own sounds.

19. Exit the Sound Recorder and open the Control Panel's Sound window.

20. Select the Maximize event, press Alt+N, and select the name of your recording from the list of sounds.

21. Click the OK command button. Resize the Control Panel window, then double-click the Control Panel's title bar to maximize the window, and you'll hear your message.

JUST A MINUTE

For fun and frolic in the office, secretly assign a voice message to one of your co-worker's Windows 95 events.

22. You may keep the sound or assign another sound to the Maximize event. Close the Control Panel for now.

Step 3: Review

The Sound Recorder application records your own voice. Once you create sounds, you can embed those sounds in other document files or save the sounds in the Windows Media folder so that you can add the sounds to Windows 95's repertoire of possible sound events. The Sound Recorder works just like a tape recorder but lets you add special effects, and even cut and insert sections of sounds within one another.

21

WINDOWS MINUTE

Embedding Sound Files

If you want to see how to embed a sound file in a document, open WordPad. Select **I**nsert | **O**bject. Click the Create from **F**ile command and type the name of your sound file or click **B**rowse to find the file. Windows 95 then finds and inserts your sound file into the document and puts a speaker icon where the sound goes. Figure 21.6 shows such a document.

The speaker icon works like any character in a document. You can cut and paste, as well as move, the icon around in the file. When someone reading the document wants to hear the sound file's contents, he or she needs only to double-click the speaker icon.

Figure 21.6.

A WordPad document with an embedded sound file.

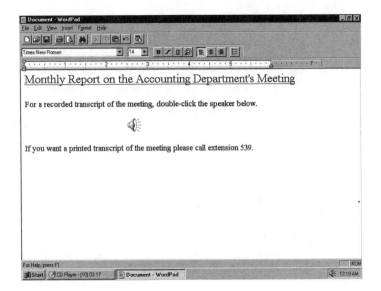

Summary

This hour explained what Windows 95 events are and how you can attach sounds to them. Windows 95 comes supplied with several sounds, or you can turn off all sounds from all events, if you prefer.

To help customize your own sounds and store different collections of event sounds, you can create sound scheme files. When you want to use one of the sound schemes for a particular Windows 95 session, you need only to select that sound scheme from the list, and Windows 95 assigns all the sounds to the proper events.

21

The Sound Recorder lets you make your own recordings. It works like a digital tape recorder. You can edit the sounds that you make and add special effects to them. Perhaps the most important use for the Sound Recorder is to make recordings that you can embed in other kinds of documents, such as a word processor or spreadsheet document.

Workshop

Term Review

analog recording   All sounds coming from a sound source are stored as continuous analog noise impulses that cannot be reproduced or changed without loss of quality. There are some modern-day digital tape recorders in use, but most tape recorders use an analog signal, so you cannot make copies of recordings without losing some quality, the opposite of *digital recording*.

digital recording   All sounds coming from a sound source are stored as discrete digital impulses that can be reproduced or changed without loss of quality, the opposite of *analog recording*.

event   Windows 95 actions you perform, such as opening and closing windows or displaying a menu.

Sound Recorder   The Windows 95 application with which you can record and edit sounds.

sound scheme   A collection of customized Windows 95 event sounds. Once you add sounds to Windows 95 events, you can save that collection of sounds in a sound scheme file.

Q&A

Q Why would I want event sounds?

A Event sounds can be fun, but they also can, over time, get irritating in the wrong environments. Some people, understandably, do not want to hear a bell ring every time they see an error message. Other people like to hear sounds sometimes to help reinforce certain events that take place. There are visually-impaired individuals who can benefit from event sounds, because the sounds provide audible feedback that certain events took place, either successfully or unsuccessfully. (If you use screen savers, you'll still hear event sounds so you'll know if you get an e-mail message.)

21

If you don't want to hear sounds every time you start a program or maximize a window, you may do one of two things: turn off all event sounds, using the Control Panel's Sound dialog box, or remove sounds from common events but keep them available for those rare events that you really want to know have happened.

Q How can I tell what a sound sounds like if I assign a sound to an event that rarely happens?

A The Sound dialog box lets you preview any sound. Select a sound for an event and click the play button beneath the Preview box to hear it. If you like what you hear, leave the assignment, and if you do not like the sound, you may assign another one.

Q Can I add my own sounds to Windows 95 events?

A Of course. You can purchase sound files, download sound files from online services, such as Microsoft Network, and record your own sounds, using the Sound Recorder. Assign the name of the sound file to an event, just as you have been doing with predefined sounds from Windows 95.

In addition, the Microsoft Plus! Windows 95 add-on program includes a large collection of additional event sounds.

Q I share my computer with my family. My kids like system sounds and we, the parents, don't. How can we coexist in harmony?

A I'm not sure that I can tell you how to coexist in perfect harmony, but I can solve the computer sound conflict. Open the Sound dialog box and select No Sounds. Save your scheme under the name *Dad and Mom*. Let your kids then assign their favorite sounds to Windows 95 events and save their sound scheme under the name *Crazy kids*. When you use Windows 95, open the Sound dialog, and select your sound scheme. You'll be able to work without the sounds. When your kids use the computer, they can select their sound scheme, so they can beep and chime all they want while computing.

(You know that Windows 95 event sounds aren't the real problem, don't you? It's all those games they play that really make noise!)

21

PART IV

Hour 22

Hardware: Big and Small

This hour introduces you to the concept of *Plug and Play*. Plug and Play is the name Microsoft created to describe the steps you must go through when installing new hardware on your computer. Before Windows 95, you would have to set jumper switches and make operating system settings. Often hardware and software conflicts would occur, creating many hours of debugging headaches. With Plug and Play, you simply plug new hardware components (memory, disk drives, CD-ROM drives, and expansion boards) into your computer, and Windows 95 immediately recognizes the change and sets everything up properly.

Plug and Play requires almost no thought when installing new hardware to your system. At least that's the theory. In reality, you may still encounter problems, as this hour explains. If Plug and Play does not perform as expected, Windows 95 provides a hardware setup wizard that you can use to walk you through the new hardware's proper installation.

Windows 95 has not only made it easier to change hardware on one system, but it also has added a program for aiding in the change of entire machines! Many people work on multiple PCs. Perhaps you have a laptop and also a desktop computer. Perhaps you work both at home and at the office. Whatever your situation, the Windows 95 *Briefcase* will help you synchronize your document files so they remain as current as possible.

The highlights of this hour include:

- ☐ What Plug and Play is all about
- ☐ Which components must be in place for Plug and Play to work
- ☐ How Plug and Play benefits both you and hardware companies
- ☐ Why automatic configuration for mobile computing environments is so important
- ☐ How direct cable connection makes connecting together two computers virtually trouble-free
- ☐ Why the My Briefcase icon is one of the most important icons on the Windows 95 desktop for users of both portable and desktop computers

Plug and Play

Some computer users actually refer to Plug and Play as *Plug and Pray*; these users are actually making a good point. Despite the industry hype over Plug and Play, it simply does not always work. If you attempt to install an older board into your computer, Windows 95 might not recognize the board, and you could have all kinds of hardware problems that take time to correct.

Things do not always go right when installing non–Plug-and-Play hardware. You often have to set certain hardware switches correctly. You may also have to move certain jumpers so that electrical lines on your new hardware flow properly to work with your specific computer. The new hardware can conflict with existing hardware in your machine. Most hardware devices, such as video and sound boards, often require new software support contained in small files called *drivers* that you must install and test.

JUST A MINUTE

Hardware designed before the invention of Plug-and-Play specifications is called *legacy hardware*.

22

Before Plug and Play can work in Windows 95, these two Plug and Play items must be in place:

☐ A Plug-and-Play-compatible Basic Input Output System (called the *BIOS*) in your computer's system unit. The computer manual's technical specifications or technical support should be able to tell you if the BIOS is Plug-and-Play-compatible.

☐ A Plug-and-Play-compatible device to install

You are running Windows 95, which is Plug-and-Play-compatible. If you do not have the Plug-and-Play BIOS inside your computer (most computers made before 1994 will have no form of Plug and Play compatibility), then you have to help Windows 95 with the installation process by answering some questions posed to you by a new hardware setup wizard. When you purchase new hardware in the future, try to purchase only hardware rated for Plug and Play compatibility.

TIME SAVER

One key in knowing whether or not the hardware is designed for Plug and Play is to make sure the Windows 95 logo appears on the new hardware's box or instructions. Before a hardware vendor can sell a product with the Windows 95 logo, that product must support Plug and Play compatibility. Microsoft calls Windows 95-compatible hardware *PC 95 hardware*. If you have older hardware already installed under Windows 3.1, you will not have to reinstall this hardware.

CAUTION

Make sure the next computer you buy is Plug-and-Play-compatible. As long as you run Windows 95 on a computer with a Plug-and-Play BIOS, you'll have little trouble installing additional hardware, whether or not the new hardware you're installing supports Plug and Play.

If you run Windows 95, own a computer with a Plug-and-Play BIOS, and purchase only Plug-and-Play hardware, the most you should ever have to do is turn off the computer, install the hardware, and turn the computer back on. Everything should work fine after that. (Perhaps to be on the safe side, you should also Plug and Pray.)

Plug and Play to Play and Play!

The Plug and Play standard should help both you and computer companies. Think of these benefits, if Plug and Play delivers as designed:

☐ Installing new hardware will no longer be troublesome.

☐ You will have less computer downtime and will be able to get back to work faster. (Perhaps we should rethink this Plug and Play business!)

☐ Hardware companies will have to staff fewer technical support people.

☐ Hardware companies will not have to buy as many support phone lines.

☐ Hardware companies will be able to cut costs.

☐ Hardware products will come down in price, due to the decrease in the support costs just mentioned.

☐ You will have more money in your pocket to vacation in Italy!

Plug and Play works both for newly installed hardware and for removed hardware. If you remove a sound card that you no longer want, or remove memory and replace that memory with a higher capacity memory, Plug and Play ought to recognize the removal and reconfigure the computer and operating system automatically. Again, Plug-and-Play is not always perfect and does not always operate as expected, but as long as you run a Plug-and-Play BIOS and install Plug-and-Play hardware, there should be little installation trouble ahead for you.

JUST A MINUTE

Plug and Play does *not* make legacy hardware obsolete. If you install Windows 95 in a computer that has older non-Plug-and-Play legacy hardware, Windows 95 and the hardware should work fine together.

Some Hardware Help

If you install hardware and find that Windows 95 does not properly recognize the change, double-click the Add New Hardware icon in the Control Panel window. Windows 95 starts the Add New Hardware Wizard, shown in Figure 22.1, which helps walk you through the installation process.

JUST A MINUTE

This hour is not as task-oriented as the rest because the hardware differences among all the readers would make following specific tasks virtually impossible.

Figure 22.1.

*The Add New Hardware
Wizard helps you install
non-Plug-and-Play
hardware.*

22

The wizard goes through a series of tests and attempts to detect the newly added hardware. Suppose you added an internal modem, but you cannot communicate with the modem. The Add New Hardware Wizard may realize that you have a new internal modem after running through its series of tests, but may not be able to determine exactly what kind of internal modem you have. You and the wizard together should be able to determine the proper configuration.

CAUTION

If you add a new modem to a serial port or a printer to a parallel port, you should not run the Add New Hardware Wizard. The wizard works only for hardware you physically connect to the system unit. If you plug a modem into an existing serial port, that serial port will already be installed, so you don't need to run Add New Hardware. You will, however, have to double-click the Control Panel's Modems icon and select your modem from the list of modems displayed.

Mobile Computing

The Microsoft programmers understood the need for *mobile computing environments* when they developed Windows 95. Mobile computing environments refer to those environments in which portable computers such as laptops are used. In the past year or two, companies have begun developing *docking stations* for computer users who take a laptop with them on the road, and then come home and plug the laptop directly into a docking station. The docking station is a connecting device that connects the laptop to a full-size color screen, printer, mouse, and keyboard. Therefore, the computer user would use the laptop on the road, and then use the laptop's system unit at home or in the office, with regular-size peripheral equipment.

Windows 95 can detect whether or not a computer is docked and make appropriate adjustments instantly and accordingly. When undocked, Windows 95 can use the laptop's screen, and when docked, Windows 95 can immediately adjust the screen to a larger and higher-resolution monitor.

CAUTION

> If your hardware is not Plug-and-Play—compatible, you will have to re-boot your computer before Windows 95 can reconfigure itself to the docking. If, however, you have full Plug-and-Play compliance, you don't have to reboot for Windows 95 to recognize the change in docking status.

Windows 95 often can recognize that a computer has been docked, but some hardware does not allow you to undock your PC without Windows 95 knowing about the undocking. If Windows 95 does not recognize the fact that you've undocked, you can select Eject PC from the Start menu, and Windows 95 will know to reconfigure for the undocking and use the laptop's own configuration.

If you have a laptop or desktop with a PCMCIA card, you can plug PCMCIA cards directly into the laptop, changing a PCMCIA hard disk to a PCMCIA modem, and Windows 95 will adjust itself automatically.

JUST A MINUTE

> Most hardware manufacturers now shorten the term *PCMCIA card* to *PC card.*

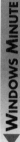

Additional Hardware Support

Windows 95 uses a *registry* and *hardware tree* to keep track of the current and changeable hardware configuration. The registry is a central repository of all possible hardware information for your computer. The hardware tree is a collection of hardware configurations, taken from parts or all of the registry, for your computer. (In addition, your registry holds software settings, as well.)

Luckily, you don't have to know anything about the registry, because Windows 95 keeps track of the details for you. If, however, you want to look at the hardware tree currently in place on your computer, you can display the Control Panel and double-click the System icon. Windows 95 displays the System Properties tabbed dialog box, shown in Figure 22.2. The hardware tree shows the devices currently in use.

Figure 22.2.

The Device Manager tabbed dialog box under the Systems Properties box.

22

Windows 95 also supports a feature called *Dial-Up Networking* that lets you, when on the road, dial up your office or home computer and work just as if you were on the home or office computer network. The interface to you as a laptop user will be no different than if you plugged the network cable into the back of your laptop. The only difference is that you might be 1,000 miles away, and things will run as if you were attached to the office network. You'll find a Dial-Up Networking wizard in the Accessories menu.

CAUTION

Full dial-up networking is possible only if the computer you call also is running Windows 95.

If you attach a high-speed parallel or serial cable to two computers, those computers can share files and hardware resources with one another. This is a simple replacement for an expensive network if you want only two computers to share resources.

The Direct Cable Connection option should be available in the Accessories menu. (If the Direct Cable Connection option is not installed, run the Windows Setup option from the Control Panel's Add/Remove Programs icon if you need to install Direct Cable Connection.) Once you select Direct Cable Connection, Windows 95 initiates the wizard shown in Figure 22.3. After answering the wizard's prompts, your two computers will be linked together.

CAUTION

The two computers connected using a direct cable connection must use the same type of port. Therefore, you must connect two parallel ports together or two serial ports together, but not a parallel port to a serial port.

Figure 22.3.

The Accessories menu contains the Direct Cable Connection wizard.

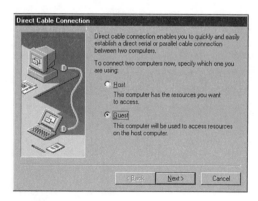

The Windows 95 Briefcase

When on the road, you want to work with the most up-to-date data files possible. Therefore, users often copy the latest files from their desktops to portable PCs before leaving on a trip. The direct cable connection, described at the end of the last section, is a great way to copy those files. (Users also use floppy disks to transfer data between two computers.)

Once they return, those users often have to reverse the process and copy their latest laptop data files over the ones on the desktops to refresh the desktop's files so that both computers stay in synchronization with each other. Until Windows 95, the only way to ensure that you were working with the latest data files was to look at the file date and time values and work with only the latest. At best, trying to maintain the latest files was a hassle and often caused confusion and errors as well.

The Briefcase application does all the nitty-gritty for you and synchronizes two computers that you have connected together via a network or by cable. You'll find the Briefcase application on your desktop. The first time you double-click the My Briefcase icon, Windows 95 runs the Welcome to the Windows Briefcase wizard, shown in Figure 22.4.

Figure 22.4.

The first time you run Briefcase, you'll have to tell Briefcase some details.

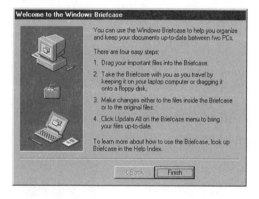

22

JUST A MINUTE

The Briefcase icon appears on the desktop and not on the Control Panel or within the Start menu so that you can drag files onto the Briefcase from Explorer or from an Open dialog box.

22

Briefcase acts just like a briefcase that you take between your office and home. Before leaving in the morning, you put important papers in your briefcase. In the Windows 95 environment, before going on the road with your laptop, you should drag all data files that you want to work with to the Briefcase.

Suppose you copy two files to the Briefcase icon. After loading the Briefcase welcome screen, shown in Figure 22.4, close the screen to see the My Briefcase work area ,shown in Figure 22.5. Figure 22.5 shows two files in the Briefcase window ready to be transferred to a laptop computer. Close the Briefcase work screen so you can move the Briefcase files.

Figure 22.5.

There are two document files in Briefcase at the moment.

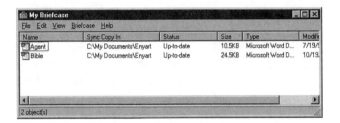

If you are using a floppy disk for the Briefcase intermediary storage media, move the My Briefcase icon to the floppy disk. You can display the floppy disk by displaying the Explorer window or Control Panel and then dragging the My Briefcase icon to the floppy disk.

Insert the floppy disk into your laptop's disk drive. While on the road, you can work with those files in the Briefcase. If you save a Briefcase file to the laptop's hard disk, be sure to return the file to the laptop's Briefcase before you reconcile the files on your primary desktop computer later.

Once you get back to the desktop, insert the floppy disk into the desktop's disk drive and double-click the desktop's My Briefcase icon once again. Select **B**riefcase | Update **A**ll or select only those files you want to update, and then press the **B**riefcase | **U**pdate Selection from the menu. Briefcase will synchronize the desktop's files by doing one of three things:

☐ If your desktop does not have one or more Briefcase files, then the Briefcase application copies those files to the desktop computer.

☐ If your desktop already has those files on its disk, then Briefcase transfers files from the Briefcase *only* if the Briefcase's files are newer than the desktop's.

☐ If your desktop already has one or more Briefcase files and the files are older than the Briefcase versions, the Briefcase application copies the newer versions over the old ones on the desktop.

TIME SAVER

If you want to update files using a direct cable connection or network instead of an intermediary floppy disk, make the physical connection first to the laptop with a direct cable or plug the laptop into your network. Then drag the files from the desktop computer to the laptop's My Briefcase icon. This sends the files to the Briefcase on the laptop. While on the road, work with the files inside the Briefcase icon. When you reconnect to the desktop or network, you can select the **B**riefcase | Update **A**ll menu command to bring the desktop up to date.

Summary

This hour got fairly technical during the discussion of hardware. An operating system must run through several operations before it can recognize and work with new hardware. Fortunately, the Plug-and-Play process makes such work slightly easier and sometimes trouble-free.

As long as you purchase Plug-and-Play hardware and have a Plug-and-Play–compatible computer, you can add all kinds of new hardware to your computer, and Windows 95 should be able to recognize the change and update itself accordingly. Windows 95 includes support for docked laptop computers, so the configuration changes whenever you dock and undock.

If you do not use 100 percent Plug-and-Play hardware, the Add New Hardware Wizard will walk you through each installation and help make the hardware easier to install. If you are simply plugging devices into a serial or parallel port, you do not need to worry about installing new hardware, but you will have to set up a modem or printer driver, using appropriate Control Panel windows.

The interconnection possible in Windows 95 means that you'll be connecting more computers together than ever before. With those connections comes confusion, however. A desktop and laptop computers' files can get out of synchronization. Generally, you want to work with the latest version of a file, but comparing dates and times yourself is tedious and error-prone. The My Briefcase icon solves that problem by making the time and date comparisons for you and refreshing any laptop or desktop files that need refreshing to make sure both systems have the latest versions of document files.

22

Workshop

Term Review

BIOS Stands for Basic Input Output System and refers to the system unit's ROM-based code that handles I/O devices.

Briefcase The Windows 95 application that synchronizes the document files from two computers so that you can always have the most up-to-date files at any time.

Dial-Up Networking The ability of a remote laptop computer to dial into a network over the phone lines and work as if connected to the network by cable.

direct cable connection The connection between two computers with a cable attached to both parallel or serial ports.

docking station A device into which you can insert some laptop computers that instantly connects the laptop to a full-size screen, keyboard, mouse, and printer.

drivers Software files that often accompany hardware to tell the computer how to control the hardware when you install it.

hardware tree A collection of hardware configurations, taken from parts or all of the registry, that your computer may require.

I/O Stands for *input and output.*

jumpers Special routing connections that a lot of older, legacy hardware requires to change the electrical path flows so the hardware works properly on your specific machine.

legacy Older hardware that was designed before engineers invented the Plug-and-Play specification.

mobile computing environments The computer environment that includes laptop computers and desktop docking stations for the laptops.

PCMCIA Cards Also called *PC Cards.* Small credit card sized I/O cards that add functionality such as modems and memory to laptops and to some desktop systems.

PC 95 hardware Hardware that has been tested and approved by Microsoft to work with Windows 95 and support such features as Plug and Play.

Plug and Play The name Microsoft gives to hardware that you can install without making any hardware or software changes. The Windows 95 Plug-and-Play feature will take care of setting up things correctly for you.

registry A central repository of all possible information for your hardware.

Q&A

Q How do I know if I have Plug and Play?

A You have Windows 95, which means that installing hardware ought to be easier than with previous operating systems and previous versions of Windows. Perhaps the best way to see if you have Plug and Play is to plug the next device you get for your computer into the computer, power on your machine, and see what happens. (Of course, you should read the new hardware's installation instructions to learn the correct way to install the device.)

If you turn on your computer and the computer responds to the new device properly, you have, for all intents and purposes, all the Plug-and-Play–compatibility you need. You have Plug and Play, at least, for that one device. Just because Windows 95 and your BIOS are Plug-and-Play–compatible, does not mean that the hardware you install will also be Plug-and-Play–compatible. Some hardware might be Plug-and-Play–compatible and some may not be.

Q I cannot seem to use the Dial-Up Networking feature to network to my home computer while on the road. What do I do?

A Dial-Up Networking works only if the computer you call is running Windows 95 and is itself attached to a network.

Q I don't want to buy and install a network in my house, but how do I easily connect my laptop to my desktop to share files between them?

A Use the Windows 95 direct cable connection. Connect a parallel or serial cable to both parallel or serial ports. Your laptop will be able to access the desktop's shared files.

Q I often cross time zones and change my laptop accordingly. Will Briefcase be affected by the time changes?

A It is possible for Briefcase to make incorrect decisions when copying files using different time zones. You can do very little to make Briefcase happy when you move across time zones. The best thing you can do is resist the temptation to change the laptop's clock while on the road. Keep your laptop clock set the same as your desktop computer, so that when you return to the desktop, Briefcase will have no trouble reconciling your files.

22

Hour **23**

Exchange Faxes and Mail

This hour introduces you to the world of electronic mail and faxes using Windows 95. This hour explains how to expand the use of Windows 95 to manage electronic mail and faxes. Of course, you will need to have a fax and modem combination to take advantage of this technology. Most modems sold in the last five years have fax send and receive capabilities.

This hour teaches you how Windows 95 *improves* upon the standard electronic mail and electronic faxing that you might already be doing. The Windows 95 application named *Microsoft Messaging* (Microsoft Messaging is called *Microsoft Exchange* in some versions of Windows 95) contains a *universal Inbox* that acts as a repository of electronic mail you can send and receive. To Windows 95, electronic mail can be more than simple messages and files. Microsoft Messaging supports the management and exchange of all kinds of electronic mail, including faxes and files, and it provides support for virtually any online service you might use.

In conjunction with Microsoft Messaging, you might want to use the Windows 95 Microsoft Fax application to send and receive faxes. Microsoft Fax uses Microsoft Messaging's universal Inbox for storing sent and received faxes. Therefore, you'll be able to track all your sent and received messages, including faxes and e-mail.

The highlights of this hour include:

- [ ] What Microsoft Messaging is all about
- [ ] How Microsoft Messaging's central storage location collects all your messages and faxes
- [ ] Where to access the Personal Address Book
- [ ] How to send faxes
- [ ] Why different fax recipients might receive your faxes in different ways

Microsoft Messaging Command Center

It is common for computer users to access more than one online service. Perhaps you work on the Internet as well as on CompuServe. Each morning you might log on to the Internet to get incoming messages and send your outgoing Internet messages. Once finished, you might log on to CompuServe to send and receive those messages. The burden of managing that electronic mail grows as more people sign up for more online services.

JUST A MINUTE

Are we living in a *paperless society*, as promised by the Management Information System gurus of the early 1970s? Not a chance. Computers help us use *more* paper and at a *faster* rate than ever before. It's often said in the computer industry that, despite the prevalence of electronic mail, we'll have paperless bathrooms before we'll have a paperless society!

Wouldn't it be nice to tell your computer to send and receive all your electronic mail without any intervention on your part? The computer could store all received mail in a central location; you could then manage, sort, print, respond to, or delete from there. Windows 95 has the answer: Microsoft Messaging.

Microsoft Messaging is a Windows 95 program that features a central repository, called a universal Inbox, where you store, receive, and send all electronic mail from virtually any source. Once you collect your electronic mail in the universal Inbox, you can sort and filter the mail any way you like.

23

TIME SAVER

As soon as Windows 95 recognizes that you have messages in the universal Inbox, an envelope icon appears next to the taskbar clock to alert you that you have new mail.

Using Microsoft Messaging

The Microsoft Messaging program uses a document file format named *rich-text format (RTF)*. You can send an RTF document over a phone line, and different programs might exchange those files.

Unlike straight text files, RTF files can be formatted with special characters and properties. You do not have to know how to convert your document files to the RTF format, because Windows 95 does the conversion automatically, as needed.

WINDOWS MINUTE

23

JUST A MINUTE

This hour discusses both Microsoft Messaging and Microsoft Fax. The distinction between these two programs becomes cloudy at times because they work so closely together. When you send and receive faxes, you use Microsoft Fax for the transmission. Those faxes are stored in Microsoft Messaging's universal Inbox before you send them and after you receive them. If you use a third-party program such as WinFax Pro, your program probably integrates with the Microsoft Messaging Inbox as well, so you'll still be able to track sent and received faxes.

Along with Microsoft Messaging, you get a Personal Address Book that can contain all of the following:

- ☐ E-mail addresses
- ☐ Names, mailing addresses, and voice/fax phone numbers
- ☐ Contact information and notes

If developers of Windows 95 applications choose to do so, and hopefully they will, they can write their applications to access Windows 95's Personal Address Book instead of building one of their own. Therefore, if you want to use someone else's fax software instead of Microsoft Fax, the other fax software can read your Personal Address Book so that you don't have to keep two sets of address books up to date.

JUST A MINUTE

Due to the wide variety of e-mail services that different readers of this book will use, it's impossible to list tasks that make sense for everybody. Therefore, these tasks acquaint you with the different things you can do with Microsoft Messaging and then, from Microsoft Messaging, you can explore Microsoft Messaging with your own specific needs in mind.

One of the problems associated with a book of this kind is that the book can demonstrate the services provided by Microsoft only for the Windows 95 product. If you want to add services not supplied by Microsoft, such as America Online or CompuServe, you must obtain Microsoft Messaging *profile* disks from those services so that Microsoft Messaging can exchange electronic information with the service. As long as you get the profile disks from your online service, Microsoft Messaging can read that profile disk and work with that service.

In addition, you'll hear a lot about Microsoft's new product named Microsoft Outlook, which comes with Office 97. Outlook somewhat replaces the Windows 95 Messaging Inbox by giving you additional address book fields and keeping track of your message logs. Outlook's name and address phone book (called the Contacts database) is more complete than Windows 95 Messaging's address book and integrates well with Microsoft Word. This book will not discuss Outlook, because Outlook is not included with Windows 95, but you should check out Outlook's features if you often send and receive electronic mail and faxes from your computer. You might like the extra features Outlook provides for a central messaging center.

Task 23.1: Getting Started with Microsoft Messaging

Step 1: Description

Microsoft Messaging is a service that provides a central mailbox for all your electronic correspondence. When you first installed Windows 95 with Microsoft Messaging, Microsoft put a message or two in your mailbox; assuming that you or someone else hasn't erased these initial messages, this task shows you how to start Microsoft Messaging and read from your universal Inbox.

Step 2: Action

1. Display the Start menu.
2. Select **P**rograms.
3. Select Microsoft Messaging (or Microsoft Exchange if you do not see an entry for Microsoft Messaging). After a brief pause, an introductory screen appears.

Microsoft Messaging displays your universal Inbox with any incoming messages
that might be waiting for you, as shown in Figure 23.1. If you do not see the list of
Microsoft Messaging folders to the left of your messages, click the Show/Hide
Folder List toolbar button (the second toolbar button from the left).

Figure 23.1.

*The universal
Inbox, with
messages waiting
for you.*

JUST A MINUTE

Your incoming messages might be different from those described here,
depending on the date of your Windows 95 release.

TIME SAVER

The Inbox is usually available as an icon from your Windows 95 desktop.
Therefore, you can bypass the Start menu if you want to start the Inbox
program from the desktop screen.

Obviously, Microsoft Messaging did not poll all the online services available and
retrieve these messages when you started the program, because you see no modem
action occurring when you start Microsoft Messaging. When you installed Windows 95, the installation program made sure that one or two initial messages (such
as those shown in Figure 23.1) were waiting for you. Nevertheless, once you set up
Microsoft Messaging to work with your own online services (by obtaining these
services' profile disks), you'll see messages just like these when you retrieve mail
from your universal Inbox.

4. The Inbox folder is highlighted so that you know you're viewing incoming mail.

   In the right-hand window, the sealed envelopes next to messages indicate that you
   haven't read that message. As with any Windows 95 dialog box that contains a list
   of items, you can sort on any column in the window by clicking the column name.

   Open the first message to read the contents. You might have an advertising message
   from Sprint. Double-click the Sprint message to read the text.

5. If you read the entire message, you'll find that you can double-click on the Sprint icon and the message automatically hotlinks to the modem and downloads (via a free call) a message to you from Sprint. Sure, Sprint is trying to sell you a service here, and the service may or may not be right for you, but the important thing to note here is that the RTF contained an embedded OLE object (the Sprint icon). After you double-clicked the icon, the document began executing a small program that retrieved additional information for you through the modem.

The paper clip next to Microsoft Messaging's Sprint message indicated that this file contained an embedded object.

If you had outgoing mail, you could make sure that mail appears within the Microsoft Messaging list to be sent by clicking the Outbox folder.

Handling RTF Documents

The RTF documents used by Microsoft Messaging are flexible enough to contain virtually any kind of data or hotlink to an embedded OLE object. If you send an RTF file to another Windows 95 user as e-mail, that user receives the file as an RTF document. If, however, you send the RTF file to a user who does not run Windows 95 and who uses a text-based service, such as a textual Internet provider, Microsoft Messaging transforms your mail into text and *attaches* embedded objects as external files that the user will download along with the text file.

You can drag any or all of the messages you receive to any other Microsoft Messaging folder or to any drive or folder on your computer. Once you drag the file to a location not inside Microsoft Messaging, Windows 95 stores the file with a .MSG filename extension. Windows 95 uses the extension to tell itself how to read the file if you double-click the file's icon to open the file or use a Quick Viewer to look at the message file from Explorer. All the sender and recipient information stays with the message file even after the file leaves Microsoft Messaging so that you'll always know who sent messages to you.

6. Slowly move the mouse across the toolbar at the top of the document to read the hovering help and to see what the buttons do. Sometimes you may want to reply to the sender of a message or reroute the message to others. The toolbar buttons enable you to do those things and more.

7. After closing the Sprint message by double-clicking the message window's control button, drag the Sprint message *header* (the one-line message description) to the Deleted Items folder. All items remain in the Deleted Items folder until you specifically delete them from the Deleted Items folder. When you delete items from the Deleted Items folder, those items are gone permanently. Windows 95 does not send deleted messages to the Recycle Bin.

8. If you want to read the next sample message, you can do so. The message contains no OLE-embedded attachment. Send the message to the Deleted Items folder when done.

23

TIME SAVER

To delete items permanently from the Deleted folder, open the folder by double-clicking the folder's icon. Click over the message you want to delete or use Ctrl+click to select multiple messages. Once you select the message or messages you want to delete, right-click the mouse button and choose **D**elete to delete the messages.

Step 3: Review

This task got you started using Microsoft Messaging. The next task explains how to work with the Personal Address Book so you can begin to add your business associates and friends to the address database.

Task 23.2: Maintaining the Personal Address Book

Step 1: Description

You access the Personal Address Book through the Microsoft Messaging window. Although other programs might use the Personal Address Book, the Microsoft Messaging is where you'll manage and update the Personal Address Book to keep the information current.

Step 2: Action

1. Click the Address Book toolbar button to display the Personal Address Book. If this is the first time you or anyone else on your computer has accessed the Personal Address Book, your Personal Address Book will be empty, as is the one shown in Figure 23.2.

Figure 23.2.

The Personal Address Book holds many kinds of details.

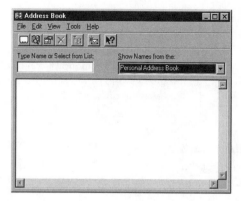

That Personal Address Book screen looks empty, doesn't it? If you want to, you can add some information to the Personal Address Book now. To get you started, the next few steps walk you through the addition of a sample entry.

2. Press the left-hand toolbar button labeled New Entry. Personal Address Book displays the New Entry dialog box. For your first few entries, you'll be adding new names and addresses to the entry type labeled Other Address. Double-click Other Address now.

You would choose Fax if you were sending a document as a fax, and you would choose Personal Distribution List if you were creating a single address book entry for more than one recipient (such as co-workers in a department).

CAUTION

Don't add anything to the entries beneath the group labeled Microsoft Network. Only after signing up for the Microsoft Network can you work with the Microsoft Network group. You might see additional entries if you use WinFax Pro, Outlook, or other messaging service programs.

3. For this entry's display name, type `Peter Parker`. Type `12345,567` for the e-mail address. Type `CompuServe` for the e-mail type.

Leave the checkmark next to the option at the bottom of the screen for this entry. As long as this recipient retrieves his e-mail from CompuServe using Windows 95 and Microsoft Messaging, the RTF file format will be the best format to use.

4. Click the tab marked Notes. Enter the following for the note on Mr. Parker: `A student at ESU studying the effects of radiation`.

5. Click the Phone number tab and enter all the phone numbers for Mr. Parker.

TIME SAVER

Suppose you aren't sure of the recipient's address information. Call the recipient by entering any phone number you know for the recipient, and press the **D**ial command button next to that number. Windows 95 dials the number and displays the message box shown in Figure 23.3. When the recipient answers, click **T**alk or, if there is no answer, click Hang **U**p.

Figure 23.3.

Let the Windows 95 fingers do the walking!

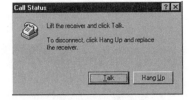

23

To dial the number, Windows 95 loaded the *Phone Dialer* application. You can initiate the Phone Dialer from the Start menu if you wish. After entering several numbers into your Personal Address Book, however, you'll probably make all your calls from the Personal Address Book (which loads Phone Dialer, as you see here).

Once you terminate the call, the dialing window goes away, but the taskbar keeps the Phone Dialer loaded, in case you want to dial another number using the dialer or using the Personal Address Book command buttons. If you press the Phone Dialer taskbar button, you'll see the phone pad shown in Figure 23.4.

Figure 23.4.

Your computer is also your phone.

When you finish this book, you can return to the Phone Dialer and add some speed-dial numbers so you can win all those radio call-in contests.

6. If you changed to the Phone Dialer at the end of the previous step, return to the Personal Address Book. If this is a business associate, click the Business tab and fill in the information there. Depending on your release of Windows 95, you may have to edit the name so that the first and last names fit in their appropriate categories. After filling out the information, your screen might look something like the one shown in Figure 23.5.

Figure 23.5.

The information is now complete.

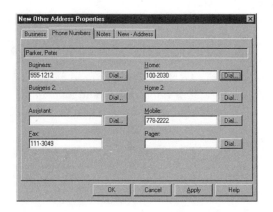

23

7. Now that you've entered the initial information, press the OK command button to close the Personal Address Book information. The Personal Address Book now contains its first entry. You can add more of your own names and numbers if you like. Close the Personal Address Book now to prepare for the next task.

Step 3: Review

The Personal Address Book is an integral part of Microsoft Messaging. Not only does the Personal Address Book support Microsoft Messaging but also the Phone Dialer and all other communications applications on your system that read the Personal Address Book. Over time, the information you store in the Personal Address Book will be very valuable, because you'll use that information for so many things.

TIME SAVER

> If you use Microsoft Word's mail merge capabilities, you can access the Personal Address Book from within Word. You then don't have to keep a separate address book for each program.

Task 23.3: Creating New Messages To Send to Others

Step 1: Description

This task shows you how to create your own mail to send to others over the Microsoft Network or using your own online service. You won't actually send the message in this task, because you may use one of several online services, and Windows 95 does not come with the other online services' profiles. Therefore, you'll have to wait until you sign up for the Microsoft Network or get your online service's Microsoft Messaging profile disk before you can send the mail you create here.

Step 2: Action

1. Select the Outbox to create new mail that you want to send.

2. Click the New Message toolbar button (the third button from the left). Microsoft Messaging displays the New Message dialog box, shown in Figure 23.6.

3. Press the To command button to display a window directly related to your Personal Address Book entries, and highlight a recipient in the left window. (If you've entered only Peter Parker, go ahead and select him, because this task will not actually send the message.)

23

Figure 23.6.

Here's where you create new mail to send.

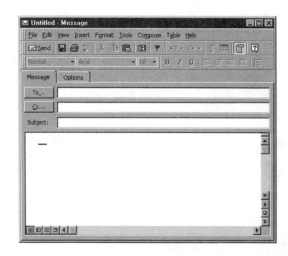

23

4. Press To to add the recipient's name to the Message recipients window. You could send the message to multiple recipients if you send several recipient messages to the Message recipients window.

   If you want a *carbon copy* sent (a copy of the message to one or more recipients), you can add additional recipients in the **Cc** window.

5. There are many more options you'll want to explore when you have time. For now, press the OK command button to display the New message window again. Enter a subject and press Tab to move the text cursor to the large message area. Type the message you that want to send.

6. Click the far-left toolbar button to send the message. Microsoft Messaging won't actually send the message, because you are not hooked to an online service yet. You can find the message in your Microsoft Messaging Sent Items folder.

Step 3: Review

This task briefly explored how to send e-mail. Once sent, your messages remain in the Sent Items folder. You can move the messages to the Deleted Items folder or to the Outbox to send them again.

Introduction to Microsoft Fax

Microsoft Fax is capable of turning your computer into a fax command center as long as you have a combined fax and modem. When you install your fax/modem, you'll be able to select that fax/modem instead of a printer from within your favorite Windows 95 word processor. You can also fax directly from Microsoft Messaging by running the fax wizard contained in Microsoft Messaging.

If you send a document fax to another user who happens to have Windows 95 answering his fax modem, Microsoft Fax actually sends the document itself so that the receiver gets the fax *not* as a fax but as a document inside the universal Inbox. If the recipient has a standard fax machine or a computer fax not using Windows 95, the recipient gets a standard fax transmission.

TIME SAVER

As soon as you start Microsoft Messaging, Windows 95 turns on the faxing support in the background. A fax machine will appear next to your taskbar's clock. You can click the fax machine icon to see the fax options that are currently set.

Task 23.4: Faxing Easily

Step 1: Description

Much of the time, sending a fax means using your word processor to type what you want to send and then printing to the fax/modem connected to your computer. If the document's already saved to the disk and you're using Microsoft Messaging, you can fax directly from within Microsoft Messaging to any recipient in the Personal Address Book.

Step 2: Action

1. Start WordPad and type a paragraph of text.

2. Select **F**ile | **P**rint.

3. Display the dropdown listbox labeled Name, and select Microsoft Fax for your destination printer. Microsoft Fax begins with the Compose New Fax window.

4. Click the **N**ext command button to display the Compose New Fax dialog box, shown in Figure 23.7.

Figure 23.7.

Microsoft Fax is getting ready to send your fax.

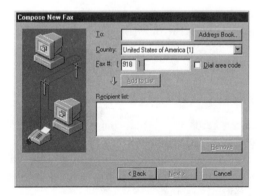

23

5. If the recipient's name and fax number appear in your Personal Address Book, press the Address Book button to switch to the Personal Address Book, and then select the name. Otherwise, type a name and number to whom you want to send the fax and press **Add** to List to add the name to the list of recipients at the bottom of the screen. You can enter additional recipients if you like.

6. Click the **Next** command button and choose the cover page style that you want. Microsoft Fax includes several standard cover pages of varying importance, or you can choose **No** to send only the document without a cover page. In addition, the Start menu's Fax menu includes a Cover Page Editor program with which you can edit the cover pages that come with Microsoft Fax or create your own by using the text and drawing tools available in the program.

   If you want to send the fax at a time in the future, press the **O**ptions button to set the sending time (don't change any of the options now).

7. Click the **Next** command button twice to send the fax. You can do something else in Windows 95 while the Microsoft Fax sends the fax.

23

TIME SAVER

> If you want to send a fax from Microsoft Messaging, select Compose New Fax from the Microsoft Messaging menu. There is also a Microsoft Fax menu on the Accessories menu, from which you can design your own cover pages, compose a new fax without first working in a word processor or Microsoft Messaging, and control the way you receive faxes from fax-retrieval services.

8. Microsoft Fax tells you when the fax is finished, and you then can close the application or resend the fax if the line was busy or didn't answer. If the line was busy or didn't answer, double-click the fax sheet by the taskbar clock to send the fax again.

Step 3: Review

Microsoft Fax makes faxing almost as easy as printing a document on a printer. Fax all your documents and graphic files from Windows 95. If the recipient is also using Windows 95, the recipient will receive the file in the file's native format.

JUST A MINUTE

> There are options within the Microsoft Fax program that you can set to send a fax as a standard fax instead of as an RTF document, even if Windows 95 answers the recipient's phone.

Task 23.5: Receiving Faxes

Step 1: Description

Unless you are already set up to receive faxes, Windows 95 does not make the receive fax designation obvious. If you don't see a fax machine icon to the left of your taskbar's clock, you cannot receive faxes. To set up your computer to receive faxes, follow this task.

Step 2: Action

1. Start Windows 95 Messaging (you can double-click your desktop's Inbox icon to start Windows 95 Messaging).

2. Select **T**ools | Microsoft Fa**x** Tools | **O**ptions.

3. Click the Modem tab to display the Modem dialog box, shown in Figure 23.8.

Figure 23.8.

Setting up the modem to receive faxes.

4. Click your fax modem to highlight the modem name if it is not already highlighted.

5. Click **P**roperties to display the Properties dialog box.

6. To receive only faxes, click the **A**nswer after option and enter the number of rings you want to occur before Microsoft Fax receives the fax. If you receive both faxes and voice calls on the line, click the **M**anual option. When you get a call, Microsoft Fax will display a command button that you can click to answer the fax, or you can pick up the phone if the call is a voice call. (You'll have to know when you're expecting a fax in order to click when needed.) The **D**on't Answer option makes Microsoft Fax ignore all incoming calls.

7. Click OK twice to close the dialog boxes and return to Microsoft Messaging.

Step 3: Review

If you don't see a fax machine icon on your Windows 95 taskbar, you will see the icon after you complete this task. The Microsoft Fax program both sends and recieves faxes but must
▲ load Microsoft Fax first.

TIME SAVER

If you've turned off the receipt of faxes, you can still receive a fax that you know is incoming on the line by selecting Request a Fax from the Fax menu on the Accessories Start menu.

23

JUST A MINUTE

You might want to change the *redial properties* on the Microsoft Fax properties sheet's Dialing page. The redialing properties determine how many retries to attempt when a faxed number is busy or does not answer and specifies the time to wait between retries.

Disable Call Waiting!

If you have call waiting, you'll need to disable the feature before using your modem for fax or data transmissions. Fortunately, you can disable call waiting very easily. Open the Modems dialog box from the Control Panel and click the **D**ialing Properties button to see the dialog box shown in Figure 23.9. Click the option labeled This location has call **w**aiting, and then enter the code to disable your call waiting feature; this code is usually *#70*. When you close the Dialing Properties dialog box, Windows 95 will disable call waiting before each call.

Figure 23.9.

You can disable call waiting.

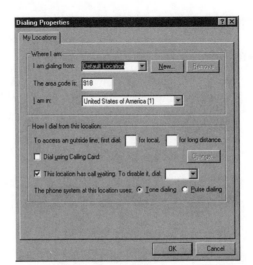

CAUTION

#70 usually, but not always, disables the call waiting feature. Check with your local phone company to make sure that you enter the correct code. Often you'll find the call waiting disabling dialing sequence in the front of your phone book.

Summary

This hour explained how to use Microsoft Messaging to work as the central messaging center for your computer. As you add online services to Microsoft Messaging's profile settings, you'll be able to let Microsoft Messaging send and receive all your e-mail messages instead of having to log on to every service and do the job yourself.

Microsoft Messaging integrates itself with the Phone Dialer application, as well as with Microsoft Fax and the Personal Address Book. This enables you to have one command center for all your communications.

Microsoft Fax integrates your fax/modem to work with all Windows 95 applications that print. Instead of going to the printer, the fax documents will route through Microsoft Fax so that you can send the document to a recipient within the Personal Address Book or to a new recipient whose fax number you enter. One of the most interesting features of Microsoft Fax is the recipient analysis that Microsoft Fax makes. If the recipient is running Windows 95, the recipient receives your fax as a normal Windows 95 document file instead of as a fax. That way the recipient has more flexibility in working with the file than if he or she received the document as a paper fax.

Workshop

Term Review

attach   Add a binary file to an e-mail message so the receiving user can receive the binary file or load the file using tools available to the receiving user.

carbon copy   A secondary recipient that gets a copy of someone's e-mail message.

e-mail Message files sent electronically to others, who receive the messages via a modem. E-mail stands for *electronic mail.*

header   A one-line message that describes the sender information for electronic messages.

23

Microsoft Messaging   The application that uses a universal Inbox to log on to all your electronic mail sources and to send and receive any waiting mail.

Microsoft Fax   A program that uses your fax modem to send and receive faxes, as well as to create cover pages and provide for viewing of received faxes.

paperless society   The lofty and incorrect prediction from the early 1970s that said electronic mail and files would replace most of the paper used in the workplace and homes.

Personal Address Book   A central address book that holds people's names, phone numbers, addresses, fax numbers, e-mail numbers, and notes.

profile   A file that describes a specific online service to Microsoft Messaging. Once Microsoft Messaging reads an online service's profile, Microsoft Messaging can manage that service's information, using the Windows 95 universal Inbox.

redial properties   Determines how many retries and the time between retries Microsoft Fax attempts when a called fax number is busy or does not answer.

Rich-Text Format (RTF)   A file format that enables different applications to exchange formatted documents.

universal Inbox   A central repository of electronic mail where you can send, receive, and manage all your electronic mail and faxes.

Q&A

Q How do I copy my old phone dialing program's address book to Personal Address Book?

A Unfortunately, there probably is no way to import such older address book files unless your phone dialing software company supplies you with a conversion program.

Q I don't know whether or not I'm faxing to a recipient running Microsoft Fax under Windows 95. Do I fax or send my file as e-mail?

A As long as you have a recipient's fax number, go ahead and fax the document. If the recipient is running Windows 95, your copy of Windows 95 will know that right away and, instead of sending a fax, automatically will send a document as if it were e-mail. If the recipient does have a standard fax machine, your Windows 95 system will know that, too, and send the document using a standard fax signal.

Hour 24

Windows 95's Internet Explorer

In today's world, the Internet is much more a part of computer users' lives than ever before. When Windows 95 was introduced in late 1995, even Microsoft underestimated the Internet's impact. The company soon released Internet Explorer, an Internet *browser* that lets you access the Internet from within Windows 95.

If you don't have Internet Explorer, Microsoft lets you download the program free of charge from its Web site (www.microsoft.com). Of course, if you have no Internet access available to you, how can you download the file? Fortunately, Microsoft does sell Internet Explorer in stores and through mail-order outlets at a low cost if you have no access to the program and already have Windows 95 without Internet Explorer.

This hour winds down the book's 24-hour clock by giving you a crash Internet course and by teaching you some of the ways Windows 95 integrates with the Internet. In addition, you'll learn how to use Internet Explorer. Microsoft has promised to integrate Internet Explorer even more completely into subsequent Windows 95 updates by making Internet Explorer a part of the Windows 95 interface—at which point, Microsoft may rename Windows 95 to something else.

The highlights of this hour include:

- [ ] What makes the Internet such an important online tool
- [ ] Why modern Internet access techniques, such as Web pages, make the Internet more manageable
- [ ] How to start and use Internet Explorer to surf the Internet
- [ ] How you can navigate the Internet and view the multimedia information you find there
- [ ] Where you must go to obtain Internet access
- [ ] How to specify search criteria so that you can locate the exact Internet information you need

The Internet

The Internet is a world-wide system of interconnected computers. Whereas your desktop computer is a stand-alone machine, and a network of computers is tied together by wires, the Internet is a world-wide on-line network of computers connected as well to stand-alone computers through modems. Hardly anyone understands the Internet because the Internet is not one system but a conglomeration of systems.

The Internet began as a government and university-linked system of computers, but it has now grown to a business and personal system that contains almost an infinite amount of information. The Internet is so vast that nobody would be able to access all of its information today.

JUST A MINUTE

There is no central Internet computer anywhere. Instead, the Internet is a system of connected computers. *Internet* is the term given to the entire system. The term *Web* is given to the interconnected system of Internet information pages that you can access to read specific information, as described throughout this hour.

24

TIME SAVER

> For an in-depth look at the Internet, you might want to read *The Internet Unleashed 1997* (ISBN 1-57521-185-8) published by Sams.net.

The Internet's vastness almost caused its downfall. How does one access or find information on the Internet? Fortunately, Internet technicians began standardizing Internet information when it became apparent that the Internet was growing and becoming a major information provider.

The WWW: World Wide Web

The *WWW*, or *World Wide Web*, or just *Web*, is a collection of Internet pages of information. Web pages can contain text, graphics, sound, and video. Figure 24.1 shows a sample Web page. As you can see, the Web page's graphics and text organize information into a magazine-like readable and appealing format.

24

Figure 24.1.

Web pages provide Internet information in a nice format.

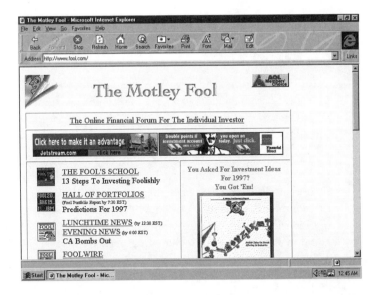

Generally, a Web site might contain more information than will fit easily on a single Web page. Therefore, many Web pages contain links to several additional extended pages, as well as other linked Web pages that may be related to the original topic. The first page you view is called the *home page*, and from the home page you can view other pages of information.

JUST A MINUTE

Each Web page has a unique location that includes the source computer and the location on that computer but such locations would be difficult to keep track of. Therefore, the Internet has standardized Web page locations with a series of addresses called *URLs*, or *Uniform Resource Locator addresses*. You can view any Web page if you know its URL. If you do not know the URL, the Internet provides several *search engines* that find Web pages when you search for topics.

TIME SAVER

Surely you've run across computer addresses that look like this: www.microsoft.com and www.mcp.com; these are URLs that access the Web pages for Microsoft Corporation and Macmillan Computer Publishing.

Introducing the Internet Explorer Web Browser

Before you can access and view Web information, you need a program that can display Web page information including text, graphics, audio, and video. The program you need is called a *Web browser*—or just a *browser*. Although several companies offer browsers, Windows 95 integrates one of the best Web browsing programs, called *Internet Explorer*.

In many Windows 95 installations, Windows 95 comes with the Internet Explorer browser program. Again, if you don't have Internet Explorer, you'll have to get it before you can follow these examples. If you've installed another vendor's browser, such as Netscape Navigator, you can use that browser from Windows 95 to access Web pages. This hour's figures and tasks use Internet Explorer because it integrates so nicely with Windows 95 and because newer Windows 95 installations include Internet Explorer.

JUST A MINUTE

Remember that Microsoft developers have stated they plan to integrate Internet Explorer more and more into the Windows 95 environment. Perhaps Microsoft will even do away with Explorer in future operating systems and will use a form of Internet Explorer to browse both Internet pages and files on your computer.

24

Before you can access the Internet's Web pages, you'll need to get Internet access through an *ISP*, or *Internet Service Provider*. One of the easiest ways to get access is through the Microsoft Network, which has access programs that are available with all Windows 95 installations. If you want Internet access through another ISP, such as a local Internet provider, your provider will tell you how to use Internet Explorer or another Web browser to access the ISP's Internet system.

Task 24.1: Starting Internet Explorer

Step 1: Description

Internet Explorer is easy to start. You literally can access the Internet with one or two clicks by running Internet Explorer. This task explains how to start Internet Explorer. You must already have Internet access through the Microsoft Network or another provider and you must know the phone number to that provider. (Your provider will have to give you the specific access and setup details.)

Step 2: Action

1. Double-click the Windows 95 desktop icon labeled The Internet. If you get an Internet Connection Wizard dialog box, you must contact your service provider to learn how to hook up Internet Explorer to the Internet.

2. If you access the Internet through the Microsoft Network provider, you'll see Figure 24.2's dialog box.

Figure 24.2.

You may need to log into the Microsoft Network to use Internet Explorer.

Enter your Microsoft Network Member ID and password and click **C**onnect to dial up the Internet. If you use another Internet provider, Windows 95 will either automatically call your Internet number or display another log on dialog box similar to the one in Figure 24.2.

3. Assuming that you have Internet access and you've been set up with a provider, Internet Explorer will now dial your provider and display the page set up to be your initial browser's *start page*. Depending on the amount of information and graphics on the page, the display may take a few moments or may display right away.

JUST A MINUTE

Internet Explorer's toolbar button labeled Home displays your start page. You can return to Internet Explorer's start page by clicking the Home button. You can change your start page address by entering a new start page within the **V**iew | **O**ptions dialog box's Navigation page. When you enter a new start page address, Internet Explorer will return to that page whenever you click the Home toolbar button or start Internet Explorer in a subsequent session.

Step 3: Review

Using Internet Explorer to access the Internet and Web pages requires just one or two clicks. Internet Explorer automatically displays an initial start Web page from which you then can access additional Web pages and surf the Internet!

Task 24.2: Managing the Internet Explorer Screen

Step 1: Description

TASK

Internet Explorer makes it easy to navigate Web pages. Before looking at a lot of Internet information, take a few minutes to familiarize yourself with the Internet Explorer screen.

Step 2: Action

1. Study Figure 24.3 to learn the parts of the Internet Explorer screen. Internet Explorer will display your start page and will list the start page's address in the address area.

2. Some Web site addresses are lengthy. Drag the Address text box left or right (giving more or less room to the link buttons) to adjust the address display width.

3. Click the down arrow at the right of the address entry to open a list of recently traversed site addresses. If this is the first time you or anyone has used your computer's Internet Explorer, you may not see sites other than the current start page sites.

4. Adjust the scroll bar to see more of your start page. Most Web pages take more room than will fit on one screen.

Figure 24.3.

Learn the Internet Explorer screen so that you can maximize the Internet Explorer browser.

Menu bar   URL address entry/display   Toolbar   Links to common Web sites

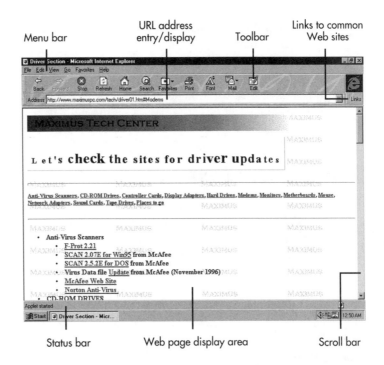

Status bar   Web page display area   Scroll bar

5. Use the **View** menu to get rid of the toolbar and status bar. As Figure 24.4 shows, the address list box goes away as well. Getting rid of the toolbar and status bar gives you more display room for the Web page. You can still enter site addresses that you want to traverse from the **File** menu.

Figure 24.4.

Although you can gain more screen room, you'll probably miss the toolbar and status bar.

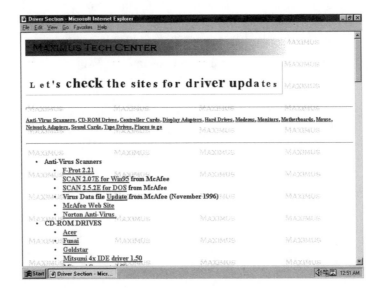

6. Display the toolbar and status bar once again by clicking the appropriate **View** menu options.

Step 3: Review

Familiarize yourself with Internet Explorer's screen elements. As you traverse the Internet, Internet Explorer will aid you—as you'll see throughout the rest of this chapter. By adjusting the screen's elements, you can see more or less of large Web pages you encounter.

Surfing the Internet

Remember that the Internet's Web is a collection of inter-connected Web pages. Almost every Web page contains links to other sites. These links (often called *hot links* or *hypertext links*) are often underlined. You'll be able to locate these links by moving your mouse cursor over the underlined description. If the mouse cursor changes to a hand, you can click the hand to move to that page. After a brief pause, your Web browser will display the page.

TIME SAVER

A link is nothing more than a URL address to the other Web site. The link often displays a description and not a technical URL address. (As you move your mouse cursor over a link, your Web browser's status bar displays the actual URL address to the link.) Therefore, you can traverse related Web pages without worrying about addresses; just click link descriptions to move to those sites.

Suppose you view the home page of your financial broker. The page might include links to other related pages, such as stock quotation pages, company financial informational pages, and order-entry pages in which you can enter your own stock purchase requests.

One of the most useful features of Internet Explorer and every other Web browser is the browser's ability to return to sites you've visited both in the current session and in former sessions. The toolbar's Back button takes you back to a site you just visited and you can keep clicking the Back button to return to pages you've visited this session. The Forward toolbar button returns you to pages from where you've backed up.

At any point, you can click the Address dropdown listbox to see a list of URL addresses you've visited. (See Figure 24.5.) You'll find addresses from the current as well as previous Internet Explorer Web sessions.

24

Figure 24.5.

Internet Explorer keeps track of recent Web page addresses you've visited.

Recent URLs ──

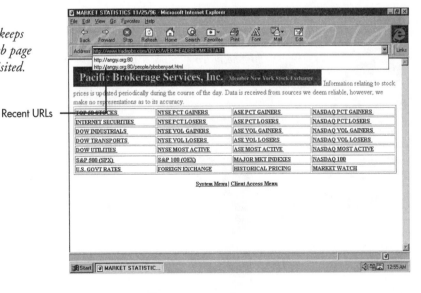

If you know the address of a Web site you want to view, you can type the site's address directly in the Address textbox. When you press Enter, Internet Explorer takes you to that site and displays the Web page. In addition, you can select **F**ile | **O**pen to display Figure 24.6's dialog box and enter an address in the dialog box. When you click OK, Internet Explorer displays the page associated with that address.

Figure 24.6.

You can enter a Web address in this Open dialog box.

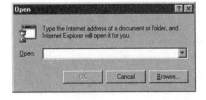

JUST A MINUTE

As discussed previously, Microsoft will probably integrate Internet Explorer more fully into Windows 95 and Windows 95 applications. Most of the Office 97 products, for example, include an Internet Explorer-like interface in many areas, and they link directly to Internet Explorer when you perform certain Internet-related tasks from within an Office 97 product. In some cases, you can bypass Explorer when you want a file listing or when you want to view a file while surfing the Internet Web pages. Select **F**ile | **O**pen to display the Open dialog box (refer to Figure 24.6). Instead of entering a URL address, type a disk, pathname, and filename. If Internet Explorer recognizes the file's registered type, you'll see the file's contents, *from within the Internet Explorer browser,* as shown in Figure 24.7.

Figure 24.7.

Internet Explorer displays files as well as Web page contents.

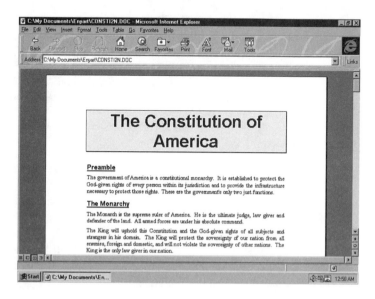

If you find a location you really like, save that location in Internet Explorer's Favorites list. (Often, these Favorites lists are called browser *bookmarks*.) For example, if you run across a site that discusses your favorite television show and you want to return to that site again quickly, click the Favorites toolbar button and add the site to your Favorites list. The Address history does not keep track of a lot of recently visited addresses; you can, however, store your favorite sites in the Favorites folders so that you can quickly access them during another Internet session.

TIME SAVER

Many non-browser products, such as Microsoft Office 97, let you add Web links to non-Internet documents such as Word documents. When you type a URL address in Word, Word will underline the address. If you—or someone who reads your document from within Word—clicks on the URL link, Word automatically starts Internet Explorer (or whatever browser you use); as soon as Internet Explorer locates the page, it appears on-screen.

24

Task 24.3: Moving Between Pages

Step 1: Description

This task lets you practice using the Internet Explorer browser to move between Web pages. After you visit a site, you can return to that site very simply.

Step 2: Action

1. If you have not started Internet Explorer, start it and log onto the Internet.

2. Click the Address listbox to highlight your start page's URL address.

3. Type the following Web page address: http://www.mcp.com. You'll see Macmillan Publishing's home page appear, as shown in Figure 24.8. (Depending on the changes that have been made to the site recently, the site may not match Figure 24.8 exactly.)

CAUTION

> Often, you'll see Web addresses prefaced with the text http://. This prefix lets you and your browser both know that the address to the right of the second slash is a Web page's URL address. Be sure to type forward slashes and not the MS-DOS backslashes you are used to typing on PCs.

Figure 24.8.

Macmillan Publishing's home page.

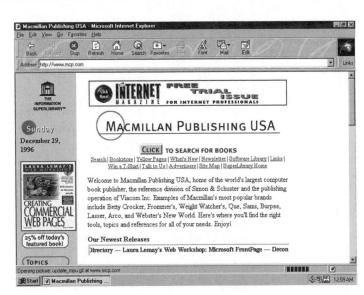

4. Click any link on the page. After a brief pause, you'll see the linked Web page.

5. Click the toolbar's Back button. Almost instantly, the first page appears.

JUST A MINUTE

> Internet Explorer (as well as most browsers) keeps a history of Web page content in memory and on your disk. Therefore, if you revisit a Web site that you've recently viewed, your browser will most likely still have that site in its storage buffer. Instead of waiting for a long download once again, the page appears quickly because your browser actually reloads the page from memory and not from the original site.

6. Once back at Macmillan Publishing's home page, practice building a favorite site list by clicking the Favorites toolbar button.

7. Click the **Add** To Favorites option. Internet Explorer displays the Add to Favorites dialog box.

8. Enter a description for the page. Make the description something you will remember the page by (such as `Macmillan Computer Book Publishing`).

9. Click OK.

10. Click the Favorites toolbar button once again. You'll see the new entry. When you select the favorite entry, Internet Explorer will look up that entry's stored URL address and will go to that Web page.

Step 3: Review

The toolbar makes it easy to visit and revisit Web sites that interest you. You can return to previous sites and move forward once again. The Favorites toolbar button lets you add descriptions to your favorite Web sites so that you can return to those sites by clicking your mouse over the site's description in the Favorites list.

JUST A MINUTE

> If you add too many favorites, your favorites list might become unmanageable. When you add to your favorites list, you'll be able to create folders from the Add to Favorites dialog box's **C**reate In button. By setting up a series of named folders named by subjects, you can group your favorite Web sites by subject.

24

TIME SAVER

Visit Microsoft's site often. Microsoft will give you advanced information on Windows 95 correction files available, as well as information on future products and helpful tips you can use to make your life with Windows 95 better.

Speeding Web Displays

You'll find that some Web pages take a long time to display. Often, Web pages contain a lot of text and graphics and that data takes time to arrive on your computer. Therefore, you might click to a favorite Web site but have to wait a minute or longer to see the entire site.

To speed things, Internet Explorer will attempt to show as much of the page as possible, especially the text on the page, before downloading the graphic images. Internet Explorer puts placeholders where the graphic images will appear. For example, Figure 24.9 shows a Web page with placeholders. This page appears quickly. If you view this page for a few moments, the placeholders' images begin to appear until the final page displays in its entirety, as in Figure 24.10.

Figure 24.9.

Placeholders let you see the overall Web page design and text.

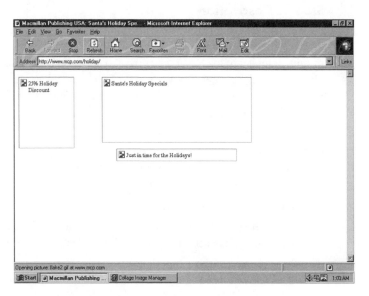

Figure 24.10.

After the images all arrive, the placeholders turn into graphic images.

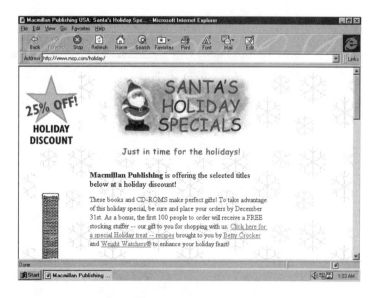

Task 24.4: Refreshing and Stopping the Display

Step 1: Description

As you saw in the previous task, Internet Explorer saves recent Web page contents in a memory buffer. Therefore, even if a Web page contains lots of information and requires a minute or longer to load, if you return to that page in a subsequent session, your browser will often display the in-memory Web page. Although the memory buffer speeds things up, you may not want to see the buffer's Web page. You might, instead, want to see the original page in case the site has changed since your last visit.

Step 2: Action

1. Return to Macmillan Publishing's Web site once again (`http://www.mcp.com`, in case you did not save the site).

2. Click on a link from that site.

3. Click the Back button to go right back. The site should appear almost instantly because you are actually viewing the site from your stored memory buffer.

4. Suppose you suspect that data has changed on the site and you want to see the real address's site once again. Click the toolbar's Refresh button. Internet Explorer will reload the Web page from its original location. After the page loads, you'll see the page once again with any updates that may have been applied since your last visit.

5. Click the Refresh button once again to redisplay the page, but then immediately click the toolbar's Stop button. Instantly, Internet Explorer stops refreshing the

24

page. Any graphic images not yet loaded will remain as placeholders and will not appear no matter how long you view the page. The Stop button is useful for stopping the loading of a slow-loading Web page. If you have no need to see the images but you're only interested in the text that quickly appears, you can reduce the Internet traffic by stopping the page before it completely loads. Obviously, you will not want to stop the loading process unless you are familiar with the page's contents.

Step 3: Review

Use the Stop and Refresh buttons to control the loading of Web pages. The Stop button keeps Web pages from fully loading. You can click Stop as soon as you see as much of the page as you want to see. Click Refresh if you view a Web page from your memory buffer but want to reload the page from its URL address. If you suspect that a Web page has been updated since you last visited the page, click Refresh so that you can be assured you've seen the most recent version.

24

Search for the Information You Need

How can you expect to find any information on a vast network of networks such as the Internet? Web pages offer linked sites in an appealing format that lets you comfortably view information and see related pages, but you must know the location of one of the site's pages before the links can help.

Fortunately, Internet Explorer (as well as most Internet Web browsers) offers a searching mechanism that helps you locate information on the Web. By clicking the Search toolbar button, you can access the Microsoft Web page shown in Figure 24.11.

CAUTION

> The Web page you see may differ from the one in Figure 24.11 because Microsoft changes the page quite often.

The search Web page offers the benefit of multiple *search engines.* A search engine is a Web program that lets you enter words and phrases to search for, and then the search engine scans the vast information on the Web to locate sites that contain the phrase. The accuracy of the search depends on the words and phrases you enter, as well as the capability of the search engine. For example, some search engines you can choose from will search only Web pages while others will search *newsgroups* (discussion areas that hold files and messages related to topics).

Figure 24.11.

Select from one of several Web search engines.

TIME SAVER

If you find that one of the search engines locates information for you better than the others, you can make that search engine the default by clicking the Set Default command button. If you do not set a default search engine, Internet Explorer will select a different one from the list each time you visit the search site. Even if you don't set a default, you can select whatever search engine you want to use by clicking on it when the search page appears.

After the search page concludes the search, Internet Explorer displays from zero to several address links on which you can click to find information about your topic. For example, Figure 24.12 shows the result of one search. By scrolling down the page (and by clicking the additional pages of links if your search turns up a lot of sites), you can read the descriptions of the pages (the descriptions often contain the first few lines of the located Web page text).

Each search engine locates information differently and each search engine has its own rules for the words and phrases you enter. Keep in mind that the more specific your search phrase is, the more accurately the search engine can find information that will help you.

TIME SAVER

If your search failed to locate information you think is on the Web, or if the search turned up too many sites and you want to narrow the search, you can often click the site list's pages Options or More Information button to read the search criteria rules for that search engine.

24

Figure 24.12.
The results of a search might produce several pages of Web sites.

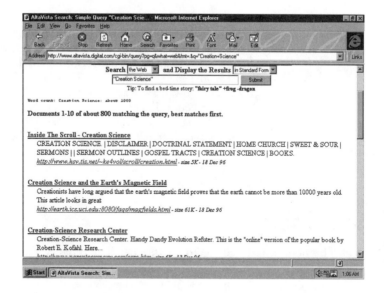

Generally, you can use these guidelines with most search engines:

- Enclose a multiple word phrase in quotation marks if you want the search engine to search for those words in the order you list. For example, if you enter `"Bill Clinton"`, the search engine searches for that specific name. If, however, you enter `Bill Clinton` (without the quotes), most search engines locate every site that contains the word *Bill* and every site that contains the word *Clinton,* most of which would have nothing to do with the man you originally wanted to locate.

- Place the word AND between the words or quoted phrases when you want to search for Web sites that contain every word and phrase in the list. For example, entering `"Rush Limbaugh" AND Congress` would find *only* those sites that contain the name *Rush Limbaugh* and the word *Congress,* but would not find sites that listed only one or the other.

- Place the word OR between the words or quoted phrases if you want to search for sites that contain one or more of your words and phrases. For example, entering `"Bill Clinton" OR "Rush Limbaugh"` would locate any and every site that contains the name *Bill Clinton* or that contains the name *Rush Limbaugh* or that contains both names.

Remember that these search criteria rules are only guidelines that often work. Some of the search engines follow slightly different rules and you'll have to look up that search engine page's help references for specific information if the previous rules do not seem to work the way you expect.

JUST A MINUTE

Most of the search engines are *case sensitive* when you mix uppercase and lowercase characters in your search; that is, you need to type words and phrases exactly as you expect them to appear if you want the search to match your search case exactly. Otherwise, if you enter a search criteria in all lowercase letters, the search engines generally do not base the match on case. Therefore, if you want to locate the city named *Flint* (in Michigan), enter `Flint`. Otherwise, if you enter the name in all lowercase letters, the search engine will probably search both for the city name as well as the rock.

Summary

This hour introduced you to the Internet. The Internet is a vast collection of inter-related computers all around the world. You can access the Internet as long as you have access through an Internet Service Provider. Although Internet information appears in many forms, the most useful Internet often appears on Web pages that contain text, graphics, sound, and video.

Windows 95 supports the Internet Explorer Web browser with which you can view Web pages. Internet Explorer includes searching tools as well as a history system that keeps track of recent Web pages. Not only can you view Web pages with Internet Explorer, but you can also view other kinds of files on your computer. As the Internet becomes more organized and as Internet access gets faster and cheaper, you will make the Web browser more and more of your daily computing routine. One day, you'll find that you do most of your work from Web browsing software such as Internet Explorer.

Workshop

Term Review

bookmarks   Web sites you've stored in the Favorites area so that you can easily return to the sites without knowing their addresses.

browser   Software that searches for, loads, and displays information from Internet Web pages. Browsers display the text, graphics, sound, and even video that appear on modern Web pages.

home page   A Web site's foundational page from which all other pages connect. Often, your browser's start page will be the home page of a Web site such as Microsoft's home page.

hot links (Also called *links* and *hypertext links*) Web page items with descriptions that you can click to display other Web pages. Often, a Web page will contain several links to other sites that contain related information.

hypertext links See *hot links.*

Internet A collection of networked computer systems that you can dial into by using a modem that contains a vast assortment of information.

Internet Explorer The Web browsing software that Microsoft gives away to Windows 95 users.

search engine A program that locates information on the Web.

site The location of a Web page or set of related Web pages.

start page The page your Web browser initially shows when you first log onto the Internet.

URL address (Stands for *Uniform Resource Locator*) The technical address of a Web page's location. When you enter the URL address in your browser's Address textbox, the browser will locate that address's Web page and display the Web page's contents.

Web A system for formatting Internet information into readable and manageable pages of text, graphics, video, and sound.

WWW (Stands for *Wide World Web*) See *Web.*

24

Q&A

Q I've clicked the Internet icon but I don't see Web pages. What do I have to do to get on the Internet?

A Do you have Internet access from Microsoft Network or from another Internet service provider? Generally, unless you work for a company that offers Internet access to its employees, you'll have to sign up for Internet access, get the access phone number, pay a monthly fee (most Internet Service Providers offer unlimited access for a flat monthly rate), and set up your browser, such as Internet Explorer, to access that provider.

If you want to use Microsoft Network, you can sign up and get access by following the wizard that you'll see when you click the Windows 95 desktop's Microsoft Network icon.

Q Does all Internet information appear on Web pages?

A The Internet is standardized only because of a series of loosely compatible *de facto* standards that appeared as more people began using the Internet in the late 1980s and early 1990s. One of the newest of these home-grown standards to appear is Web pages.

The Internet's information appears in many forms, sometimes in a form known as an *FTP site* or a newsgroup. The Web page standard has become one of the most popular ways to organize and view Internet information. As more people began using the Web page standard, more modern technology let that standard evolve into a uniform container of multimedia-based information. Therefore, with a Web browser, one can view all kinds of information over the Web.

Q How do I know if I'm viewing a Web page from the memory buffer or from the actual site?

A If the page appears almost instantly after you enter the address, the chances are great that you are looking at the page from your browser's memory. In most cases, the memory's page will match the actual Web site. Nevertheless, if you want to make sure you're viewing the latest and greatest version of the Web page, click the Refresh toolbar button. Refresh forces Internet Explorer to reload the page from the actual site's address.

Q Which Internet browser should I use?

A Because Microsoft now supplies Internet Explorer with all versions of Windows 95, and because Microsoft has strongly suggested that Internet Explorer will become more of a part of Windows 95-like operating systems in the future, readers of this book will likely find that Internet Explorer works well with Windows 95. I have tried most Web browsers and, due to its tight integration with Windows 95 (as well as the free price tag), prefer Internet Explorer over its competitors for working from within the Windows 95 environment.

Most Web browsing programs offer the same standard features described in this hour's chapter. Nevertheless, not all Web browsers contain the advanced technical features of Internet Explorer—especially a new technology called *Java*. Java is a programming language that lets one store small programs on Web pages; the downside is that users surfing those pages must have a Java-aware Internet browser in order to view Java-based Web pages properly. Internet Explorer seems to do a good job supporting Java, as well as other advanced features such as ActiveX controls. It seems that Microsoft has committed itself to Internet Explorer and will continue to support the product and keep it up-to-date as new Internet technology arrives on the scene.

24

PART V

Appendixes

Hour

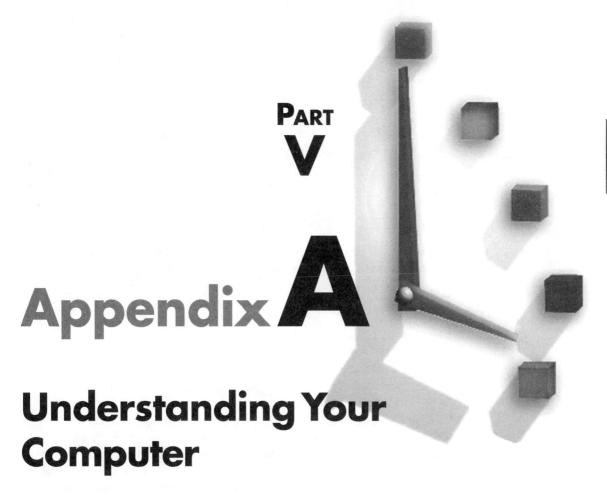

Appendix A

Understanding Your Computer

Perhaps you are brand new to computers. If so, you are in luck because Microsoft, the company that wrote Windows 95, wrote the Windows 95 operating system with you in mind. As a matter of fact, Microsoft used several new computer users to thoroughly test Windows 95 during the product's design.

This appendix will not make you an expert at computers. In fact, this appendix only briefly introduces computers. If, however, you have not used a computer much and have *no* idea what an operating system is, this appendix will certainly make you feel more comfortable in front of your computer. After you finish this appendix, you will have more insight into the world of computers, and you'll understand better how Windows 95 helps you work with your computer.

Often, desktop and laptop computers are called *PCs,* which stands for *Personal Computers.* Whether you have a full-sized desktop PC or a small laptop PC, the background in this appendix applies to either.

The Computer's Hardware

Your computer is made up of several *hardware* components. The hardware consists of the physical devices that you can touch and see. All of the following are hardware devices:

- The system unit
- The disk and CD-ROM drives
- The keyboard
- The screen
- The printer
- The mouse

Figure A.1 contains a diagram that illustrates each of these hardware components. The disk and CD-ROM drives, keyboard, screen, printer, and mouse are often called *peripheral devices* because they plug into the system unit and support the computer's operation. Peripheral devices are either *input devices, output devices,* or *input/output devices* (sometimes called *I/O devices*), depending on the data flow direction between the device and the system unit. If data flows out from the system unit to a device such as the printer, that device is an output device. The keyboard is an input device because data goes from the keyboard into the system unit. Disk drives are I/O devices because data flows in both directions between the system unit and the disk drives.

Figure A.1.

Your computer is made up of many hardware devices.

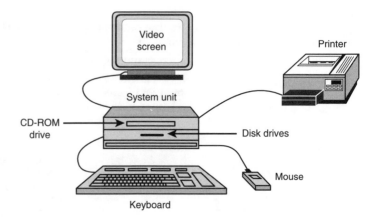

A

The System Unit

The system unit is the primary controlling unit of your computer. Often the system unit is a large box that sits on the floor or on your desktop. Many people put their video screens on top of their system units. The system unit holds the following elements:

☐ The *CPU,* which stands for the *Central Processing Unit.* The CPU controls the rest of your computer and processes all the data that goes through the machine. The CPU resides on a wafer-like *integrated circuit chip* that is small enough to fit in the palm of your hand. The small size of the CPU makes laptop computers and pocket calculators possible.

☐ The *memory* that stores short-term data. There are two kinds of memory: *RAM* and *ROM*.

The most important is RAM, which stands for *Random Access Memory.* Before your CPU can process data and run programs, that data and those programs must be in RAM. As a secretary creates a document using a word processor, that document lives in RAM memory and is saved permanently, only if the secretary saves the document to a disk drive. When you purchase a computer, you should buy as much RAM as you can afford because the more RAM that your computer has the faster the computer typically runs. Windows 95 requires eight megabytes of memory to run well.

ROM stands for *Read Only Memory* and is a secondary memory that contains some system start-up instructions.

☐ The power supply that ensures your computer gets enough continual power to perform its computing tasks.

The system unit is the actual computer. When you buy a computer, try to buy the latest system unit and as much memory as possible, even if it means settling for a less-expensive video screen and printer. Later, you can always upgrade the screen and printer. If you cannot afford more than eight megabytes of memory you can add more later.

Disk and CD-ROM Drives

The two kinds of disk drives are: *Hard disk drives,* which are non-removable, fast, and hold a considerable amount of information; and *floppy disk drives,* which are slower than hard disks and do not hold as much information, but you can use removable *diskettes* in the floppy disk drives so that you can transfer and share data between two or more computers.

JUST A MINUTE

> The term *drive* refers to the box in which you insert diskettes and CD-ROMs. Hard disk drives contain non-removable disk platters that hold data and programs.

The disk drives provide for long-term memory. When you power off your computer the data on the disks remains on the disks. Like a cassette tape, the data leaves a disk drive only when you issue commands to remove that data. Disk data is often called *non-volatile memory*. The contents of RAM disappears when you turn off your computer.

The disks and RAM work in tandem with each other. When you need to run a program, such as a word processor, you'll instruct the computer to load that program from a disk drive into RAM memory. Once loaded into RAM, your CPU can then execute the instructions in that program.

JUST A MINUTE

> Programs are discussed more fully in a later section.

Disks, even large hard disks, rarely hold as much information as CD-ROM drives. A CD-ROM drive holds compact disks that look just like the audio CDs you've seen and listened to. As a matter of fact, all of today's CD-ROM drives play music from audio CDs as easily as they read data from CD-ROMs that contain computer data and programs. A CD-ROM drive typically holds over 600 million characters of information. Although CD-ROMs are slow, their capacity makes them almost a staple item in today's computers. *Multimedia* (the audio and video capabilities of computers) often requires the huge storage capacities of CD-ROM drives to hold motion video and sound.

JUST A MINUTE

> Memory and disks are measured by their storage capacities. Generally, the more data they hold, the better and more expensive disks and memory are. Today's disks and memory hold so much data that computerists have developed a shortcut that represents the amount of data a device can hold.
>
> One character of storage is called a *byte*. One thousand bytes is often called a *kilobyte*. Actually one kilobyte (or 1KB for short) is exactly 1,024 bytes because the internal nature of today's digital memory requires that memory amounts fall on a power of 2 boundary.
>
> One million bytes is called a *megabyte* or *meg*, or M for short. One billion bytes is called a *gigabyte* or *gig* for short. Therefore, if a CD-ROM holds approximately 600 million characters of data, that CD-ROM is known as a *600-meg CD-ROM drive*.

A

New kinds of disk drives are appearing every day. Today you can purchase a removable disk drive that falls somewhat between a hard disk and a floppy disk. The storage capacity exceeds that of many hard disks (you can get more than 1 gigabyte of removable disk storage), and these disk drives use removable disk cartridges that act and look a lot like floppy disks. In addition, advanced CD-ROM technology is making CD-ROMs available in a writeable format so that you can record your own CD-ROMs. The CD technology is progressing in storage capacity also so that CDs in the future will be able to hold much more storage than today's.

The Keyboard

New users rarely have a problem adapting to computer keyboards because the keyboard works almost exactly like a typewriter's keyboard. There are several *alphanumeric* keys that hold the numbers and letters laid out identically to a typewriter's alphanumeric keys. Figure A.2 shows a typical computer keyboard.

Figure A.2.

Computer keyboards look like typewriter keyboards with some additional keys.

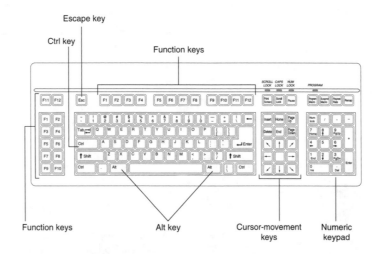

The Enter key often works like a carriage return key on a typewriter. You'll sometimes press Enter at the end of a line to signal that you're finished entering that line of text. In most word processors, you will press Enter at the end of a paragraph of text, but not at the end of a line because the word processors usually offer a feature called *word wrap* that automatically brings the cursor to the start of the next line of text as you type.

Often there is a *numeric keypad* to the right of the keyboard. The numeric keypad contains number keys as well as common operator keys that hold an equal sign, plus sign, minus sign, division sign (a slash), and multiplication sign (an asterisk). The keypad allows for quicker numeric data entry than is possible using the numbers across the top of the alphanumeric section of the keyboard.

There are usually two Shift keys for uppercase letters. To type an uppercase *A* you would hold Shift, then press A before releasing both keys. Often, such a combined keystroke is referred to as *Shift+A*. A CapsLock key enables you to lock the keyboard into an uppercase state (all letters appear shifted) until you press CapsLock once again.

In addition to Shift, there are these additional *modifier keys:* Alt and Ctrl. The Alt key (meaning *alternative*) and Ctrl (meaning *control*) give two more levels of shift states. Therefore, you can press A, Shift+A, Alt+A, or Ctrl+A. Different programs use these modifier keys differently. For example, Alt+F might display a list of file options or select an item on the screen.

You'll find 10 or 12 keys labeled *F1* through *F10* (or *F12*). They are called *function keys.* A function key often performs several tasks depending on what you're doing at the time. Each program that you run responds differently to the function keys.

The Esc key (known as the *escape key*) often lets you back up one step when working on your PC. For example, if you start to print a document you can often press Esc to cancel the printing. As with the function keys, each program that you run handles the Esc key differently.

There are always at least four keys with arrows on them. These are the *cursor-movement keys.* A cursor is a blinking underscore, straight vertical line, or box, that indicates where the next typed character will appear on the screen. Often you can move the cursor around the screen using the Up, Down, Left, and Right arrow keys.

JUST A MINUTE

Actually there are two cursors. The *text cursor* (more accurately known as a *caret*), normally a vertical bar, indicates where the next typed character will appear on the screen. The *mouse cursor* is usually a pointing white arrow (although Windows 95 lets you change the mouse cursor to a different shape) that indicates the current position of the mouse on the screen.

Four additional cursor-movement keys, the Home, End, PageUp, and PageDown keys move the text cursor around on the screen. Each of these keys behaves differently depending on how the programs you run react to those keystrokes. During the movement of the text cursor, you can often press the Ins and Del keys to change text already on the screen by inserting and deleting text.

A

The NumLock key is used for converting the numeric keypad from numbers to cursor-movement keys and back again. Hour 18, "Aid via the Accessibility Options," describes a second and more specialized use for NumLock. The ScrollLock key is not used much these days but sometimes controls the *scrolling* of the screen's display. If you are displaying a large document and only part of that document fits on the screen at one time, you can scroll the screen up and down the document to bring other parts of the document into view.

Windows 95 uses the PrtSc key (meaning *print screen*—it may be spelled out on your keyboard) to save a copy of the screen. You can later print or store that screen image to the disk drive.

Keyboards often come with built-in mice or trackballs that give you more room on your desk. In addition, companies are manufacturing more *ergonomically balanced* keyboards. Such keyboards are designed to ease strain on your hands and wrists, and they're a great help for people who use their computers a lot.

The Screen

The computer's video screen is sometimes called a *monitor*. These days almost every screen is capable of displaying color graphics. Without color graphics, Windows 95 would be fairly useless. Windows 95 is known as a *GUI*, or *graphical user interface*, so graphics are an integral part of the nature of Windows 95.

The quality of graphics is measured by a screen's *resolution*. The resolution determines the number and density of dots that combine to create graphics and text. The lowest resolution sold today is called *VGA* (which stands for *Video Graphics Array*), but most computers support higher resolutions such as *super-VGA* standards. As long as your monitor is capable of displaying VGA-resolution graphics, you will be able to work with all Windows 95 features.

CAUTION

Your computer's system unit contains a *video card* into which you plug your video screen. Both your video card and the monitor must be capable of displaying VGA resolution before you will see VGA on your screen.

The Printer

Many kinds of printers are available. Windows 95 supports over 1,600 printer makes and models. Although many printers exist, almost every printer connected to a PC today falls into one of these three categories:

☐ Dot-Matrix: A printer that produces graphics and text by printing dots onto the page much like the way your screen displays output by combining small dots together. Dot-matrix printers are inexpensive and often support a *letter-quality* mode that helps smooth curved lines and make the printer's output look more like typeset letters.

☐ Ink-Jet: This printer prints text and graphics on the page by shooting ink onto the paper. Ink-jet printers are fairly inexpensive and produce high-quality output. Many of today's ink-jet printers also print in color. The low cost and high quality of ink-jet printers has lessened the demand for dot-matrix printers.

☐ Laser printer: This printer draws graphics and text on the page using a laser beam to burn ink into the page. The output quality of laser printers is extremely good, and laser printers are fast. Laser printers are often more expensive than dot-matrix and ink-jet printers, but their prices are coming closer to the lower-end printer prices every day.

JUST A MINUTE

You also can find color versions of ink-jet and laser printers. Color ink-jet printers produce fairly good quality output. Color laser printers produce high-quality output, but are fairly expensive.

The Mouse

Although you can enter several kinds of information using the keyboard, the mouse is the fundamental controlling input device for Windows 95. Due to the graphical nature of Windows 95, you need the mouse for pointing and moving graphics around the screen.

JUST A MINUTE

Hour 1, "What's Windows 95 All About?," explains how to use the mouse.

If you have a desktop computer, be sure to clear plenty of room (about one square foot is good) for mouse movement. Some people use a *trackball,* which is a stationary mouse that takes up less desk space. Many of today's laptop computers contain mice or trackballs that are built into the keyboards or attached to the side of the computer.

A

The Computer's Software

The computer's software consists of programs and data. The term *program* has already been used often in this appendix during the discussion of hardware. Programs fall into the category of software. A program is a set of instructions that direct the computer. The CPU interprets those instructions and either activates one of the hardware devices (such as the printer) or processes data given to the program.

Programs and data reside both on disk drives and in memory. The software on disk drives is safe and remains stored on the disk until you erase the software and data. If you want to run a program (which causes the computer to execute the program's instructions) you'll have to instruct the computer to load the program from the disk into RAM. Only when the program is in RAM can the computer run it.

Windows 95 is an *operating system* that controls all the computer's input and output. Windows 95 is just a program, but it is a program that controls other programs and that enables you to control your computer. Windows 95 turns the computer into a *multitasking* computer, which means that you can run more than one program at once. If you want to work on a word processor and print payroll checks, you can do both at the same time by starting both the word processor program and the payroll program.

JUST A MINUTE

The checks produced by the payroll program, as well as the document that you create inside the word processor, make up the data that resides inside the computer's memory at the time.

Figure A.3 shows what your memory looks like when using a computer and Windows 95. Notice that memory is consumed by Windows 95, by one or more programs, and by data sections that go with each program. The amount of memory not used is known as *free memory* and is available for other programs and data.

JUST A MINUTE

If you do not have enough memory to run several programs at once, Windows 95 can often use disk storage to simulate memory. Windows 95 then swaps data and programs to and from the disk drive as you run the multiple programs. The more memory your computer has, the less swapping that Windows 95 has to perform, and the faster your programs will run.

Figure A.3

The typical contents of RAM.

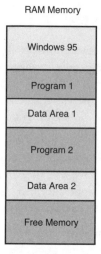

All data and programs reside on your disk drive in *files*. A file is a program or a data document of related information. Files have unique names to distinguish them from one another.

Summary

Most of this appendix dealt with hardware because the rest of the book explains how to use your computer's software. Windows 95 is the controlling element, and Windows 95 must always be loaded and reside inside your computer before you can take advantage of its features, such as multitasking.

Now that you've been introduced to the computer's elementary hardware and software concepts, you're ready to begin using Windows 95. Turn now to the first hour and start Windows 95. You'll be a productive computer user (and computer lover) quickly!

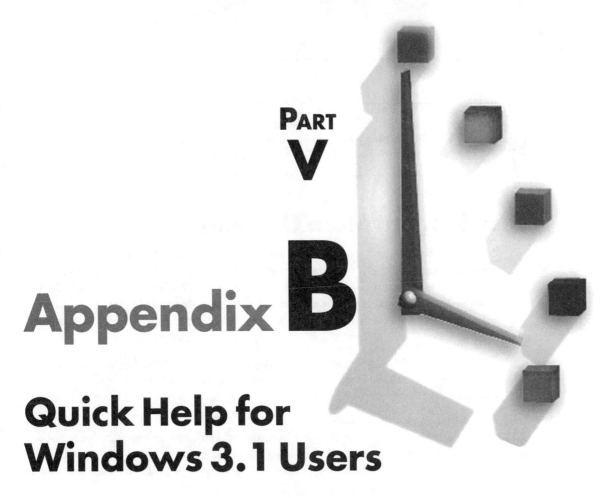

Appendix B

Quick Help for Windows 3.1 Users

If you're a Windows 3.1 expert, you can probably boot Windows 95 and begin using it without any further assistance. "*Different, better, and still the same*" best describes how Windows 95 compares to Windows 3.1. Despite the similarities, you should know ahead of time about some major Windows 95 differences so that you can use Windows 95 the way it was designed to be used.

Throughout this book, you'll find *Windows 3.1 Step-Up* sections. These sections were written with you, a current Windows 3.1 user, in mind. This appendix will serve to give you a quick overview of the major changes you will face when you move from Windows 3.1 to Windows 95. Think of this appendix as an overview that provides you with the big picture, whereas the rest of the book explains Windows 95's details.

TIME SAVER

Glance through this appendix to get a feel for Windows 95. Once you've completed this appendix, you will have seen a few of the ways Microsoft improved upon the Windows 3.1 paradigm.

Less System, More Usability

So much of Windows 3.1's technical nature is gone in Windows 95. For example, you have perhaps tinkered with .INI files when you installed or changed or deleted programs on your disk. Windows 95 still recognizes .INI entries but uses the Windows 95 *registry* to hold true Windows 95 information. The registry is a vast database that includes both hardware and software. Every time you install a Windows 95 program, the installation procedure updates your registry.

The registry modifications are much more automatic than some of the .INI file modifications that used to be common. Rarely, if ever, will you have to change your registry. Most registry changes occur automatically as you modify your system's hardware and software.

In addition, Windows 95 needs no AUTOEXEC.BAT or CONFIG.SYS files. Although Windows 95 will respect these files when needed (such as when older legacy hardware's device drivers need real address space that Windows 95 will not easily give up), it does not need these files. In addition, only Windows 95's MS-DOS windows will look at the contents of your system files.

JUST A MINUTE

As you progress through this book, keep in mind that Windows 95 is a complete operating system. Older Windows versions resided on top of MS-DOS, but Windows 95 *includes* MS-DOS.

TIME SAVER

Although Windows 95 eliminates many of the reboots that were so necessary under Windows 3.1, Windows 95 respects your reboot requests more easily. Windows 95 completely freezes up much less and you can often reboot a single program (and not your entire computer system) when a program crashes.

B

The Task at Hand

The single most important Windows 95 feature is the taskbar. Windows 3.1 did not have a similar feature. Figure B.1 shows a sample taskbar. The taskbar resides at the bottom of your screen as you work with Windows 95 programs. If you want to switch to another running program, simply click that program's icon on the taskbar. The taskbar acts like a jukebox for programs from which you can select whatever program you want to activate next.

Figure B.1.

The taskbar lets you quickly switch between running programs.

Running applications

When you start an application, Windows 95 adds that application's icon and command button to the taskbar. When you close an application's window, Windows 95 removes the program from the taskbar.

JUST A MINUTE

> You can still switch between running programs using the Alt+Tab keystroke.

Windows 95 gives you all kinds of ways to modify the behavior, size, shape, and location of the taskbar. Part I of this book explains the taskbar in detail.

Good-bye File and Program Manager

Windows 95 includes updated versions of both File Manager and Program Manager. There is absolutely *no* reason to start either program! As a matter of fact, run, don't walk, to your nearest computer and delete these programs from the disk drive!

The taskbar, described in the previous section, includes the Start button at the left of the taskbar. When you click the Start button, Windows 95 displays a pop-up Start menu. The Start menu's **P**rograms command displays yet another menu. The Start menu continues to cascade as shown in Figure B.2. These cascaded menus supplant the program groups used by Program Manager. For example, if you want to start the Windows 95 Paint program, you would follow these steps to produce the menu shown in Figure B.2:

Figure B.2.

*The cascading menus
make program selection
easy.*

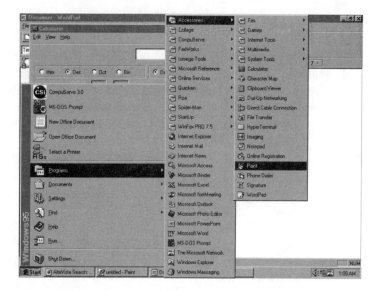

1. Press the taskbar's Start button to display the Start menu.

2. Select **P**rograms to display the Programs menu. (You can select the **P**rograms
    option with the mouse or keyboard.)

3. Select the Accessories menu (analogous to the Accessories program group in the
    Windows 3.1 Program Manager).

4. Select Paint from the last menu to start Paint.

If you've used the Windows 3.1 File Manager, you'll have to agree with the observation that
File Manager is sluggish, awkward, slow, and hard to learn well. (Other than that, File
Manager's a *great* program!) Microsoft does offer an updated version of File Manager in
Windows 95, but Microsoft also offers a brand new utility program named *Explorer* that
completely replaces File Manager and makes File Manager completely obsolete.

Instead of opening a single window for each disk drive, Explorer opens a window for your
entire computer. Windows 95 does not focus on disk drives because *you* don't focus on disk
drives. You don't work on a bunch of disk drives; you work on a *computer.* Explorer attempts
to be a computer manager that includes not only your disks and files, but also your CD-ROM
drive, printers, and even hardware devices such as modems.

Figure B.3 displays the Explorer screen. The computer system used in Figure B.3 is a relatively
simple computer with a single hard disk and floppy disk. In the right-hand window, you'll
see a scrolling list showing the drive C's top-level file *folders* (the name Windows 95 uses for
subdirectories). If you want to copy a file from drive C to A, you only need to drag the file

B

from the right-hand window to the A: icon in the left-hand window. Using Windows 3.1's File Manager, you would have to open two windows for the two selected drives before dragging the file.

Figure B.3.

The entire computer system appears in the left-hand Explorer window.

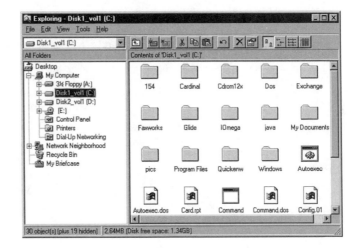

If you want to print a file, you can double-click over the Printer icon in the left-hand window to open a printer folder and then drag the file from drive C to a printer icon. Virtually everything you do inside the Explorer utility program is visual and more intuitive than an equivalent task inside Windows 3.1's File Manager.

CAUTION

Don't initially use Windows 95's File Manager and Program Manager thinking that you will convert to the Windows 95 equivalents later, once you've become accustomed to the new environment. The best way to learn the Windows 95 environment is to use the taskbar and Explorer.

Hour 6, "Explore the Windows 95 System," explains in detail how to use Explorer.

Unlimited Filenames

Windows 3.1 followed the long-standing MS-DOS tradition of requiring that filenames consist of one to eight characters followed by a one to three letter extension. All of the following names are valid under Windows 3.1:

```
ACCTG.DAT
REPORT1.DOC
APRSALES.TXT
LETRBOB.DOC
```

The 8.3 limitation doesn't appear too constricting does it? After all, you can probably figure out what these files contain from their names.

Windows 95 lets you give names to files that contain from 1 to 255 characters. All of the following are valid filenames as well:

```
Accounting data for the Nevada division
Report for the First National Bank Building Fiscal Quarter 1997
April sales data for the Marketing Department
Letter for Robert Barkley regarding his home purchase
```

Which group of filenames, the first group that follows the 8.3 rule or the second group of filenames, provides the most information? Obviously, the longer filenames are superior and let you describe exactly what a file contains.

JUST A MINUTE

> Windows 95 creates an internal table for the long filenames and also stores all files using the regular 8.3 rule as well. While inside Windows 95, you can refer to the file's long filename. If you copy the file to another computer and that computer does not contain Windows 95, the file will go to that computer with an abbreviated filename that follows the standard 8.3 convention.

Find What You Want

Have you ever created a file and forgot the filename? Windows 95 contains a **F**ind option on the Start menu that searches your computer for a file that matches a certain filename pattern (using wildcards), a specific modification and creation date, and even searches every file's contents for a word or phrase that you know is in the file.

JUST A MINUTE

> Not only does Windows 95 search one disk, but it will also search all your computer's storage devices, including CD-ROMs and the floppy disk drives, if you want the search to extend across all storage devices.

Hour 6 explains how to use the Windows 95 Find command.

The Wizard of DOS

Windows 3.1 supported MS-DOS applications fairly well. Windows 95 supports MS-DOS applications *extremely well.* Most of the MS-DOS games and programs that brought

B

Windows 3.1 to its knees, now run flawlessly under Windows 95. Windows 95 provides more free memory for MS-DOS programs and lets you open several MS-DOS sessions at once.

One of the most important new MS-DOS support features in Windows 95 is the toolbar that appears at the top of MS-DOS windows. Figure B.4 shows an MS-DOS window with a toolbar. The toolbar provides advanced support for copying and pasting data to and from Windows 95 programs. Also, you can resize the MS-DOS window, change the MS-DOS properties, and change the font style and size used for text inside the MS-DOS window.

Figure B.4.

The MS-DOS window contains a toolbar.

Hour 14, "Activate DOS-Based Applications," explains how to use the Windows 95 MS-DOS support features.

Added Help

Microsoft completely rewrote the Help search engines. You can now search most help topics using a book and chapter approach. Help topics are organized into major categories (the books), broken down into sub-categories (the chapters), and then divided into individual screens that describe specific help topics (the pages of the chapters).

Most of the Help windows are smaller than their Windows 3.1 counterparts. Figure B.5 shows one such sample Help window. The topics are more organized and compact, so that you can focus on the subject you want help with.

In addition to being more focused, many of the Help windows contain *hyperlinks* (connections to other areas of Windows 95) that you can click to perform actions. For example, if you were to click the button towards the top of Figure B.5's Help window text, the Help engine would immediately take you to a window where you could change the background wallpaper graphic on the desktop.

Figure B.5.

The new Help windows offer better organization and hyperlink connections.

Hyperlink connection ——

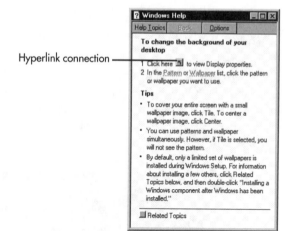

No More Plug and Pray

Windows 95 introduces the *Plug and Play* feature that lets you plug new devices into your computer *without* having to set hardware switches or determine appropriate *interrupt settings* (an interrupt signal that the computer receives to know that a device is active). Not all devices that you attempt to plug into your computer will be Plug-and-Play compatible, but almost all new devices made after the introduction of Windows 95 will support some or all of the Plug-and-Play standard.

Windows 95 continually scans your computer's hardware looking for changes in the hardware's configuration. Upon boot-up, Windows 95 will be able to detect whether or not you've installed a new hardware device. If you have, Windows 95 will automatically configure that device, make appropriate Windows 95 arrangements to control that device, and start Windows 95 without your intervention in the process.

JUST A MINUTE

If you use a laptop that supports PCMCIA cards, you usually do not even have to power-off your computer to plug new PCMCIA cards into their slots.

If you do need to install hardware that is not Plug-and-Play compatible, Windows 95 does provide a hardware installation script (called a *wizard*) that walks you through the installation process and assists with hardware and software interface settings.

Hour 22, "Hardware: Big and Small," explains how to use the Windows 95 Plug-and-Play feature.

B

Two New Folders: My Computer and Control Panel

Windows 95 provides two new windows: the *My Computer* window and the *Control Panel* window. These windows are shown in Figure B.6. The My Computer window gives you an interface to your hardware devices. You can look at files on a disk drive by clicking that drive. If you have a CD-ROM, you can view its settings by clicking on the CD-ROM drive icon. You can change the ways your printers behave, and you can change printer drivers if you need to.

B

Figure B.6.

The new My Computer and Control Panel windows.

JUST A MINUTE

Notice that the My Computer window contains an icon labeled Control Panel. The Control Panel is accessible from both the Start menu under **S**ettings and from the My Computer window. Several areas of Windows 95 are accessible from one of several places. When you need something, Windows 95 usually gives you a way to get to what you want.

The Control Panel provides the functionality of the Windows 3.1 Control Panel. You can access font information, change mouse and keyboard settings, add new software, and change the Windows 95 setup.

Hour 2, "Tour Windows 95 Now," discusses Control Panel windows, and Hour 3, "Understanding the My Computer Window," explains how to manage the Windows 95 My Computer.

Summary

This appendix only touches the surface of the new features of Windows 95. Now that you've seen an overview of the improvements that Windows 95 provides over Windows 3.1, perhaps you are more ready to tackle your new Windows 95 environment.

The best way to get acquainted with Windows 95 is, as with any new software, to try Windows 95 for yourself. Take Windows 95 on a test drive, open some windows, start utility programs, and play some games. There are several subtle, as well as drastic changes, that you will probably like. While you're testing Windows 95, take a moment to try these things:

- [ ] Double-click the clock at the right of the taskbar.
- [ ] Insert an audio CD into the CD drive and wait a couple of seconds to see what happens.
- [ ] Right-click over different parts of the Windows 95 screen.
- [ ] Start the WordPad program and select the **File | O**pen command to see the new Windows 95 dialog box style.
- [ ] Select the **H**elp command on the Start menu, click the tab marked Contents, and take the ten-minute Windows 95 tour.

What are you waiting for? Go have fun!

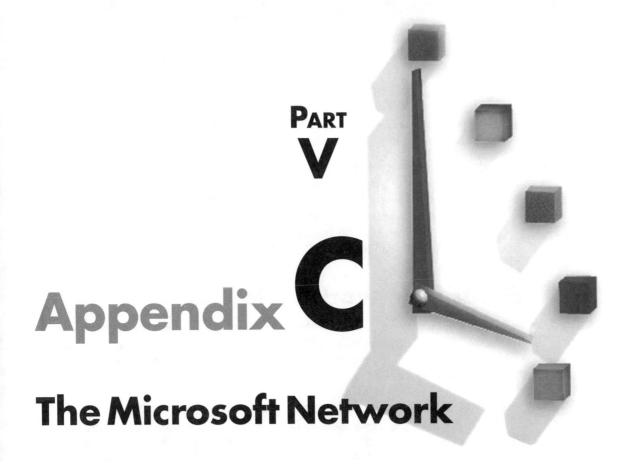

Appendix C

The Microsoft Network

This appendix introduces you to the Microsoft Network. Windows 95 supports an interface that can use the Microsoft Network in conjunction with your other applications. Many online services, such as CompuServe and Prodigy, compete with the Microsoft Network, but Microsoft Network is important to you because Windows 95 includes software that connects you to the Microsoft Network. Once you sign on to Microsoft Network with Windows 95, you can sign up for the Microsoft Network online service and begin using Microsoft Network over your phone lines right away.

One of the most important Microsoft Network features is its Internet access capability. Although you can access the Internet from other software, Microsoft Network integrates so well into Windows 95 that you should consider using Microsoft Network.

Microsoft Network is always changing. Over time, Microsoft will add new features and online locations to Microsoft Network. All you need is a basic understanding of Microsoft Network to use the network. Once connected, you can exchange e-mail, faxes, and document files with others on the system, shop without leaving your keyboard, get the latest news, sports, weather, and financial information, get help with software problems, and access an online multimedia encyclopedia.

This appendix reviews some of the fundamental Microsoft Network services so that you can see whether Microsoft Network offers services you need. Complete books have been written on the Microsoft Network; although those books provide you with every detail about Microsoft Network (and give you *information overload* sometimes), you don't need every detail to use and enjoy Microsoft Network effectively. Microsoft Network is easy to explore using the same point-and-click mouse movements you are already used to.

Microsoft Network Costs

As with most quality online services, Microsoft charges you for your connection time to the Microsoft Network. Maintaining such a service is costly, and Microsoft recaptures that cost. Perhaps the easiest way to pay for your Microsoft Network usage is to have a credit card handy when you sign up for the service.

CAUTION

The cost for the Microsoft Network changes depending on the offers currently available. This book cannot tell you what you will have to pay. Be assured that Microsoft will not be able to charge much more than similar services for your monthly access which, at the time of this writing, runs around $20 a month for unlimited access—$50 if you use a special ISDN high-speed line. If you use certain additional Microsoft Network extra-pay services, you may be charged more than the monthly minimum. You can access Microsoft Network for as little as about $7 per month if you use another Internet Service Provider and you want to access the Microsoft Network-specific locations.

Before explaining the things you can do on the Microsoft Network, you should sign up for access. If you decide that you do not want to access Microsoft Network any longer, you can cancel your access while online and not incur additional charges.

Introducing Microsoft Network

Microsoft Network's access is now completely Internet based. If you logged into Microsoft Network previously and did not like the service more than your current online service, you should try it again. Microsoft has implemented some major changes into Microsoft Network.

C

For example, Microsoft Network didn't used to be Internet based; although you could access the Internet through Microsoft Network, you did not use Microsoft Network for direct Internet access. In a way, your computer's Microsoft Network software would issue Internet commands to Microsoft Network, and then Microsoft Network would send those commands to the Internet and return the response. The end result was that you never saw the Internet directly; you only saw it through Microsoft Network's interface.

JUST A MINUTE

Now that Microsoft Network is fully Internet based, you only need to learn one interface—your Internet browser—to access both Microsoft Network and other Internet services. The common browser features such as returning to previous screens with a single click work inside the Microsoft Network. If Microsoft Network were not Internet based, you would have to learn two sets of interface commands: one for Microsoft Network and one for the Internet using your browser.

When you first log onto Microsoft Network, Windows 95 will use your Internet browser (see Hour 24 for information on Internet browsers) such as Internet Explorer. Microsoft Network's home page's Internet URL address is www.msn.com/. Although the Microsoft Network home page changes frequently, you'll see a Web page that contains features similar to those that Figure C.1 shows.

Figure C.1.

A sample Microsoft Network opening screen.

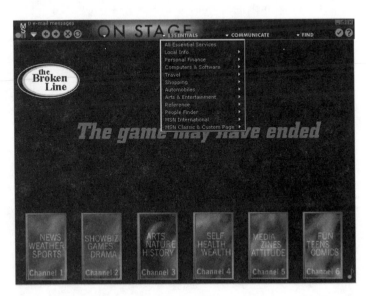

TIME SAVER

Once you begin using Microsoft Network, you may want to see special information on the opening page. For example, you may want today's weather in your area and a few stock quotes to appear on your Microsoft Network home page. If so, click the Custom Page hot spot and Microsoft Network lets you design your own Microsoft Network home page!

A Few Microsoft Network Features

At the top of Microsoft Network's home page, you'll find the following menu options:

- ☐ **On Stage.** The opening Microsoft Network home page, which might contain your customized elements. The On Stage page gives you access to six *channels* of Internet services. The next section explains each of the channels that you can "tune in" just as you tune into channels on a television for the subject you want.

- ☐ **Essentials.** Several consumer-related Microsoft Network features such as CarPoint (a car-buying service), Cinemania (a movie-review and research guide), Encarta (an online encyclopedia as shown in Figure C.2), Expedia (an online travel service), Internet Gaming Zone (a game-playing resource center), MSN International (access information for non-USA residents), Microsoft Investor (a financial service that includes an online brokerage service as Figure C.3 shows), Music Central (a music history and research area), On Computers (for computer software and hardware information), and Plaza (a new online shopping service).

- ☐ **Communicate.** Support for Internet e-mail, forums grouped by various subjects, chat rooms where you can—via your keyboard—chat with others on the Microsoft Network, and access Internet newsgroups that provide around-the-world discussion and files.

- ☐ **Find.** Searches either the Microsoft Network or the entire Internet for information you want to find.

- ☐ **Help.** Offers online help for using Microsoft Network and the Internet.

The Six MSN Program Channels

The On Stage area is grouped into six channels. When you want to access a particular subject, you can tune in to that subject's channel. When you move your mouse pointer over the On Stage area, a drop-down menu appears with the six channels from which you can select. In addition, the MSN often lists the six channels at the bottom of your MSN window; you can click on the channel icons to go directly to a channel. Each of the following sections describes the six channels you can change to.

C

Figure C.2.

Encarta provides an on-line encyclopedia.

Figure C.3.

Invest your money with Microsoft Investor.

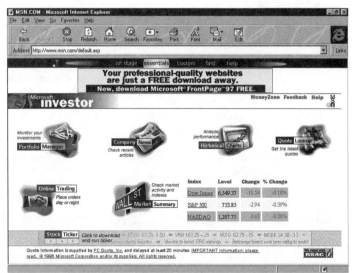

Channel 1: MSNBC: The News, Weather, and Sports Channel

One of the Microsoft Network features with the most promise is the *MSNBC* (Microsoft Network/NBC Studios) area. Microsoft designed the MSNBC Web areas to coincide with the MSNBC television news and entertainment services that are appearing on broadcast networks across the country. Often, such as in the 1996 elections, the MSNBC Microsoft Network site supplements information you watch on the MSNBC television network. In the 1996 election coverage, the Microsoft Network MSNBC site provided all the election statistics while the television network broadcasted interviews and showed election summary results.

JUST A MINUTE

Keep your eyes on the MSNBC site. It appears that Microsoft wants to integrate its network broadcast directly on the MSNBC Web pages! Therefore, you'll be able to see and view the broadcast while surfing the Internet. Although today's Internet speeds and bottlenecks do not allow for an extremely tight broadcast integration just yet, some day such a feature should be commonplace.

Channel 2: The Showbiz, Games, and Drama Channel

The second channel looks at several entertainment-related services, including the following:

- ☐ *Entertainment Tonight* **Online:** An online supplement to the popular television show that describes current events in the entertainment world.
- ☐ *Star Trek:* **Continuum:** An official *Star Trek* Internet site available for MSN subscribers only.
- ☐ **The Broken Line:** A travel adventure game with which you can win real prizes.
- ☐ **Additional entertainment-related topics:** These can change, depending on the day's events.

Channel 3: The Arts, Nature, and History Channel

The third channel supports an educational flair with topics that range from history to science to geography. Microsoft has just begun a new online magazine named *Slate* that covers current political matters in a light and often humorous format. Figure C.4 shows a typical *Slate* opening contents page.

Microsoft's new adventure magazine called *Mungo Park* enables you to explore remote regions of the world by using its multimedia capabilities. You can visit *Mungo Park* each month on Channel 3.

C

Figure C.4.

Read Slate *to invoke thought.*

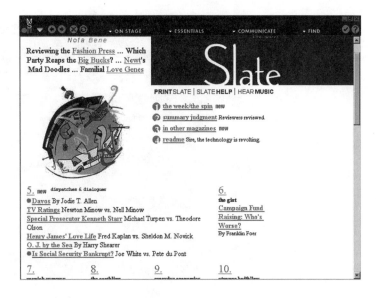

Channel 4: The Self, Health, and Wealth Channel

Relax and take a break on Channel 4 by getting advice with cooking, travel, and home; spend time with medical experts to learn more about health and illness prevention. If you're into fashion, check out *V-Style*, a new online fashion showplace and discussion area.

Channel 5: The Media, 'Zines, and Attitude Channel

Participate in powerful adult-oriented debates on current issues, the entertainment industry, and fashion. You'll find *15 Seconds of Fame*, which features several hilarious bloopers.

TIME SAVER

> If you're new to the Internet, Channel 5 offers highlights of the Internet's best sites and resources so that you can stay abreast of the latest and greatest Internet pages.

Channel 6: Fun, Teens, and Comics

A channel for young adults and teens that targets the current trends that interest teens. Channel 6 (see Figure C.5) offers entertainment and games for the younger crowds who surf the Internet after school.

Figure C.5.
Channel 6 offers an interactive high school story line.

Three special Channel 6 online features are the *Bad Advice* (dos and don'ts for teen dressing, school, and relationships), *Spike's World* (one of the most exciting interactive Internet gaming worlds on the Internet), and *High School* (an interactive story to help students cope with today's high schools).

Take a Look at Microsoft Network

Microsoft lets you try Microsoft Network for a trial period before you commit yourself to the service. Microsoft Network's promising future features (such as the MSNBC interface) make Microsoft Network a powerful contender among Internet service providers and online services. Microsoft Network experienced the fastest initial growth rate of any service, with more than one million new users signed up in its first year of operation. There's a lot good about Microsoft Network, the least of which is the strong Microsoft presence for users of Windows 95.

C

Glossary

32-bit application   A program written to take advantage of the Windows 95 interface and to integrate easily with other Windows 95 application programs.

640KB barrier   Programs written for previous Windows environments could not address more than 640KB of memory without performing memory tricks that slowed down the computer.

accelerator key   A key found on a menu, usually a function key used in conjunction with the Alt key (such as Alt+F4), that lets you initiate a menu command from the keyboard without first having to display the menu.

Accessibility Time Out   Turns off the accessibility options after a preset period of time.

accessory programs   Programs Microsoft included with Windows 95; they fall under several categories such as multimedia programs, text editors, and games such as Solitaire.

Active Movie Control   The new Windows 95 video player. If you do not see the Active Movie Control on your Multimedia menu, you can contact Microsoft or check out the company's Web site (www.microsoft.com) for an update.

analog recording   The opposite of *digital recording*, where all sounds coming from a sound source are stored as continuous analog noise impulses that cannot be reproduced or changed without loss of quality. There are some modern-day digital tape recorders in use, but most tape recorders use an analog signal so you cannot make copies of recordings without losing some quality.

anchor position   The starting coordinate pair of lines and other geometric shapes.

animated cursors   Cursors that display movement during the cursor's display, such as a cursor showing a picture of a running horse or a playing piano.

applet   A Windows 95 utility program such as the Clipboard Viewer.

attach   Add a binary file to an e-mail message so the receiving user can receive the binary file or load the file using tools available to the receiving user.

auto detect   HyperTerminal automatically detects the remote computer's technical requirements so you do not have to know anything but the remote computer's telephone number for HyperTerminal to talk to the machine.

AutoPlay   The Windows 95 feature that starts the loading and execution of a CD-ROM as soon as you place the CD-ROM in your computer's CD-ROM drive. AutoPlay plays audio CDs as well.

backscroll buffer   The memory area, adjustable in size, where HyperTerminal keeps track of previous online screens while you work on a remote computer.

backup file set   A description that contains a specific list of files that you want to back up. For example, you may have a backup file set that backs up your accounting data files only, as well as a full backup file set that backs up your entire hard disk.

baud rate   A term that describes the speed of computerized telephone communications.

BBS   An acronym for *bulletin board system.* BBS lets you connect your computer, via the phone lines, to exchange electronic mail and files with the BBS's primary computer and other computers connected to the BBS.

binary   The base-2 numbering system.

binary operators   Operators that work on two values such as the addition and subtraction operators.

BIOS   Stands for Basic Input Output System and refers to the system unit's ROM-based code that handles I/O devices.

bitmap   The technical name for a graphics file. Windows 95 often uses bitmaps for the Windows 95 wallpaper.

BounceKeys   Keeps users from producing double-keystrokes if they accidentally bounce keys several times in succession.

Briefcase   The Windows 95 application that synchronizes the document files from two computers so that you can have the most up-to-date files at any time.

bullet-proof   The term applied to Windows 95 because of its increased protection against locking up in certain situations.

burn-in   Characters left on older computer monitors begin to burn into the monitor, leaving their outlines even after the monitor's power is turned off.

byte   One character of storage.

C2-level security   File encryption that conforms to the U.S. Government's security standards.

carbon copy   A secondary recipient that gets a copy of someone's e-mail message.

cascade   The effect of neatly stacking all open windows on the screen so that each window's title bar appears.

checkbox   A Windows 95 control that appears next to each item in a list that you use to select one or more items from the list.

click   The process of pressing and immediately releasing one of the mouse buttons.

Clipboard   An area of Windows 95 that temporarily holds documents or parts of documents. The Clipboard can hold any kind of document including text, sound, and graphic images.

Clipboard Viewer   A Windows 95 applet that lets you look at the contents of the Clipboard no matter what kind of data resides on the Clipboard.

closing a window   The practice of eliminating a window from view and terminating any program that might be running within the window at the time.

command button   A Windows 95 control that appears and acts like a pushbutton on the screen.

compression   The process of squeezing your disk drive so that almost 100 percent more data fits on a disk.

connection profile   An individual remote computer site's connection-setting information. HyperTerminal keeps track of a remote computer's description, icon, phone number, and modem settings inside each connection profile.

context-sensitive   The process Windows 95 uses to respond to what you're doing.

context-sensitive help   Refers to the capability of Windows 95 to look at what actions you are currently performing (the *context*) and display help that explains how to complete those actions.

Control menu   A menu available on all windows within Windows 95 that lets you move and resize windows from the keyboard; it is accessed by clicking the window's icon in the upper-left corner of the window.

Control Panel   A folder window within the My Computer window that lets you change your computer's system settings.

coordinate   A pixel position on the screen defined by a coordinate pair.

coordinate pair   A pair of numbers of which the first represents the number of pixels from the left edge of the drawing area of an image and the second represents the number of pixels from the top edge of the drawing area. In Paint, the coordinates appear on the status bar.

copy   The process of sending a copy of an item such as a document or part of a document to the Clipboard. From the Clipboard you can place the item elsewhere, in effect making a copy of the item in at least two places on your computer system.

cross-referenced help topic   Underlined green text inside help dialog boxes that display definitions when you click them.

cursor   A pointing device, such as the arrow that represents the mouse pointer location and the insert bar that represents the Windows 95 text location. The cursor moves across the screen as you type or move the mouse.

cut   The process of removing an item, such as a document or part of a document, from somewhere in your computer system. The removed item goes to the clipboard. From the clipboard you can place the item elsewhere, in effect, moving the item.

decimal   The base-10 numbering system.

default drive and directory   When you start MS-DOS, the MS-DOS command prompt always contains a disk drive and directory. The disk drive is normally C, and the directory is the root directory called \ (backslash). You can change the default disk or directory by entering a new one at the command prompt.

deferred printing   The process of issuing print commands but delaying the physical printing of those documents until later. Sometimes deferred printing is called *delayed printing.*

deinstaller   The section of a program that removes the program from your computer.

deselect   The process of reversing a selected item so that item is no longer selected. Usually when you deselect an item the highlight around the item disappears.

desktop   The Windows 95 screen and background.

dial-up networking   The ability of a remote laptop computer to dial into a network over the phone lines and work as if connected to the network by cable.

dialog box   A window containing text and one or more screen controls that you use to issue instructions to Windows 95.

differential backup   A backup of only the files that have changed since the most recent backup. Also called an *incremental backup.*

digital recording   The opposite of *analog recording,* where all sounds coming from a sound source are stored as discrete digital impulses that can be reproduced or changed without loss of quality.

direct cable connection   The connection between two computers with a cable attached to both parallel or serial ports.

disk crash   A disk-drive failure.

Disk Defragmenter   A Windows 95 program that collects and removes blank disk space left from deleted files.

disk operating system   The program inside memory that controls all the hardware and software interactions.

docking station   A device into which you can insert some laptop computers. The docking station instantly connects the laptop to a full-size screen, keyboard, mouse, and printer.

document-centered   The concept that Windows 95 promotes by maintaining that you work with the computer's files, as if they were documents inside folders in a file cabinet.

download   The process of receiving a file from a remote computer over the phone lines.

dragging   The process of moving an image or selected text from one screen location to another using the mouse. To drag the mouse, you move the mouse while holding the mouse button. When you've dragged the item to the final position, release the mouse to anchor the item in that position.

drivers   Software files that often accompany hardware to tell the computer how to control the hardware when you install it.

DriveSpace   The name of the Windows 95 utility program that condenses the disk space so that more data fits on a disk.

e-mail   Message files sent electronically to others who receive the messages via modem. E-mail stands for *electronic mail.*

Energy Star   A name applied to monitors that comply with environmental guidelines that limit the use of continuous power applied to your monitor.

Enhanced CD   A new audio CD standard that puts graphics and text on the same CDs that your stereo plays.

event   A Windows 95 action you perform, such as opening and closing windows or displaying a menu.

Explorer   A powerful system-listing application that gives you both high-level and detailed descriptions of your computer system and the files on the system.

FAT   (*file allocation table*) Controls the placement of files on your disk.

field   A single value, such as quantity or last name, in a Cardfile record.

file extension   The end part of some filenames including a period followed by one to three characters. By giving some files the same filename extension you can group them together so that, using wildcards, you can work with those files as a collection. All major applications support their own filename extension. For example, WordPad uses the Word for Windows standard .DOC filename extension at the end of all documents you open with WordPad. You can select a different filename extension in WordPad if you prefer to work with a different type of document.

file system   The collection of disk access routines and memory.

FilterKeys   The group of keystroke aids that include RepeatKeys and BounceKeys.

firmware   The computer's internal memory, also known as *RAM*, which stands for Random Access Memory. Firmware memory is volatile, meaning that the contents remain in memory for only as long as the PC is turned on. The disk drive is hardware, not firmware, because the disk drive retains its contents after the computer is turned off.

flat-file database   A collection of data values, stored in a uniform manner, that allows for simple searching, printing, and sorting of data.

flat memory model   The term applied to the use of memory by Windows 95 so that programs can take advantage of all your computer RAM memory without slowing down to adjust for memory above the 640KB barrier.

FM synthesis   An older sound standard that produces non-realistic computer-generated sounds.

focus   The highlighted command button or control in a dialog box that Windows 95 automatically selects when you press enter.

folder   A special icon that contains other icons, which are displayed when you double-click the folder icon; a grouping of related files stored under the same subdirectory.

font   A specific typestyle. Fonts have names that distinguish them from one another. Some fonts are fancy and others are plain. Choose a font style that best serves the idea your words need to convey.

font family   Characters that take on the same typeface appearance, but that come in italics, boldfaced, and underlined versions, are all part of the same font family.

formats   Different files are stored on the disk differently depending on the nature of the file. The format is the nature of the file that determines if the file is a graphic, text, or program file.

full backup   A complete backup of your entire disk drive.

full system backup file set   A backup file set supplied by Backup that performs a full backup.

GDI   (*Graphics Device Interface*) Consists of your graphics resources.

GUI   A *Graphical User Interface*, such as Windows 95, that lets the user interact with the computer primarily through graphic images as opposed to a more traditional text-based interface that requires typed commands.

hardware tree   A collection of hardware configurations, taken from parts or all of the registry, that your computer may require.

header   A one-line message that describes the sender information for electronic messages.

hexadecimal   The base-16 numbering system.

high-contrast display   A video option that makes your screen more readable by increasing the size of icons, menus, and text, as well as changing screen colors so that the items on the display are as readable as possible.

home position   The upper-left position of a document or of a window.

host drive   A logical new drive that DriveSpace creates to hold compression information.

hot key   The combination of an Alt keypress with another key that selects command buttons. The key you press with Alt is displayed with an underlined letter in the command button you want to select.

I/O   Stands for *input and output*.

icons   Small pictures that represent commands and programs in Windows 95.

incremental backup   See *differential backup*.

index line   A line at the top of each card in the Cardfile that contains unique information that identifies the card.

insert mode   Newly typed text shifts the existing text to the right.

jumpers   Special routing connections many older, legacy hardware require to change the electrical path flows so the hardware works properly on your specific machine.

KB   The abbreviation for *kilobyte*. *8KB* refers to approximately 8,000 characters of storage.

kernel   The internal native operating system that controls the hardware and software interaction. The CPU's processor routines.

kilobyte   Approximately 1,000 characters of storage. See also *KB*.

landscape view   Shows how the document would look if displayed across the wide edge of the page. Landscape view is helpful for wide documents.

legacy   Older hardware that was designed before engineers invented the Plug-and-Play specification.

link   Pasted Clipboard contents with which Windows 95 keeps an active connection. If you change linked data in its original application, after you have pasted it elsewhere from the Clipboard, the data then also changes inside the other application(s) containing the pasted contents.

logging off   The process of typing a command that tells the remote computer you are finished using the computer and are ready to exit HyperTerminal or dial a different connection.

logging on   The process of typing an identifying name and password when you first connect to a remote computer to gain access to the remote computer's capabilities. The process that lets you gain access to a networked computer.

login name   A nickname you go by on a remote computer.

low memory   RAM below one megabyte.

maximized window   A window that you've expanded to the size of the entire screen.

media   The types of storage on which you store and back up data. Examples of media would be a diskette, a tape, and paper.

Media Player   The Windows 95 application that plays video clips.

Memory Manager   Controls the various segments of memory that Windows 95 tracks.

Microsoft Exchange   See *Microsoft Messaging*.

Microsoft Fax   A program that uses your fax modem to send and receive faxes as well as to create cover pages and provide for viewing of received faxes.

Microsoft Messaging   The application that uses a universal Inbox to log on to all your electronic mail sources and to send and receive any waiting mail.

Microsoft Network   An online service available from Microsoft.

Microsoft Plus! A Windows 95 add-on product that you can purchase that can automate the backup process (as long as you back up to tape, a network drive, or another hard disk) so that you can request a backup at any time of day or night.

MIDI Stands for *Musical Instrument Digital Interface* and reproduces musical instruments and other sounds.

minimized window A window that you've shrunk down to a taskbar icon.

mobile computing environments The computer environment that includes laptop computers and desktop docking stations for the laptops.

modifier keys The Alt, Ctrl, and Shift keys.

MouseKeys Lets you simulate mouse movements and clicks using the keyboard's numeric keypad.

MPC Stands for *Multimedia Personal Computer*. A computer hardware and software standard that has been in effect for several years. It determines the minimum hardware and software requirements for a product to be called a multimedia product that's endorsed by the MPC compliance committee.

MPC-2 A more modern version of the MPC standard that requires a double-speed CD-ROM drive.

MS-DOS command prompt When you open an MS-DOS window you must issue a command to the MS-DOS environment. The command prompt, usually shown on the screen as c:\>, indicating the current default drive and directory, accepts your MS-DOS commands as you type the commands.

MS-DOS program A program written specifically for the MS-DOS environment. MS-DOS programs do not take advantage of the graphical nature of Windows 95.

multiprocessor A system unit with multiple CPUs, and each CPU works in parallel to double or even triple the speed of single-unit processors.

multitasking The process of a computer that is running more than one program at the same time.

mutually exclusive Two or more Windows 95 controls, such as option buttons, are mutually exclusive if you can set only one option at a time.

n The number of entries in a statistical series.

non-proportional font A font in which all characters occupy the same width on the screen or printer.

octal The base-8 numbering system.

offline   A printer is offline when it is turned off or turned on, but not ready to accept output. (You might turn the printer offline when you need to feed pages through the printer manually.)

online   Information that is available interactively as you use Windows 95. Also applies to connected hardware. A printer is online when the printer is turned on and ready to accept output.

opening a window   The process of starting a program in a window or double-clicking an icon to display a window.

Option buttons   A Windows 95 control that appears next to each item in a list that you use to select one and only one item from the list.

orientation   The way the document appears on the page. The orientation is either the portrait view (vertical) or landscape view (horizontal).

overtype mode   Newly typed text overwrites existing text.

paperless society   The lofty and incorrect prediction from the early 1970s that said electronic mail and files would replace most of the paper used in the workplace and homes.

parallel port   A connector on your computer where most printer cables plug into.

paste   The process of sending the contents of the Clipboard to another area of the computer system such as to a specific folder or to the Windows 95 desktop.

PC 95 hardware   Hardware that has been tested and approved by Microsoft to work with Windows 95 and support such features as Plug-and-Play.

PCMCIA Cards   (also called *PC Cards*) Small credit card-sized I/O cards that add functionality—such as modems and memory—to laptops and to some desktop systems.

Personal Address Book   A central address book that holds people's names, phone numbers, addresses, fax numbers, e-mail numbers, and notes.

pixel   Stands for *picture element*. A pixel is the smallest addressable dot on your screen.

Plug-and-Play   The name Microsoft gives to hardware that you can install without making any hardware or software changes. The Windows 95 Plug-and-Play feature will take care of setting up things correctly for you.

point   A measurement of 1/72 inch (72 points equals one inch). Most computers' on-screen and printed text measures from 9 to 12 points in size. Another name for *coordinate*. The action made by the screen's mouse cursor when you move the mouse.

portrait view   Shows how the document would look if displayed down the page, as a novel's text is typically printed.

print codes   Special characters that dictate how printers output and format characters.

print jobs   Every document that you print creates a print job on the print spooler.

Print Preview   A full-screen representation of how your document will look when you print the document.

printer drivers   Small descriptor files that allow Windows 95 to communicate properly with specific printers.

printer subsystem   A program automatically started by Windows 95 that controls the way output appears on the printer.

profile   A file that describes a specific online service to Microsoft Messaging. Once Microsoft Messaging reads an online service's profile, Microsoft Messaging can manage that service's information using the Windows 95 universal Inbox.

proportional font   A font that generally makes for a more natural appearance of text. The letters within the text do not all consume the same screen width. For example, the lowercase letter *i* consumes less space than the uppercase *M*.

protocol   The technical connection details that must be in place before two computers can communicate with each other.

queue   A list, such as the list of print jobs, that you see in the Printer window when you double-click a printer icon.

real device drivers   Hardware device driver files that reside in low memory.

reboot   The process of restarting your computer through the keyboard (by pressing Alt+Ctrl+Del) without shutting off the computer's power.

record   A single card image from the Cardfile program. If the Cardfile describes an inventory of parts, each part has its own card with a description of that part, the quantity, and the price. Those values form that inventory item's record. In the Cardfile program a record is a Cardfile image with data.

Recycle Bin   A special location in Windows 95 that temporarily holds all the files that you delete. Until you empty the Recycle Bin, you can recover the deleted files just as you can remove trash from your office trash can until the can's contents are taken away by the janitor.

redial properties   Determines how many retries and the time between retries Microsoft Fax attempts when a called fax number is busy or does not answer.

registered   A file is registered when you've associated an application with that file's extension.

Registry   A central repository of all possible information for your hardware.

remote computer   The computer you are trying to connect to using HyperTerminal.

RepeatKeys   Users can turn on or off the repetition of keys, so that holding down a key does *not* necessarily repeat that keystroke.

resolution   A measurement that specifies how close together individual screen dots can be. The higher the resolution, the closer together the dots that form characters and graphic images, and the better the picture will be.

rich-text format (RTF)   A file format that enables different applications to exchange formatted documents.

ROM   Stands for *Read-Only Memory* and refers to devices or memory that you can read from but not write to, delete from, or change.

Roving Help   Windows 95 lets you point to items on dialog boxes and click the window's question mark command button to get help about that item. You also can display this Roving Help by right-clicking over an item to see a description of that item and learn the commands you can perform.

RTF   Stands for *Rich-Text Format* and refers to a universal file format that many different programs support. The RTF format differs from a straight text file format because RTF files can contain text encoded with special effects such as boldfacing and underlining.

running total   The Windows 95 Calculator operations, such as addition and subtraction, keep operating on the Calculator's running display. For example, if the display contains the value 87 and you press the plus sign, and then press 5, the Calculator adds the 5 to the 87 and produces the sum of 92. If you press the plus sign again and enter another value, the Calculator adds that number to the 92, producing a continuous running total. The running total continues until you clear the display or close the Calculator program.

scaleable   A font is scaleable if Windows 95 can generate characters from the font in more than one size.

scaleable user interface elements   The text, title bars, and icons enlarge to make them easier to see.

Scientific Calculator   A Windows 95 Calculator that supports trigonometric, scientific, and number-conversion operations.

scrap   A selected portion from a document that you send to the desktop.

screen saver   A program that waits in the background and executes only if you stop using your computer for a while. The screen saver either blanks your screen or displays moving text and graphics. Screen savers have, in the past, helped eliminate burn-in problems.

scroll bars Windows 95 control tools that enable you to view a window's contents more fully.

search string A string of one or more characters, such as a filename, for which you want to search.

separator page A page that prints before each print job to separate multiple print jobs on an output stack for networked printers.

SerialKeys Lets the user use a non-keyboard input device.

series A set of values on which you perform statistical operations.

shortcut When you create a shortcut by adding programs to the Start menu or by creating shortcuts within Explorer or within Open dialog boxes, Windows 95 creates a link (the *shortcut*) to that item instead of wasting disk space with two separate files that have the same contents.

shortcut key An underlined letter on a menu that you can combine with the Alt key to issue a menu command.

ShowSounds Provides visual feedback on the screen when applications produce sounds.

SlowKeys Windows 95 can disregard keystrokes that are not held down for a preset time period. This aids users who often accidentally press keys.

Sound Recorder The Windows 95 application with which you can record and edit sounds.

sound scheme A collection of customized Windows 95 event sounds. Once you add sounds to Windows 95 events, you can save that collection of sounds in a sound scheme file.

SoundSentry Sends a visual clue when Windows 95 beeps the speaker (in the case of warning or error message dialog boxes).

spooled output Output that is sent to a disk file before being routed to a printer.

Standard Calculator A Windows 95 Calculator that performs common mathematical operations.

standard scan The quickest ScanDisk version that checks your disk files for errors.

Start button The button at the left of the taskbar that displays the Windows 95 cascading menu of choices. When you click the Start button, the Windows 95 Start menu appears.

Start menu A Windows 95 system and program menu that appears when you click the taskbar's Start button.

startup disk   A disk that you create from the Control Panel. The startup disk enables you to start your computer if your hard disk's system files get corrupted due to a hardware or software problem.

startup logo   The image you see when Windows 95 loads.

statistics box   A box that holds your entered series of statistical values. (The Calculator's display can hold only a single value at a time.)

status bar   A message area at the bottom of a window that updates to show you what is happening at any given moment. For example, when you click over a menu item, the status bar tells you what that menu item will do.

StickyKeys   Lets the user press the Shift, Alt, or Ctrl keys individually instead of having to press them with their combined keystrokes.

System Administrator   The person in charge of assigning user names and setting up new users on networked environments.

System Monitor   A Windows 95 program that graphically illustrates your computer's resources as you use the computer.

system resources   The amount of CPU, memory, and disk space utilization consumed by Windows 95 and the applications you are running.

tabbed dialog box   Two or more cascaded dialog boxes appearing on the screen at the same time.

TAPI   (*Telephone Applications Programming Interface*) TAPI describes the centralized integration of Windows 95 and telephone communications, such as the universal Inbox and Phone Dialer.

taskbar   The bar at the bottom of a Windows 95 screen where running program icons appear along with the system clock.

taskbar properties menu   The menu that appears when you click the right mouse button over an empty spot on the taskbar. You can control the performance and appearance of the taskbar and Windows 95 through the taskbar properties menu.

Taskbar Properties tabbed dialog box   A tabbed dialog box that appears when you select the Properties command on the taskbar properties menu. The Taskbar Properties tabbed dialog box lets you modify the appearance and performance of the taskbar and the Start menu.

text editor   A program that creates document files but offers only primitive formatting and printing functionality.

text frame   A rectangular area where text goes when you type the text.

thorough scan   The slower, but more thorough, scan that checks the files and performs a disk surface test to verify the integrity and safety of disk storage.

thumbnail sketch   A small representation that shows the overall layout without showing a lot of detail.

tiling   The effect of placing all open windows on the screen so that the body of each window appears next to, above, or below the other windows.

title bar   A location above many Windows 95 windows (such as the Explorer right-hand window) that describes the documents you are currently viewing.

ToggleKeys   Sounds a high noise on the speaker if the CapsLock, NumLock, or ScrollLock keys are activated and a low noise when these keys are deactivated.

tool box   Paint's collection of drawing, coloring, and painting tools.

toolbar   This area of a window contains a list of icons that instantly execute pushbutton commands. Many Windows 95 applications and dialog boxes contain toolbars that make issuing commands easier for you.

tools   The individual drawing, painting, and coloring tools on the tool box represented by icons.

transfer protocol   A predetermined method of downloading and uploading files. When one computer sends another computer a file, both computers must use the same transfer protocol.

TrueType   A scaleable font that Windows 95 prints using 32-bit technology to make text look as close to typeset characters as possible.

unary operators   Operators that work on single values such as square root.

universal Inbox   A central repository of electronic mail where you can send, receive, and manage all your electronic mail and faxes.

upload   The process of sending a file to a remote computer over the phone lines.

URL   The address of an Internet Web site. URL is an acronym for *Uniform Resource Locator.*

User profile   The customized interface and file-access rules set up for each networked user.

Video for Windows   The internal player Windows 95 uses to produce full-motion video on your screen.

viewer   A Windows 95 accessory program with which you can look at documents.

virtual device drivers   Device driver files that can move themselves to high memory to leave extra low memory free.

VM   Stands for *Virtual Memory* and refers to the concept that each MS-DOS window acts like a separate PC that has access to full memory and other system resources.

wallpaper   The background graphics that appear on the Windows 95 desktop.

Wave   Also called *wavetable*. Sound that produces realistic sounds from your computer's speaker.

wildcard character   When you want to refer to more than one file, you often can use the * or ? wildcard characters. The * substitutes for zero or more characters in a filename and the ? substitutes for one character. Therefore, *.txt refers to all files whose names end in the .txt filename extension, whereas month?.txt refers only to those files that match the pattern month1.txt, month2.txt, montha.txt, month$.txt, and so on.

Windows metafile   A special Windows 95 file that ends with the .WMF filename extension. You can use Windows metafiles for separator pages that you create yourself provided that you have a program that can create metafiles with the .WMF filename extension.

wizard   A step-by-step process that leads you through the execution of a Windows 95 task. Many Windows 95 programs, such as Microsoft Word for Windows, include specific wizards of their own.

wrap   When an editor or word processor automatically moves the cursor to the start of the next line when the cursor gets to the edge of a window or Ruler margin.

INDEX

A VIACOM SERVICE

The Information SuperLibrary™

Bookstore

Search

What's New

Reference

Software

Newsletter

Company Overviews

Yellow Pages

Internet Starter Kit

HTML Workshop

Win a Free T-Shirt!

Macmillan Computer Publishing

Site Map

Talk to Us

CHECK OUT THE BOOKS IN THIS LIBRARY.

You'll find thousands of shareware files and over 1600 computer books designed for both technowizards and technophobes. You can browse through 700 sample chapters, get the latest news on the Net, and find just about anything using our massive search directories.

All Macmillan Computer Publishing books are available at your local bookstore.

We're open 24-hours a day, 365 days a year.

You don't need a card.

We don't charge fines.

And you can be as **LOUD** as you want.

The Information SuperLibrary
http://www.mcp.com/mcp/   ftp.mcp.com

MACMILLAN COMPUTER PUBLISHING USA

A VIACOM COMPANY

Technical ---- Support:

If you need assistance with the information in this book or with a CD/Disk accompanying the book, please access the Knowledge Base on our Web site at **http://www.superlibrary.com/general/support**. Our most Frequently Asked Questions are answered there. If you do not find the answer to your questions on our Web site, you may contact Macmillan Technical Support **(317) 581-3833** or e-mail us at **support@mcp.com**.

Microsoft Office 97 Unleashed, Second Edition

—Paul McFedries and Sue Charlesworth

Microsoft has brought the Web to its Office suite of products. Hyperlinking, Office Assistants, and Active Document Support lets users publish documents to the Web or an intranet site. It also completely integrates with Microsoft FrontPage, making it possible to point-and-click a Web page into existence. This book details each of the Office products—Excel, Access, PowerPoint, Word, and Outlook—and shows the estimated 22 million registered users how to create presentations and Web documents. This book also demonstrates how to extend Office to work on a network as well as the various Office Solution Kits and how to use them. The CD-ROM includes powerful utilities and two best-selling books in HTML format.

Price: $35.00 USA/$49.95 CDN   User Level: Accomplished–Expert
ISBN: 0-672-31010-4   1,200 pages

Teach Yourself Access 97 in 14 Days, Fourth Edition

—Paul Cassel

Through the examples, workshop sessions, and Q&A sections in this book, you can master the most important features of Access. In just two weeks you'll be able to develop your own databases and create stunning forms and reports. *Teach Yourself Access 97 in 14 Days, Fourth Edition* covers wizards, tables, data types, validation, forms, queries, artificial fields, macros, and more. You'll learn how to program with Access Basic and Access lingo.

Price:$29.99 USA/$42.95 CDN   User Level: New–Casual
ISBN: 0-672-30969-6   700 pages

Access 97 Unleashed, Second Edition

—Dwayne Gifford, et al.

Access, one of Microsoft's database managers for Windows, has become one of the most accepted standards of database management for personal computers. The *Unleashed* format for this book allows current and new users to quickly and easily find the information they need about new features. It also serves as a complete reference for database programmers who are new to Access. Readers learn advanced techniques for working with tables, queries, forms, and data. *Access 97 Unleashed, Second Edition* shows you how to program Access and how to integrate your database with the Internet. The CD-ROM includes Access utilities and applications as well as an electronic Access reference library.

Price: $49.99 USA/$70.95 CDN   User Level: Accomplished–Expert
ISBN: 0-672-30983-1   1,100 pages

Microsoft Internet Explorer 3 Unleashed

—Glenn Fincher, Joe Kraynak, et al.

This comprehensive guide to Internet Explorer 3 fully exploits the complete Microsoft Internet Explorer and ActiveX environment. It details the steps for using Internet Explorer to get around the Internet as well as for sending and receiving e-mail and news, using FrontPage and the Internet Assistants to create Web pages, and adding interactivity to Web pages with VBScript and JavaScript. The CD-ROM includes source code from the book as well as powerful utilities.

Price: $39.99 USA/$56.95 CDN   User Level: Accomplished–Expert
ISBN: 1-57521-155-6   1,008 pages

Microsoft FrontPage Unleashed

—William Stanek, et al.

FrontPage technologies have recently been acquired by Microsoft, who immediately reduced its retail price from a staggering $695 to $150, making FrontPage affordable for thousands of hackers and professionals. Microsoft is also launching FrontPage as its point technology for its suite of Internet products, which will undoubtedly increase demand. With that new demand in mind, this book gives readers of all levels the information they need to succeed in Web publishing with FrontPage. This book explains how to add interactivity to Web sites and shows how to integrate CGI scripting with FrontPage. The CD-ROM includes all the examples and source code from the book.

Price: *$49.99 USA/$70.95 CDN*   User Level: *Casual–Accomplished*
ISBN: *1-57521-140-8*   *1,032 pages*

Laura Lemay's Web Workshop: Microsoft FrontPage

—Laura Lemay & Denise Tyler

This is a hands-on guide to maintaining Web pages with Microsoft's FrontPage. Written in the clear, conversational style of Laura Lemay, it is packed with many interesting, colorful examples that demonstrate specific tasks of interest to the reader. The CD-ROM includes all the necessary templates, backgrounds, and materials.

Price: *$39.99 USA/$56.95 CDN*   User Level: *Casual–Accomplished*
ISBN: *1-57521-149-1*   *672 pages*

Laura Lemay's Web Workshop: Creating Commercial Web Pages

—Laura Lemay

Filled with sample Web pages, this book illustrates how to create commercial-grade Web pages using HTML, CGI, and Java. In the classic clear style of Laura Lemay, this book details not only how to create the page, but how to apply proven principles of design that will make the page a marketing tool. This book illustrates the corporate uses of Web technology, such as how to use your Web page as a catalog as well as for customer-service and product-ordering purposes. The CD-ROM includes all the templates in the book, plus HTML editors, graphics software, CGI forms, and more!

Price: *$39.99 USA/$56.95 CDN*   User Level: *Accomplished*
ISBN: *1-57521-126-2*   *528 pages*

Teach Yourself Web Publishing with HTML 3.2 in a Week, Third Edition

—Laura Lemay & Brian K. Murphy

This is the updated edition of Lemay's previous best-seller, *Teach Yourself Web Publishing with HTML in 14 Days, Premier Edition*. In it, readers will find all the advanced topics and updates—including adding audio, video, and animation—to Web-page creation. This book explores the use of CGI scripts, tables, HTML 3.2, Netscape and Internet Explorer extensions, Java applets and JavaScript, and VRML.

Price: *$29.99 USA/$42.95 CDN*   User Level: *New–Casual–Accomplished*
ISBN:*1-57521-192-0*   *624 pages*

Add to Your Sams Library Today with the Best Books for Programming, Operating Systems, and New Technologies

The easiest way to order is to pick up the phone and call

1-800-428-5331

between 9:00 a.m. and 5:00 p.m. EST.
For faster service please have your credit card available.

ISBN	Quantity	Description of Item	Unit Cost	Total Cost
0-672-31010-4		Microsoft Office 97 Unleashed, Second Edition (Book/CD-ROM)	$35.00	
0-672-30969-6		Teach Yourself Access 97 in 14 Days, Fourth Edition	$29.99	
0-672-30983-1		Access 97 Unleashed, Second Edition (Book/CD-ROM)	$49.99	
1-57521-155-6		Microsoft Internet Explorer 3 Unleashed (Book/CD-ROM)	$39.99	
1-57521-140-8		Microsoft FrontPage Unleashed (Book/CD-ROM)	$49.99	
1-57521-149-1		Laura Lemay's Web Workshop: Microsoft FrontPage (Book/CD-ROM)	$39.99	
1-57521-126-2		Laura Lemay's Web Workshop: Creating Commercial Web Pages (Book/CD-ROM)	$39.99	
1-57521-192-0		Teach Yourself Web Publishing with HTML 3.2 in a Week, Third Edition	$29.99	
❑ 3 ½" Disk		Shipping and Handling: See information below.		
❑ 5 ¼" Disk		TOTAL		

Shipping and Handling: $4.00 for the first book, and $1.75 for each additional book. Floppy disk: add $1.75 for shipping and handling. If you need to have it NOW, we can ship the product to you in 24 hours for an additional charge of approximately $18.00, and you will receive your item overnight or in two days. Overseas shipping and handling adds $2.00 per book and $8.00 for up to three disks. Prices subject to change. Call for availability and pricing information on latest editions.

201 W. 103rd Street, Indianapolis, Indiana 46290

1-800-428-5331 — Orders   1-800-835-3202 — Fax   1-800-858-7674 — Customer Service

Book ISBN 0-672-31006-6